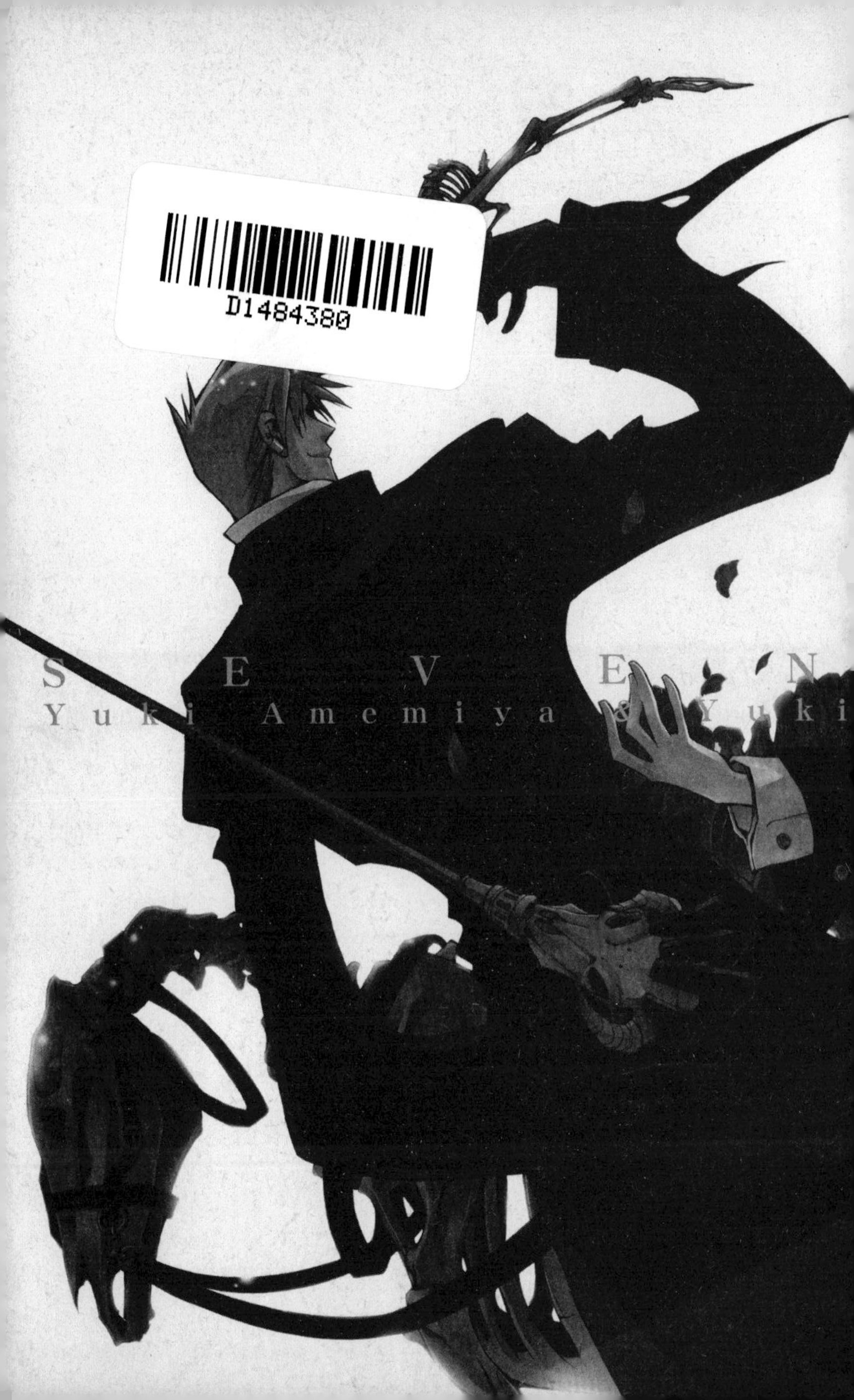
S E V E N
Y u k i A m e m i y a & Y u k i

07-GHOST

CONTENTS

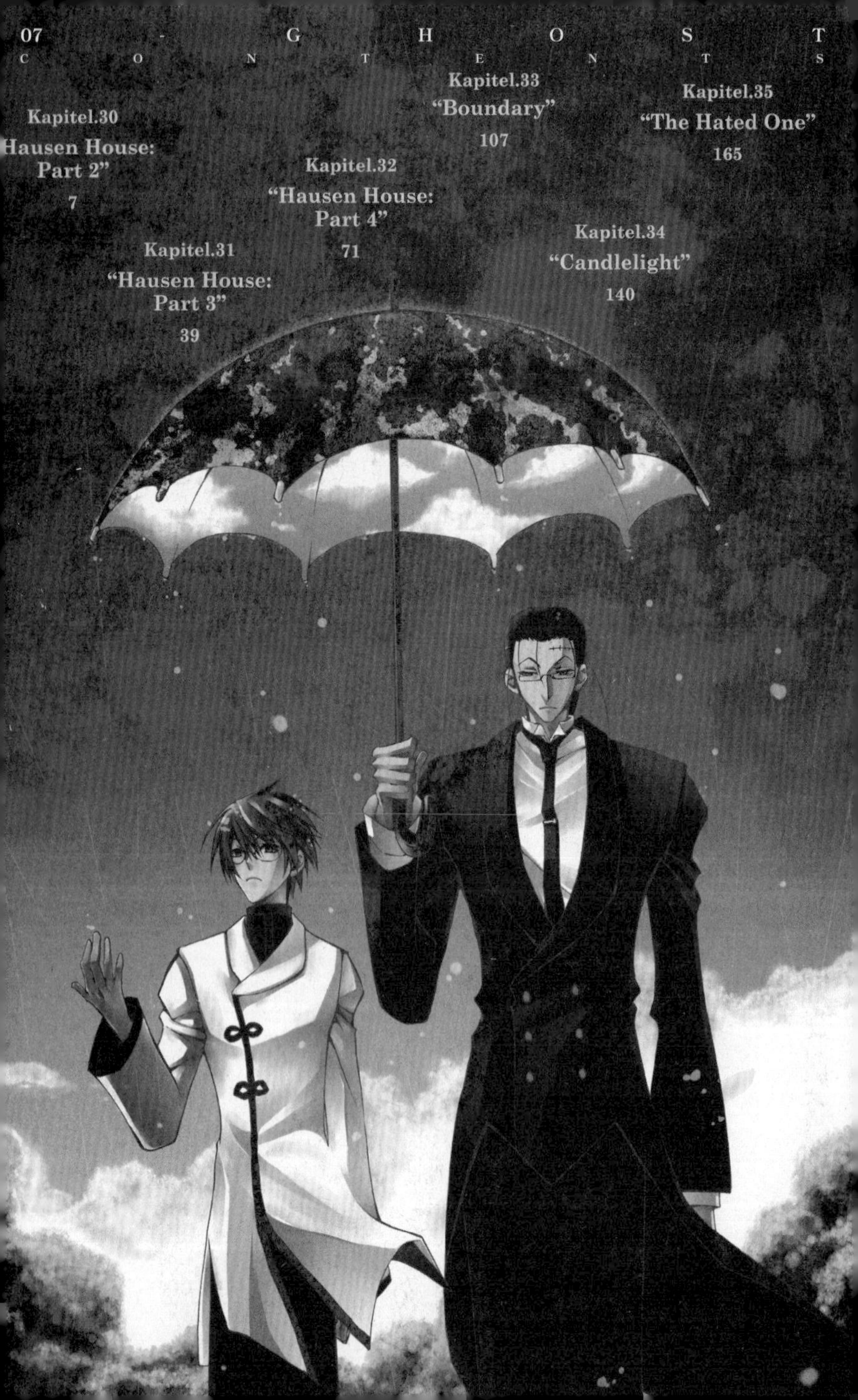

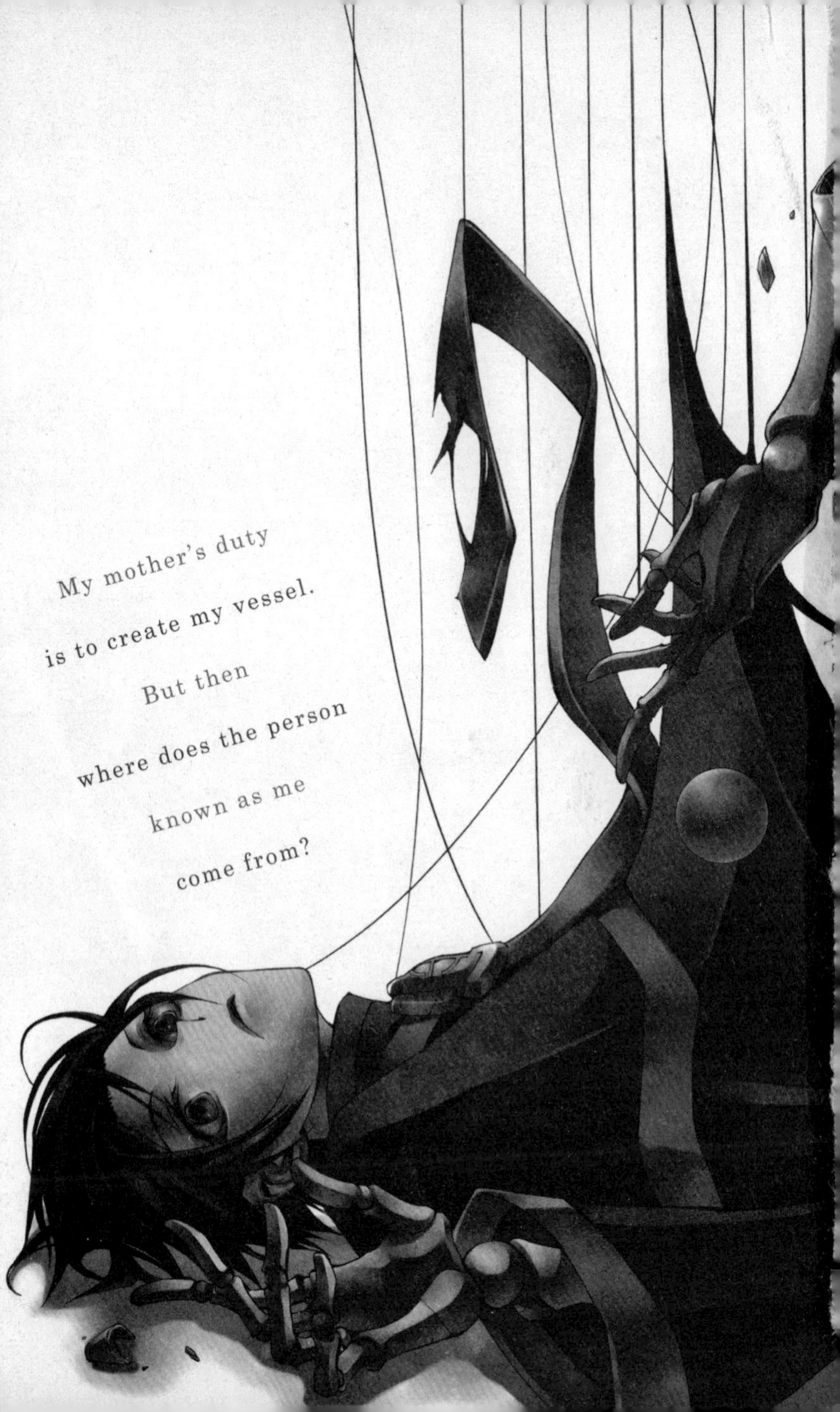
My mother's duty
is to create my vessel.
But then
where does the person
known as me
come from?

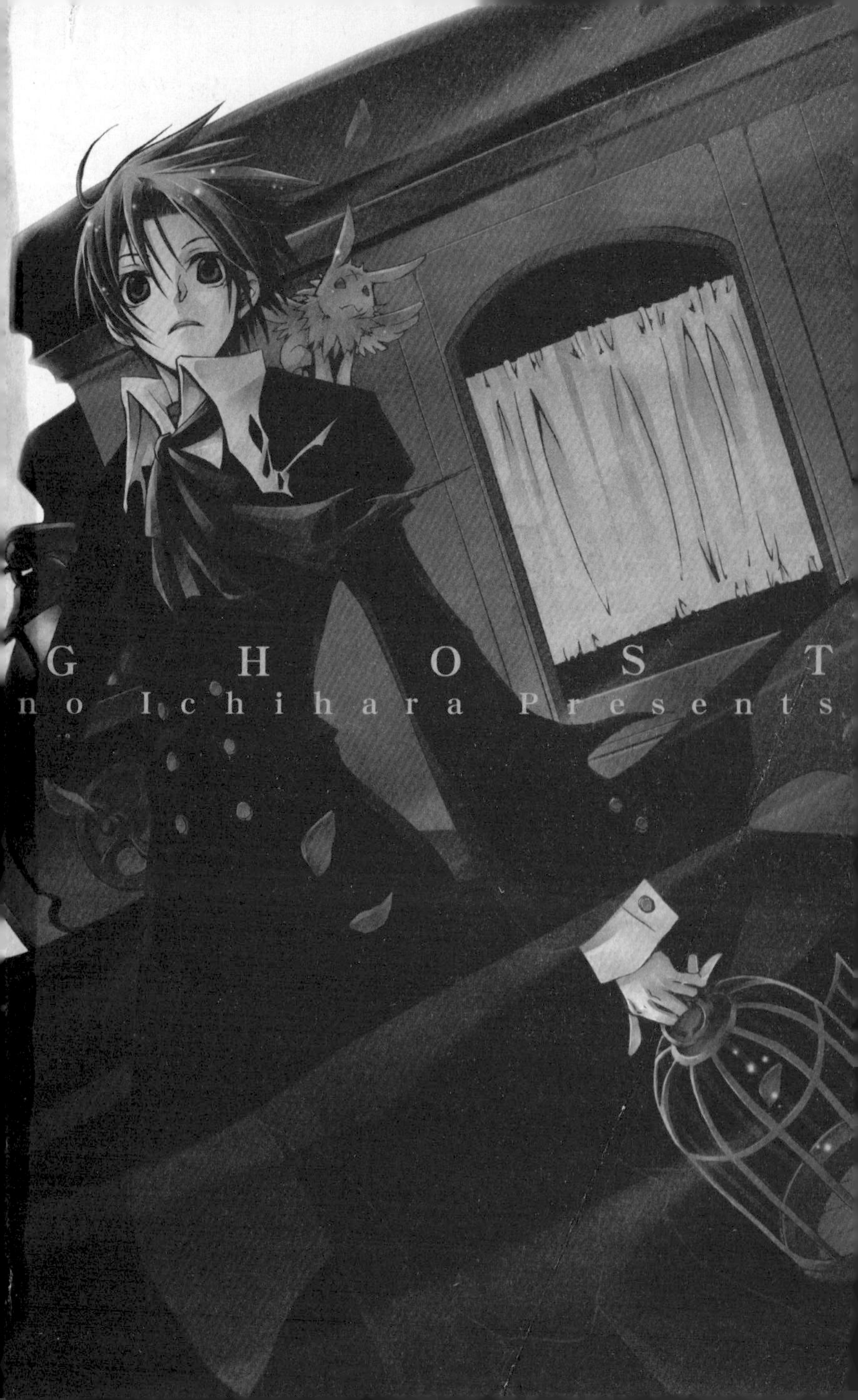
G H O S T
no Ichihara Presents

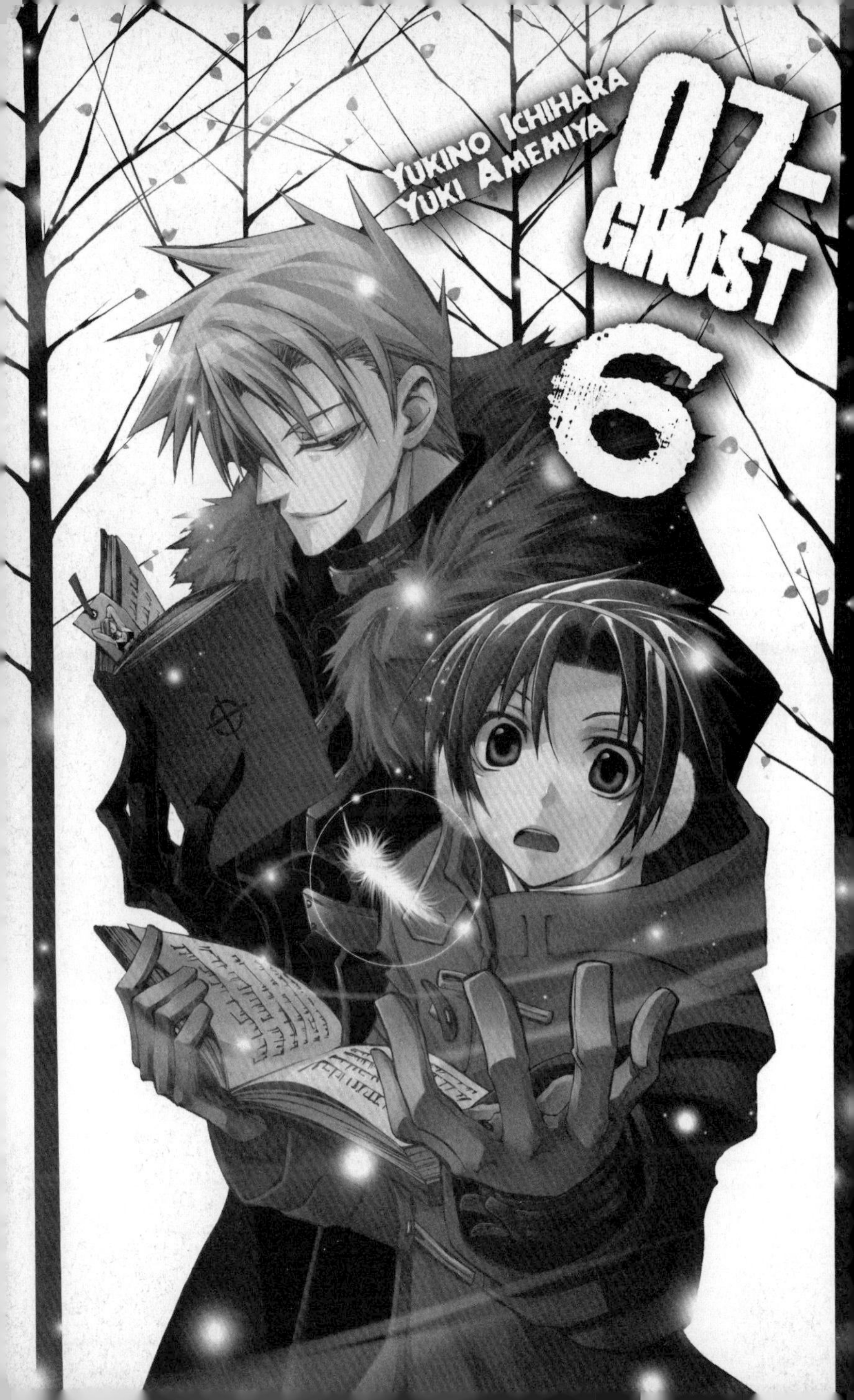

07-GHOST
6
Yukino Ichihara
Yuki Amemiya

07 GHOST Characters

One thousand years ago, two equally powerful nations coexisted. One was the Barsburg Empire, protected by the Eye of Rafael. The other was the Raggs Kingdom, protected by the Eye of Mikael. Now that the Raggs Kingdom has been destroyed, things have changed...

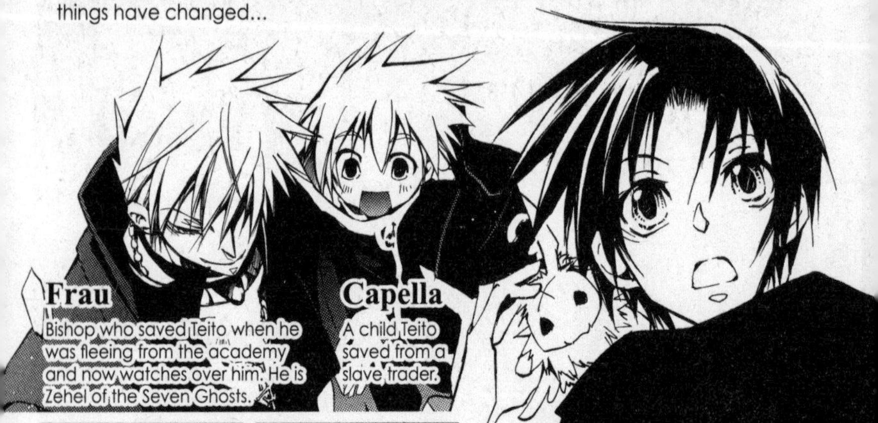

Frau

Bishop who saved Teito when he was fleeing from the academy and now watches over him. He is Zehel of the Seven Ghosts.

Capella

A child Teito saved from a slave trader.

Teito Klein

Born a prince of Raggs, Teito was stripped of his memories and raised as a soldier by the military academy's chairman. He harbored the Eye of Mikael (an artifact said to bring either the world's salvation or destruction) in his right hand until the Black Hawks stole it. Currently Frau's apprentice.

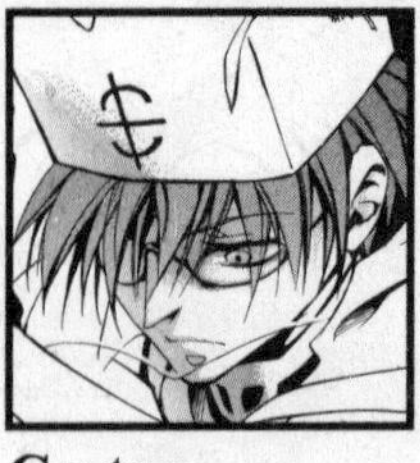

Castor

Bishop who can manipulate puppets. He watches over Teito and is Fest of the Seven Ghosts.

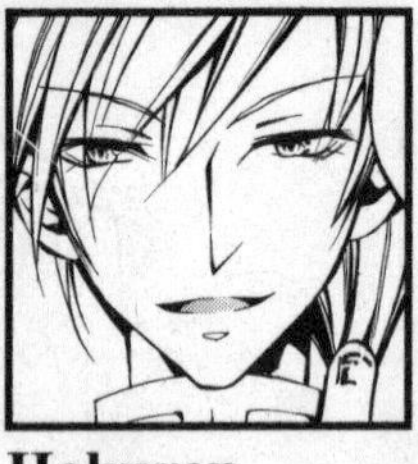

Hakuren

An apprentice bishop from the prestigious Oak family. He's Teito's friend, Castor's apprentice, and an ardent admirer of Frau.

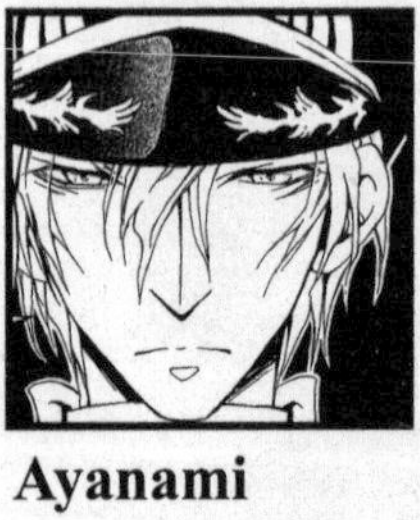

Ayanami

Imperial Army's Chief of Staff. Thief of the Eye of Mikael, and possibly responsible for the king of Raggs' death.

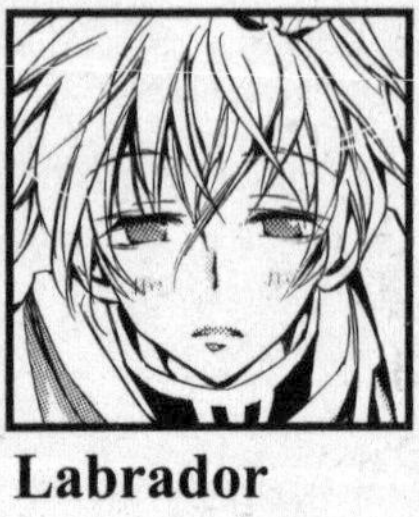

Labrador

Flower-loving bishop with the power of prophecy. One of the Seven Ghosts.

Story

Teito is a student at the Barsburg Empire's military academy until the day he discovers that his father was the king of Raggs, the ruler of a kingdom the Barsburg Empire destroyed. Teito receives sanctuary from the Barsburg Church, but loses his best friend Mikage, who Ayanami controls like a puppet to get at Teito. As a first step in avenging Mikage's death, Teito becomes an apprentice bishop to obtain special privileges. He then embarks on a journey to the "Land of Seele," which holds the key to his past and the truth about the fall of Raggs. In order to gain his first Cursed Ticket to Seele, he visits the God House in District 6.

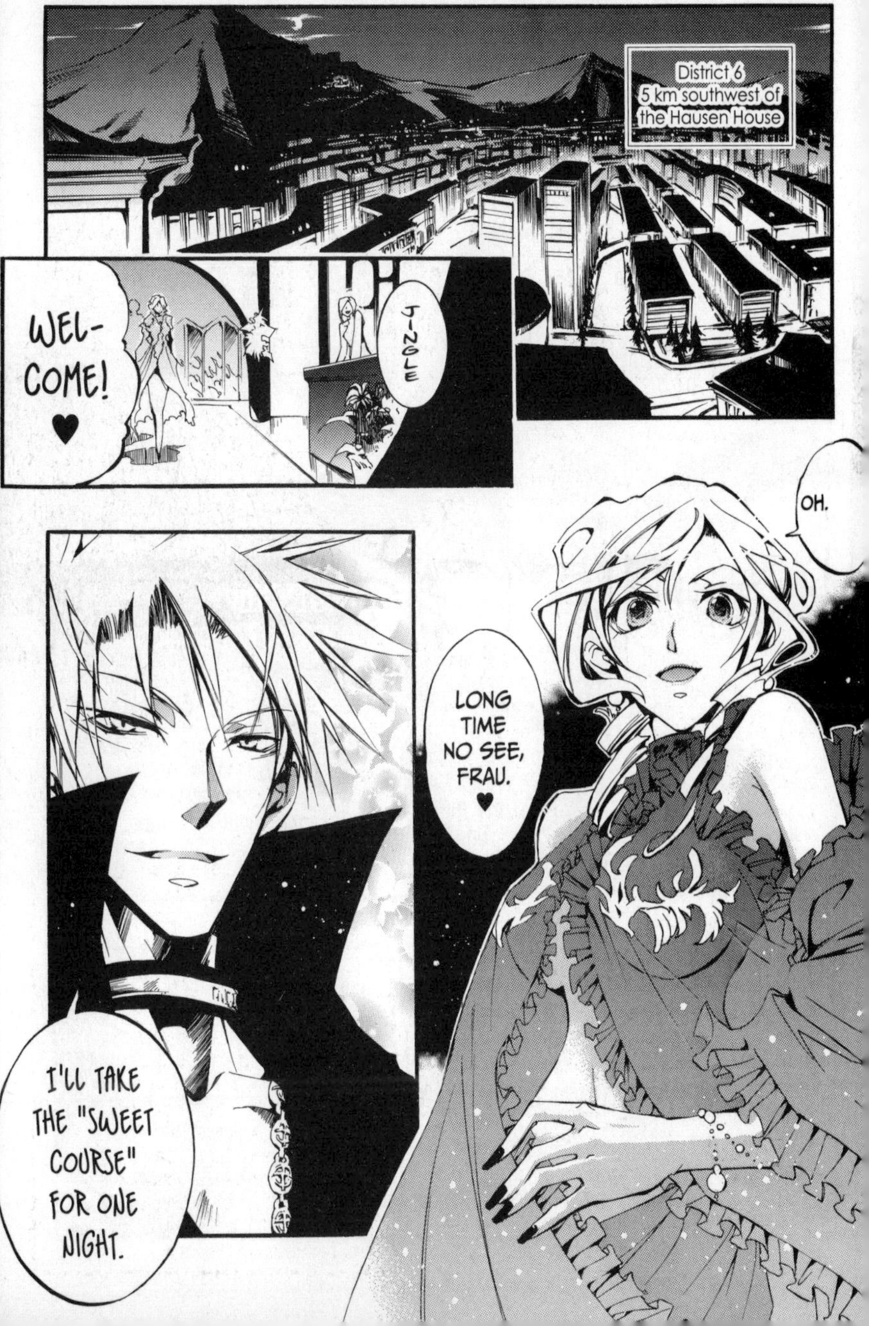
District 6
5 km southwest of the Hausen House
JINGLE
WEL-COME! ♥
OH.
LONG TIME NO SEE, FRAU. ♥
I'LL TAKE THE "SWEET COURSE" FOR ONE NIGHT.

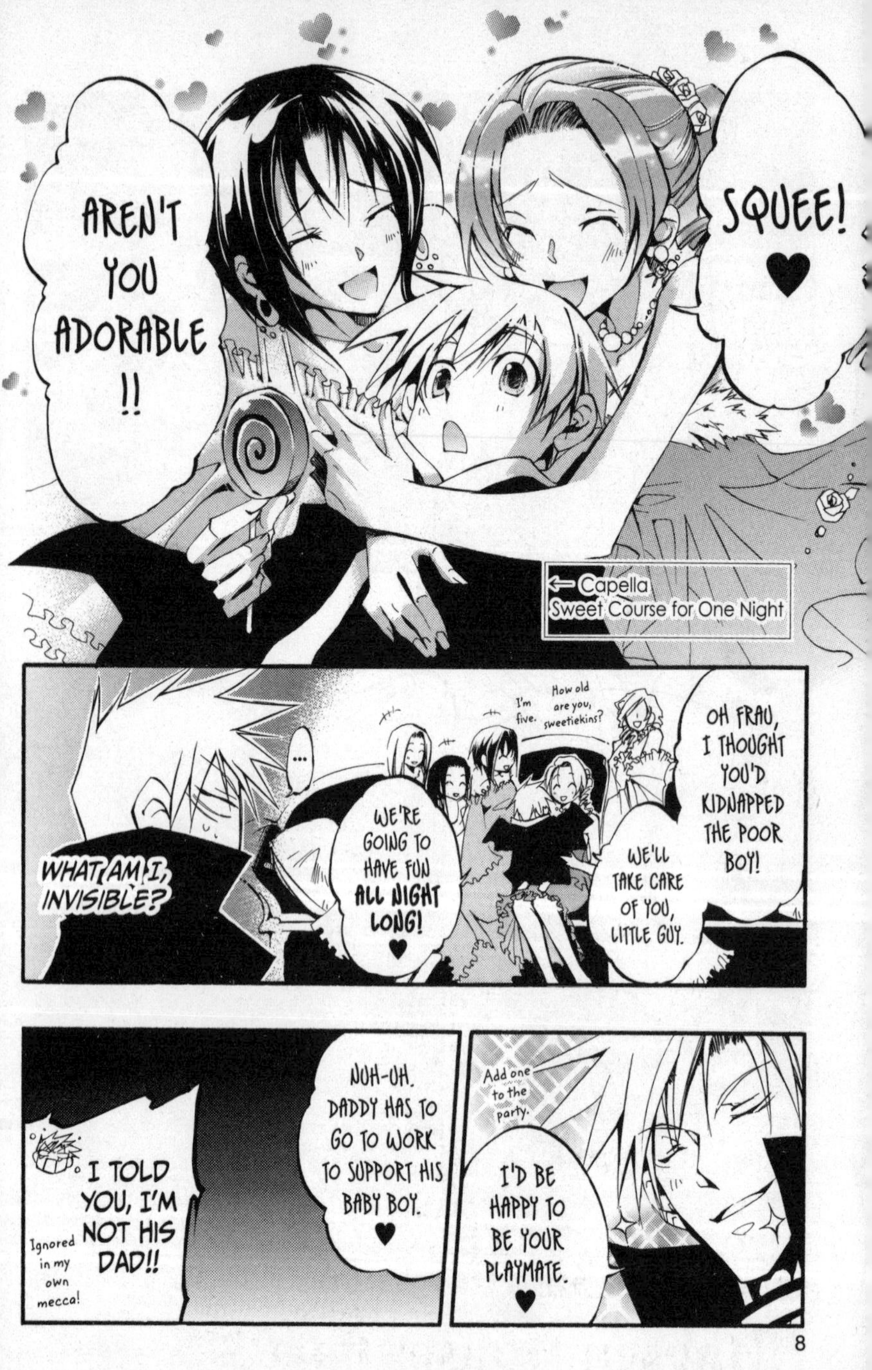
SQUEE! ♥
AREN'T YOU ADORABLE!!
← Capella Sweet Course for One Night
OH FRAU, I THOUGHT YOU'D KIDNAPPED THE POOR BOY!
How old are you, sweetiekins?
I'm five.
WE'LL TAKE CARE OF YOU, LITTLE GUY.
WE'RE GOING TO HAVE FUN ALL NIGHT LONG! ♥
...
WHAT AM I, INVISIBLE?
Add one to the party.
I'D BE HAPPY TO BE YOUR PLAYMATE. ♥
NUH-UH. DADDY HAS TO GO TO WORK TO SUPPORT HIS BABY BOY. ♥
I TOLD YOU, I'M NOT HIS DAD!!
Ignored in my own mecca!

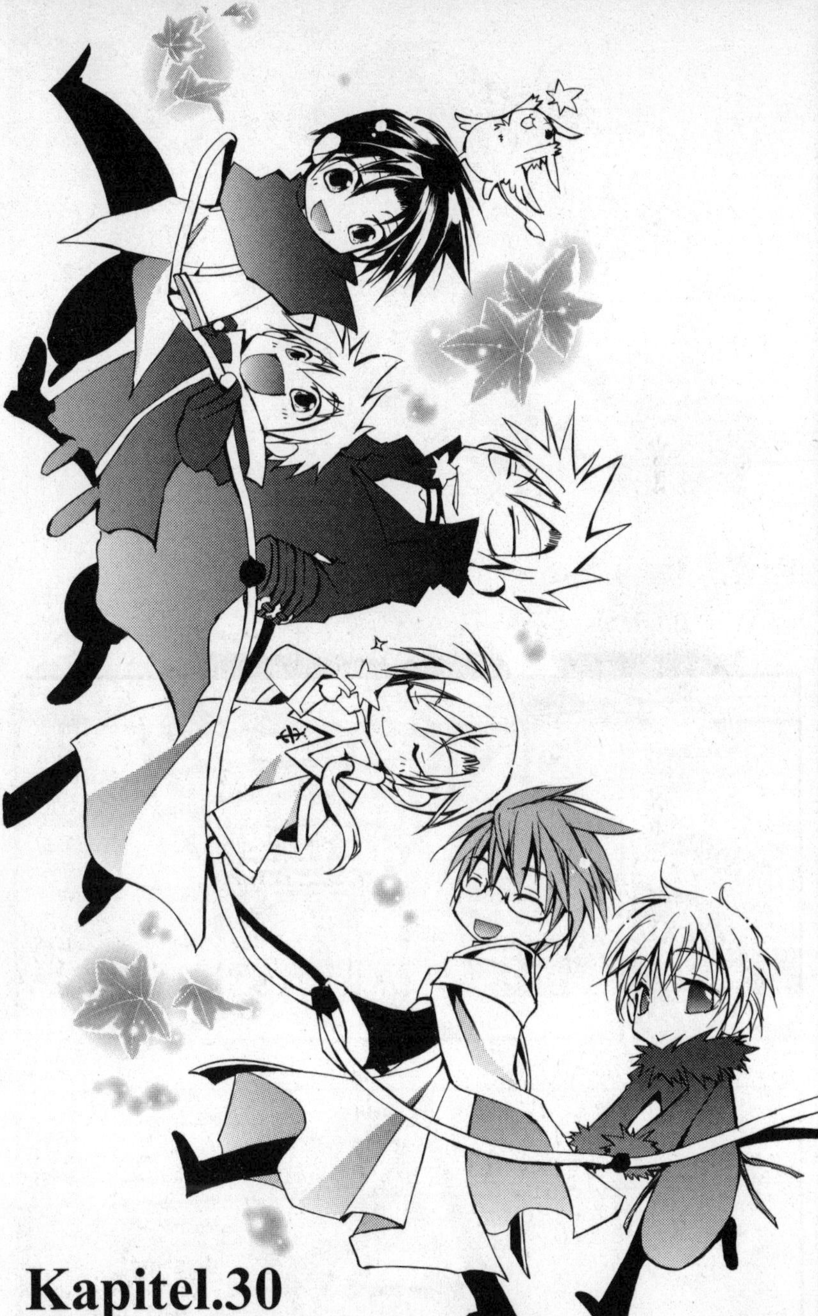

Kapitel.30
“Hausen House: Part 2”

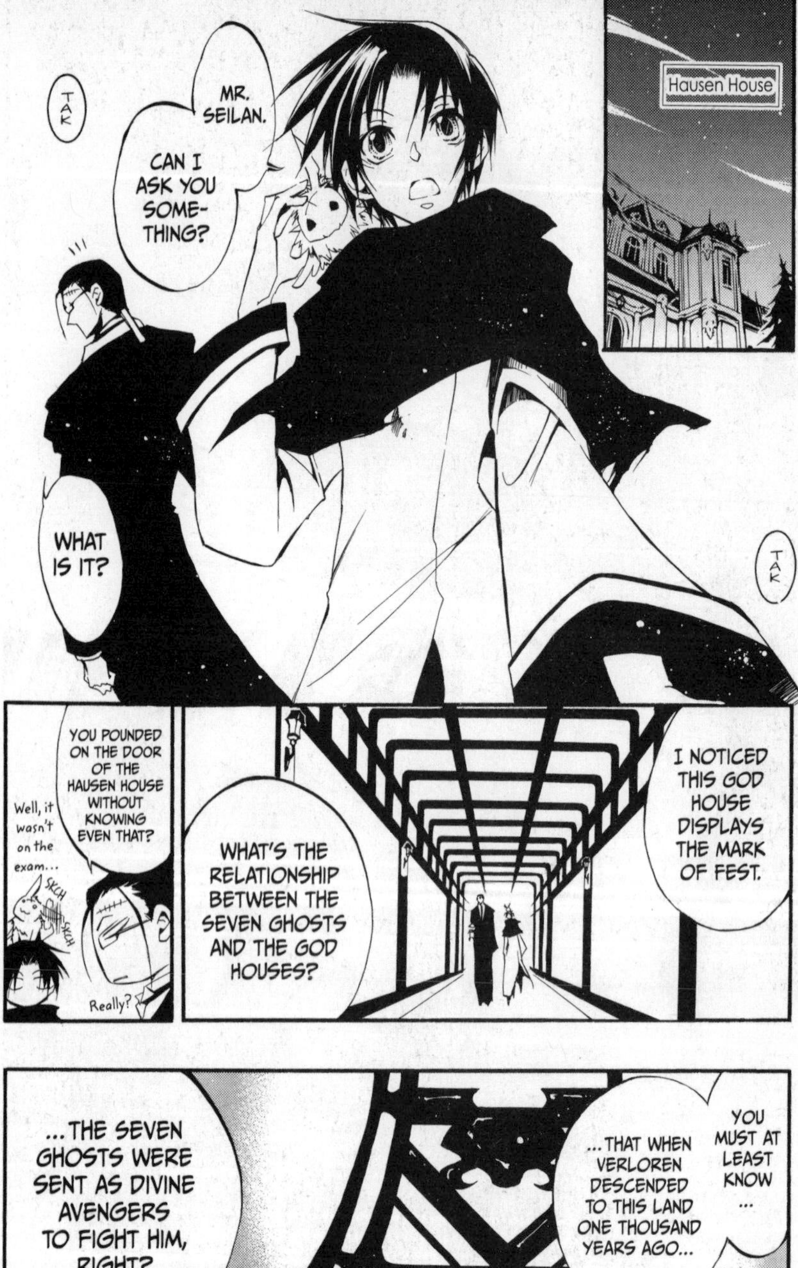
Hausen House
MR. SEILAN.
CAN I ASK YOU SOME-THING?
TAK
TAK
WHAT IS IT?
I NOTICED THIS GOD HOUSE DISPLAYS THE MARK OF FEST.
WHAT'S THE RELATIONSHIP BETWEEN THE SEVEN GHOSTS AND THE GOD HOUSES?
YOU POUNDED ON THE DOOR OF THE HAUSEN HOUSE WITHOUT KNOWING EVEN THAT?
Well, it wasn't on the exam...
SKCH
SKCH
Really?
YOU MUST AT LEAST KNOW ...
...THAT WHEN VERLOREN DESCENDED TO THIS LAND ONE THOUSAND YEARS AGO...
...THE SEVEN GHOSTS WERE SENT AS DIVINE AVENGERS TO FIGHT HIM, RIGHT?

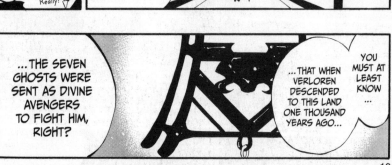

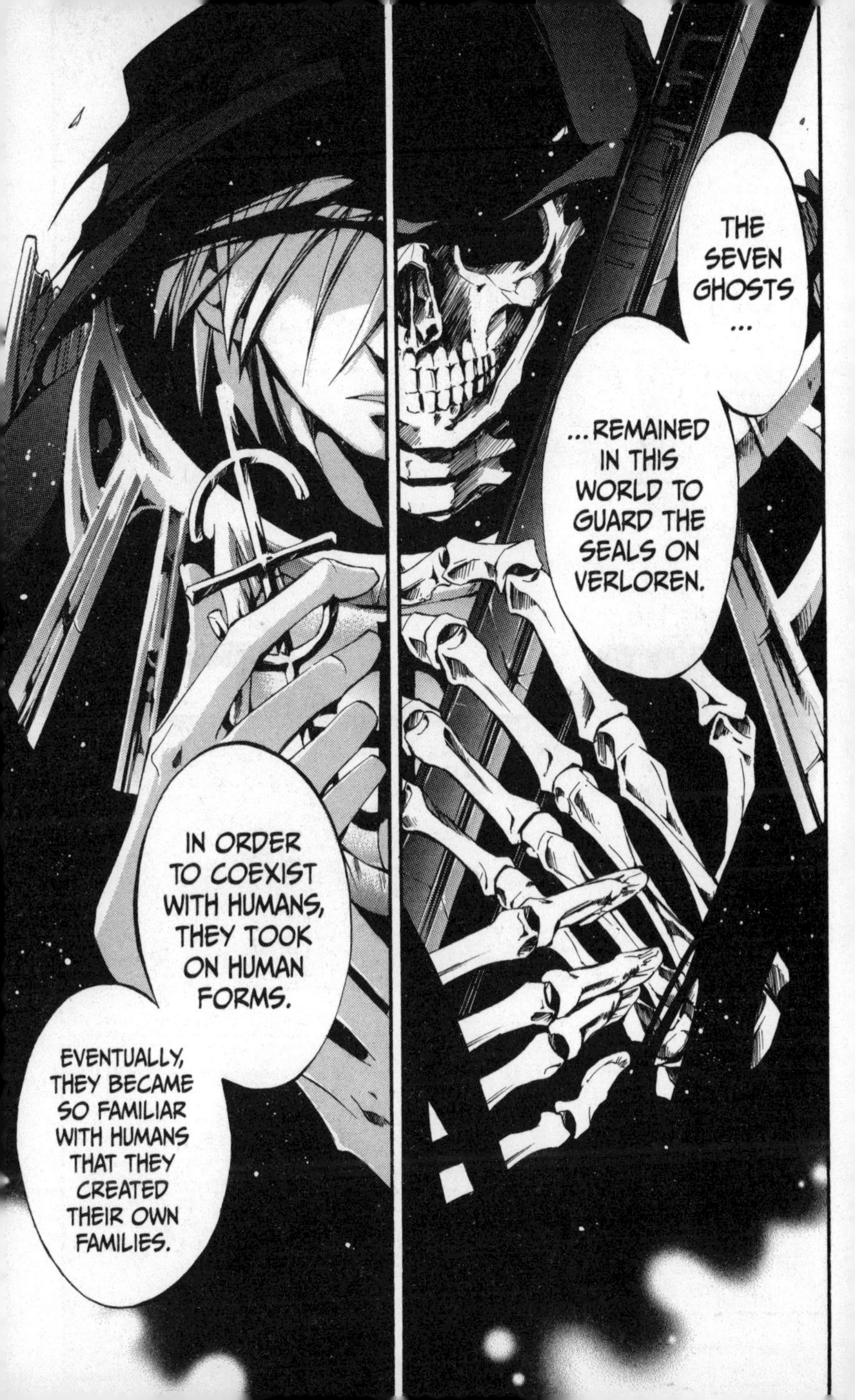
THE SEVEN GHOSTS ...
...REMAINED IN THIS WORLD TO GUARD THE SEALS ON VERLOREN.
IN ORDER TO COEXIST WITH HUMANS, THEY TOOK ON HUMAN FORMS.
EVENTUALLY, THEY BECAME SO FAMILIAR WITH HUMANS THAT THEY CREATED THEIR OWN FAMILIES.

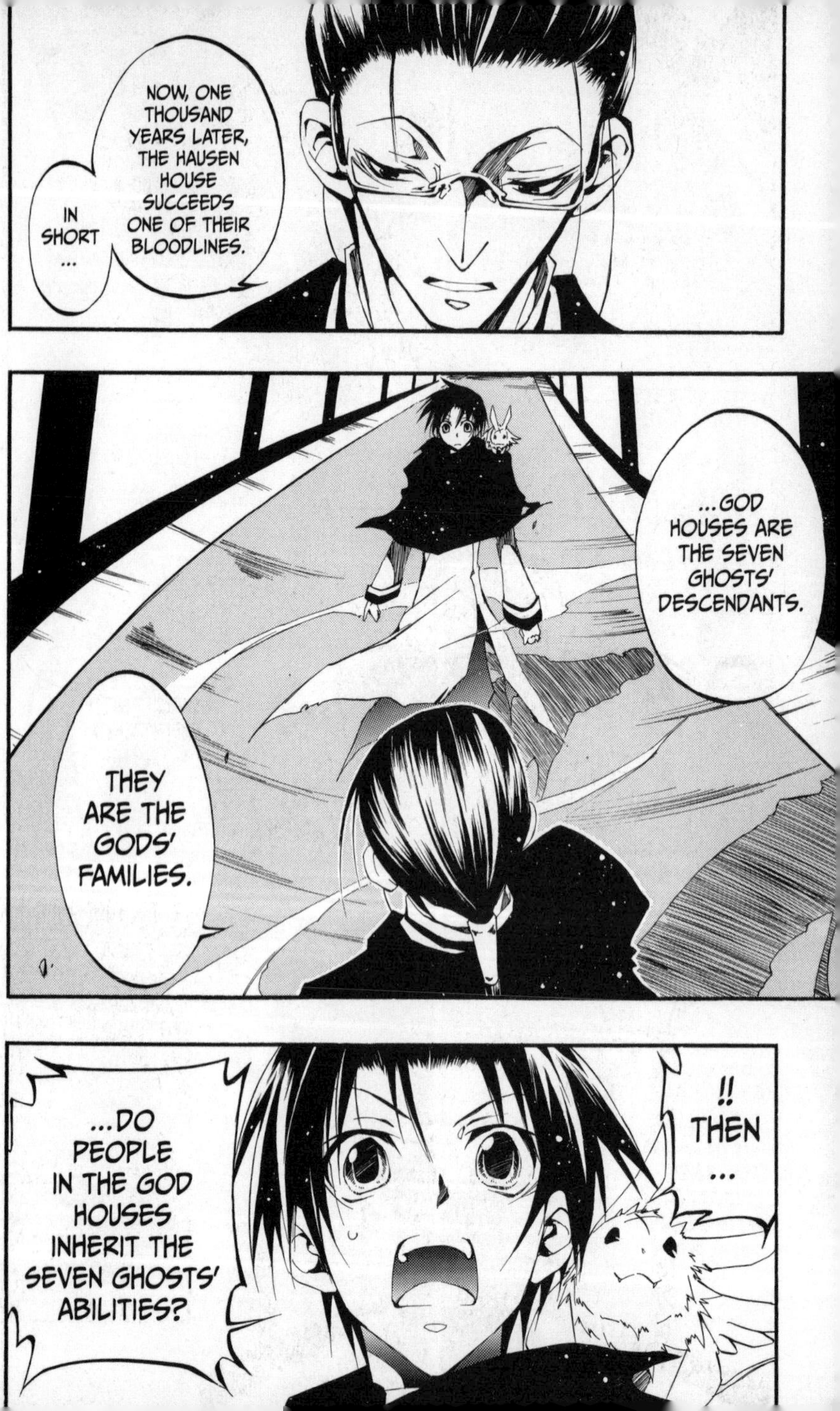
NOW, ONE THOUSAND YEARS LATER, THE HAUSEN HOUSE SUCCEEDS ONE OF THEIR BLOODLINES.
IN SHORT ...
...GOD HOUSES ARE THE SEVEN GHOSTS' DESCENDANTS.
THEY ARE THE GODS' FAMILIES.
!! THEN ...
...DO PEOPLE IN THE GOD HOUSES INHERIT THE SEVEN GHOSTS' ABILITIES?

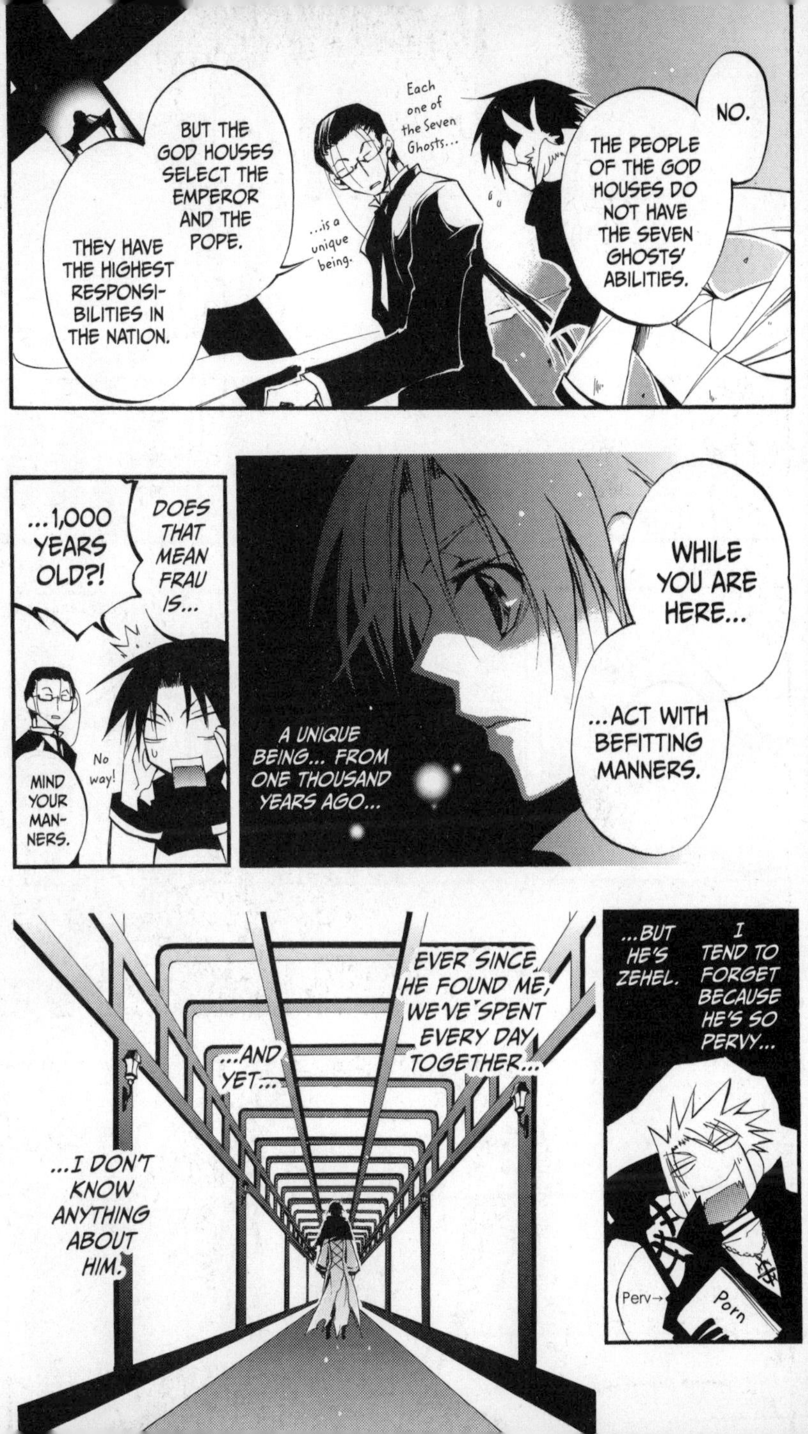
NO.
THE PEOPLE OF THE GOD HOUSES DO NOT HAVE THE SEVEN GHOSTS' ABILITIES.
Each one of the Seven Ghosts...
...is a unique being.
BUT THE GOD HOUSES SELECT THE EMPEROR AND THE POPE.
THEY HAVE THE HIGHEST RESPONSI-BILITIES IN THE NATION.
WHILE YOU ARE HERE...
...ACT WITH BEFITTING MANNERS.
A UNIQUE BEING... FROM ONE THOUSAND YEARS AGO...
DOES THAT MEAN FRAU IS...
...1,000 YEARS OLD?!
No way!
MIND YOUR MAN-NERS.
I TEND TO FORGET BECAUSE HE'S SO PERVY...
...BUT HE'S ZEHEL.
Perv→
Porn
EVER SINCE HE FOUND ME, WE'VE SPENT EVERY DAY TOGETHER...
...AND YET...
...I DON'T KNOW ANYTHING ABOUT HIM.

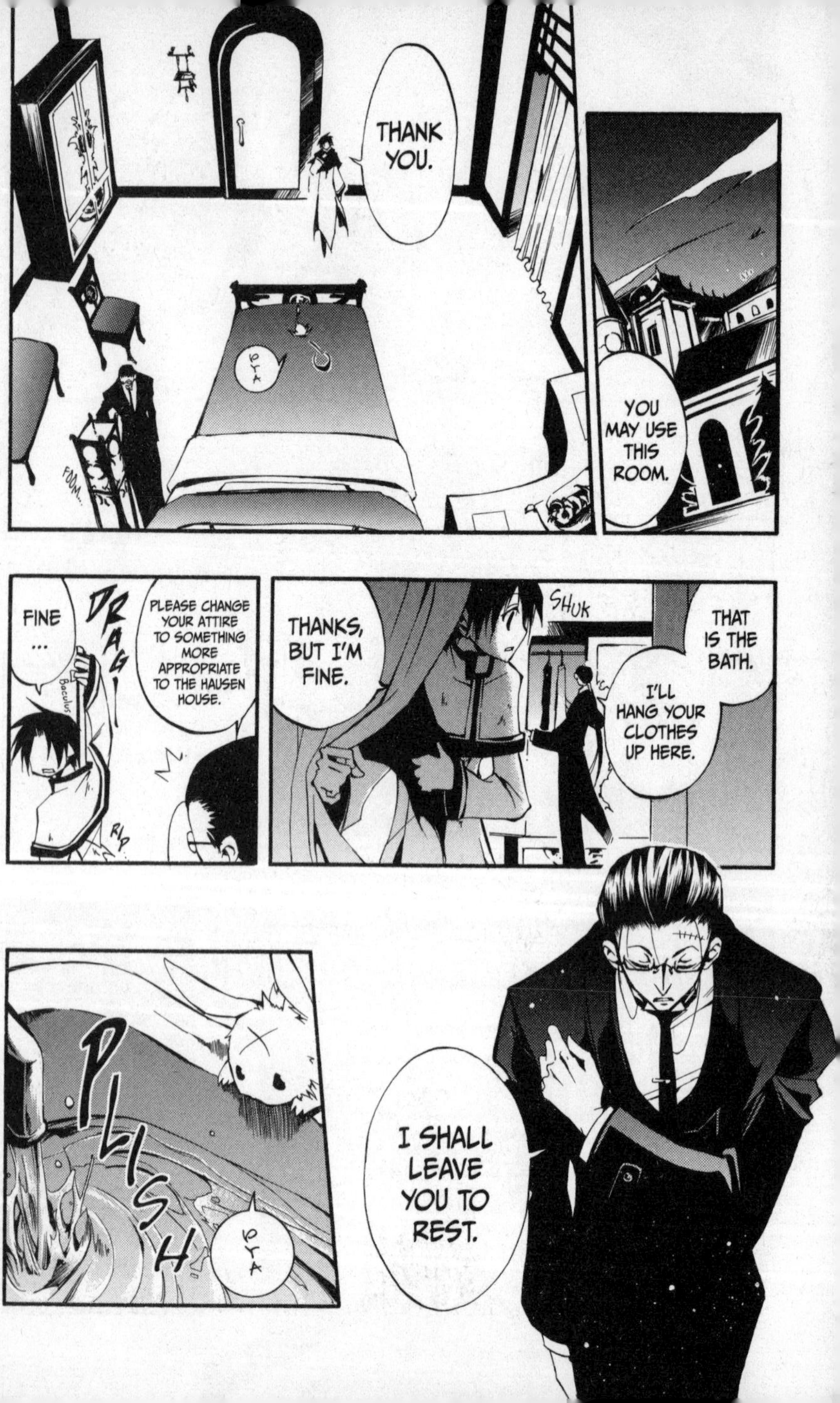
YOU MAY USE THIS ROOM.
THANK YOU.
FOOM...
SHUK
THAT IS THE BATH.
I'LL HANG YOUR CLOTHES UP HERE.
THANKS, BUT I'M FINE.
PLEASE CHANGE YOUR ATTIRE TO SOMETHING MORE APPROPRIATE TO THE HAUSEN HOUSE.
DRAG!
FINE ...
Baculus
RIP
I SHALL LEAVE YOU TO REST.
PLISH

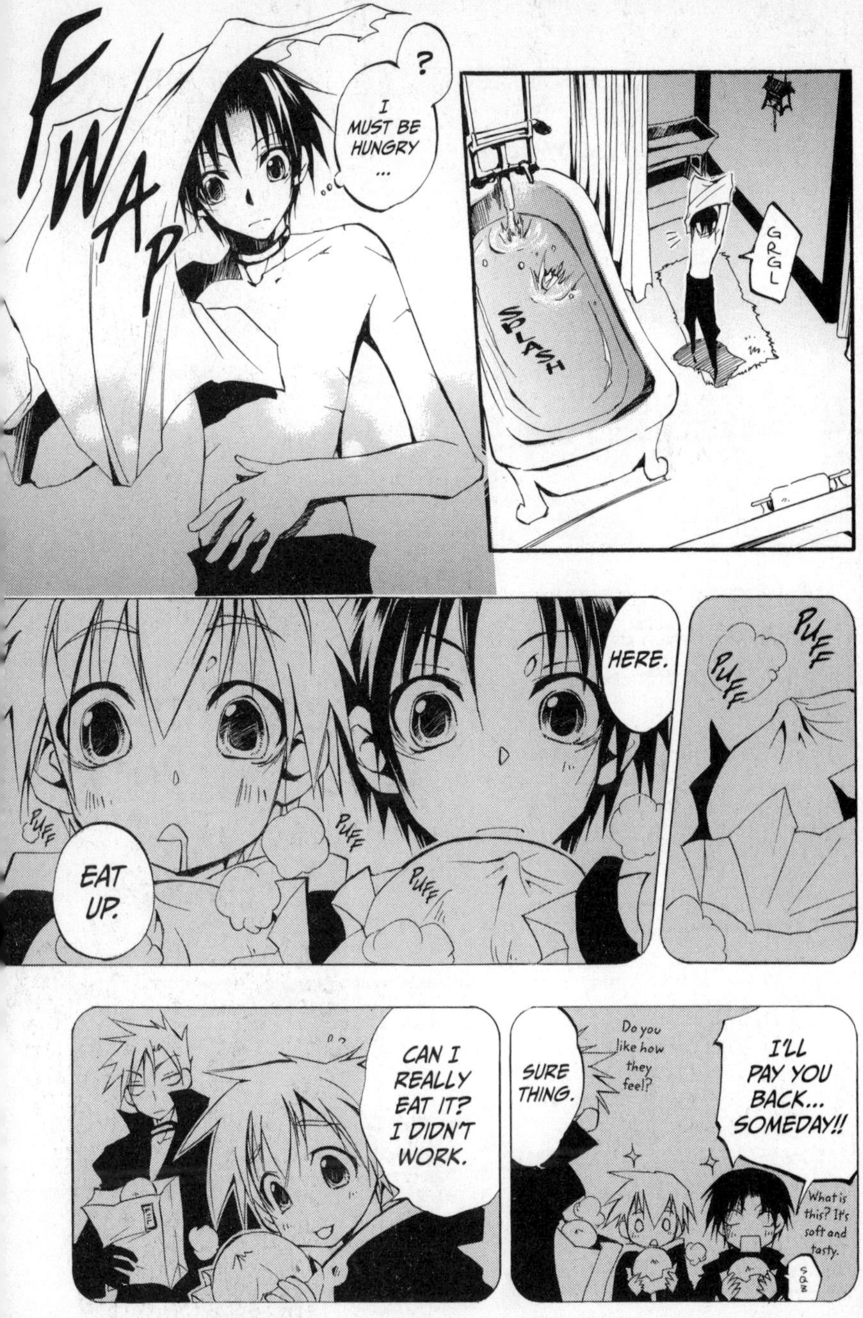
SPLASH
GRGL
FWAP
?
I MUST BE HUNGRY ...
PUFF
PUFF
HERE.
PUFF
PUFF
PUFF
EAT UP.
I'LL PAY YOU BACK... SOMEDAY!!
What is this? It's soft and tasty.
SURE THING.
Do you like how they feel?
CAN I REALLY EAT IT? I DIDN'T WORK.

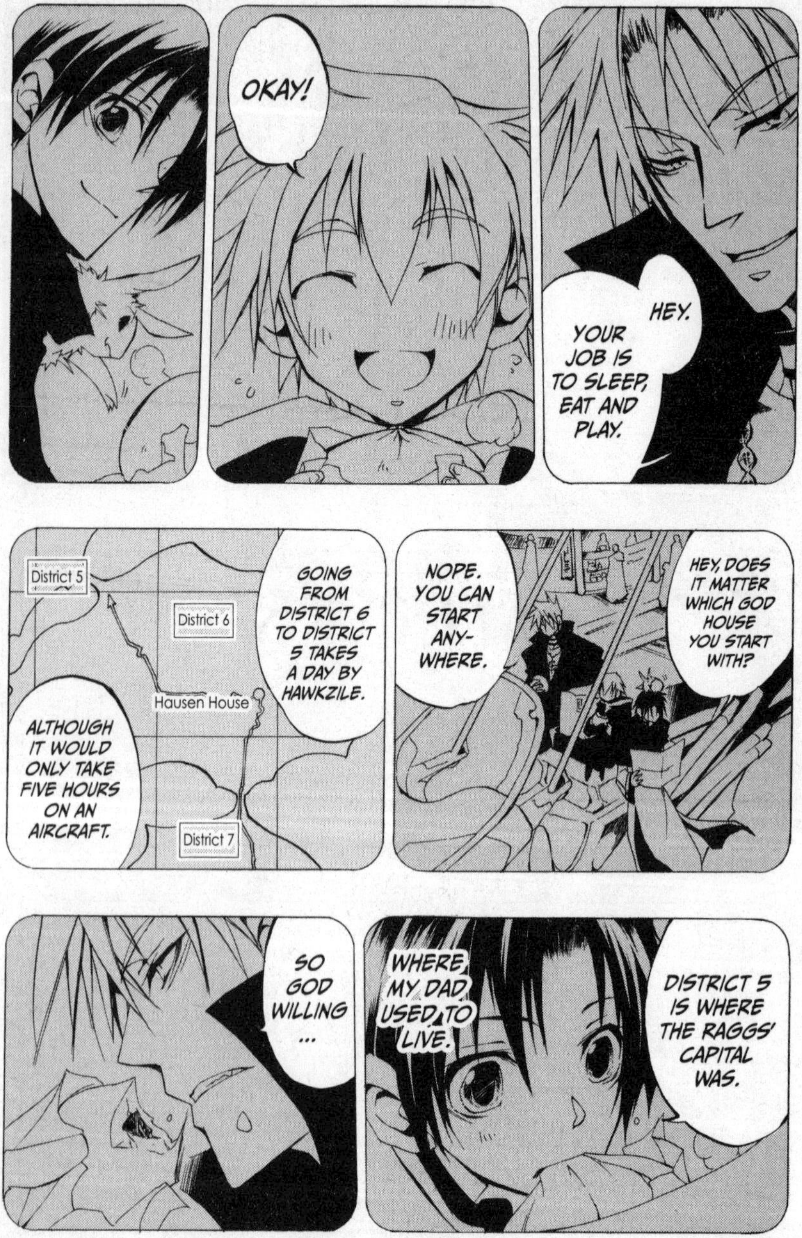
HEY.
YOUR JOB IS TO SLEEP, EAT AND PLAY.
OKAY!
HEY, DOES IT MATTER WHICH GOD HOUSE YOU START WITH?
NOPE. YOU CAN START ANY-WHERE.
GOING FROM DISTRICT 6 TO DISTRICT 5 TAKES A DAY BY HAWKZILE.
District 5
District 6
Hausen House
District 7
ALTHOUGH IT WOULD ONLY TAKE FIVE HOURS ON AN AIRCRAFT.
DISTRICT 5 IS WHERE THE RAGGS' CAPITAL WAS.
WHERE MY DAD USED TO LIVE.
SO GOD WILLING ...

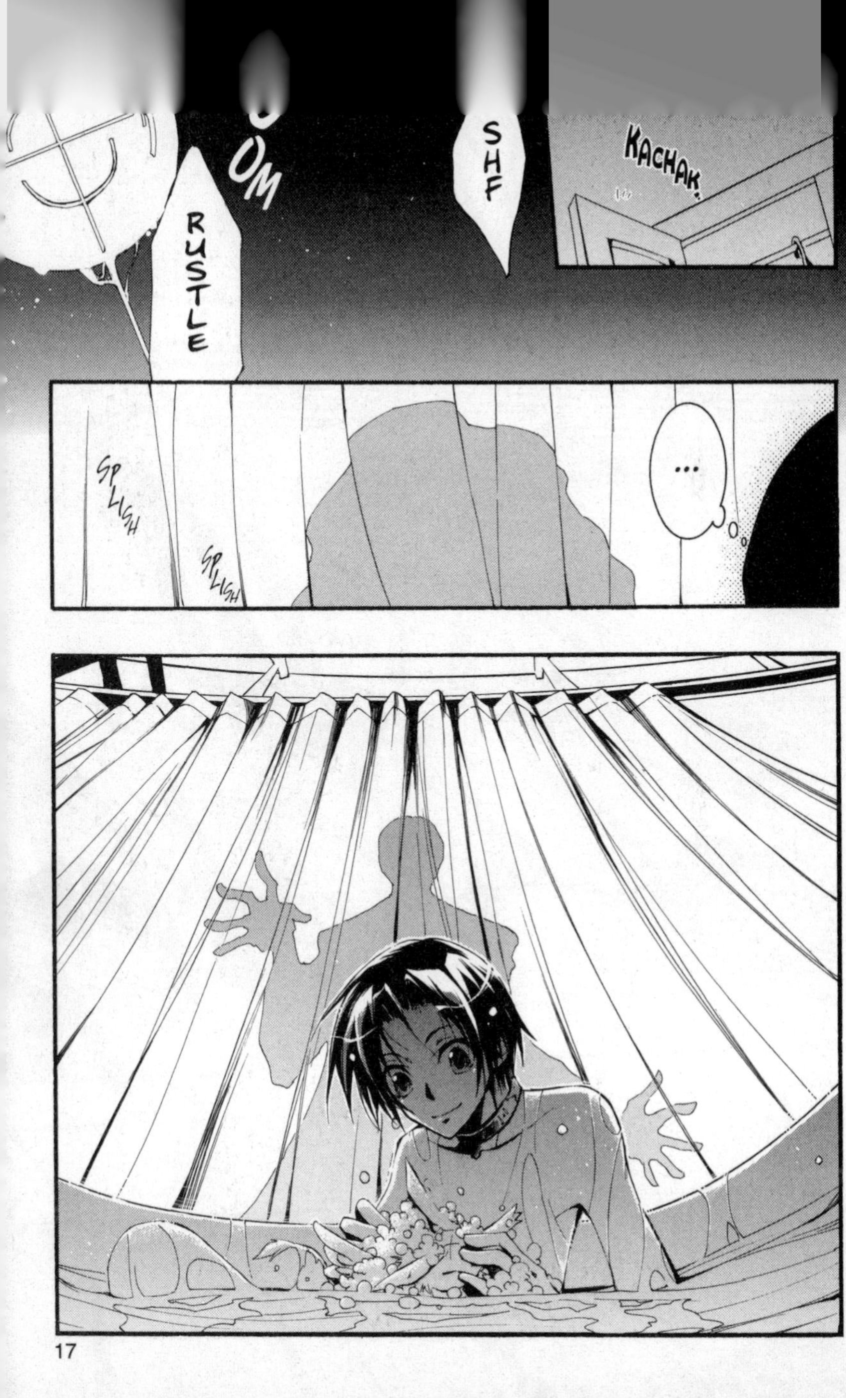
KACHAK
SHF
RUSTLE
...
SPLISH
SPLISH

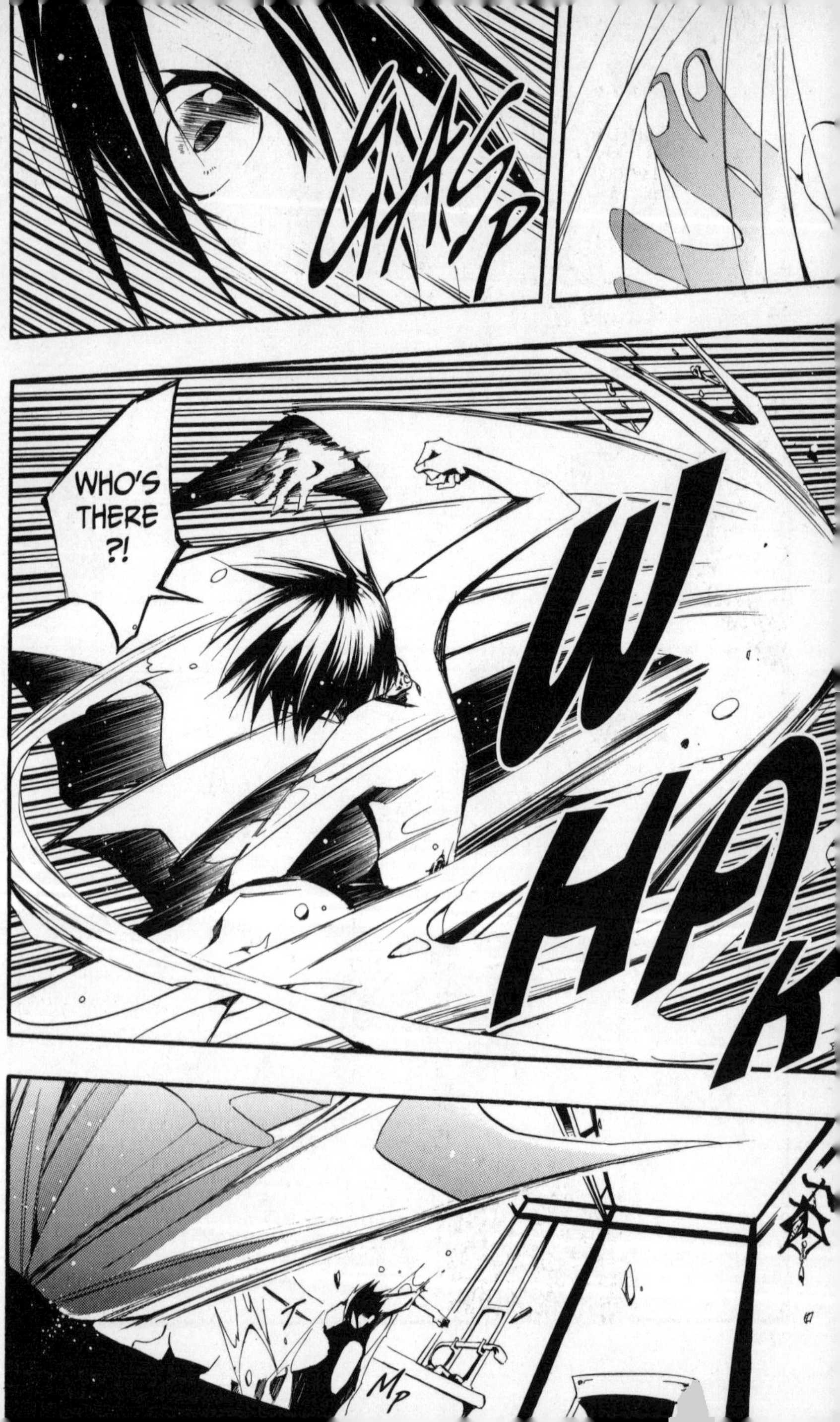
GASP
WHO'S THERE ?!
WHAK

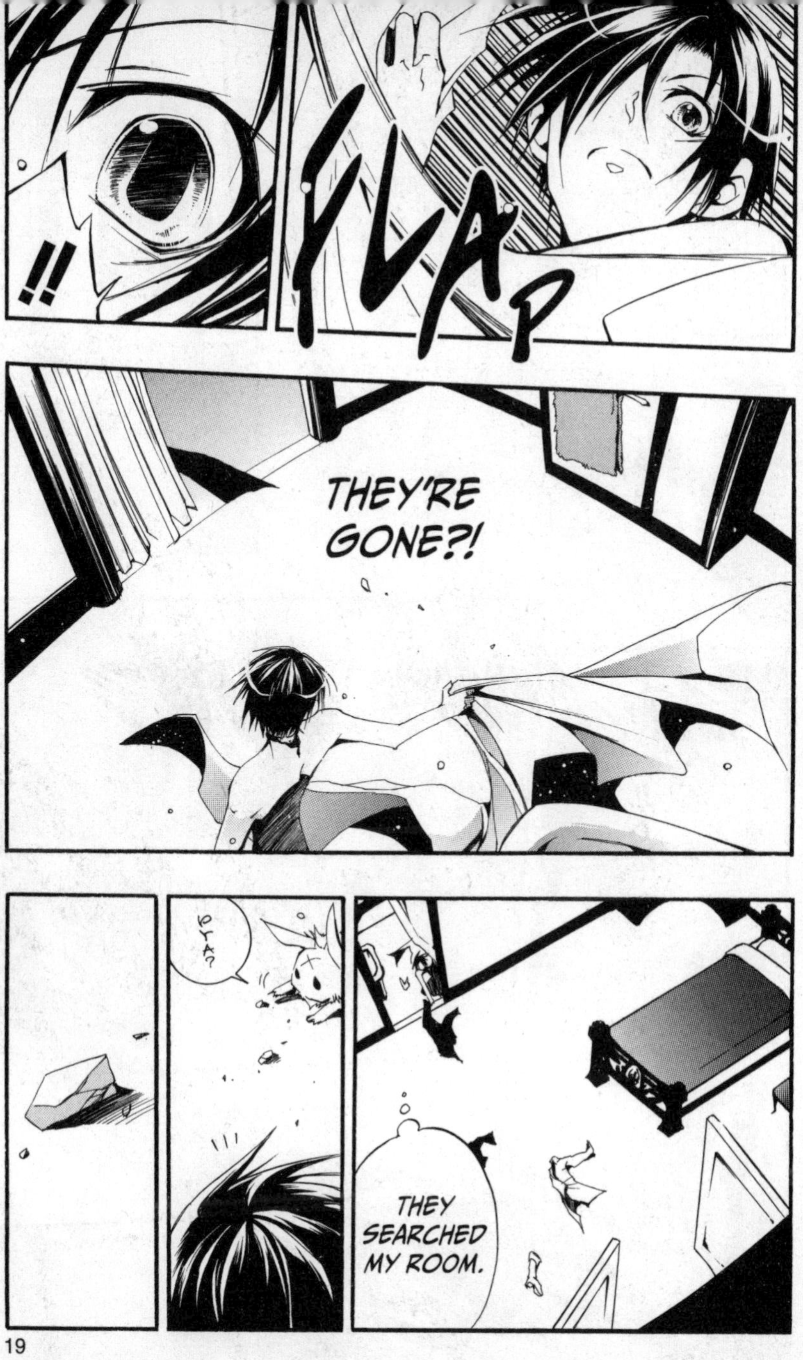
FLAP
!!
THEY'RE GONE?!
THEY SEARCHED MY ROOM.
PYA?

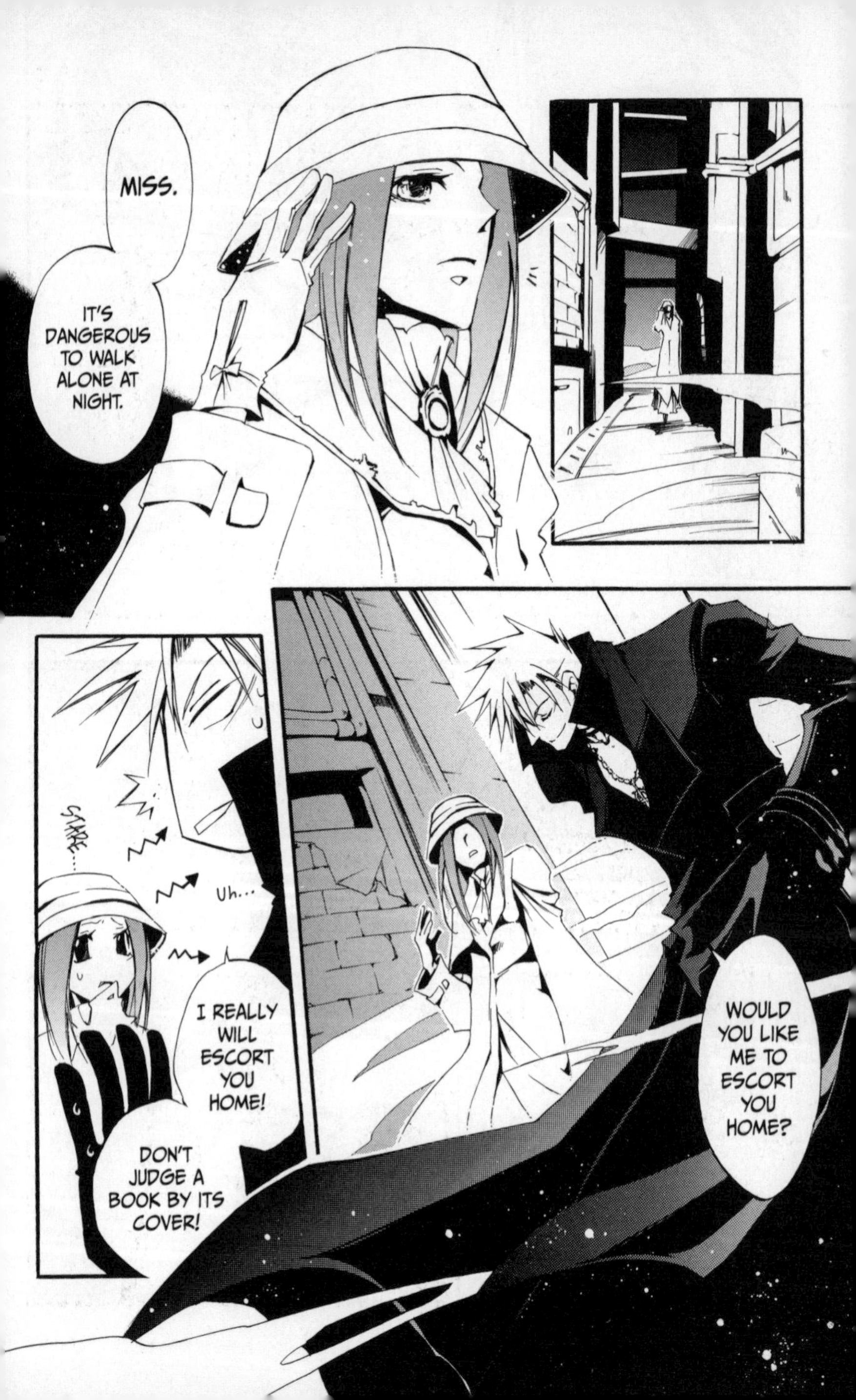
MISS.
IT'S DANGEROUS TO WALK ALONE AT NIGHT.
WOULD YOU LIKE ME TO ESCORT YOU HOME?
STARE...
Uh...
I REALLY WILL ESCORT YOU HOME!
DON'T JUDGE A BOOK BY ITS COVER!

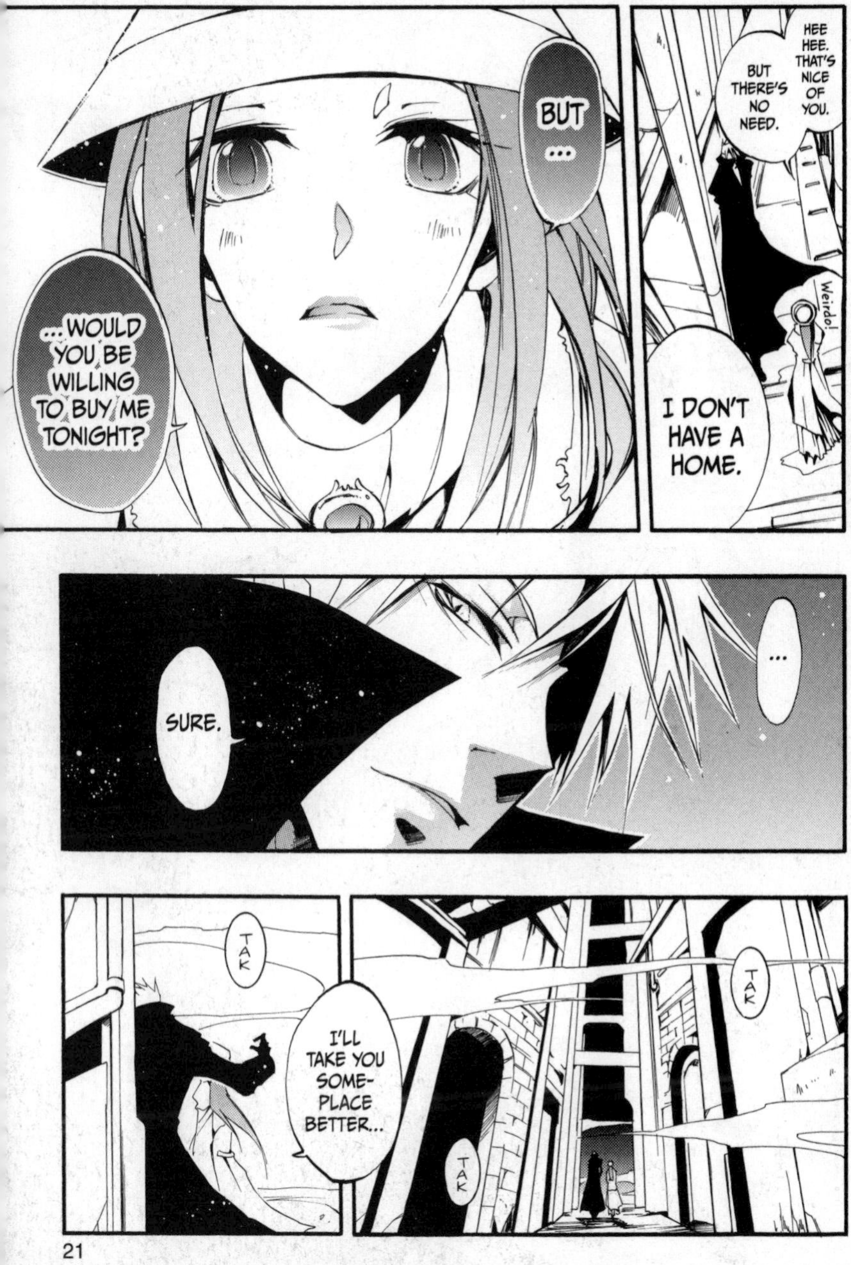
HEE HEE. THAT'S NICE OF YOU.
BUT THERE'S NO NEED.
Weirdo!
I DON'T HAVE A HOME.
BUT...
...WOULD YOU BE WILLING TO BUY ME TONIGHT?
...
SURE.
TAK
TAK
TAK
I'LL TAKE YOU SOME-PLACE BETTER...

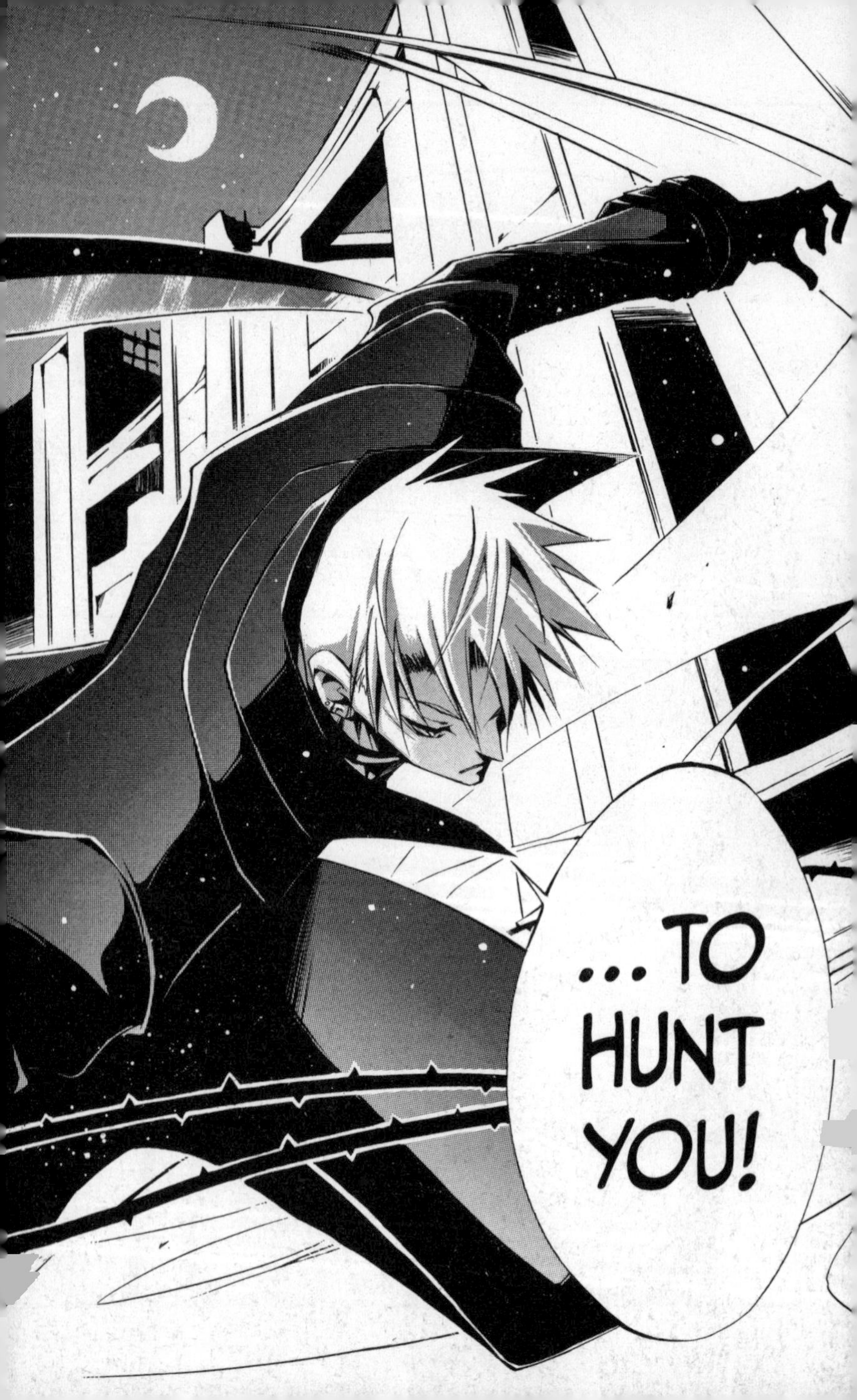
...TO HUNT YOU!

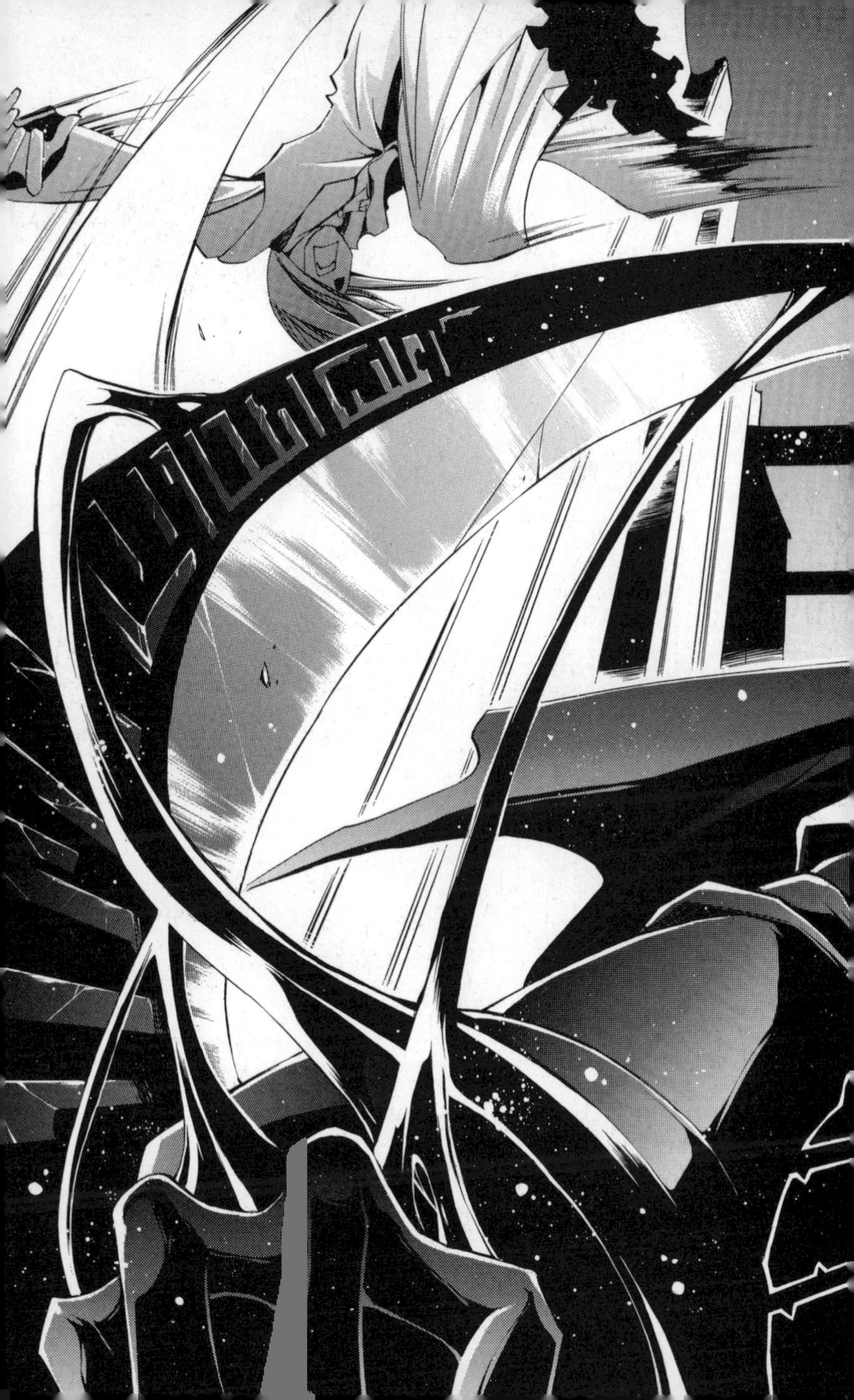

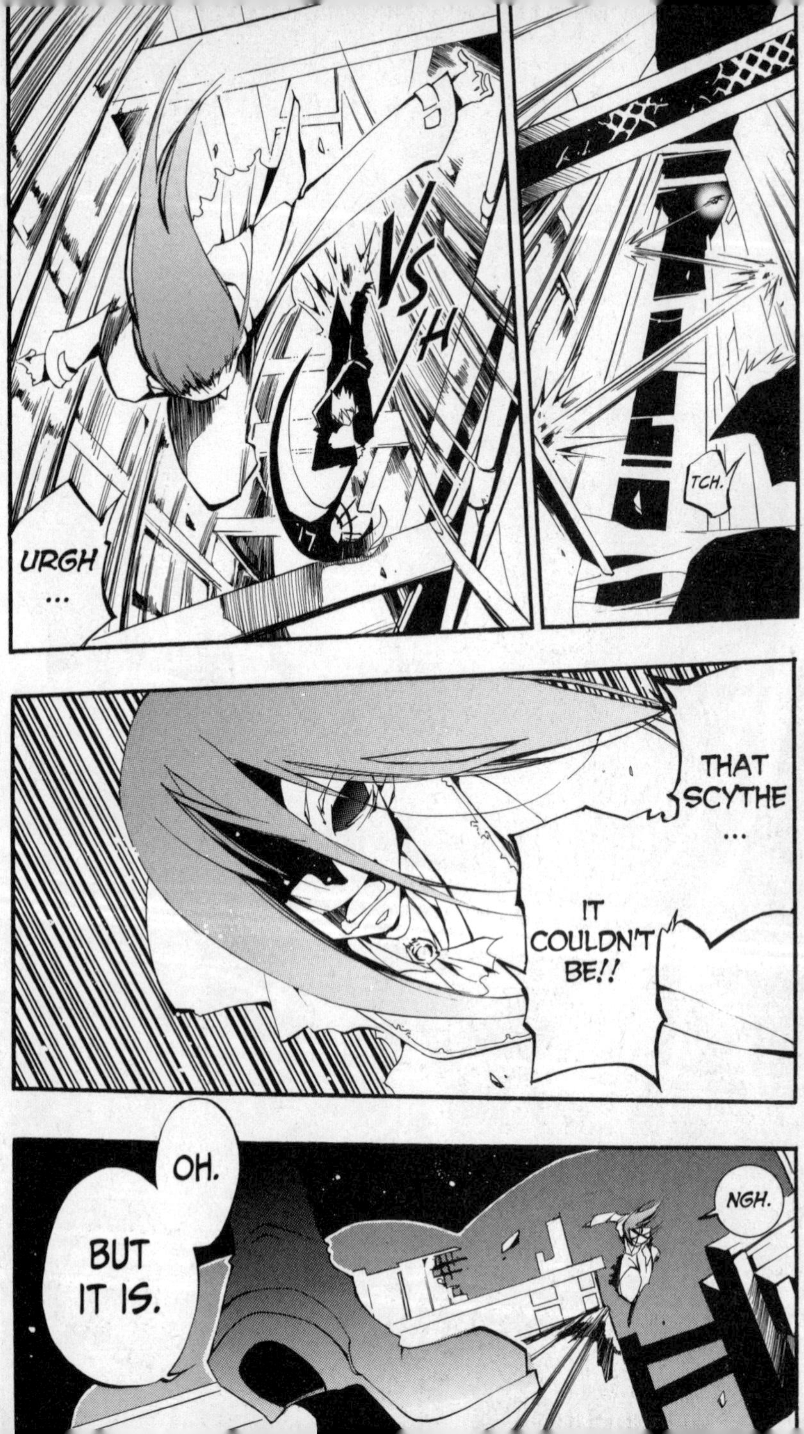
TCH.
VSH
URGH ...
THAT SCYTHE ...
IT COULDN'T BE!!
OH.
BUT IT IS.
NGH.

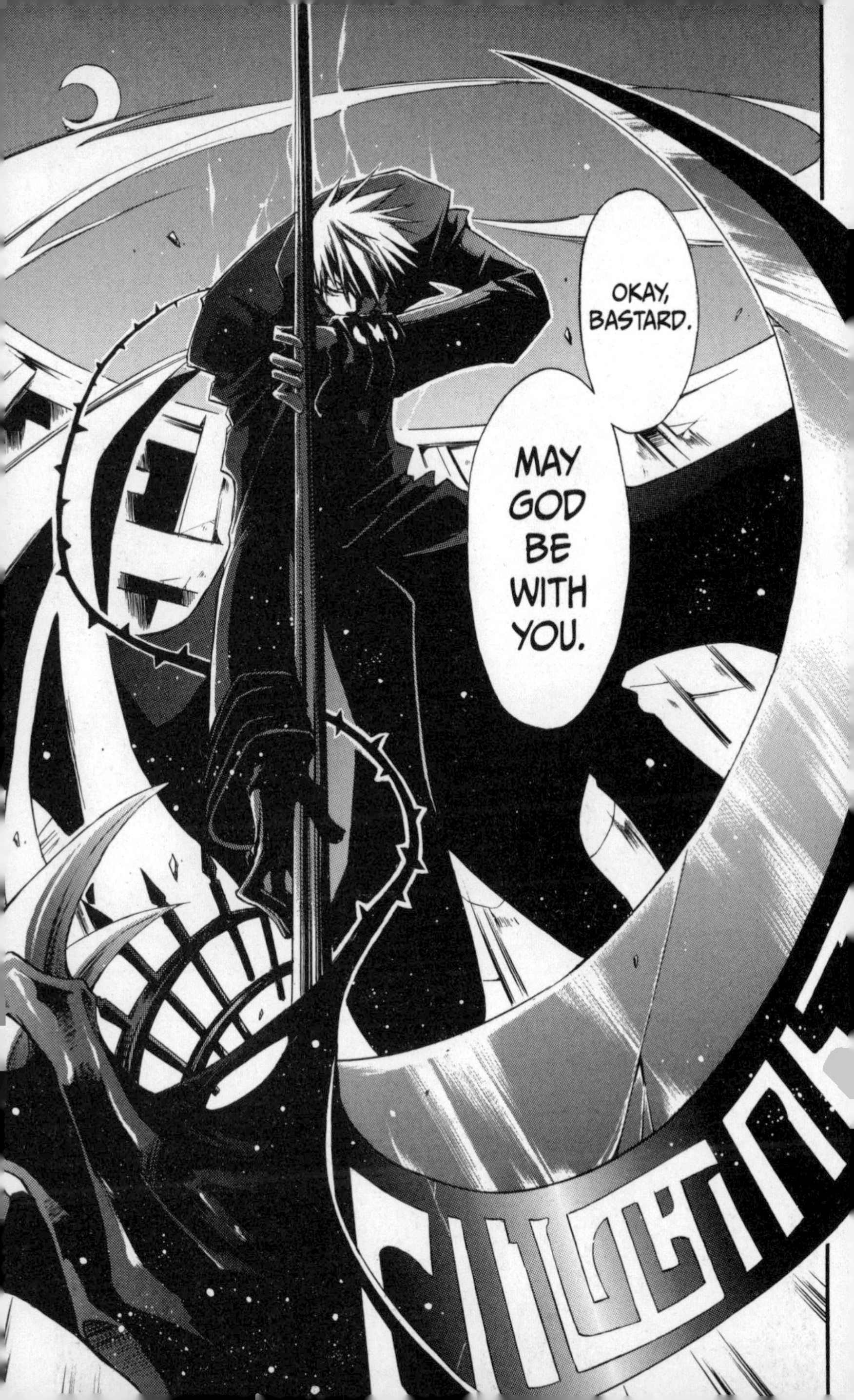
OKAY, BASTARD.
MAY GOD BE WITH YOU.

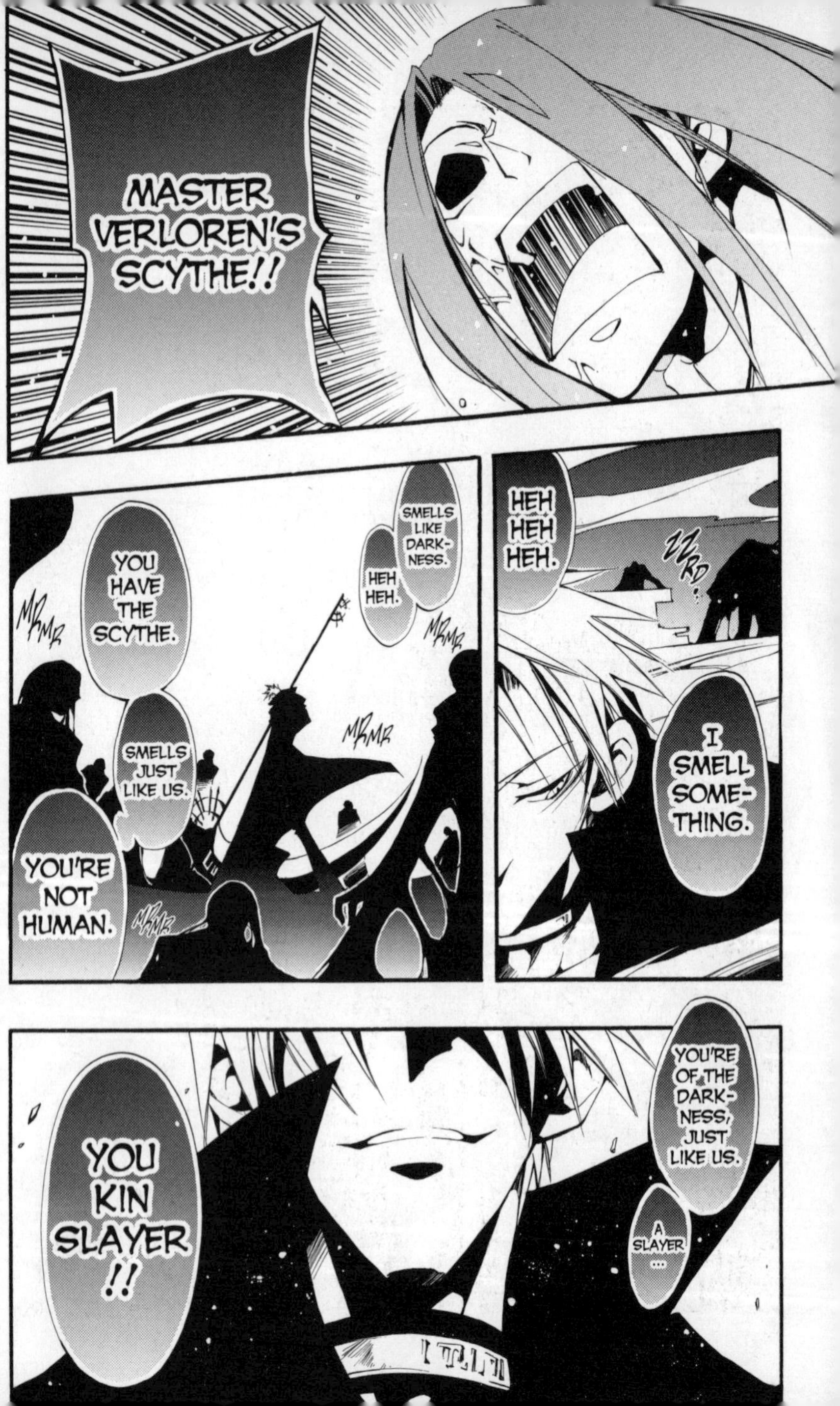
MASTER VERLOREN'S SCYTHE!!
HEH HEH HEH.
ZZRD
I SMELL SOMETHING.
SMELLS LIKE DARKNESS.
HEH HEH.
MRMR
MRMR
YOU HAVE THE SCYTHE.
MRMR
SMELLS JUST LIKE US.
YOU'RE NOT HUMAN.
MRMR
YOU'RE OF THE DARKNESS, JUST LIKE US.
A SLAYER...
YOU KIN SLAYER!!

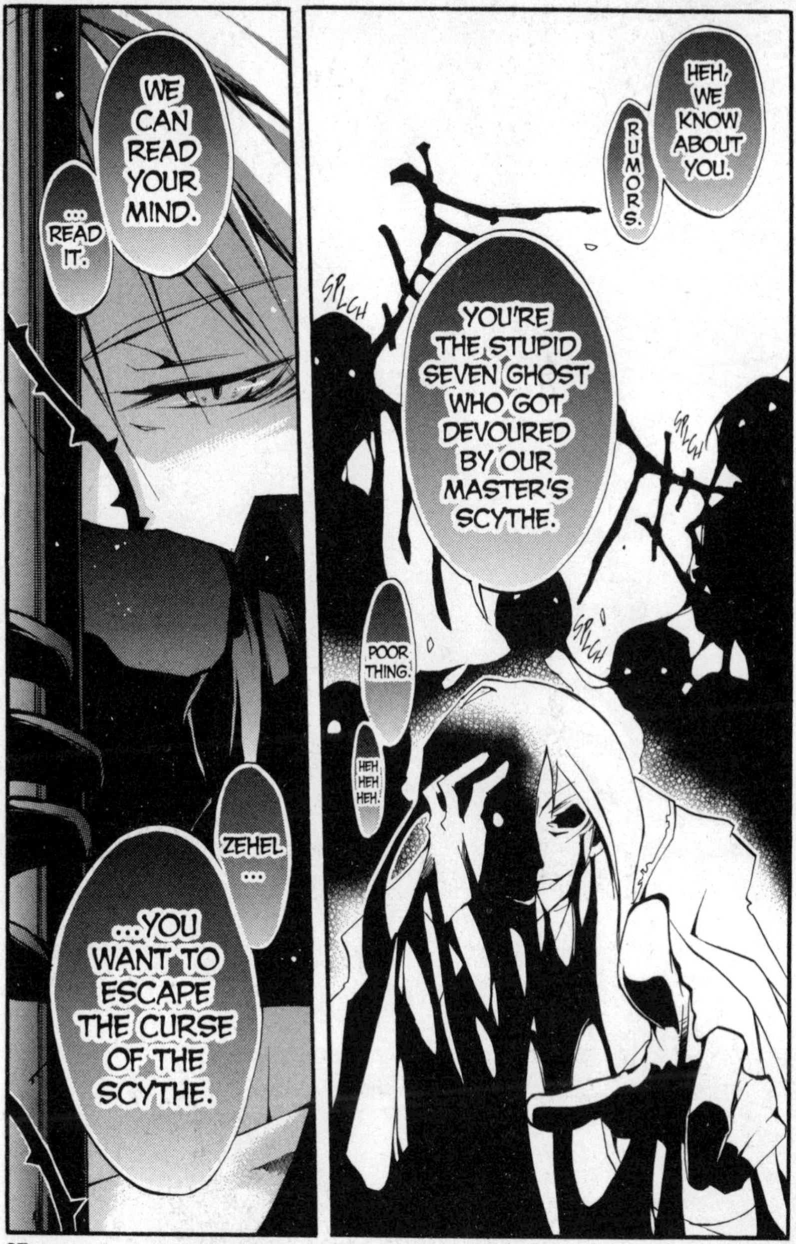
HEH, WE KNOW ABOUT YOU.
RUMORS.
SPLCH
YOU'RE THE STUPID SEVEN GHOST WHO GOT DEVOURED BY OUR MASTER'S SCYTHE.
SPLCH
SPLCH
POOR THING.
HEH HEH HEH.
WE CAN READ YOUR MIND.
...READ IT.
ZEHEL...
...YOU WANT TO ESCAPE THE CURSE OF THE SCYTHE.

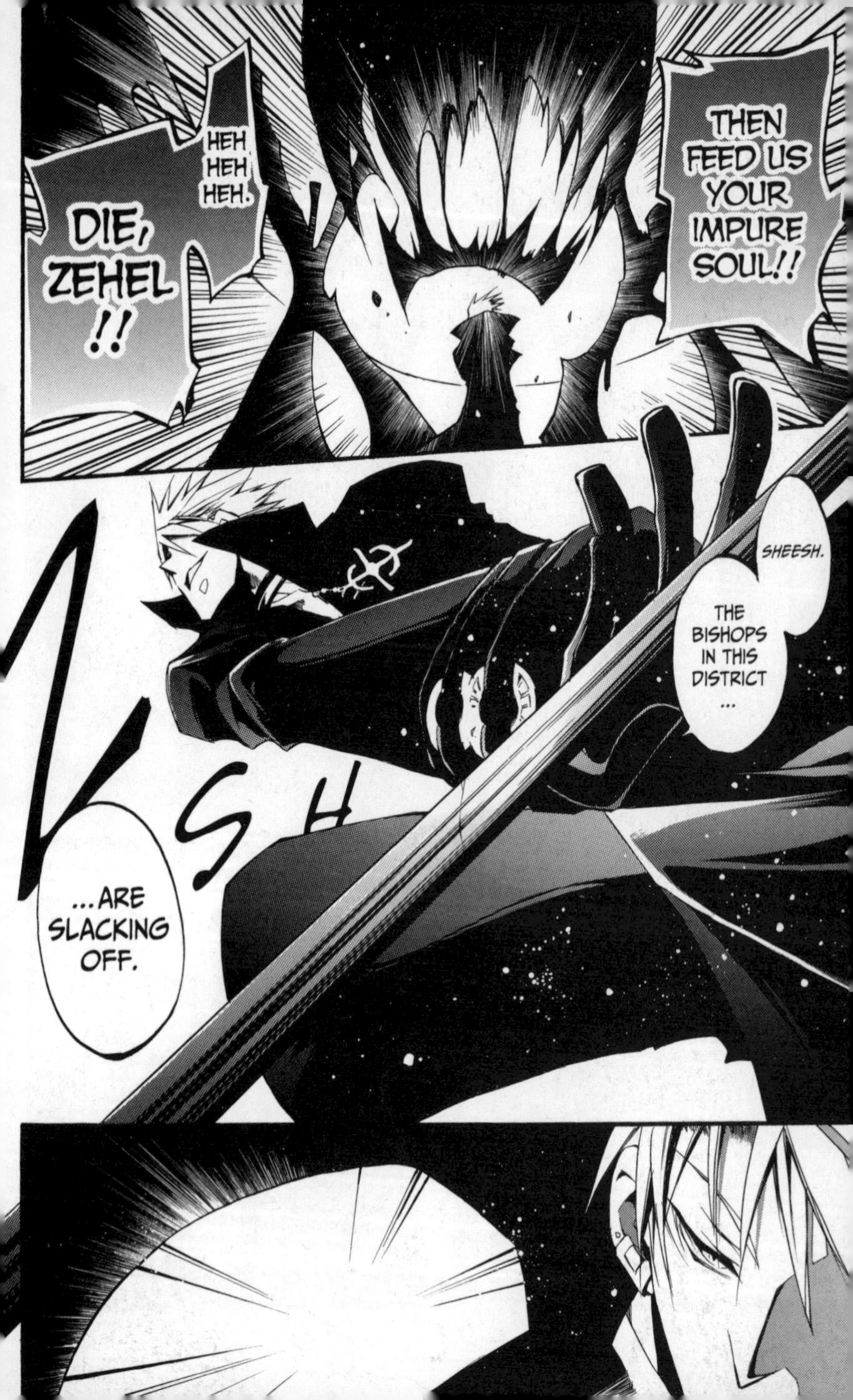
THEN FEED US YOUR IMPURE SOUL!!
HEH HEH HEH.
DIE, ZEHEL!!
SHEESH.
THE BISHOPS IN THIS DISTRICT...
VSH
...ARE SLACKING OFF.

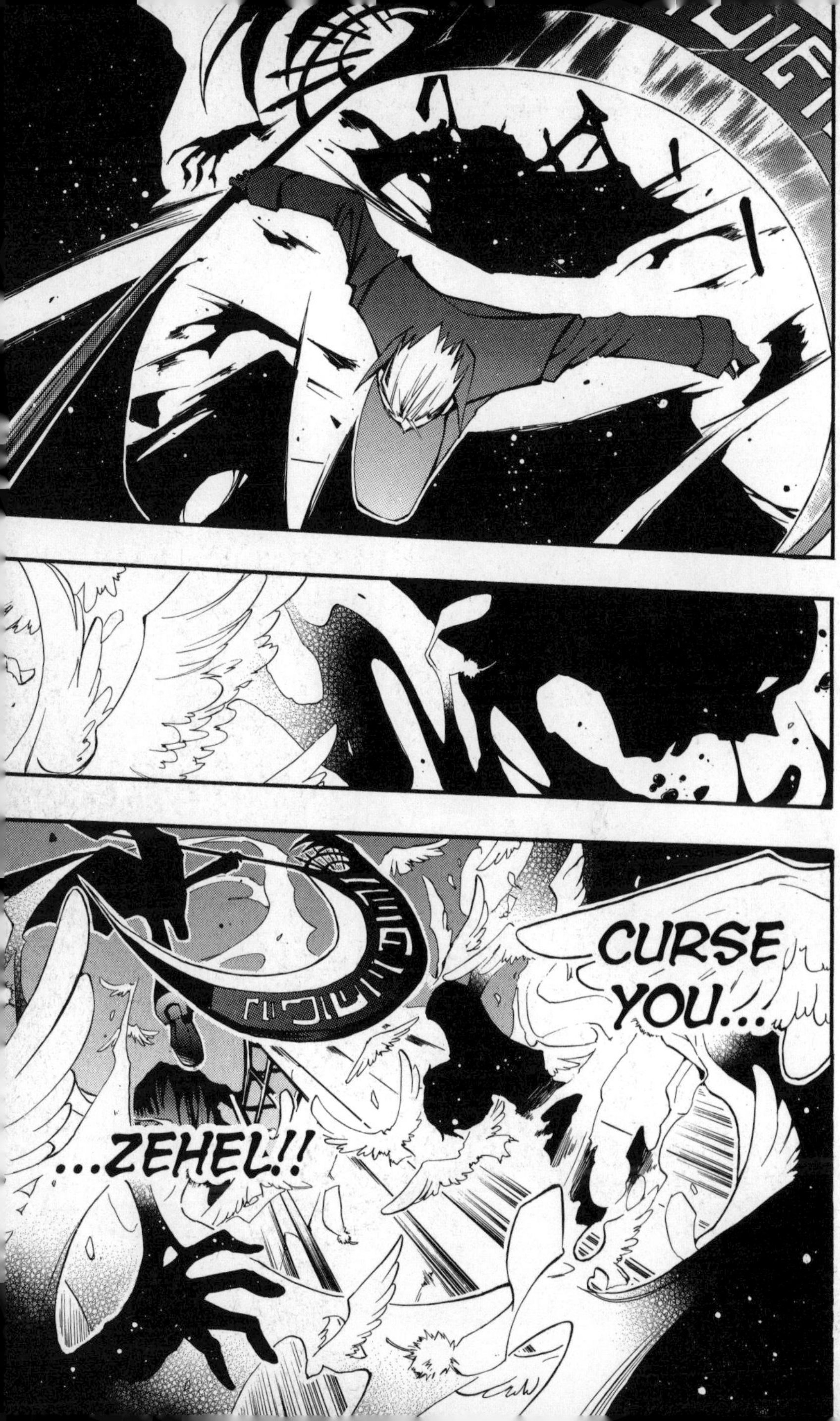
CURSE YOU...
...ZEHEL!!

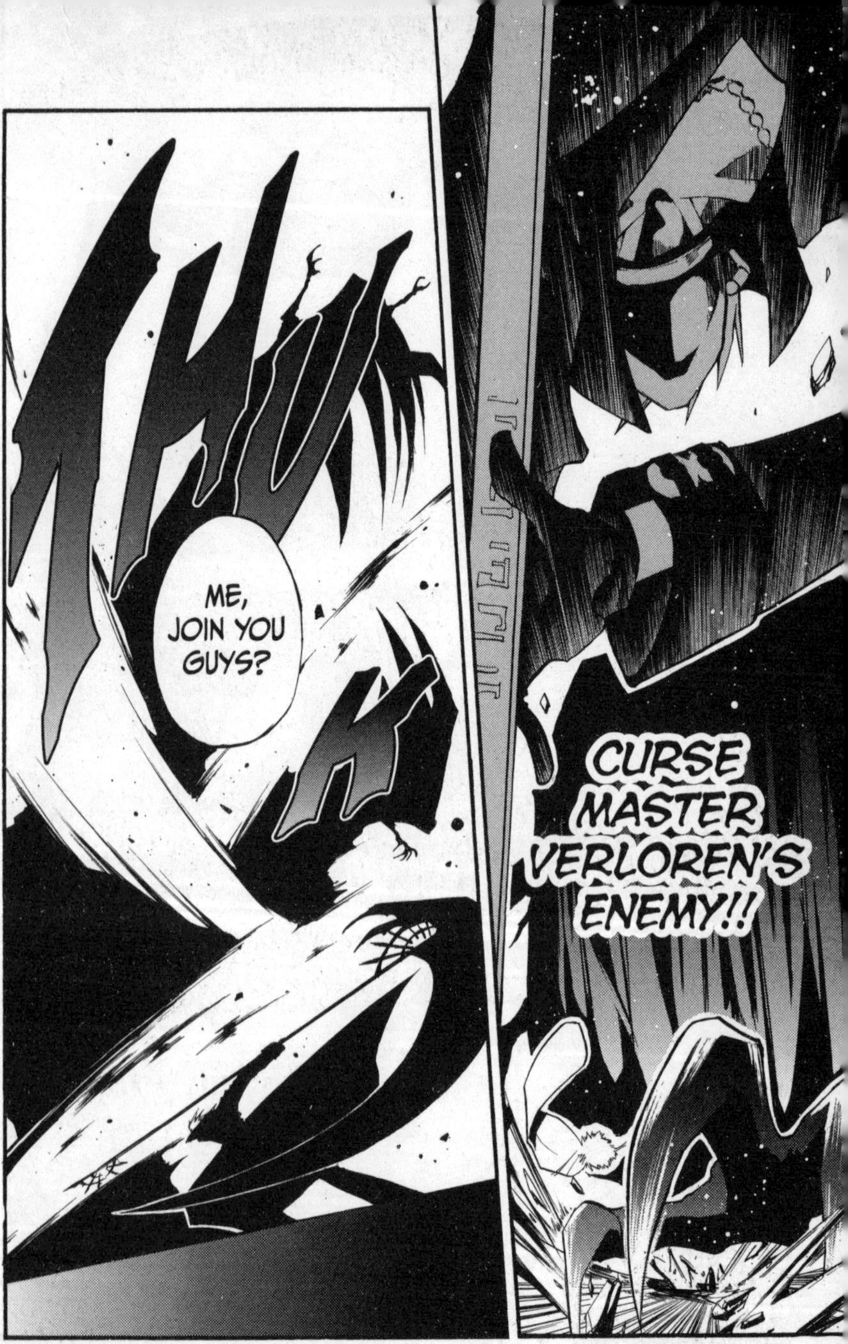
CURSE MASTER VERLOREN'S ENEMY!!
ME, JOIN YOU GUYS?

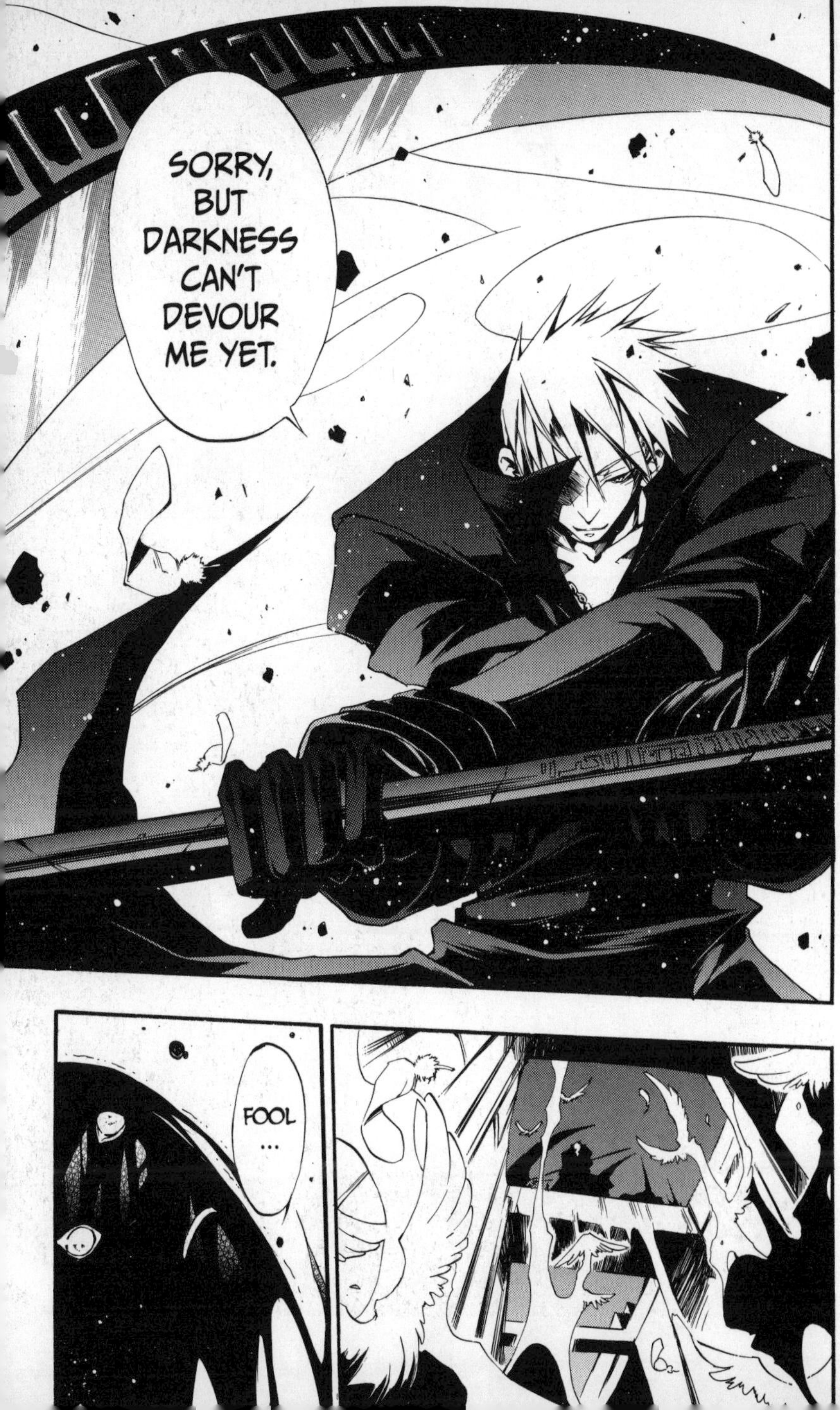
SORRY, BUT DARKNESS CAN'T DEVOUR ME YET.
FOOL ...

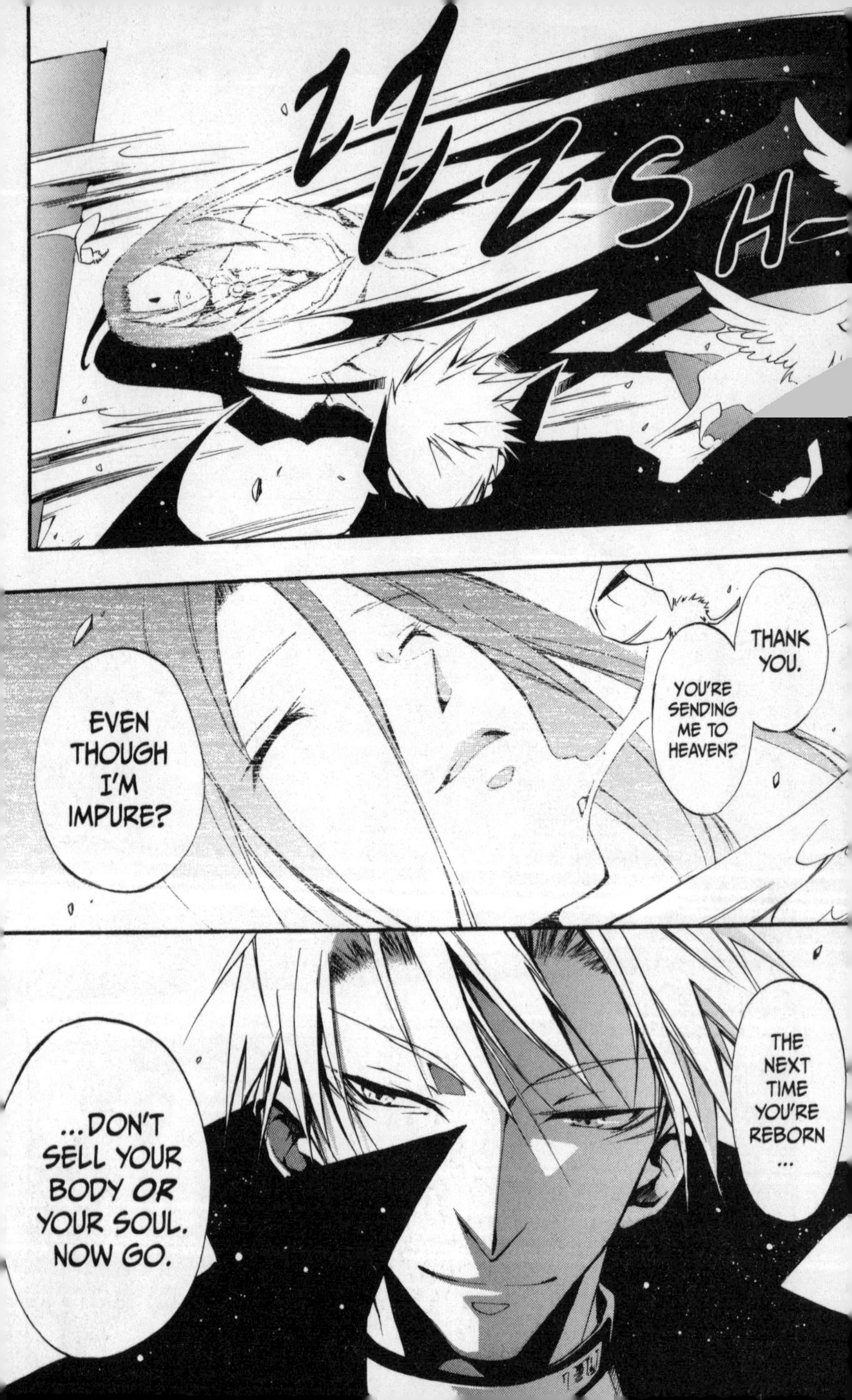
ZZZZSSH—
THANK YOU.
YOU'RE SENDING ME TO HEAVEN?
EVEN THOUGH I'M IMPURE?
THE NEXT TIME YOU'RE REBORN...
...DON'T SELL YOUR BODY OR YOUR SOUL. NOW GO.

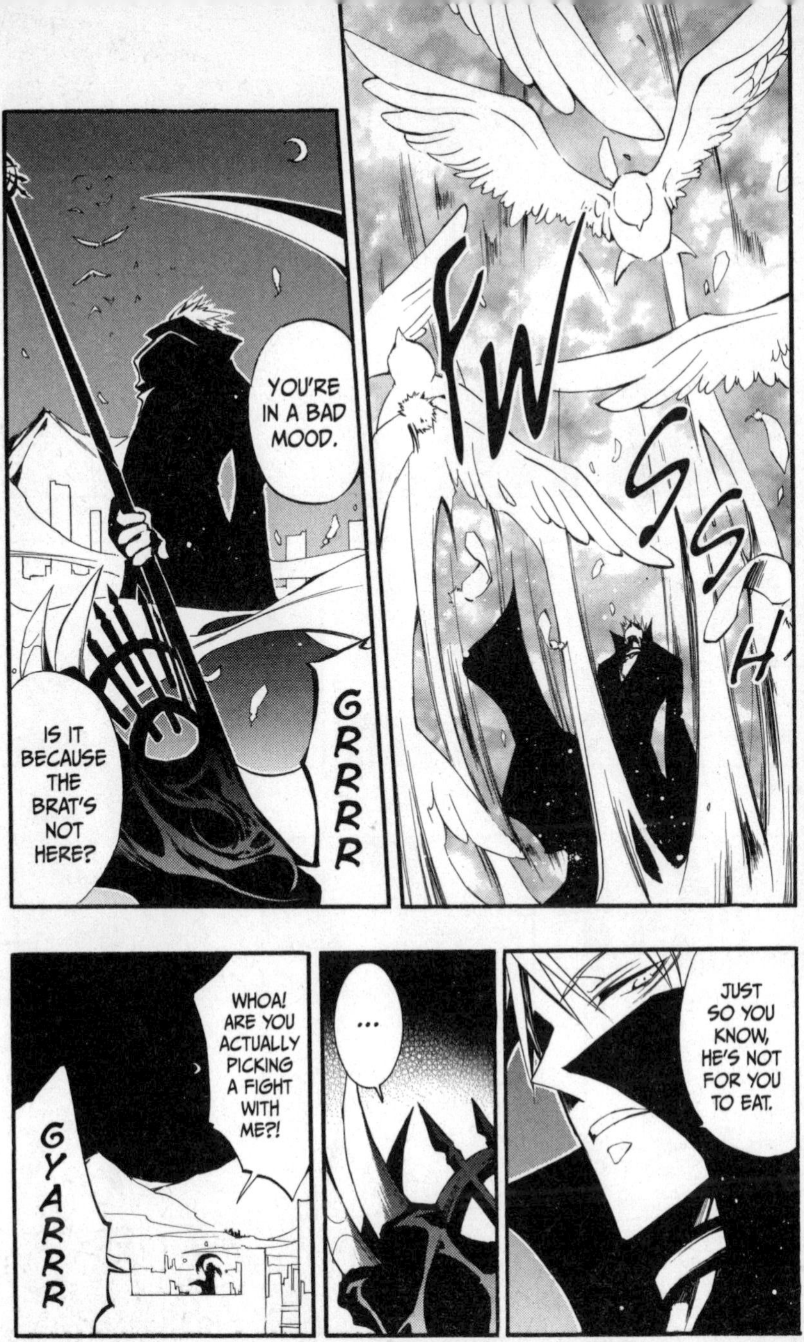
FWSSH
YOU'RE IN A BAD MOOD.
IS IT BECAUSE THE BRAT'S NOT HERE?
GRRRR
JUST SO YOU KNOW, HE'S NOT FOR YOU TO EAT.
...
WHOA! ARE YOU ACTUALLY PICKING A FIGHT WITH ME?!
GYARRR

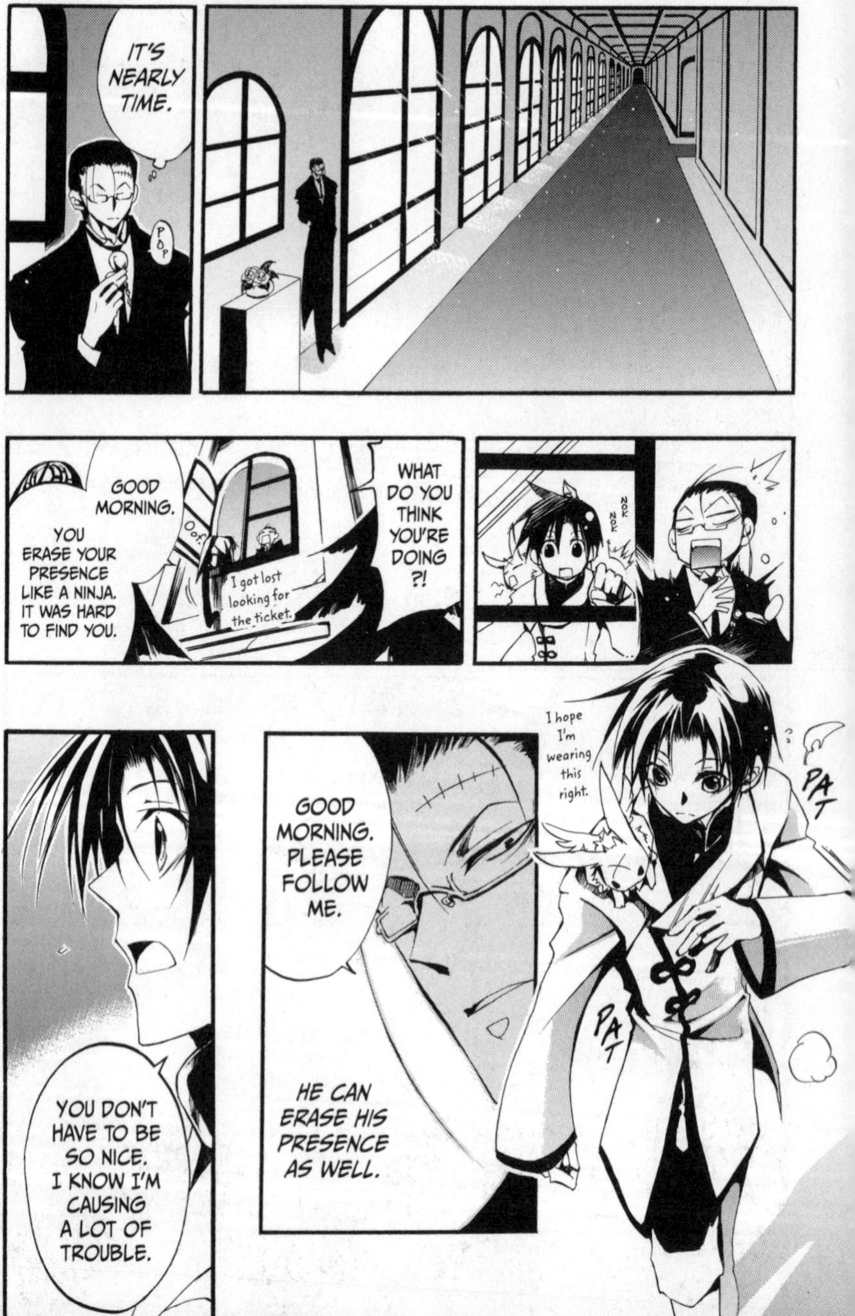
IT'S NEARLY TIME.
POP
NOK NOK
WHAT DO YOU THINK YOU'RE DOING?!
GOOD MORNING. YOU ERASE YOUR PRESENCE LIKE A NINJA. IT WAS HARD TO FIND YOU.
Oof.
I got lost looking for the ticket.
I hope I'm wearing this right.
PAT
PAT
GOOD MORNING. PLEASE FOLLOW ME.
HE CAN ERASE HIS PRESENCE AS WELL.
YOU DON'T HAVE TO BE SO NICE. I KNOW I'M CAUSING A LOT OF TROUBLE.

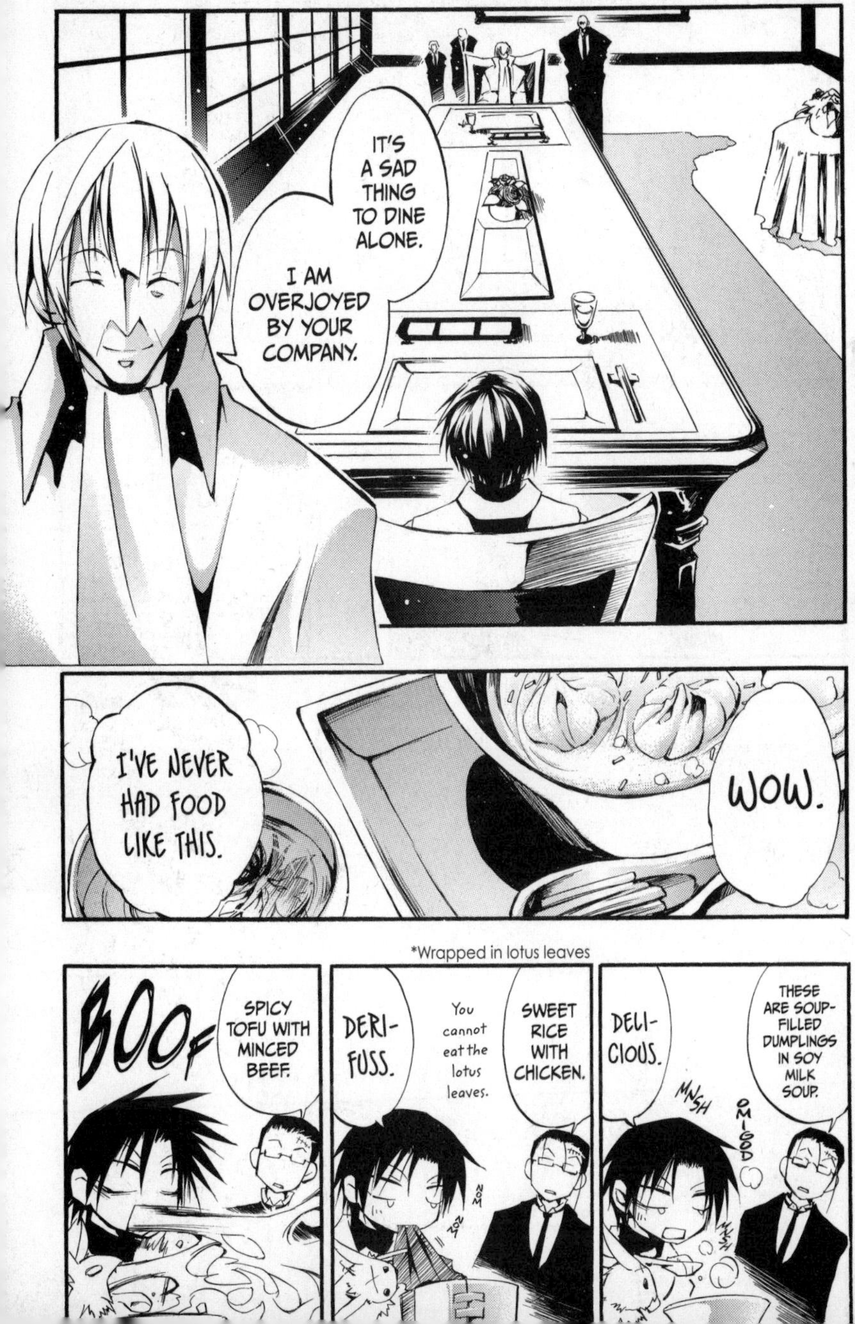
IT'S A SAD THING TO DINE ALONE.
I AM OVERJOYED BY YOUR COMPANY.
WOW.
I'VE NEVER HAD FOOD LIKE THIS.
*Wrapped in lotus leaves
THESE ARE SOUP-FILLED DUMPLINGS IN SOY MILK SOUP.
OMIGOD
DELI-CIOUS.
MNSH
MNSH
SWEET RICE WITH CHICKEN.
You cannot eat the lotus leaves.
DERI-FUSS.
NOM
NOM
SPICY TOFU WITH MINCED BEEF.
BOOF

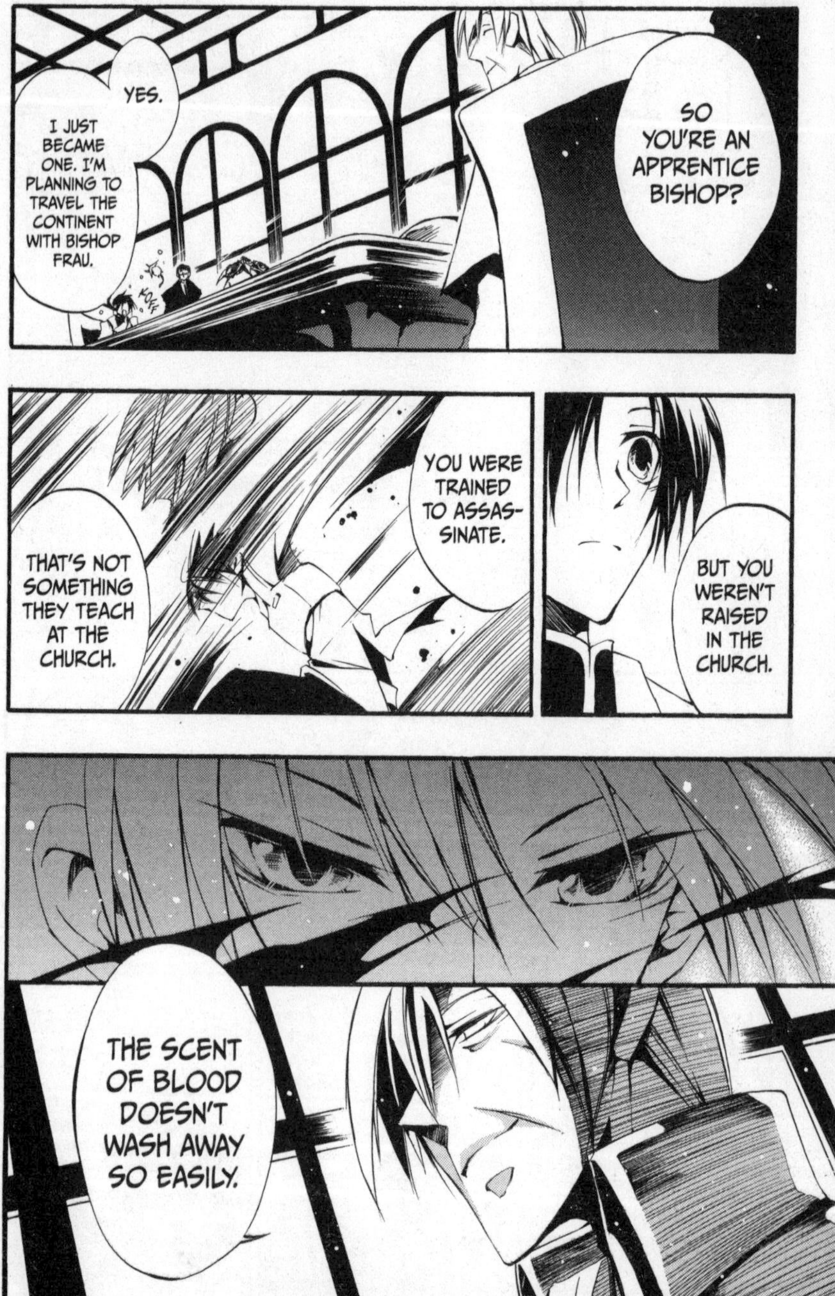
SO YOU'RE AN APPRENTICE BISHOP?
YES.
I JUST BECAME ONE. I'M PLANNING TO TRAVEL THE CONTINENT WITH BISHOP FRAU.
BUT YOU WEREN'T RAISED IN THE CHURCH.
YOU WERE TRAINED TO ASSAS-SINATE.
THAT'S NOT SOMETHING THEY TEACH AT THE CHURCH.
THE SCENT OF BLOOD DOESN'T WASH AWAY SO EASILY.

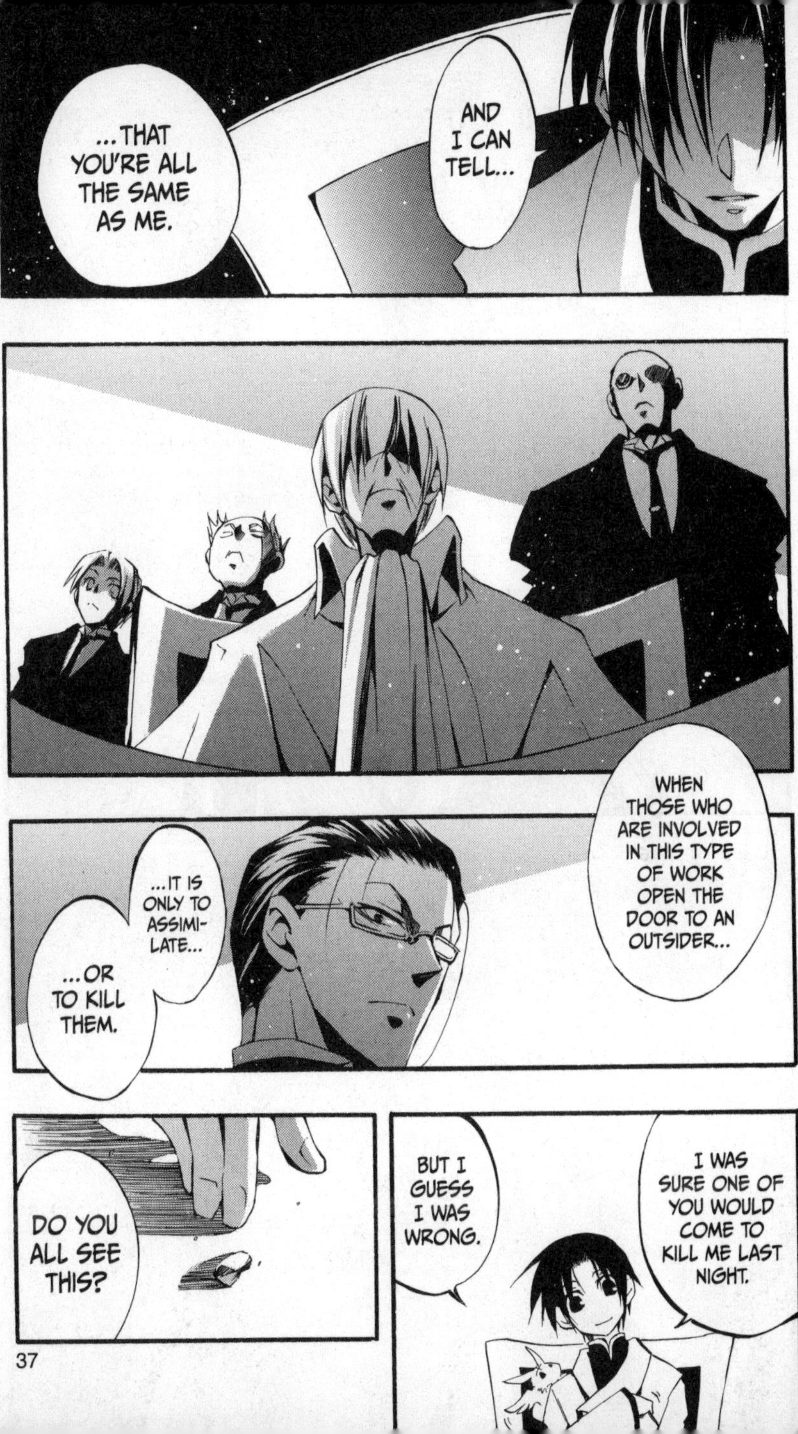
AND I CAN TELL...
...THAT YOU'RE ALL THE SAME AS ME.
WHEN THOSE WHO ARE INVOLVED IN THIS TYPE OF WORK OPEN THE DOOR TO AN OUTSIDER...
...IT IS ONLY TO ASSIMI-LATE...
...OR TO KILL THEM.
I WAS SURE ONE OF YOU WOULD COME TO KILL ME LAST NIGHT.
BUT I GUESS I WAS WRONG.
DO YOU ALL SEE THIS?

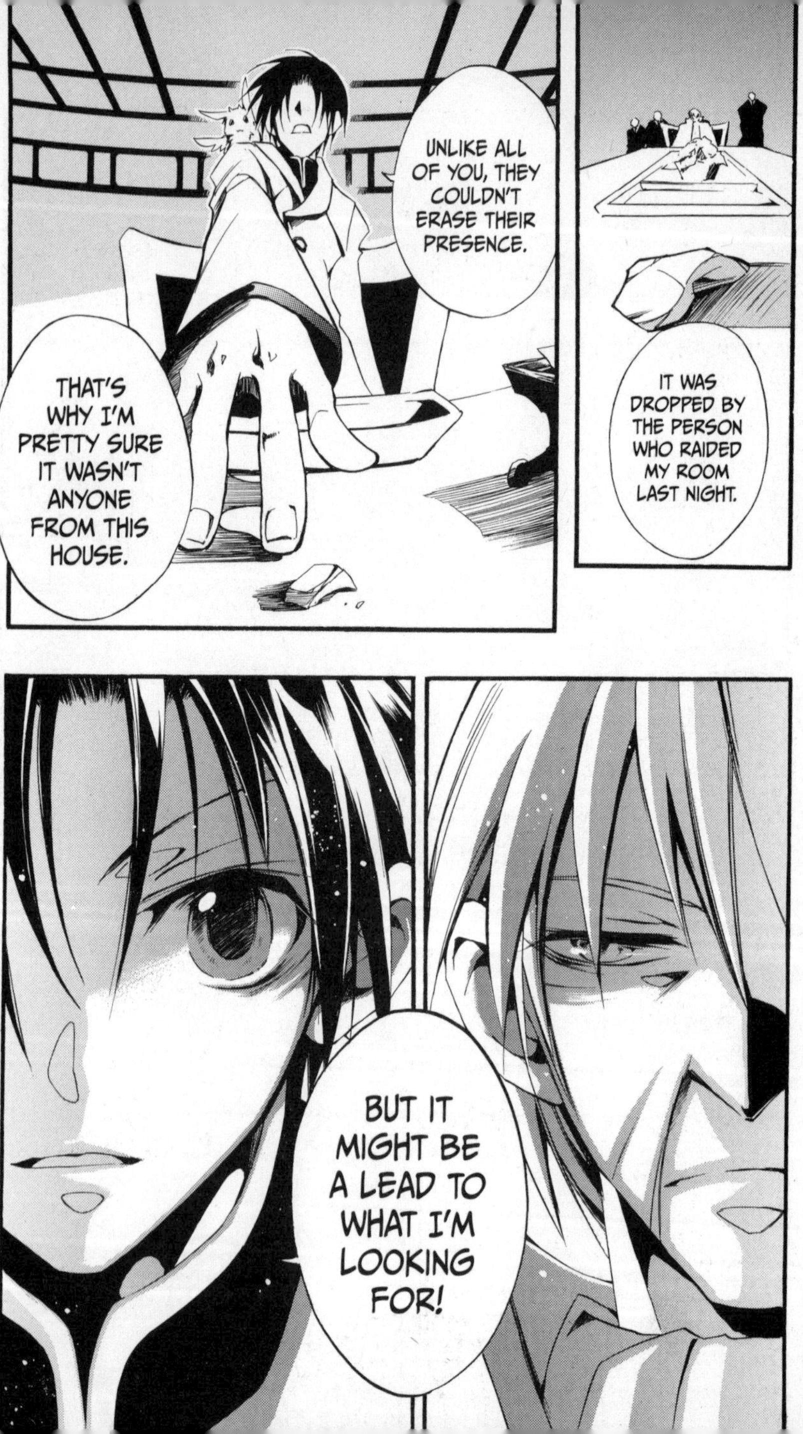
IT WAS DROPPED BY THE PERSON WHO RAIDED MY ROOM LAST NIGHT.
UNLIKE ALL OF YOU, THEY COULDN'T ERASE THEIR PRESENCE.
THAT'S WHY I'M PRETTY SURE IT WASN'T ANYONE FROM THIS HOUSE.
BUT IT MIGHT BE A LEAD TO WHAT I'M LOOKING FOR!

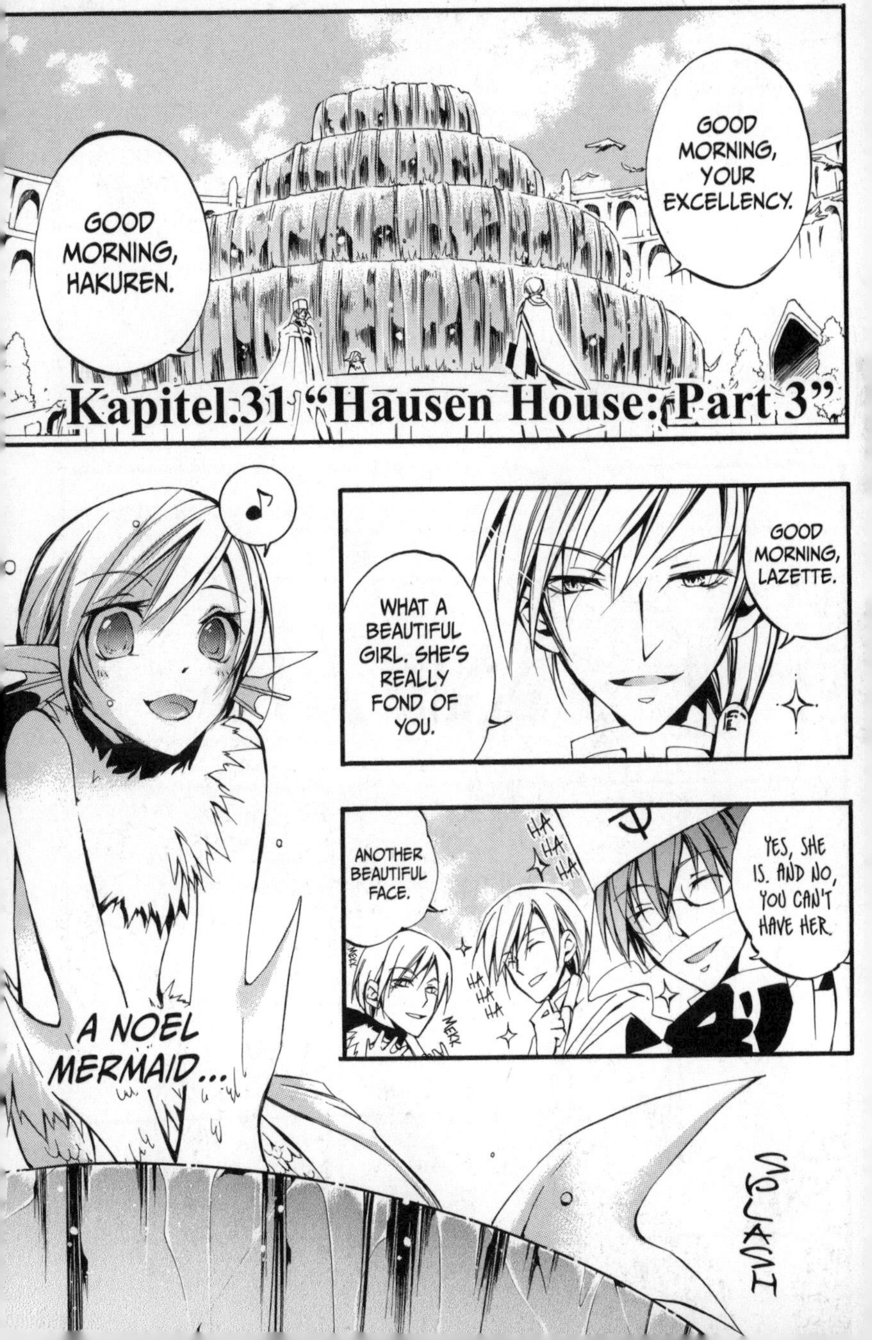
GOOD MORNING, YOUR EXCELLENCY.
GOOD MORNING, HAKUREN.
Kapitel:31 "Hausen House: Part 3"
GOOD MORNING, LAZETTE.
WHAT A BEAUTIFUL GIRL. SHE'S REALLY FOND OF YOU.
YES, SHE IS. AND NO, YOU CAN'T HAVE HER.
HA HA HA
ANOTHER BEAUTIFUL FACE.
HA HA HA
MEKK
MEKK
♪
A NOEL MERMAID...
SPLASH

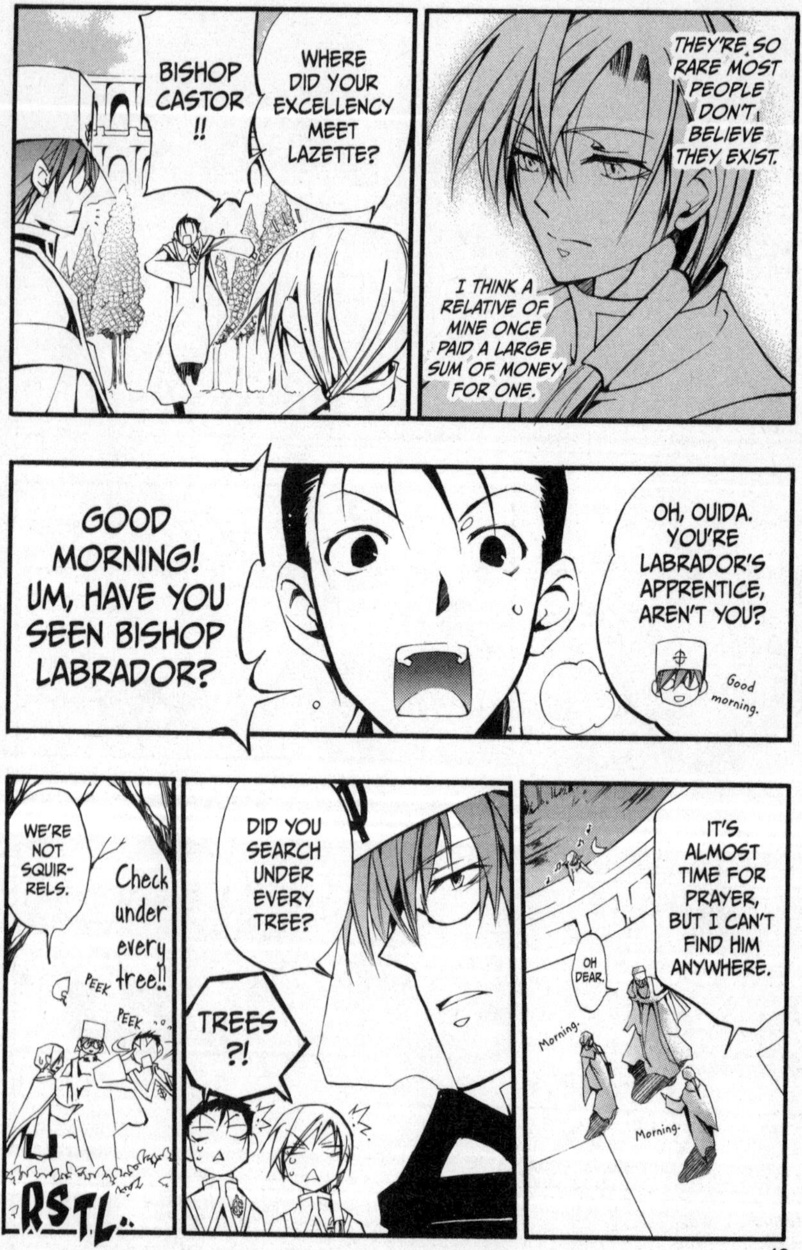

THEY'RE SO RARE MOST PEOPLE DON'T BELIEVE THEY EXIST.
I THINK A RELATIVE OF MINE ONCE PAID A LARGE SUM OF MONEY FOR ONE.
WHERE DID YOUR EXCELLENCY MEET LAZETTE?
BISHOP CASTOR !!
OH, OUIDA. YOU'RE LABRADOR'S APPRENTICE, AREN'T YOU?
Good morning.
GOOD MORNING! UM, HAVE YOU SEEN BISHOP LABRADOR?
IT'S ALMOST TIME FOR PRAYER, BUT I CAN'T FIND HIM ANYWHERE.
OH DEAR.
Morning.
Morning.
DID YOU SEARCH UNDER EVERY TREE?
TREES ?!
WE'RE NOT SQUIR-RELS.
Check under every tree!!
PEEK
PEEK
RSTL..

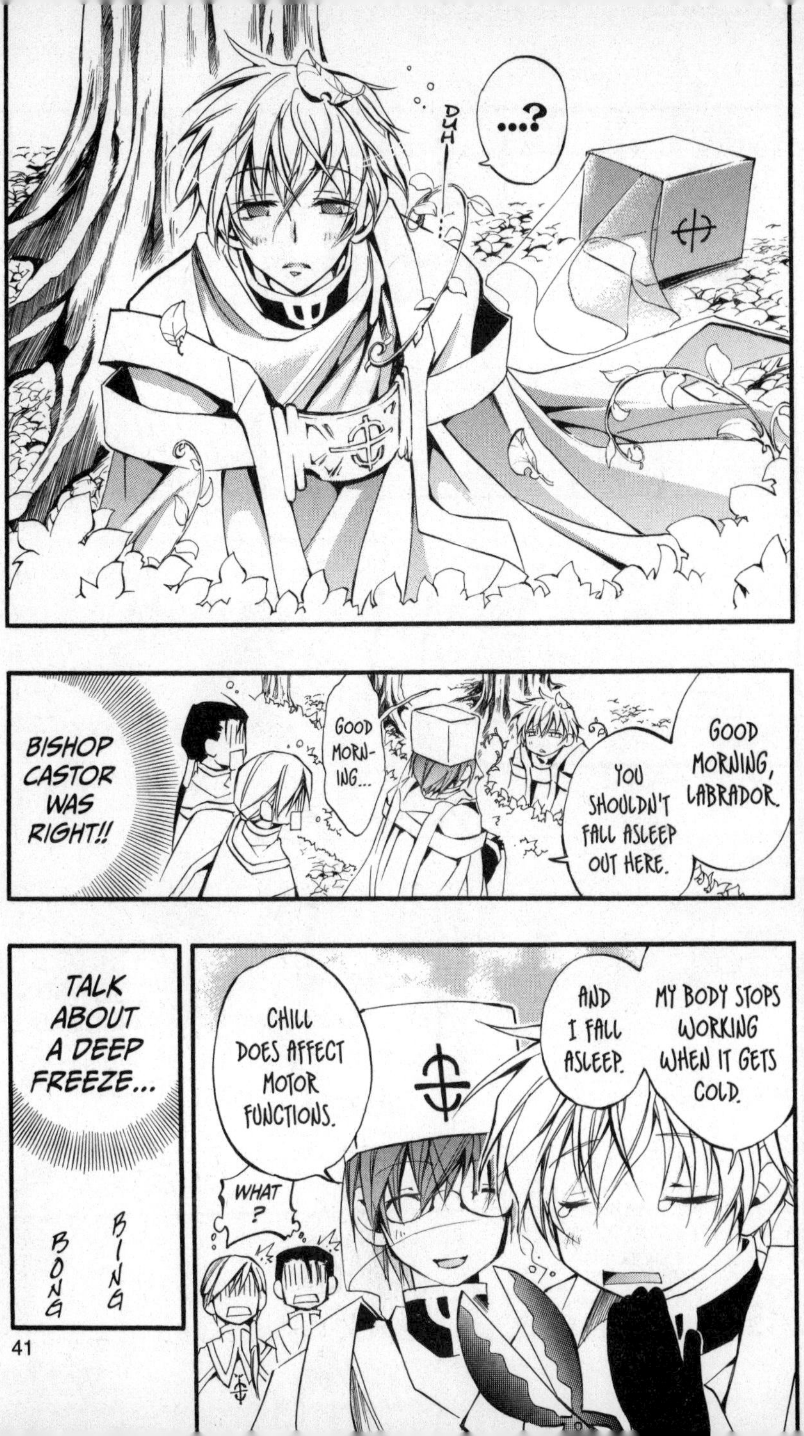
DUH
...?
GOOD MORNING, LABRADOR.
YOU SHOULDN'T FALL ASLEEP OUT HERE.
GOOD MORNING...
BISHOP CASTOR WAS RIGHT!!
MY BODY STOPS WORKING WHEN IT GETS COLD.
AND I FALL ASLEEP.
CHILL DOES AFFECT MOTOR FUNCTIONS.
WHAT?
TALK ABOUT A DEEP FREEZE...
BING
BONG

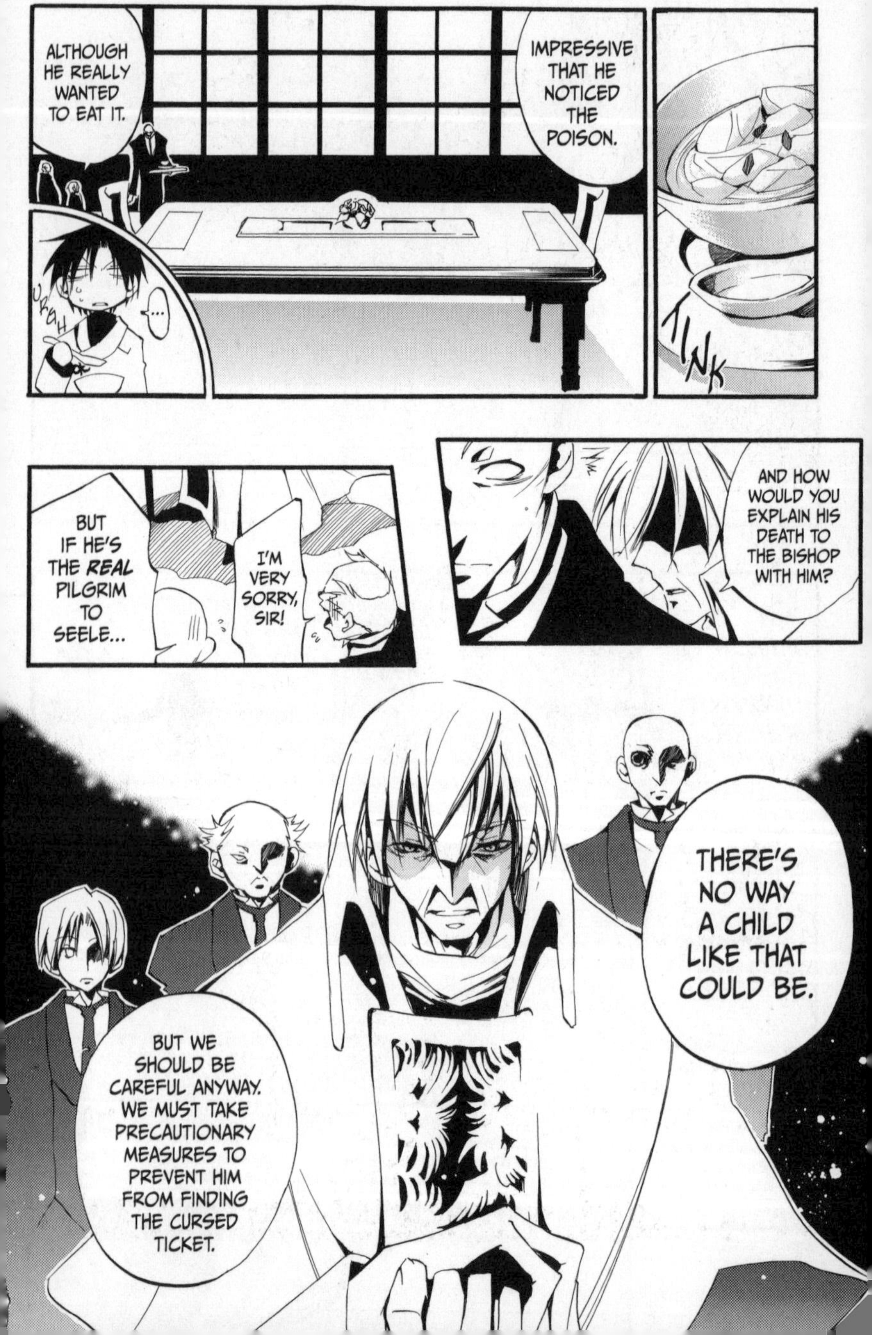
TINK
IMPRESSIVE THAT HE NOTICED THE POISON.
ALTHOUGH HE REALLY WANTED TO EAT IT.
URGH
...
AND HOW WOULD YOU EXPLAIN HIS DEATH TO THE BISHOP WITH HIM?
I'M VERY SORRY, SIR!
BUT IF HE'S THE *REAL* PILGRIM TO SEELE...
THERE'S NO WAY A CHILD LIKE THAT COULD BE.
BUT WE SHOULD BE CAREFUL ANYWAY. WE MUST TAKE PRECAUTIONARY MEASURES TO PREVENT HIM FROM FINDING THE CURSED TICKET.

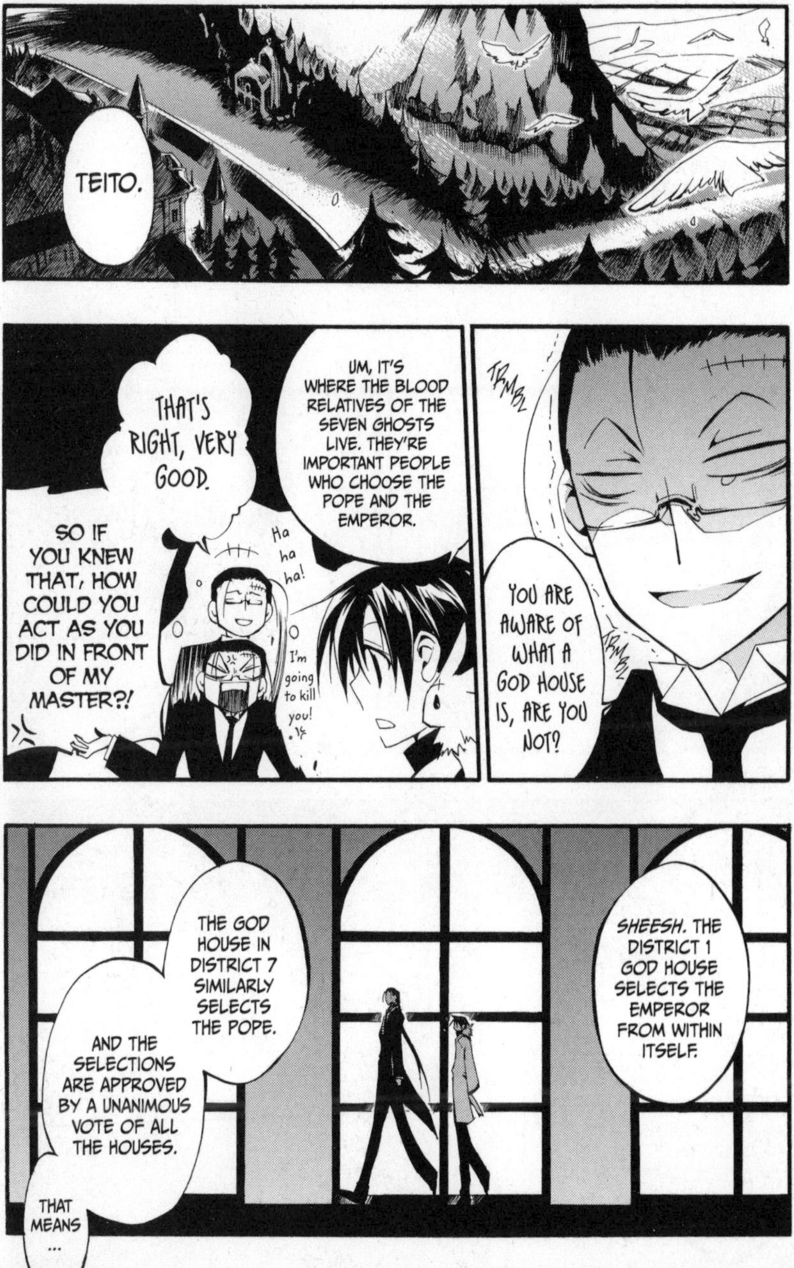
TEITO.
TRMBL
YOU ARE AWARE OF WHAT A GOD HOUSE IS, ARE YOU NOT?
TRMBL
UM, IT'S WHERE THE BLOOD RELATIVES OF THE SEVEN GHOSTS LIVE. THEY'RE IMPORTANT PEOPLE WHO CHOOSE THE POPE AND THE EMPEROR.
THAT'S RIGHT, VERY GOOD.
Ha ha ha!
I'm going to kill you!
SO IF YOU KNEW THAT, HOW COULD YOU ACT AS YOU DID IN FRONT OF MY MASTER?!
SHEESH. THE DISTRICT 1 GOD HOUSE SELECTS THE EMPEROR FROM WITHIN ITSELF.
THE GOD HOUSE IN DISTRICT 7 SIMILARLY SELECTS THE POPE.
AND THE SELECTIONS ARE APPROVED BY A UNANIMOUS VOTE OF ALL THE HOUSES.
THAT MEANS ...

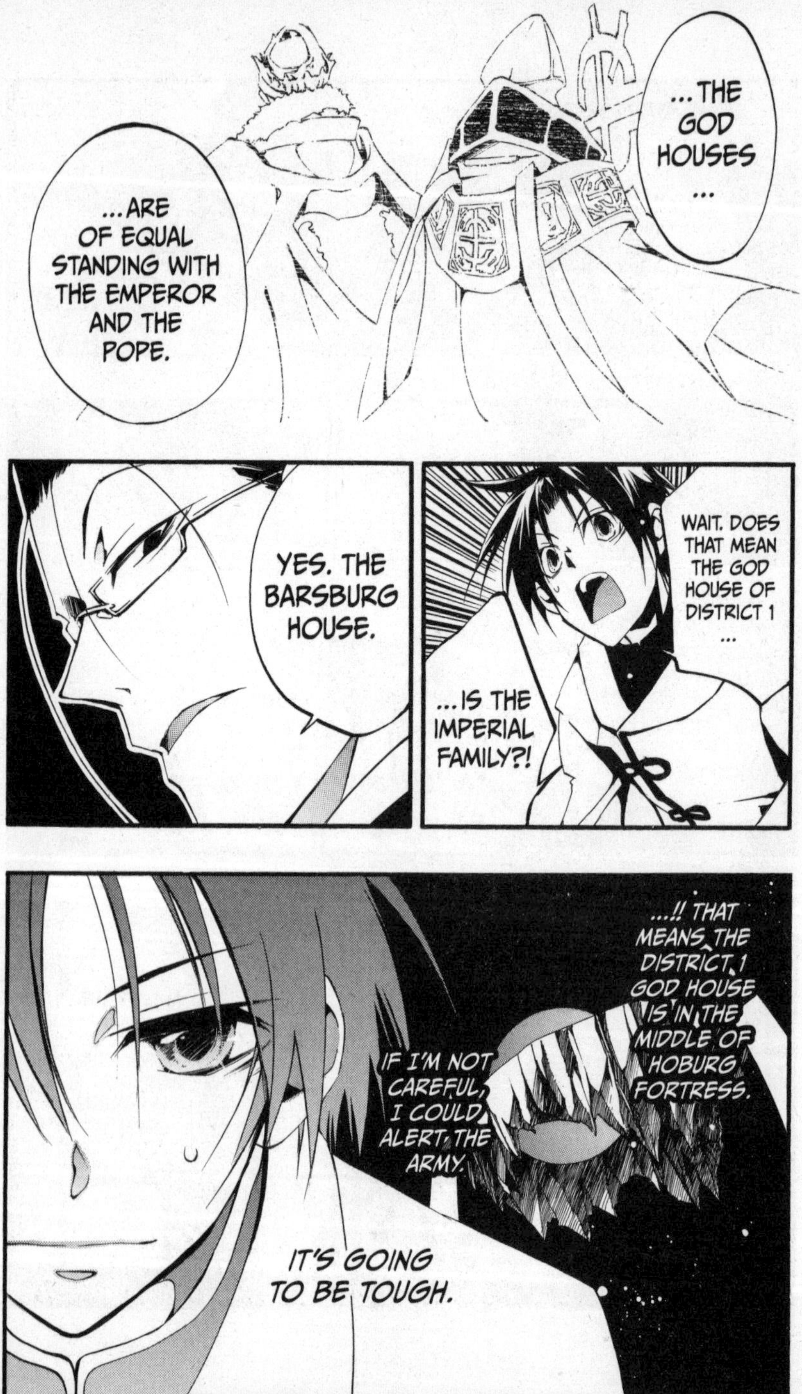
...THE GOD HOUSES ...
...ARE OF EQUAL STANDING WITH THE EMPEROR AND THE POPE.
WAIT. DOES THAT MEAN THE GOD HOUSE OF DISTRICT 1 ...
...IS THE IMPERIAL FAMILY?!
YES. THE BARSBURG HOUSE.
...!! THAT MEANS THE DISTRICT 1 GOD HOUSE IS IN THE MIDDLE OF HOBURG FORTRESS.
IF I'M NOT CAREFUL, I COULD ALERT THE ARMY.
IT'S GOING TO BE TOUGH.

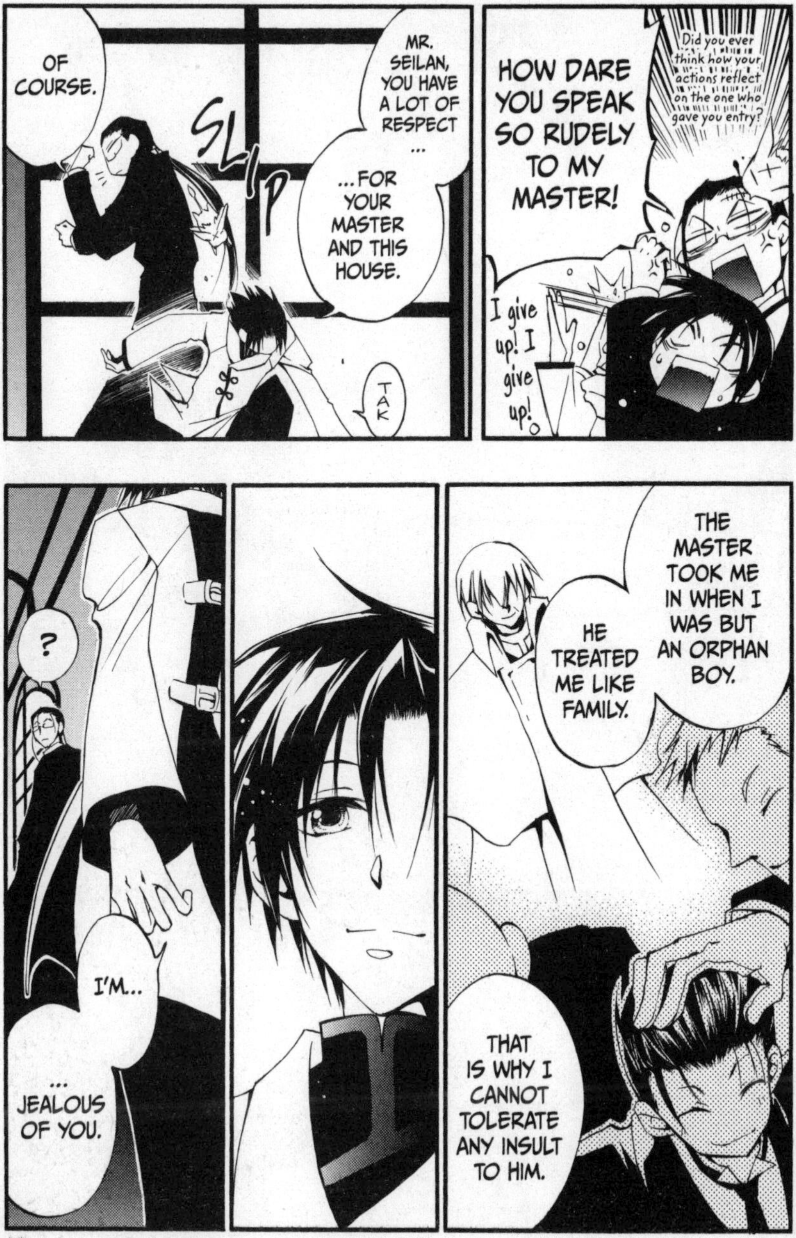
Did you ever think how your actions reflect on the one who gave you entry?
HOW DARE YOU SPEAK SO RUDELY TO MY MASTER!
I give up! I give up!
MR. SEILAN, YOU HAVE A LOT OF RESPECT ...
...FOR YOUR MASTER AND THIS HOUSE.
SLIP
OF COURSE.
TAK
THE MASTER TOOK ME IN WHEN I WAS BUT AN ORPHAN BOY.
HE TREATED ME LIKE FAMILY.
THAT IS WHY I CANNOT TOLERATE ANY INSULT TO HIM.
?
I'M...
... JEALOUS OF YOU.

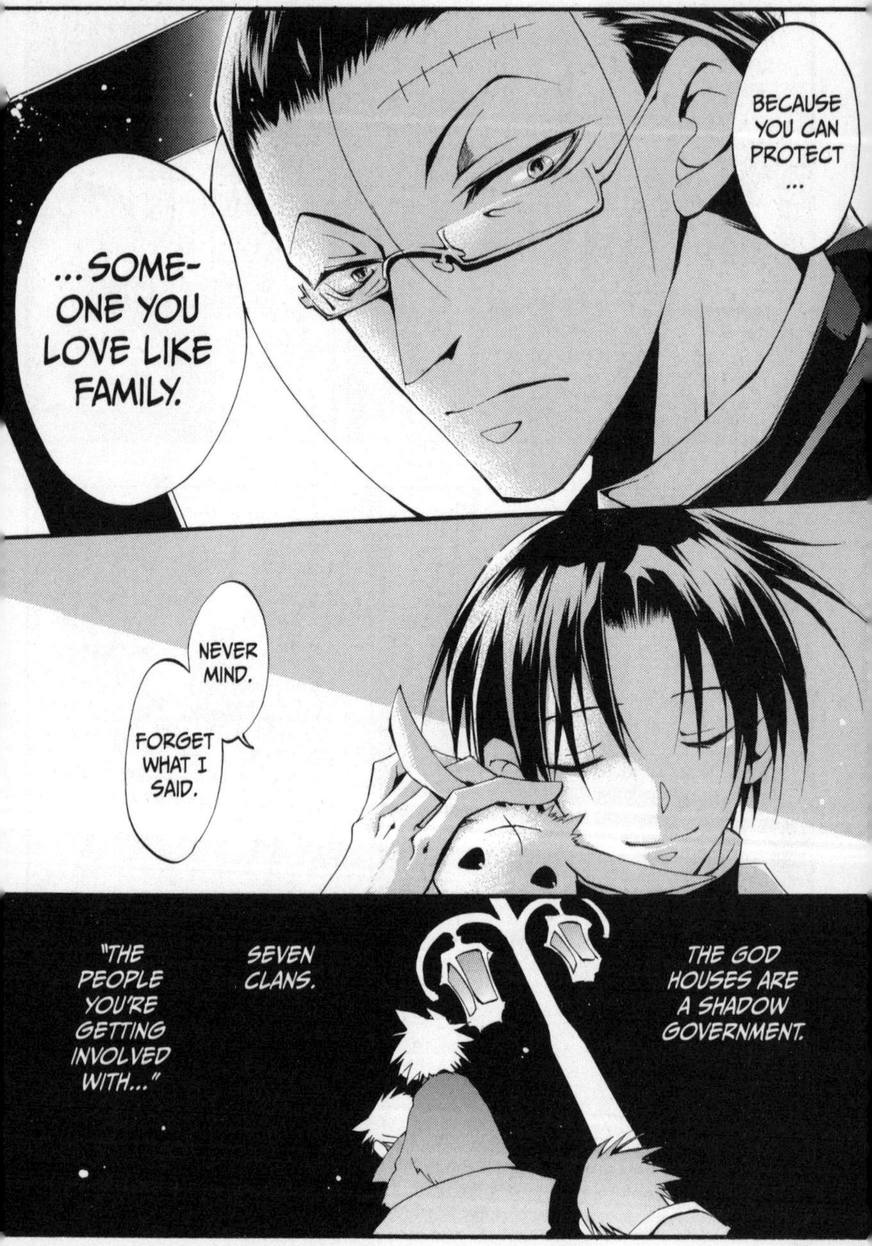
BECAUSE YOU CAN PROTECT ...
...SOME-ONE YOU LOVE LIKE FAMILY.
NEVER MIND.
FORGET WHAT I SAID.
THE GOD HOUSES ARE A SHADOW GOVERNMENT.
SEVEN CLANS.
"THE PEOPLE YOU'RE GETTING INVOLVED WITH..."

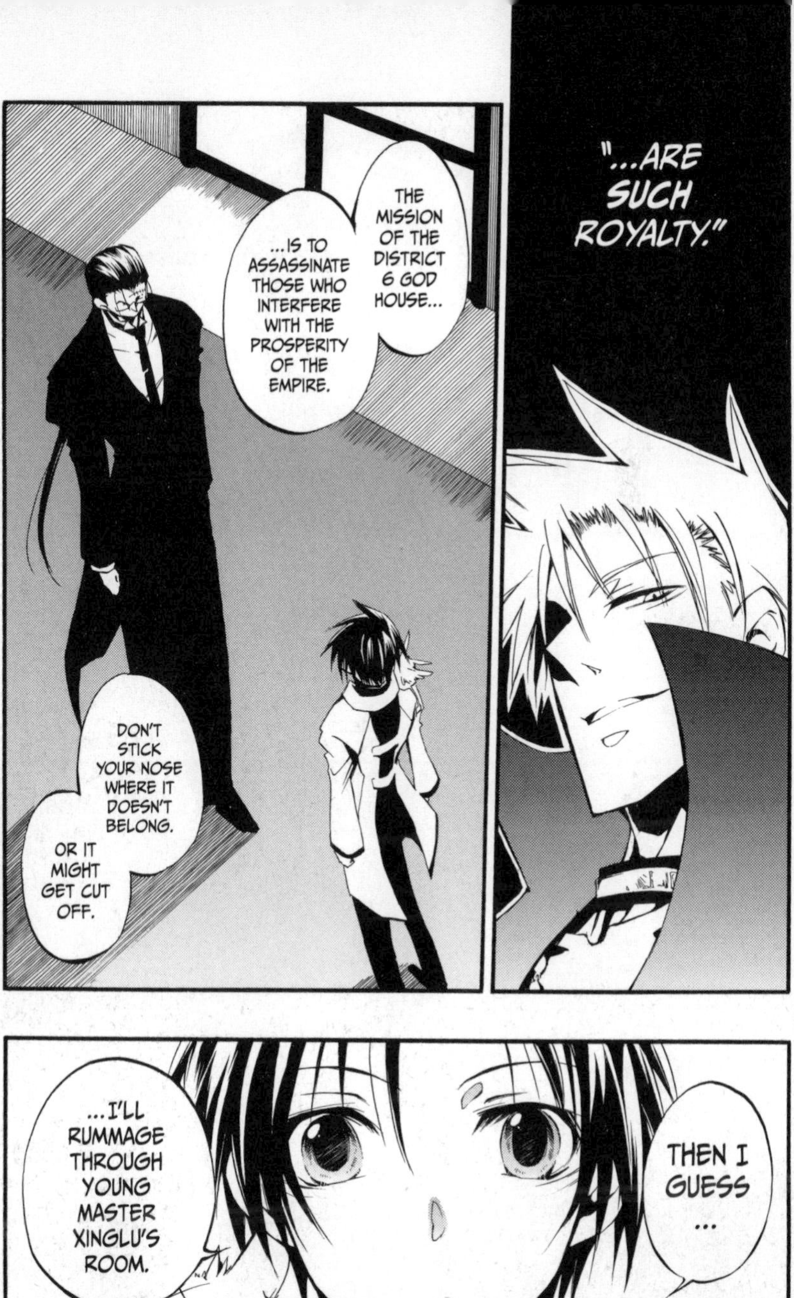
"...ARE SUCH ROYALTY."
THE MISSION OF THE DISTRICT 6 GOD HOUSE...
...IS TO ASSASSINATE THOSE WHO INTERFERE WITH THE PROSPERITY OF THE EMPIRE.
DON'T STICK YOUR NOSE WHERE IT DOESN'T BELONG.
OR IT MIGHT GET CUT OFF.
THEN I GUESS ...
...I'LL RUMMAGE THROUGH YOUNG MASTER XINGLU'S ROOM.

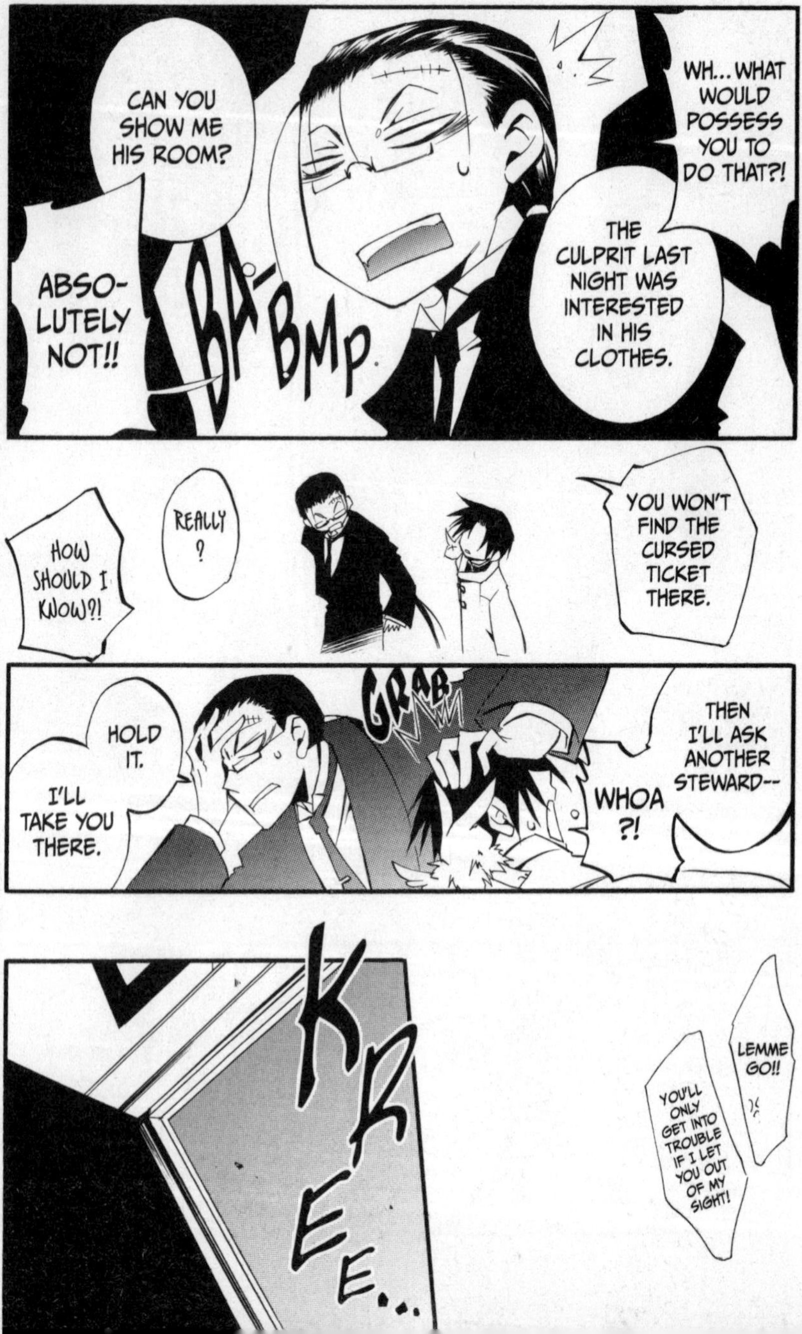
WH...WHAT WOULD POSSESS YOU TO DO THAT?!
THE CULPRIT LAST NIGHT WAS INTERESTED IN HIS CLOTHES.
CAN YOU SHOW ME HIS ROOM?
BA-BMP.
ABSO-LUTELY NOT!!
YOU WON'T FIND THE CURSED TICKET THERE.
REALLY?
HOW SHOULD I KNOW?!
THEN I'LL ASK ANOTHER STEWARD--
GRAB
WHOA?!
HOLD IT.
I'LL TAKE YOU THERE.
LEMME GO!!
YOU'LL ONLY GET INTO TROUBLE IF I LET YOU OUT OF MY SIGHT!
KREEE...

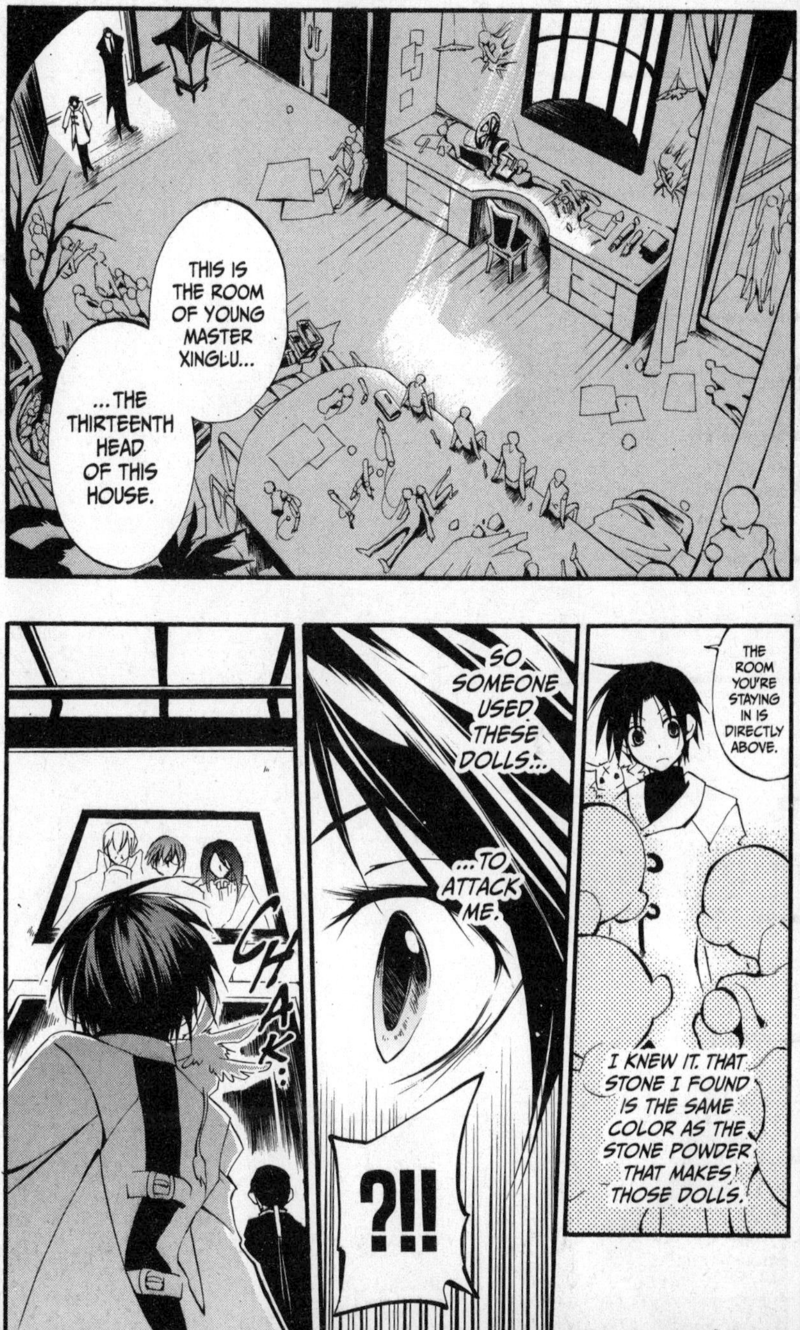
THIS IS THE ROOM OF YOUNG MASTER XINGLU...
...THE THIRTEENTH HEAD OF THIS HOUSE.
THE ROOM YOU'RE STAYING IN IS DIRECTLY ABOVE.
I KNEW IT. THAT STONE I FOUND IS THE SAME COLOR AS THE STONE POWDER THAT MAKES THOSE DOLLS.
SO SOMEONE USED THESE DOLLS...
...TO ATTACK ME.
?!!
CHAK

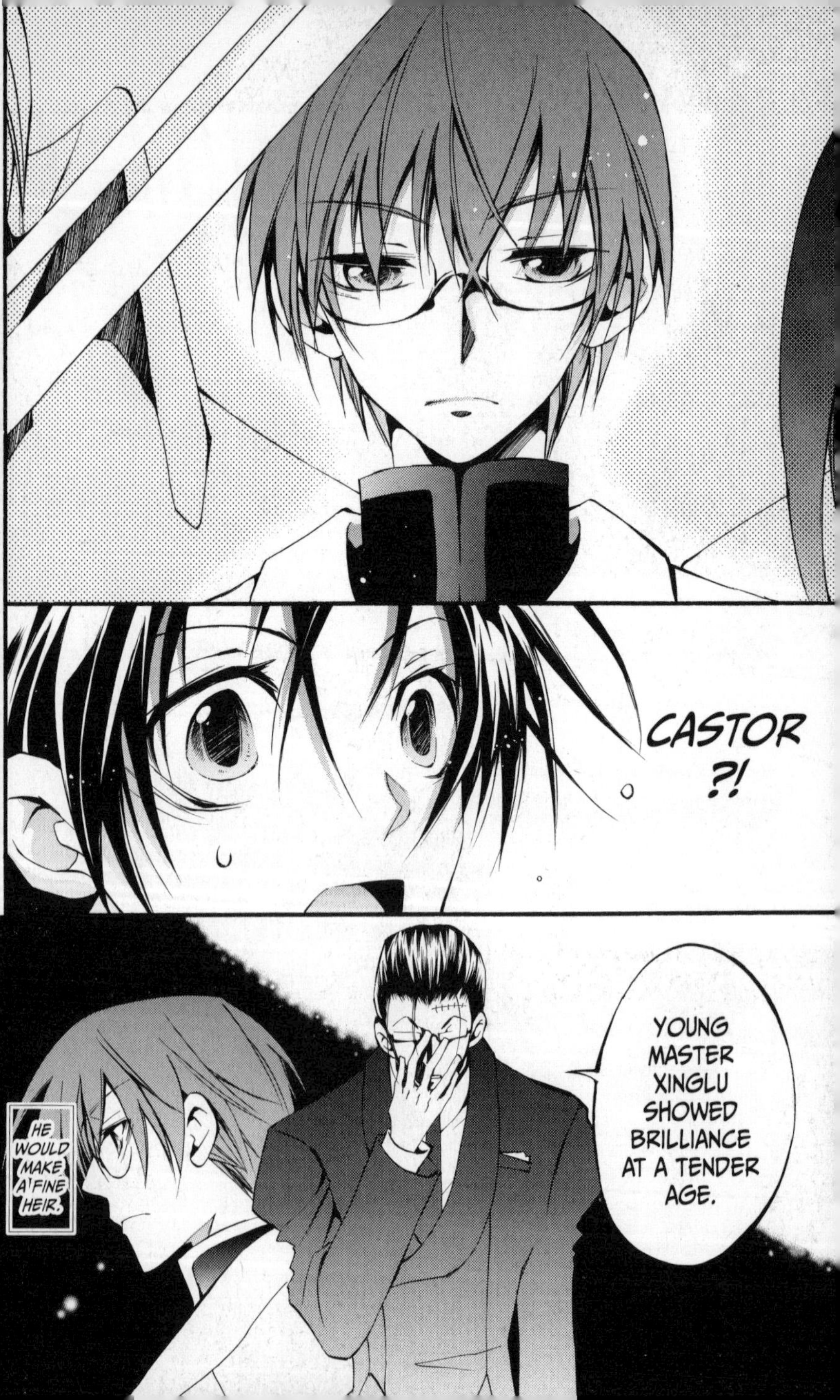
CASTOR ?!
YOUNG MASTER XINGLU SHOWED BRILLIANCE AT A TENDER AGE.
HE WOULD MAKE A FINE HEIR.

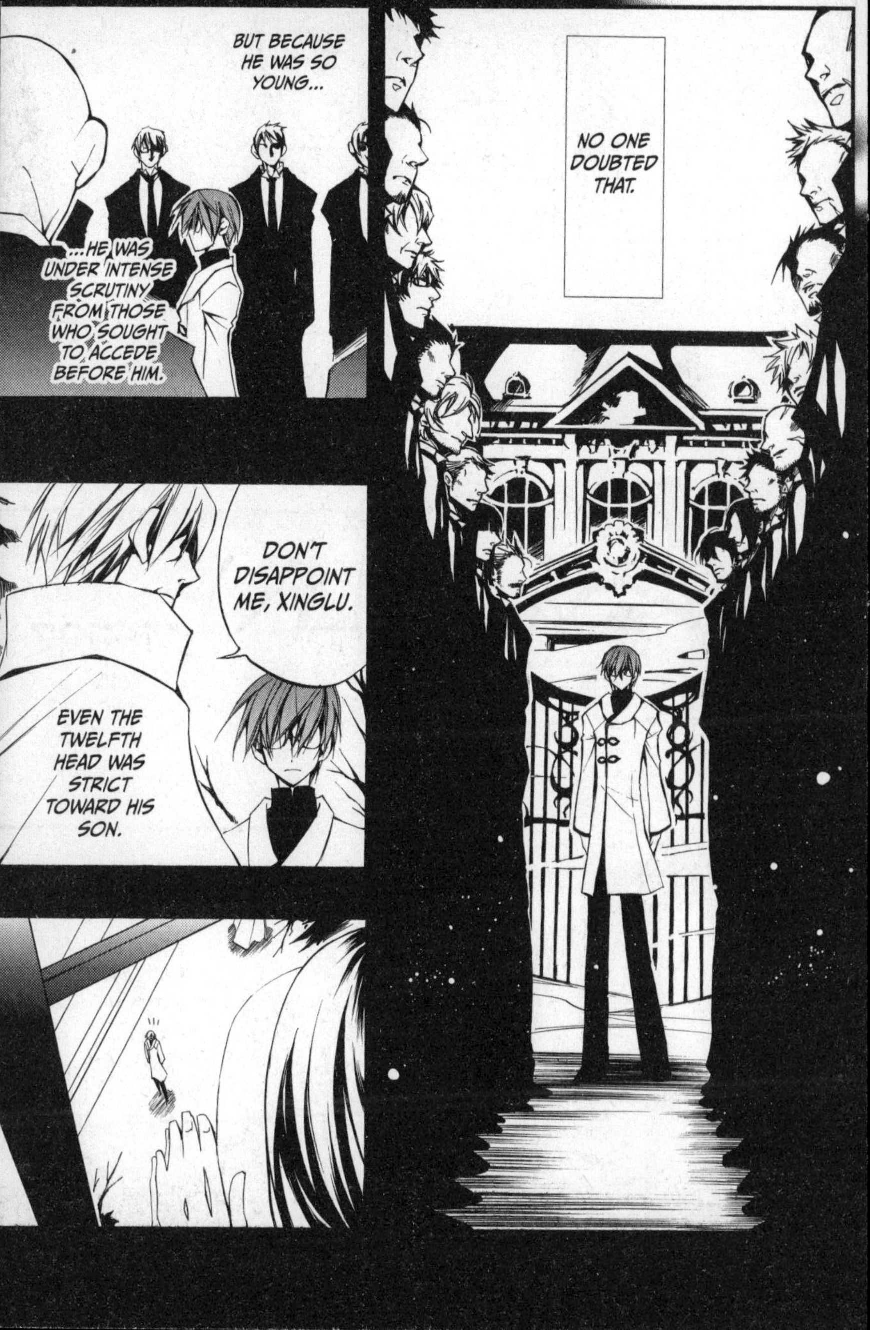
NO ONE DOUBTED THAT.
BUT BECAUSE HE WAS SO YOUNG...
...HE WAS UNDER INTENSE SCRUTINY FROM THOSE WHO SOUGHT TO ACCEDE BEFORE HIM.
DON'T DISAPPOINT ME, XINGLU.
EVEN THE TWELFTH HEAD WAS STRICT TOWARD HIS SON.

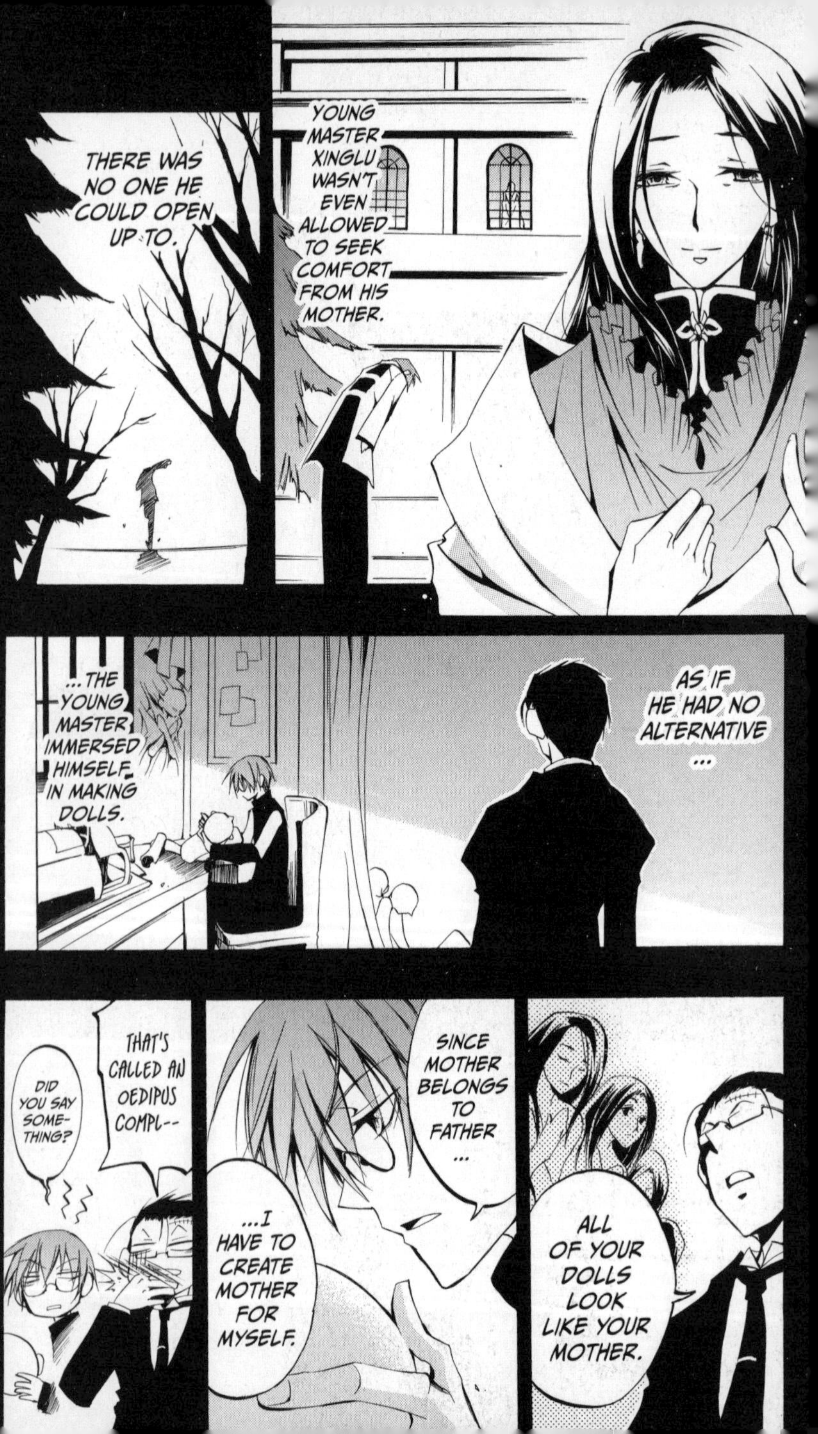
YOUNG MASTER XINGLU WASN'T EVEN ALLOWED TO SEEK COMFORT FROM HIS MOTHER.
THERE WAS NO ONE HE COULD OPEN UP TO.
AS IF HE HAD NO ALTERNATIVE ...
...THE YOUNG MASTER IMMERSED HIMSELF IN MAKING DOLLS.
ALL OF YOUR DOLLS LOOK LIKE YOUR MOTHER.
SINCE MOTHER BELONGS TO FATHER ...
...I HAVE TO CREATE MOTHER FOR MYSELF.
THAT'S CALLED AN OEDIPUS COMPL--
DID YOU SAY SOME-THING?

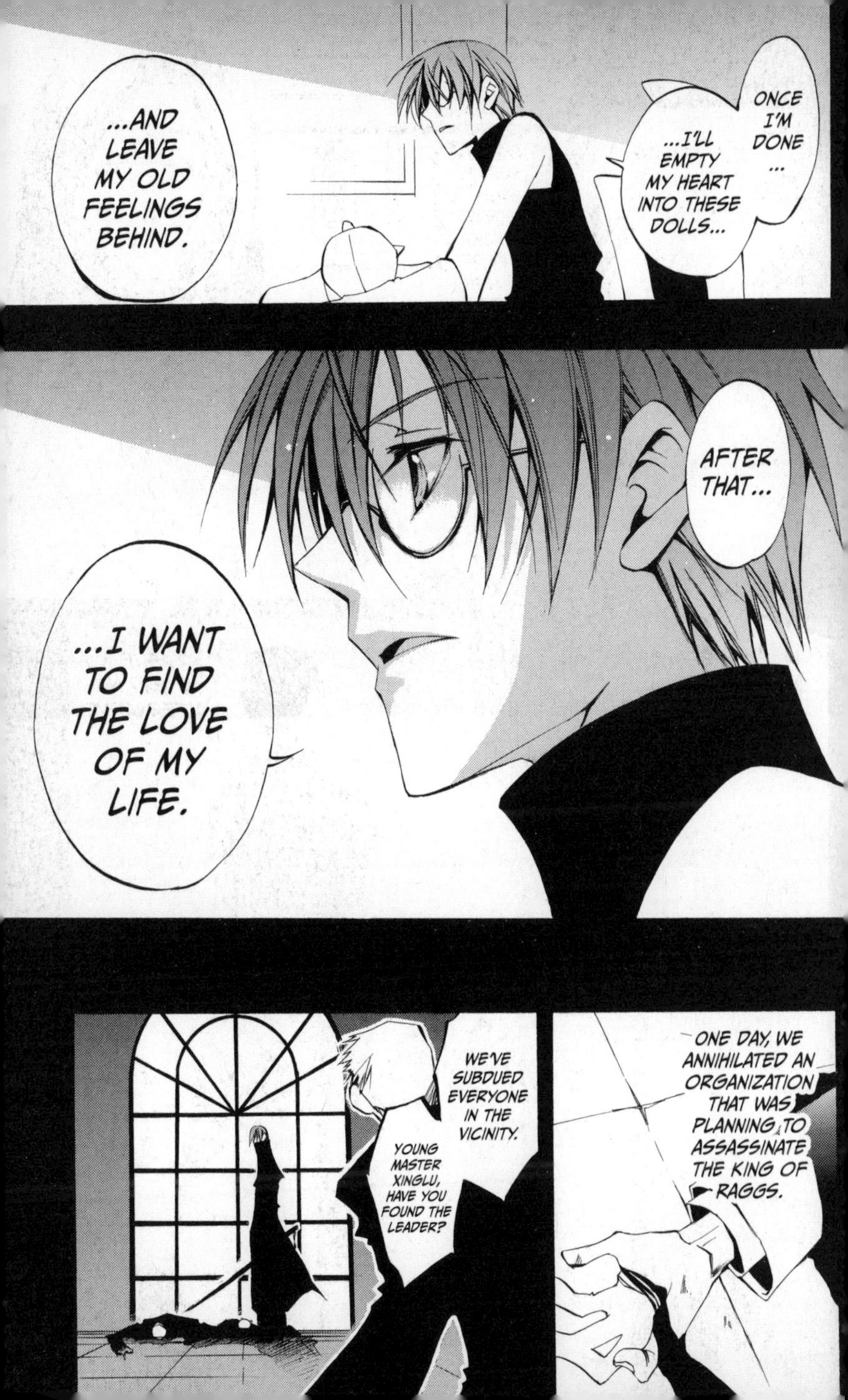
ONCE I'M DONE ...
...I'LL EMPTY MY HEART INTO THESE DOLLS...
...AND LEAVE MY OLD FEELINGS BEHIND.
AFTER THAT...
...I WANT TO FIND THE LOVE OF MY LIFE.
ONE DAY, WE ANNIHILATED AN ORGANIZATION THAT WAS PLANNING TO ASSASSINATE THE KING OF RAGGS.
WE'VE SUBDUED EVERYONE IN THE VICINITY.
YOUNG MASTER XINGLU, HAVE YOU FOUND THE LEADER?

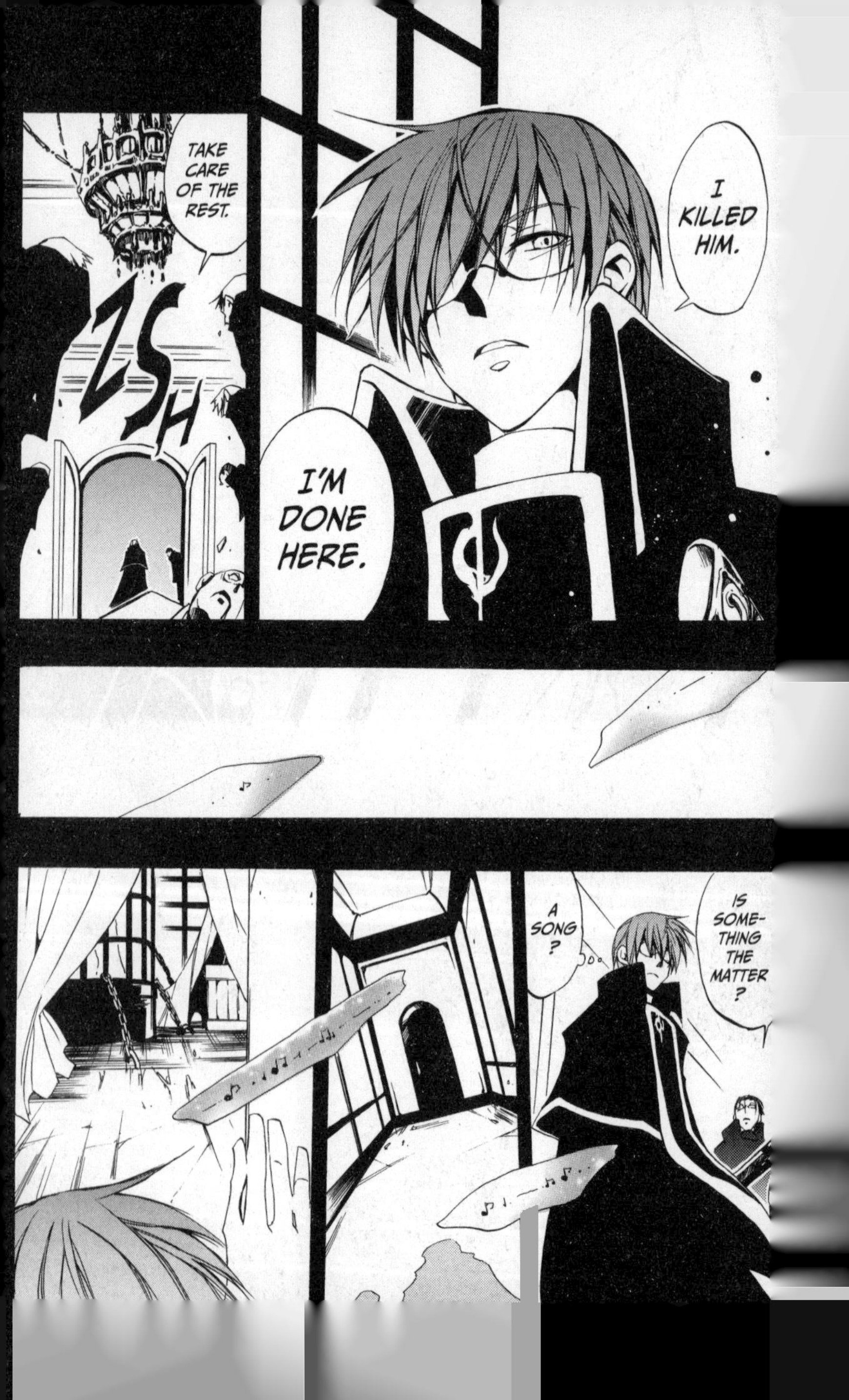
I KILLED HIM.
I'M DONE HERE.
TAKE CARE OF THE REST.
ZSH
IS SOME-THING THE MATTER?
A SONG?

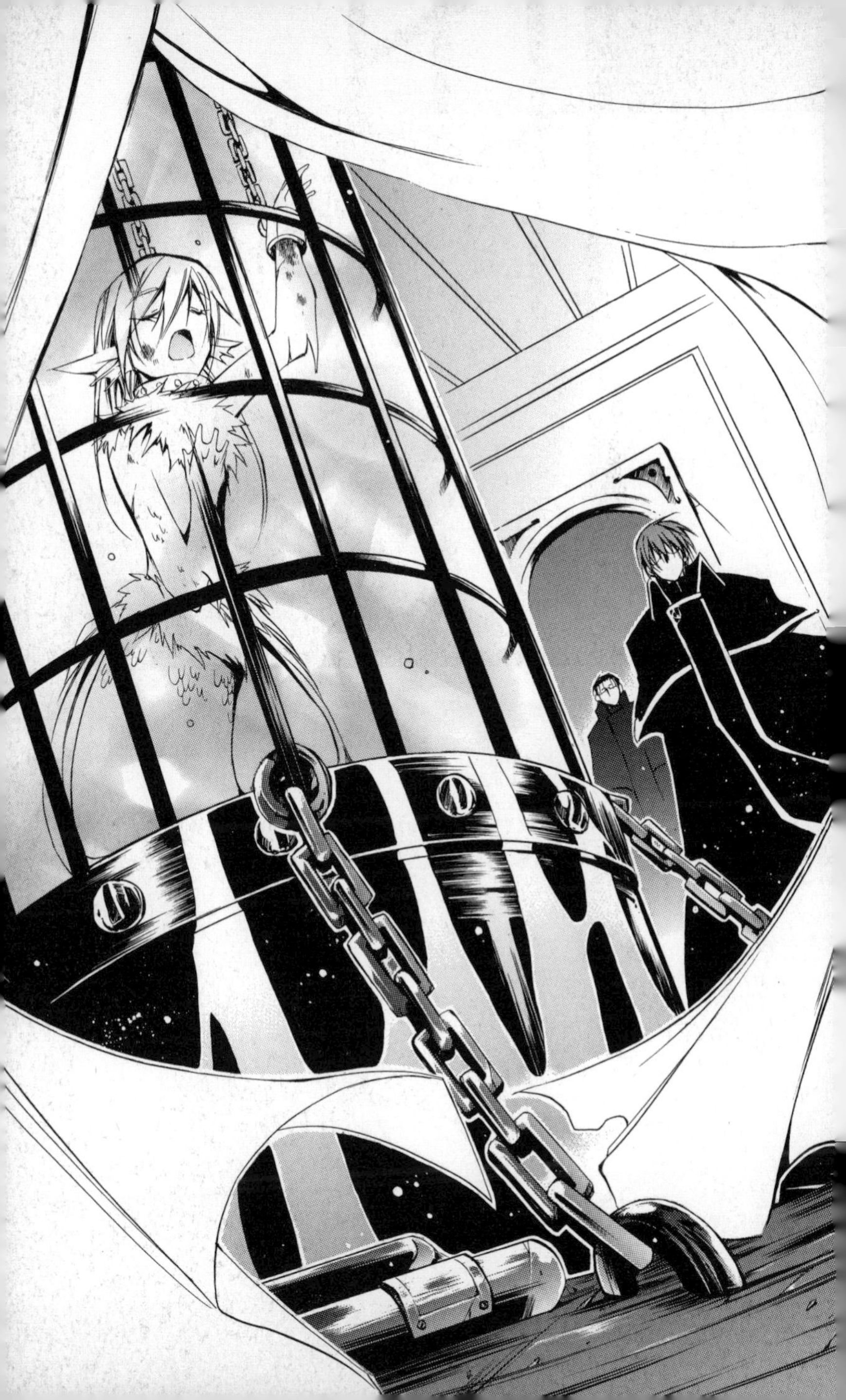

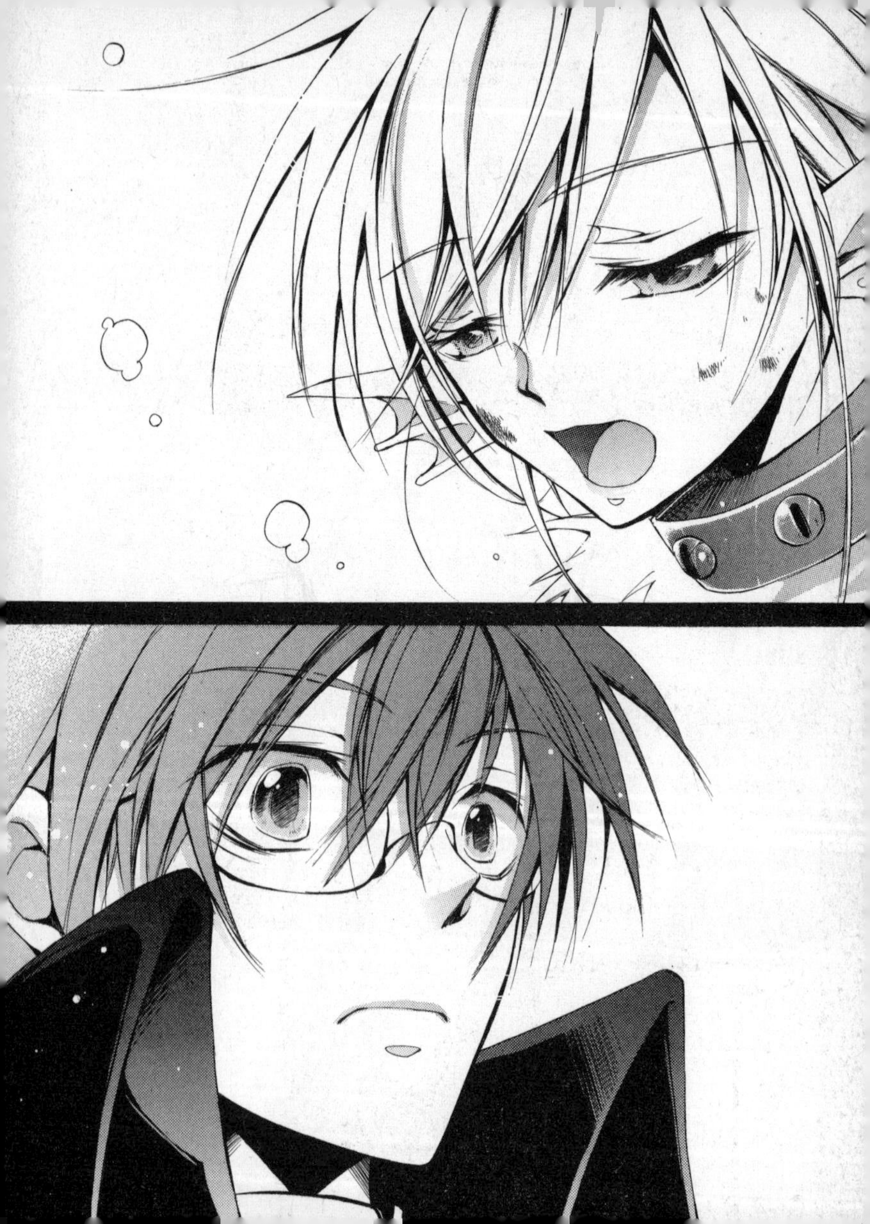

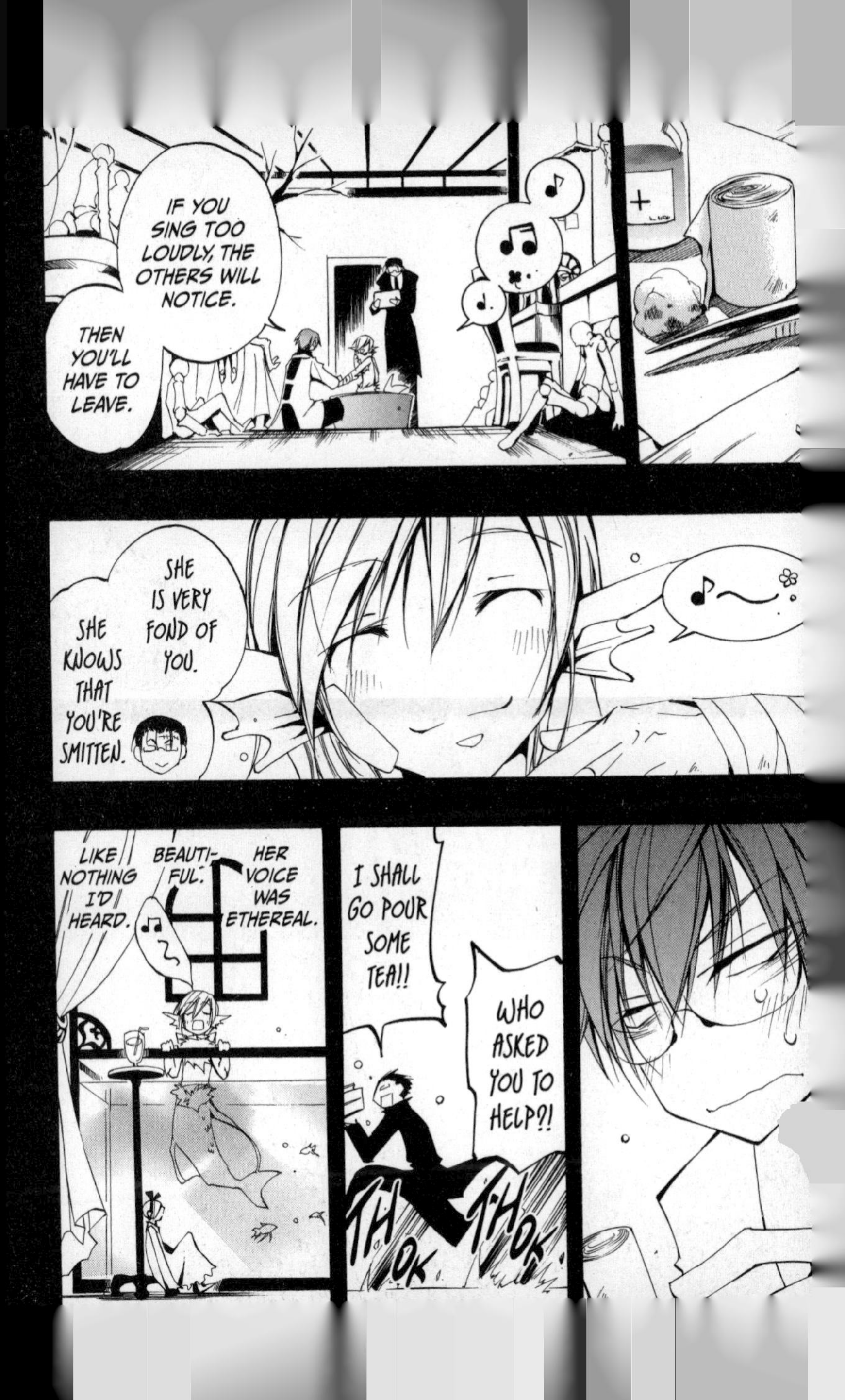
IF YOU SING TOO LOUDLY, THE OTHERS WILL NOTICE.
THEN YOU'LL HAVE TO LEAVE.
SHE IS VERY FOND OF YOU.
SHE KNOWS THAT YOU'RE SMITTEN.
I SHALL GO POUR SOME TEA!!
WHO ASKED YOU TO HELP?!
THOK
THOK
HER VOICE WAS ETHEREAL.
BEAUTIFUL.
LIKE NOTHING I'D HEARD.

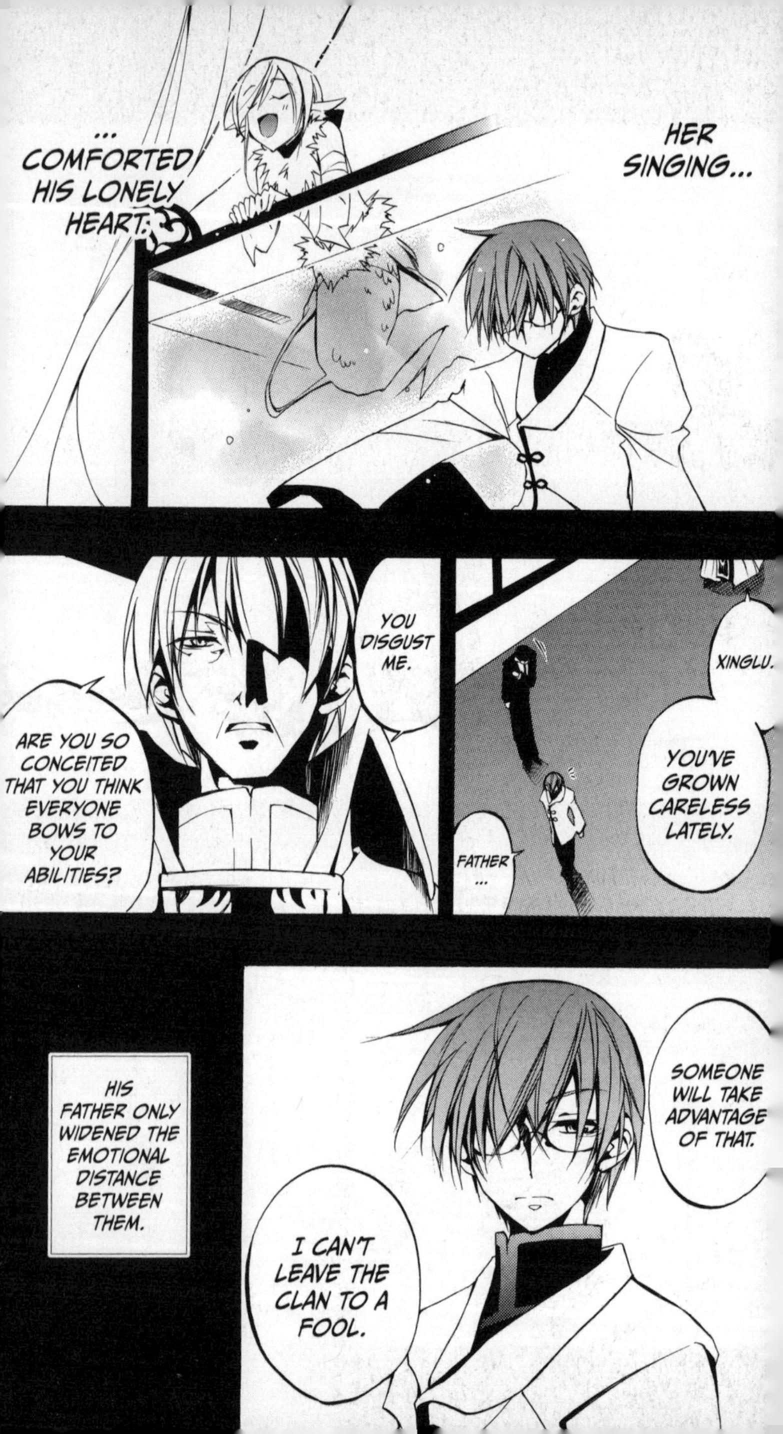
HER SINGING...
...COMFORTED HIS LONELY HEART.
XINGLU.
YOU'VE GROWN CARELESS LATELY.
FATHER...
YOU DISGUST ME.
ARE YOU SO CONCEITED THAT YOU THINK EVERYONE BOWS TO YOUR ABILITIES?
SOMEONE WILL TAKE ADVANTAGE OF THAT.
I CAN'T LEAVE THE CLAN TO A FOOL.
HIS FATHER ONLY WIDENED THE EMOTIONAL DISTANCE BETWEEN THEM.

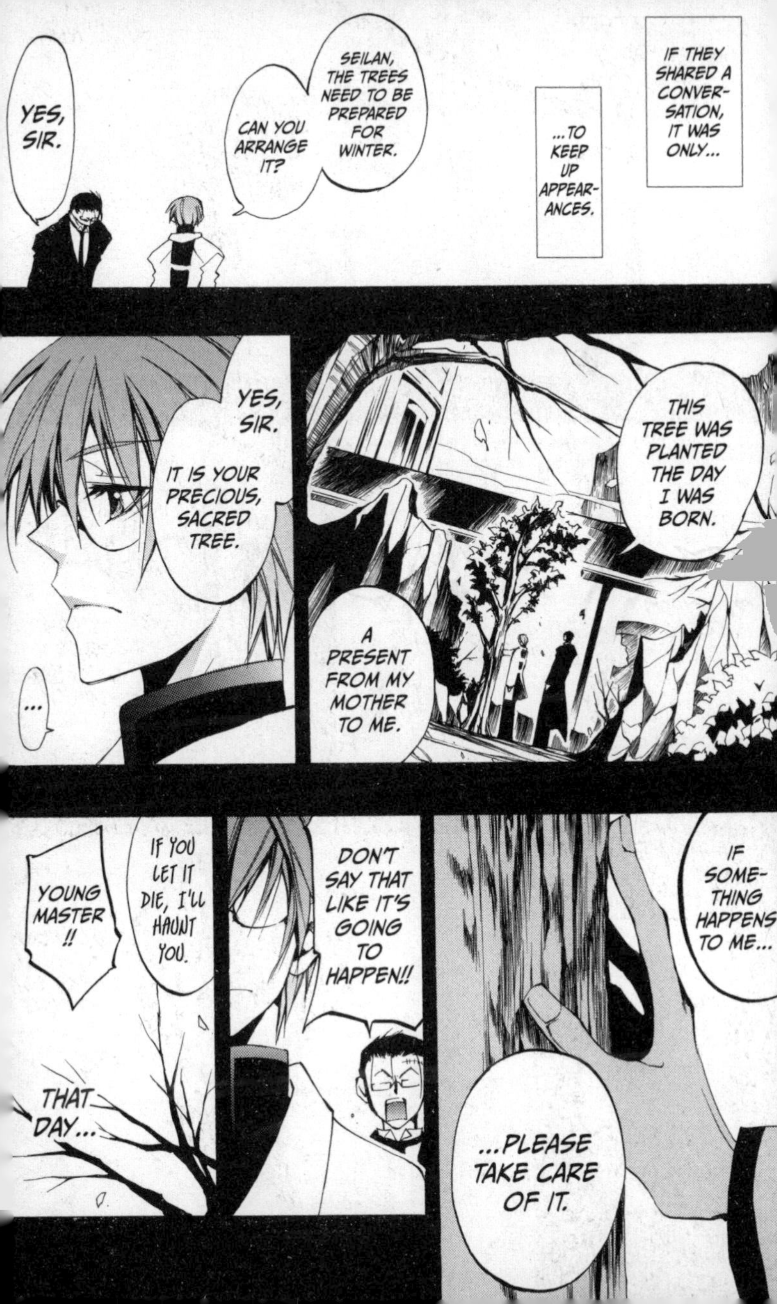
IF THEY SHARED A CONVERSATION, IT WAS ONLY...
...TO KEEP UP APPEARANCES.
SEILAN, THE TREES NEED TO BE PREPARED FOR WINTER.
CAN YOU ARRANGE IT?
YES, SIR.
THIS TREE WAS PLANTED THE DAY I WAS BORN.
A PRESENT FROM MY MOTHER TO ME.
YES, SIR.
IT IS YOUR PRECIOUS, SACRED TREE.
...
IF SOMETHING HAPPENS TO ME...
...PLEASE TAKE CARE OF IT.
DON'T SAY THAT LIKE IT'S GOING TO HAPPEN!!
IF YOU LET IT DIE, I'LL HAUNT YOU.
YOUNG MASTER!!
THAT DAY...

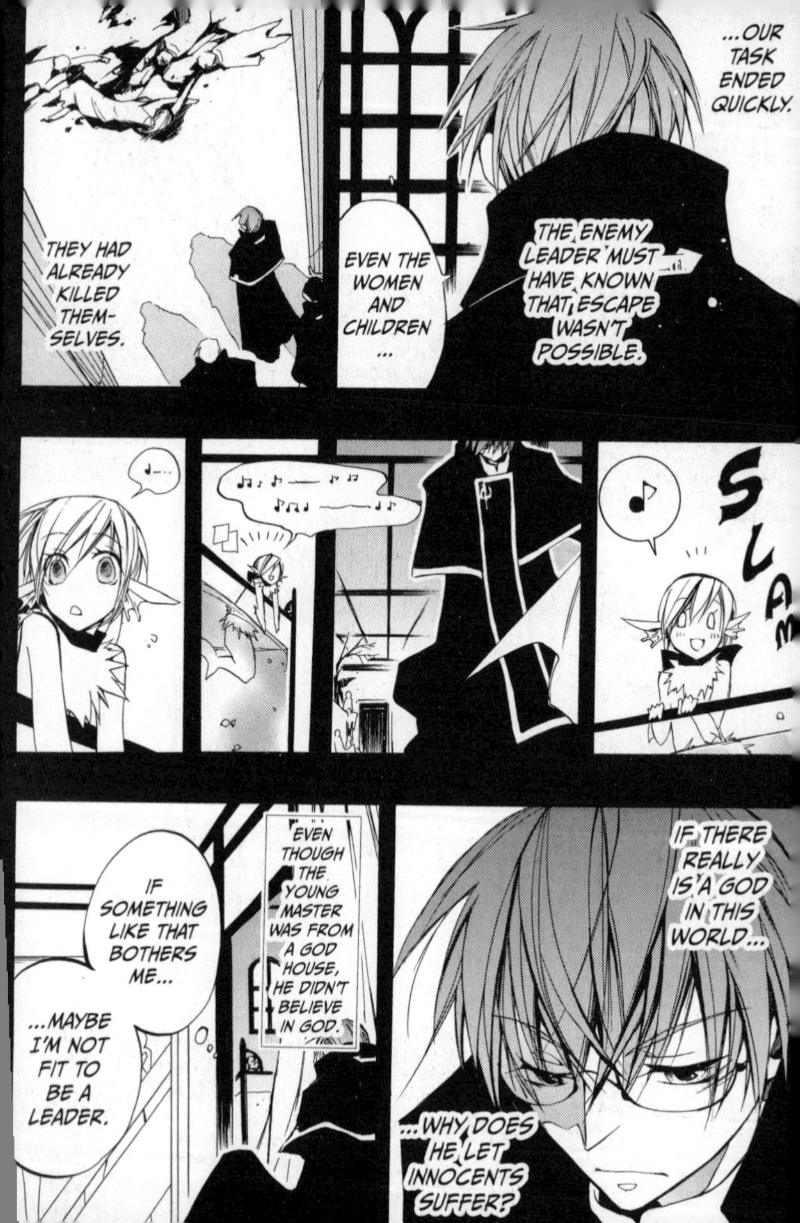
...OUR TASK ENDED QUICKLY.
THE ENEMY LEADER MUST HAVE KNOWN THAT ESCAPE WASN'T POSSIBLE.
EVEN THE WOMEN AND CHILDREN...
THEY HAD ALREADY KILLED THEM-SELVES.
SLAM
IF THERE REALLY IS A GOD IN THIS WORLD...
...WHY DOES HE LET INNOCENTS SUFFER?
EVEN THOUGH THE YOUNG MASTER WAS FROM A GOD HOUSE, HE DIDN'T BELIEVE IN GOD.
IF SOMETHING LIKE THAT BOTHERS ME...
...MAYBE I'M NOT FIT TO BE A LEADER.

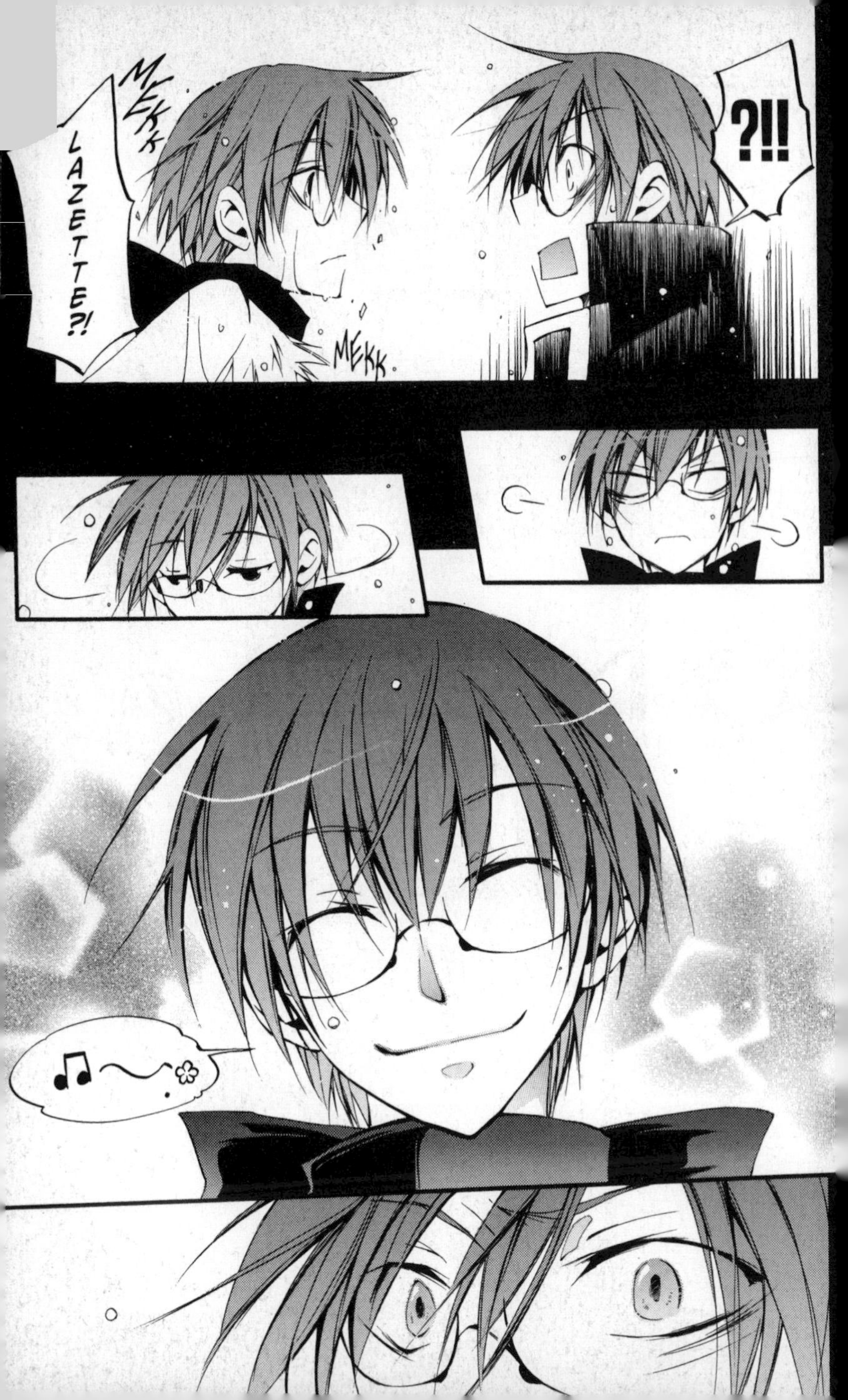
?!!
MEKK
LAZETTE?!
MEKK
♫~

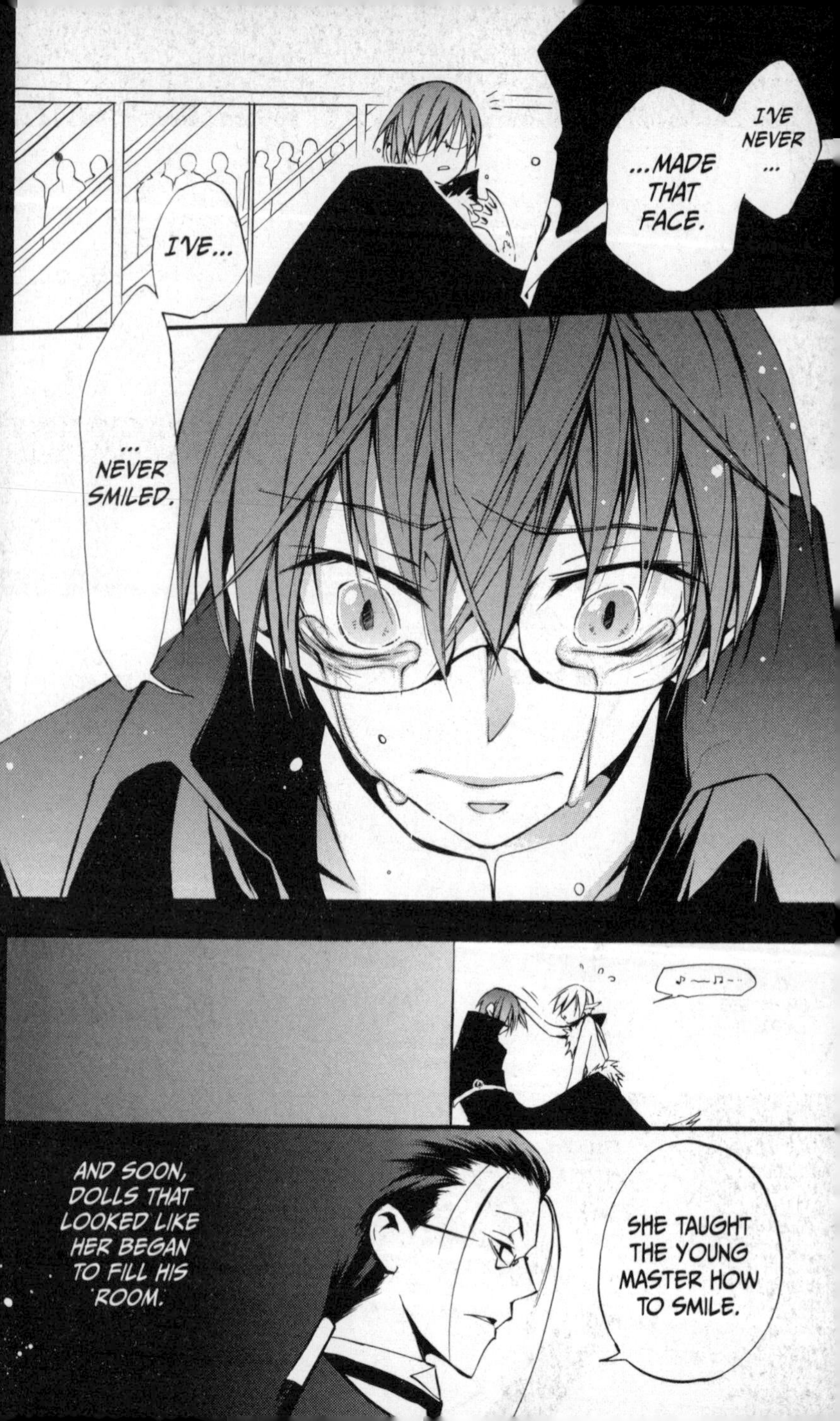
I'VE NEVER...
...MADE THAT FACE.
I'VE...
...NEVER SMILED.
SHE TAUGHT THE YOUNG MASTER HOW TO SMILE.
AND SOON, DOLLS THAT LOOKED LIKE HER BEGAN TO FILL HIS ROOM.

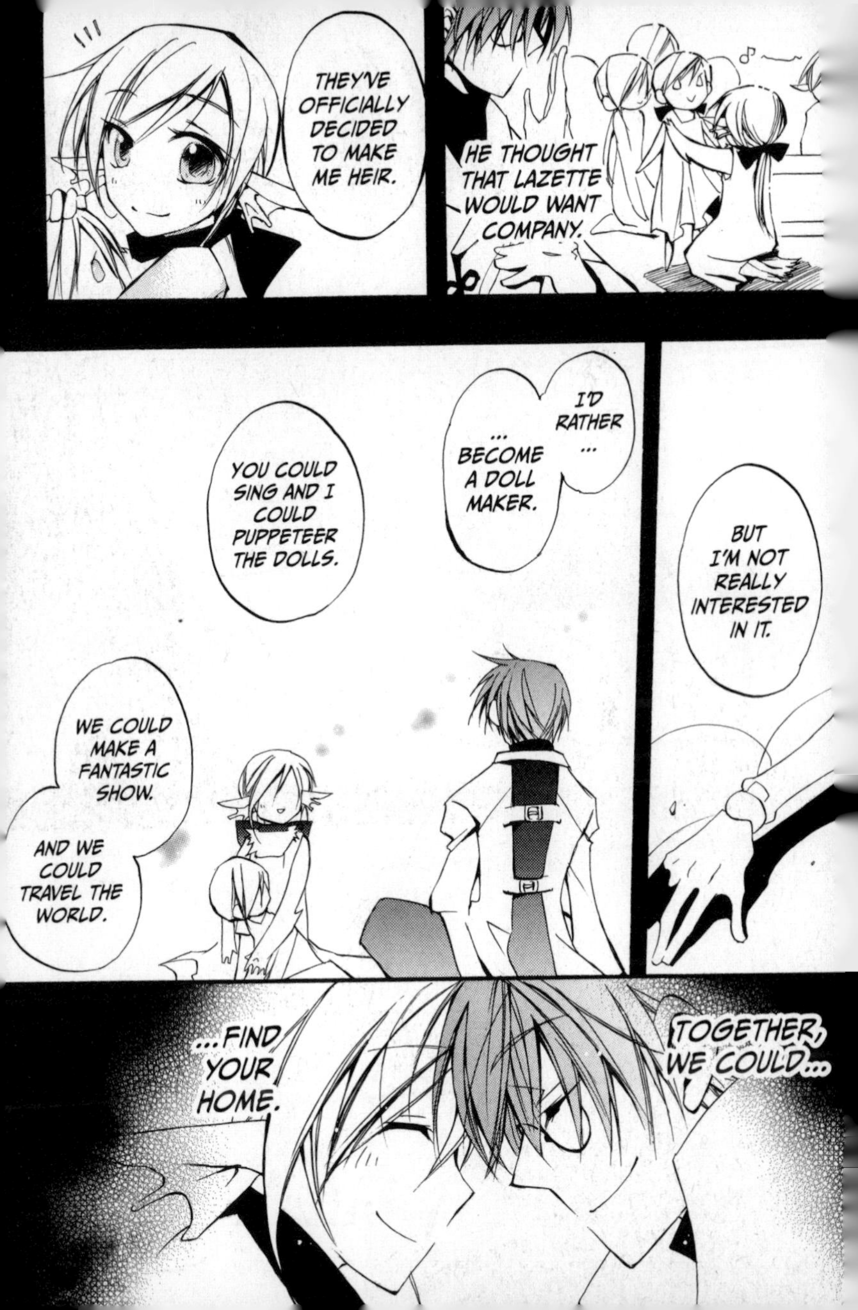
HE THOUGHT THAT LAZETTE WOULD WANT COMPANY.
THEY'VE OFFICIALLY DECIDED TO MAKE ME HEIR.
BUT I'M NOT REALLY INTERESTED IN IT.
I'D RATHER ... ... BECOME A DOLL MAKER.
YOU COULD SING AND I COULD PUPPETEER THE DOLLS.
WE COULD MAKE A FANTASTIC SHOW.
AND WE COULD TRAVEL THE WORLD.
TOGETHER, WE COULD...
...FIND YOUR HOME.

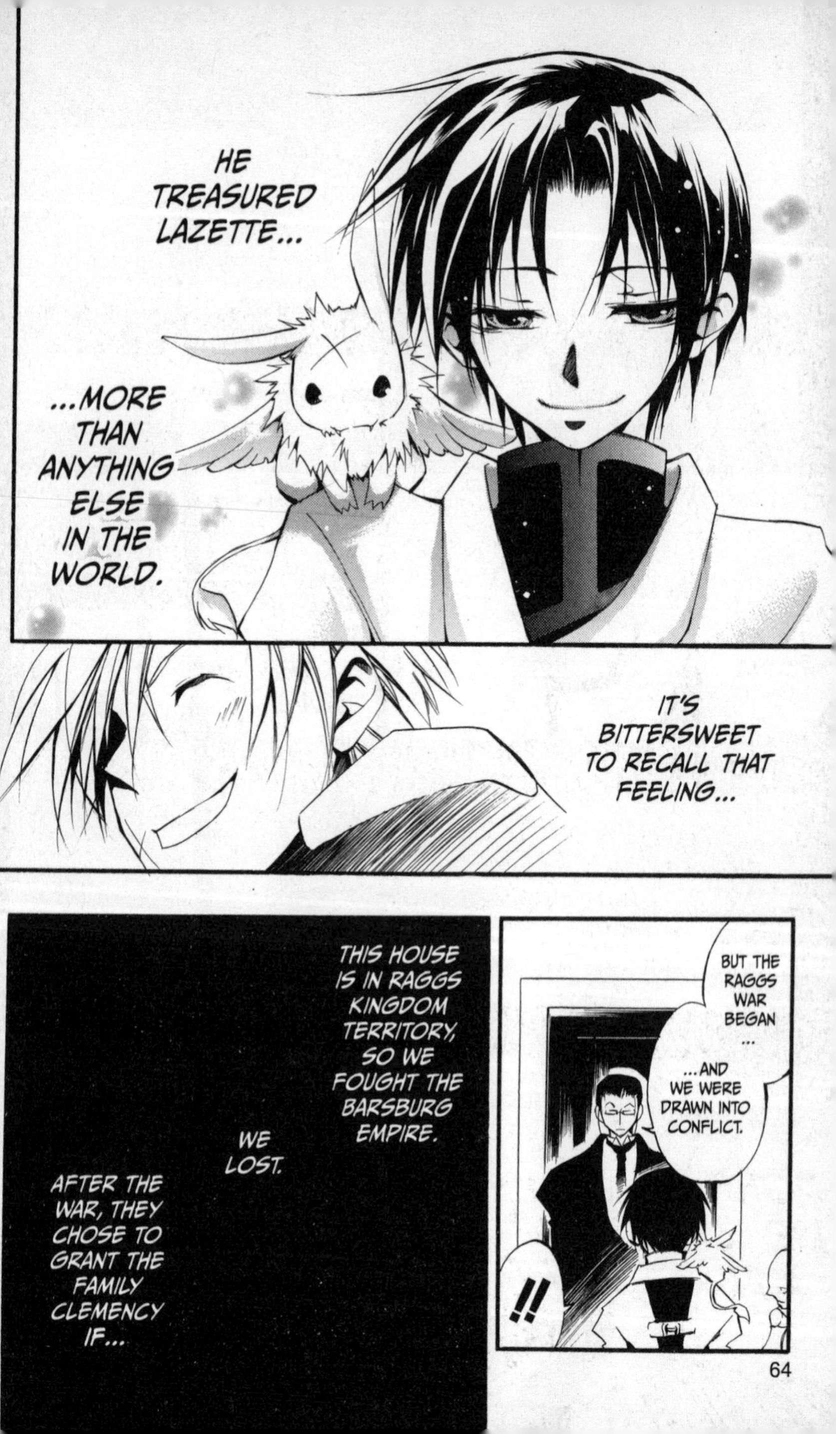
HE TREASURED LAZETTE...
...MORE THAN ANYTHING ELSE IN THE WORLD.
IT'S BITTERSWEET TO RECALL THAT FEELING...
BUT THE RAGGS WAR BEGAN...
...AND WE WERE DRAWN INTO CONFLICT.
!!
THIS HOUSE IS IN RAGGS KINGDOM TERRITORY, SO WE FOUGHT THE BARSBURG EMPIRE.
WE LOST.
AFTER THE WAR, THEY CHOSE TO GRANT THE FAMILY CLEMENCY IF...

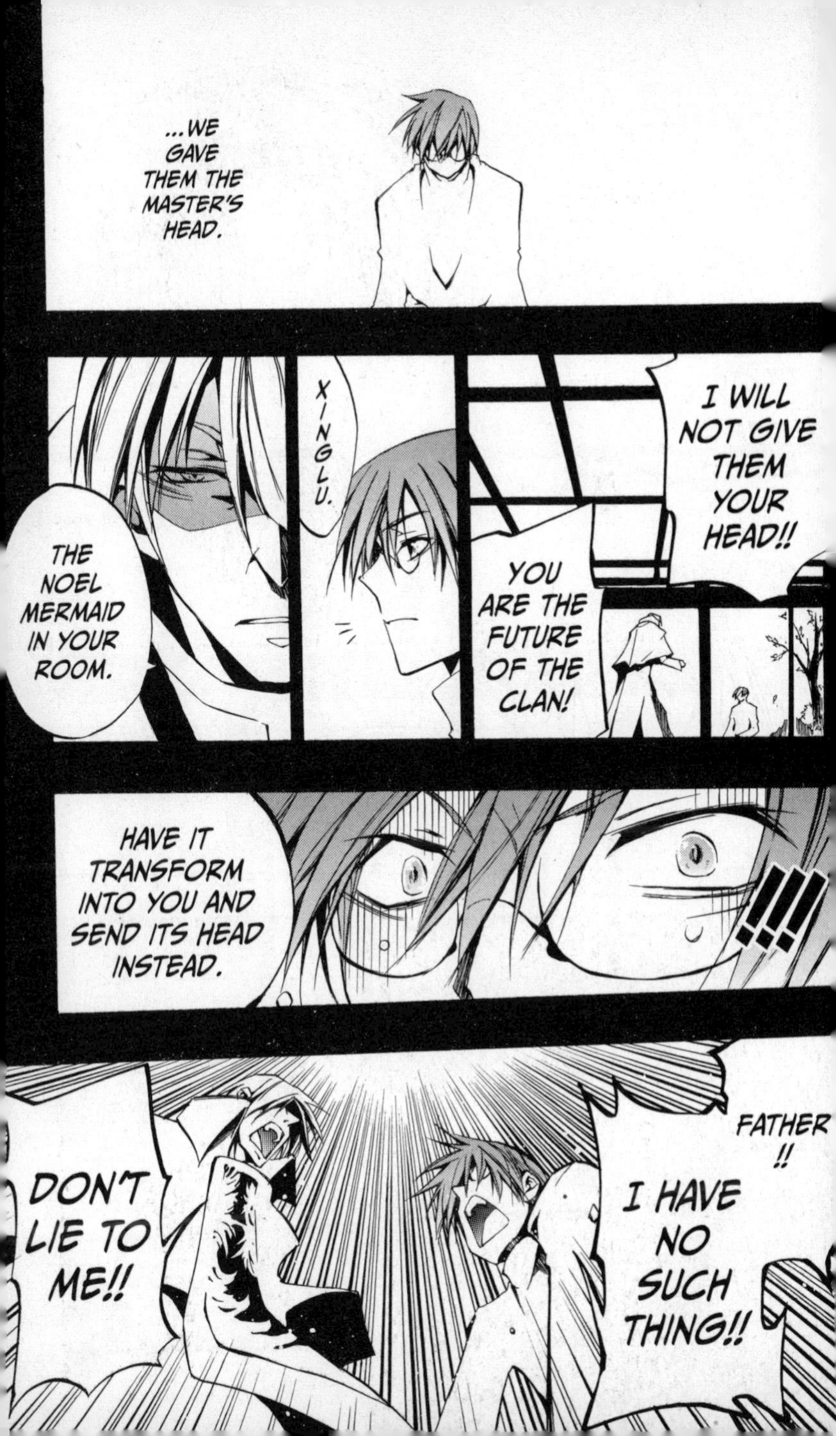
...WE GAVE THEM THE MASTER'S HEAD.
I WILL NOT GIVE THEM YOUR HEAD!!
YOU ARE THE FUTURE OF THE CLAN!
XINGLU.
THE NOEL MERMAID IN YOUR ROOM.
HAVE IT TRANSFORM INTO YOU AND SEND ITS HEAD INSTEAD.
!!!
FATHER!!
I HAVE NO SUCH THING!!
DON'T LIE TO ME!!

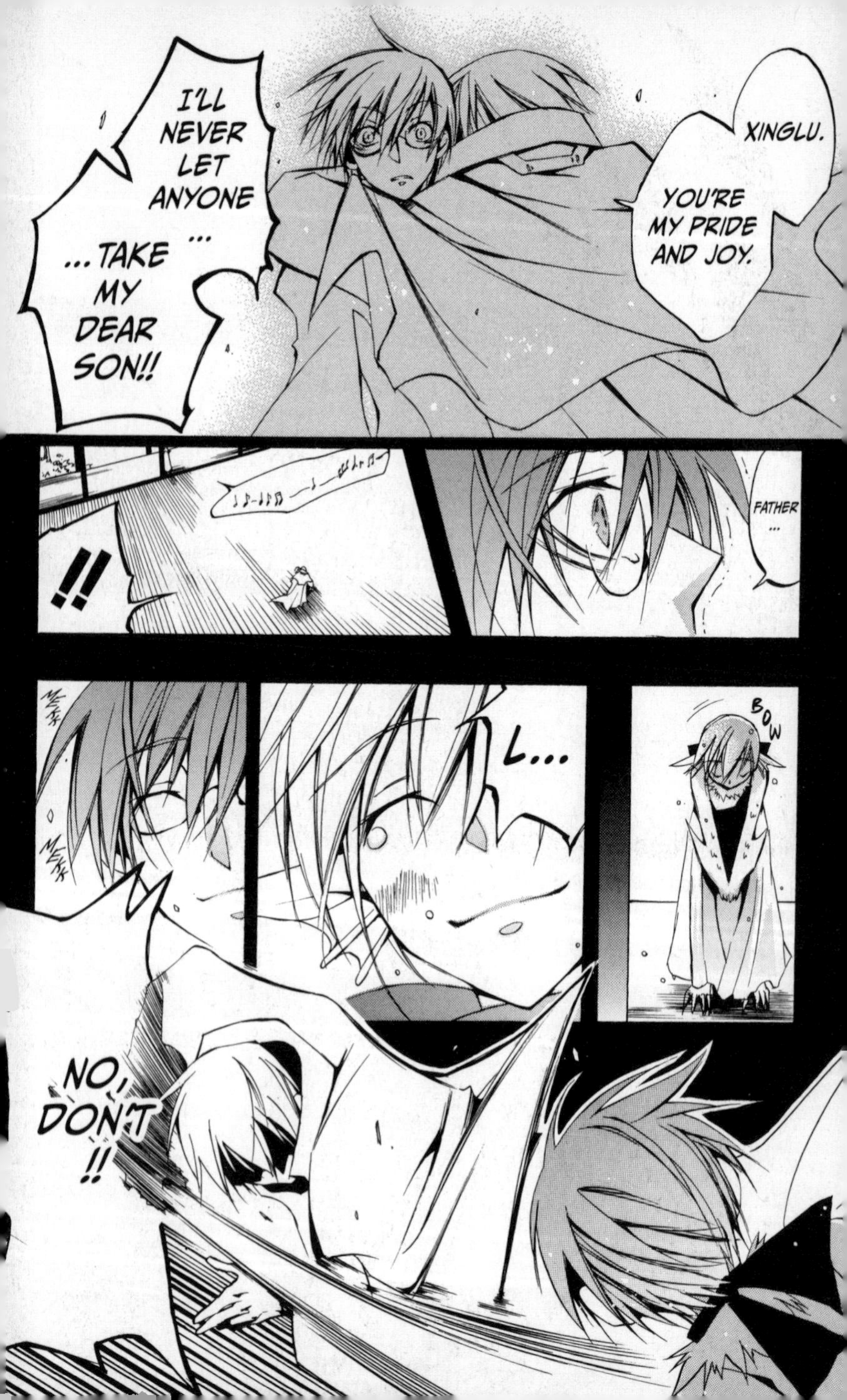
XINGLU.
YOU'RE MY PRIDE AND JOY.
I'LL NEVER LET ANYONE ...
...TAKE MY DEAR SON!!
FATHER ...
!!
BOW
L...
MEKK
MEKK
NO, DON'T!!

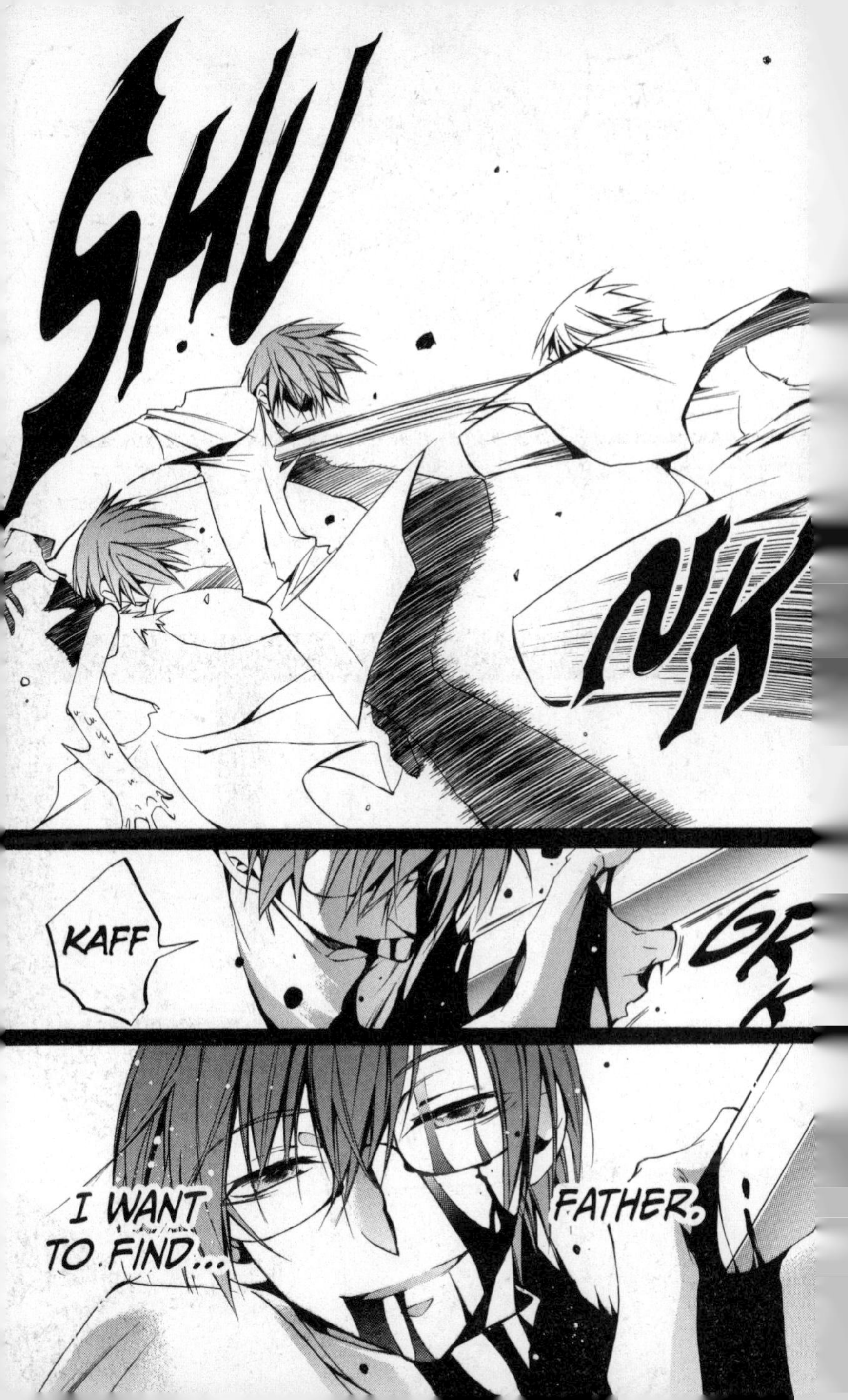
SHU
NK
GRK
KAFF
I WANT TO FIND...
FATHER.

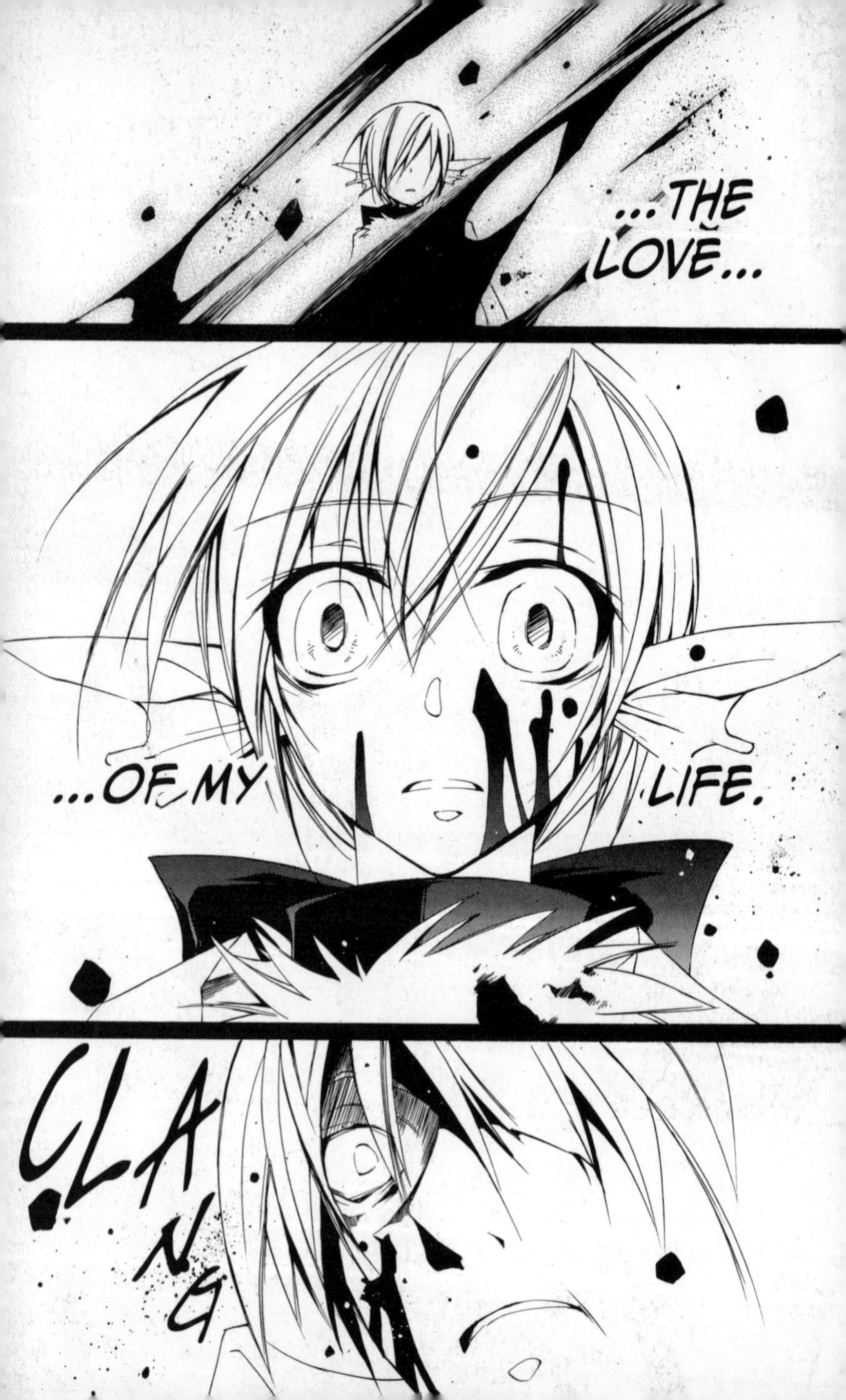
...THE LOVE...
...OF MY
LIFE.
CLANG

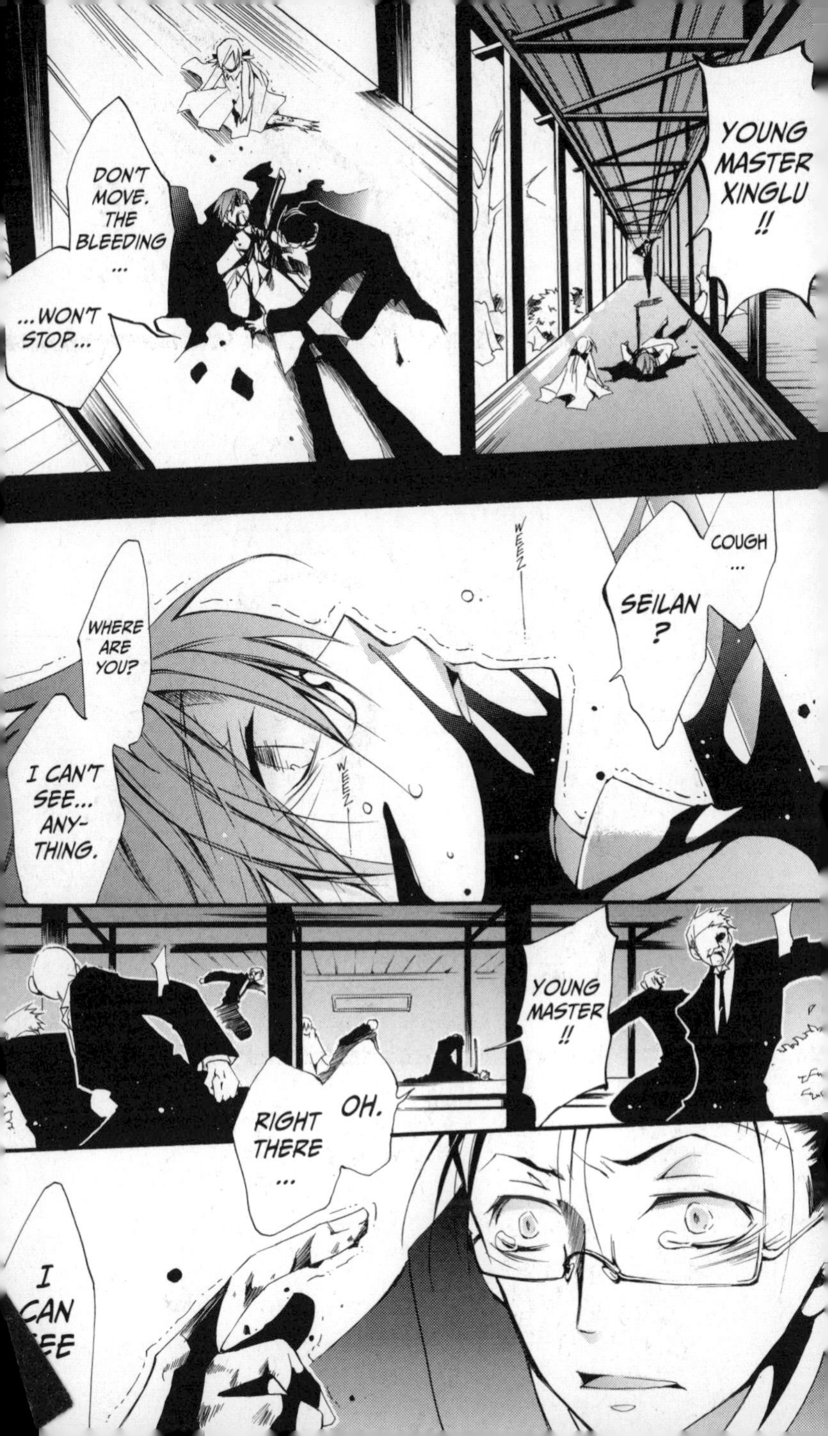
YOUNG MASTER XINGLU !!
DON'T MOVE. THE BLEEDING ...
...WON'T STOP...
WEEZ
COUGH ...
SEILAN ?
WHERE ARE YOU?
WEEZ
I CAN'T SEE... ANY-THING.
YOUNG MASTER !!
OH.
RIGHT THERE ...
I CAN

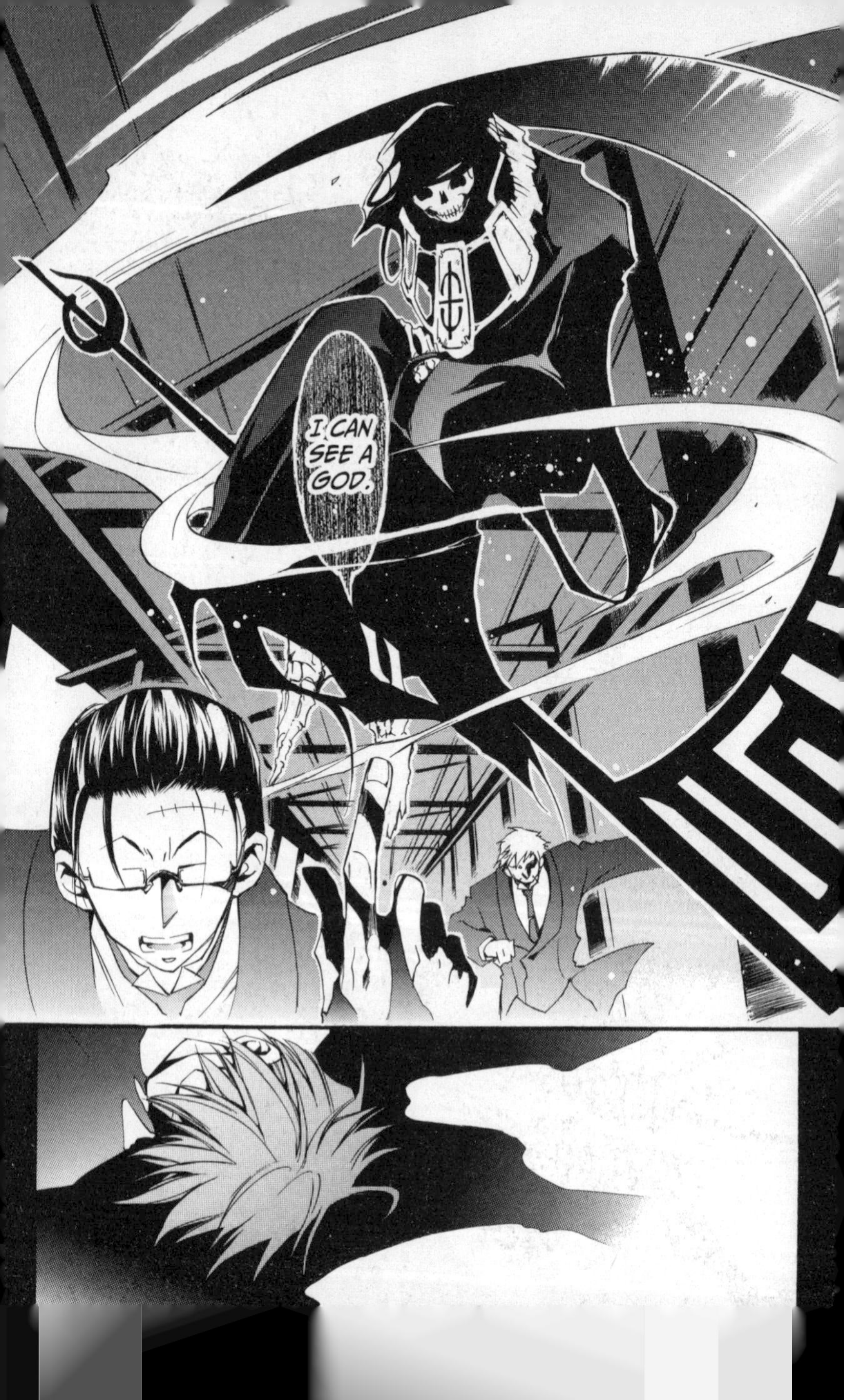
I CAN SEE A GOD.

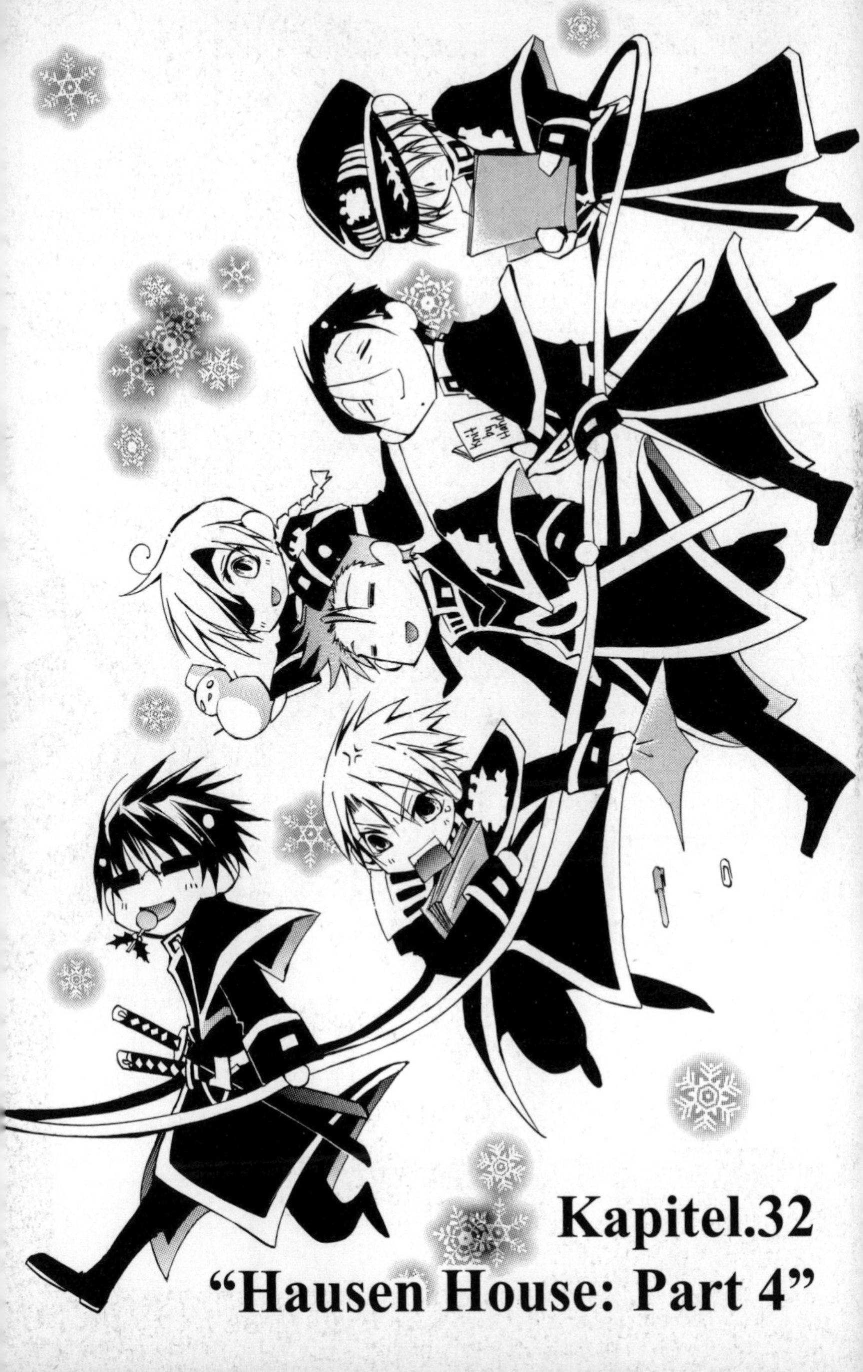
Knit by Hand

Kapitel.32
"Hausen House: Part 4"

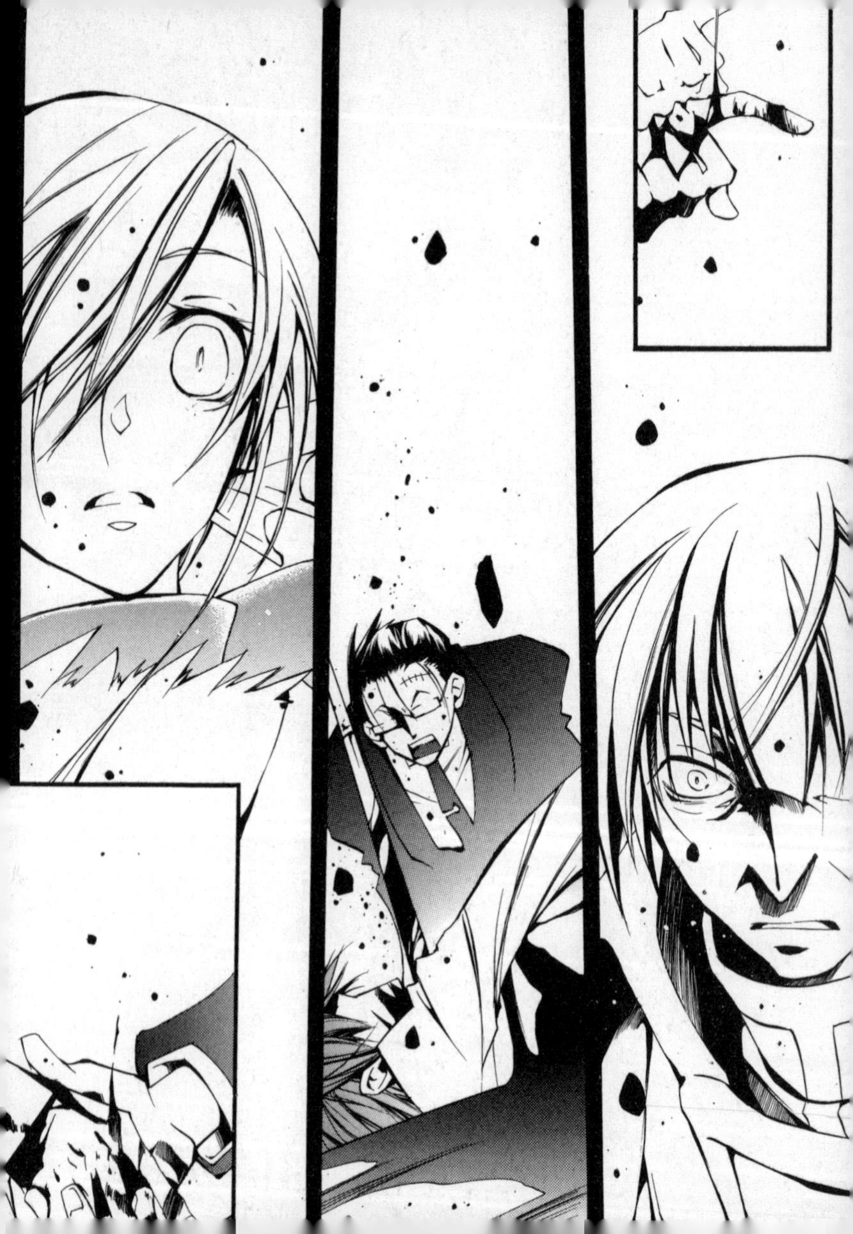

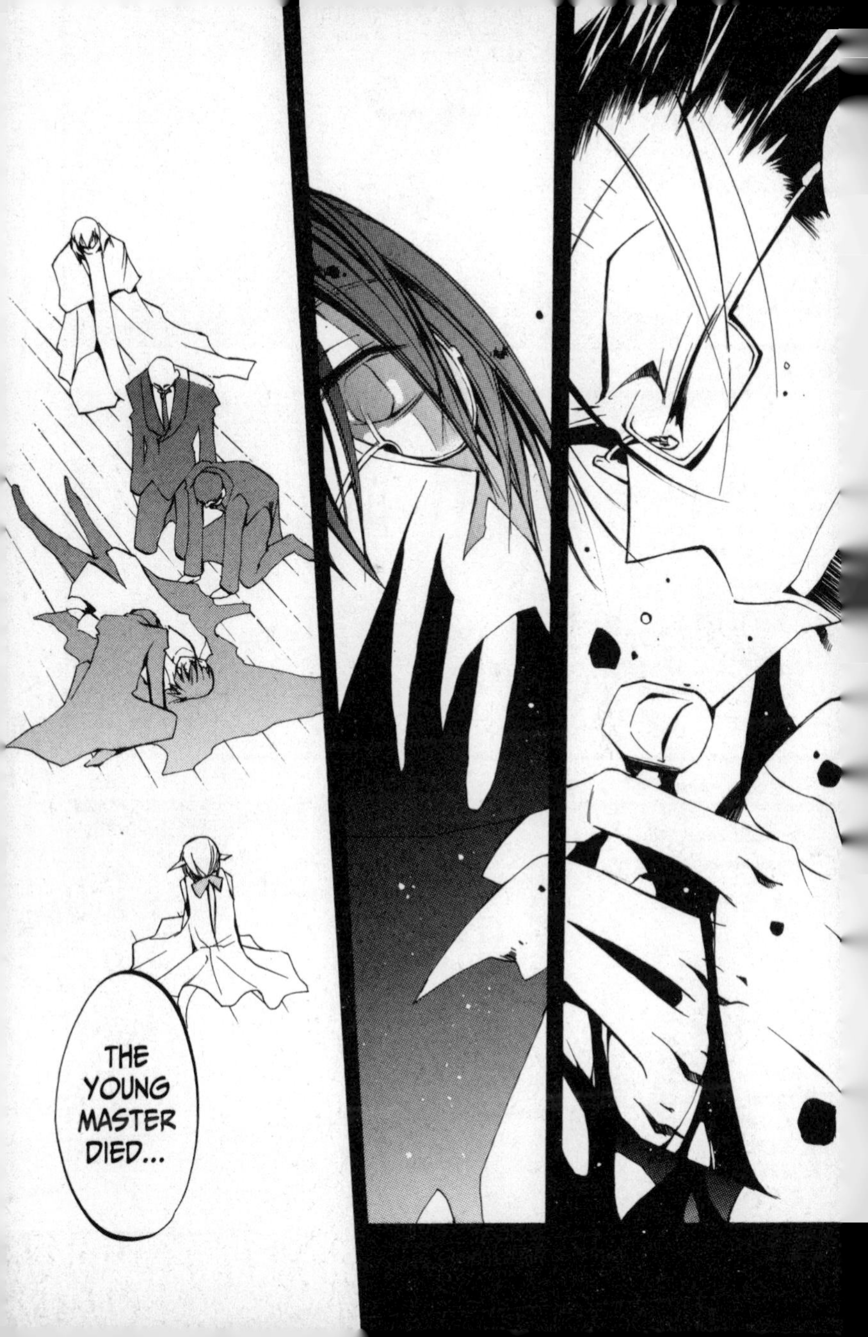
THE YOUNG MASTER DIED...

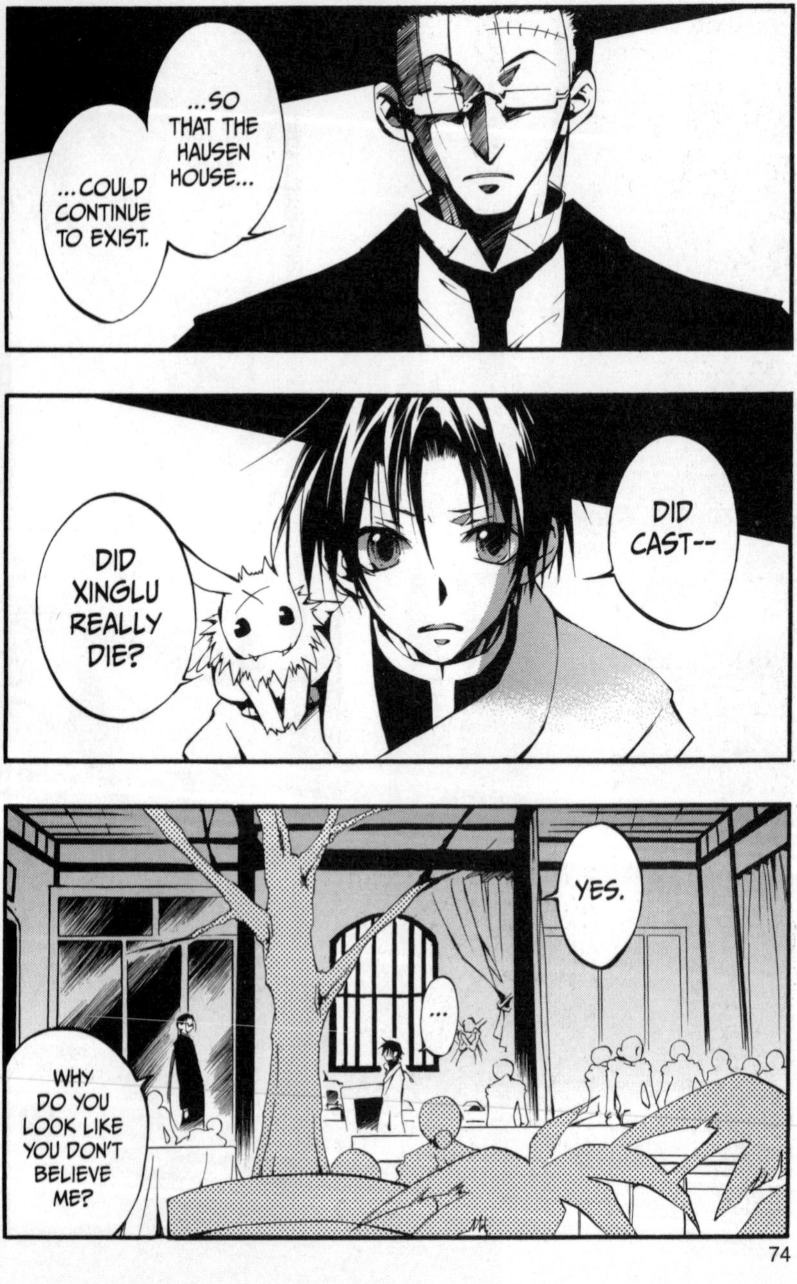
...SO THAT THE HAUSEN HOUSE...
...COULD CONTINUE TO EXIST.
DID CAST--
DID XINGLU REALLY DIE?
YES.
...
WHY DO YOU LOOK LIKE YOU DON'T BELIEVE ME?

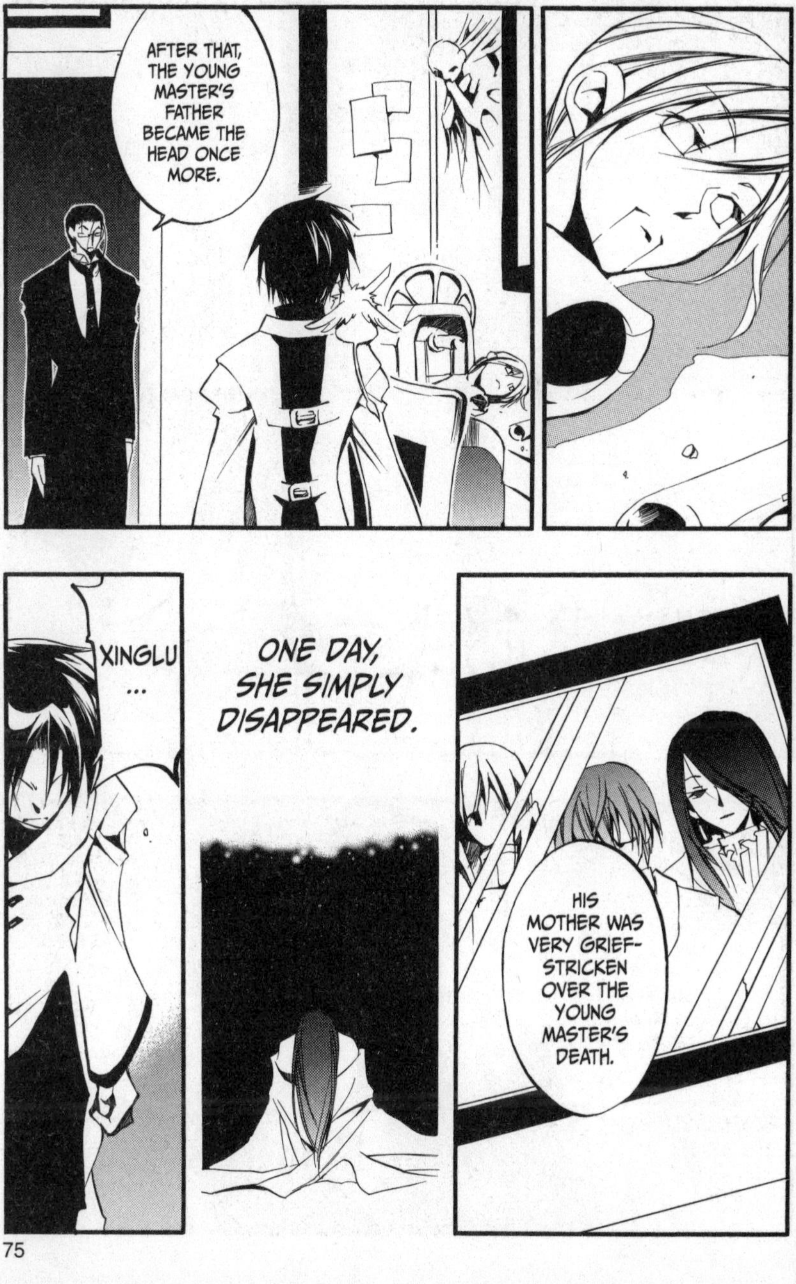
AFTER THAT, THE YOUNG MASTER'S FATHER BECAME THE HEAD ONCE MORE.
HIS MOTHER WAS VERY GRIEF-STRICKEN OVER THE YOUNG MASTER'S DEATH.
ONE DAY, SHE SIMPLY DISAPPEARED.
XINGLU ...

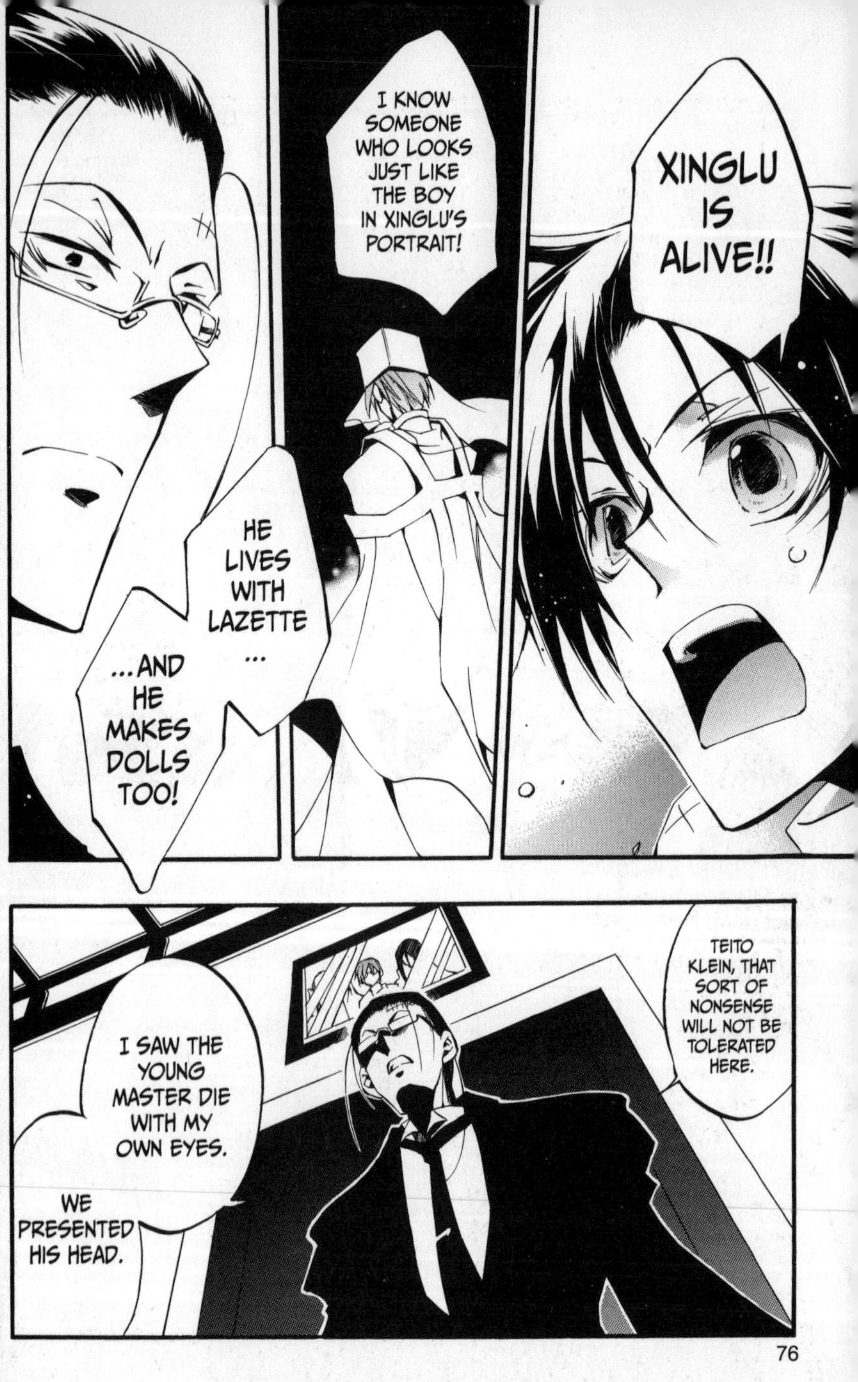
XINGLU IS ALIVE!!
I KNOW SOMEONE WHO LOOKS JUST LIKE THE BOY IN XINGLU'S PORTRAIT!
HE LIVES WITH LAZETTE...
...AND HE MAKES DOLLS TOO!
TEITO KLEIN, THAT SORT OF NONSENSE WILL NOT BE TOLERATED HERE.
I SAW THE YOUNG MASTER DIE WITH MY OWN EYES.
WE PRESENTED HIS HEAD.

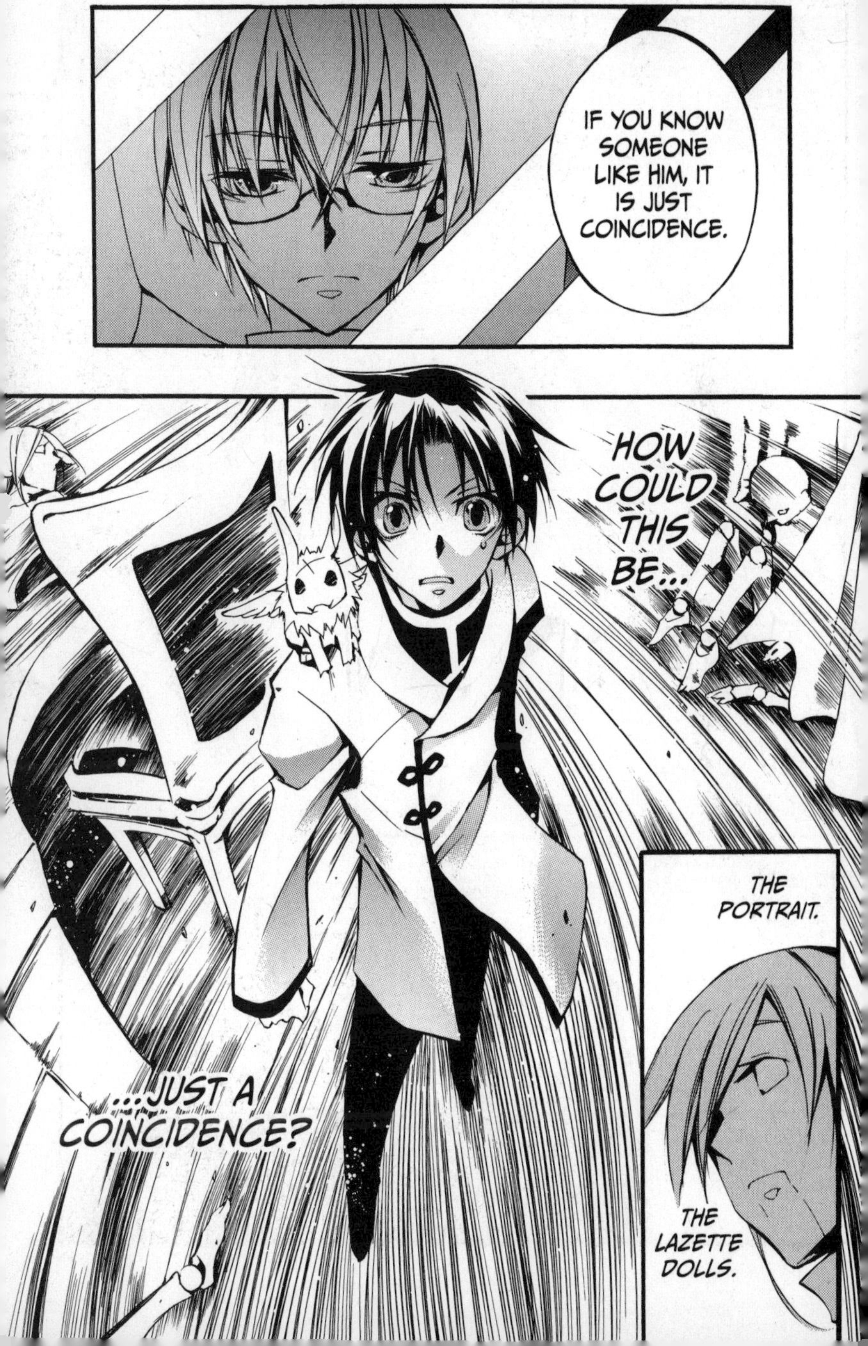
IF YOU KNOW SOMEONE LIKE HIM, IT IS JUST COINCIDENCE.
HOW COULD THIS BE...
THE PORTRAIT.
THE LAZETTE DOLLS.
...JUST A COINCIDENCE?

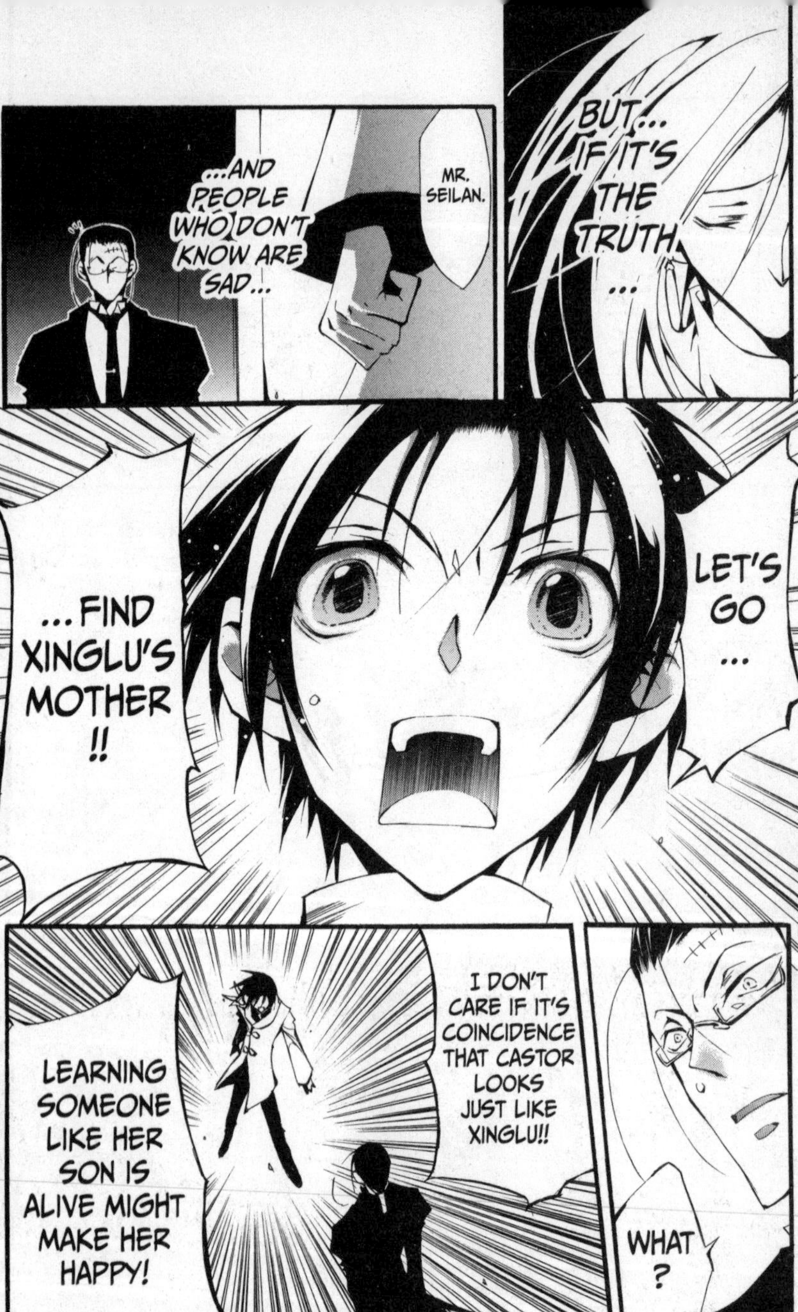
BUT... IF IT'S THE TRUTH...
MR. SEILAN.
...AND PEOPLE WHO DON'T KNOW ARE SAD...
LET'S GO...
...FIND XINGLU'S MOTHER!!
WHAT?
I DON'T CARE IF IT'S COINCIDENCE THAT CASTOR LOOKS JUST LIKE XINGLU!!
LEARNING SOMEONE LIKE HER SON IS ALIVE MIGHT MAKE HER HAPPY!

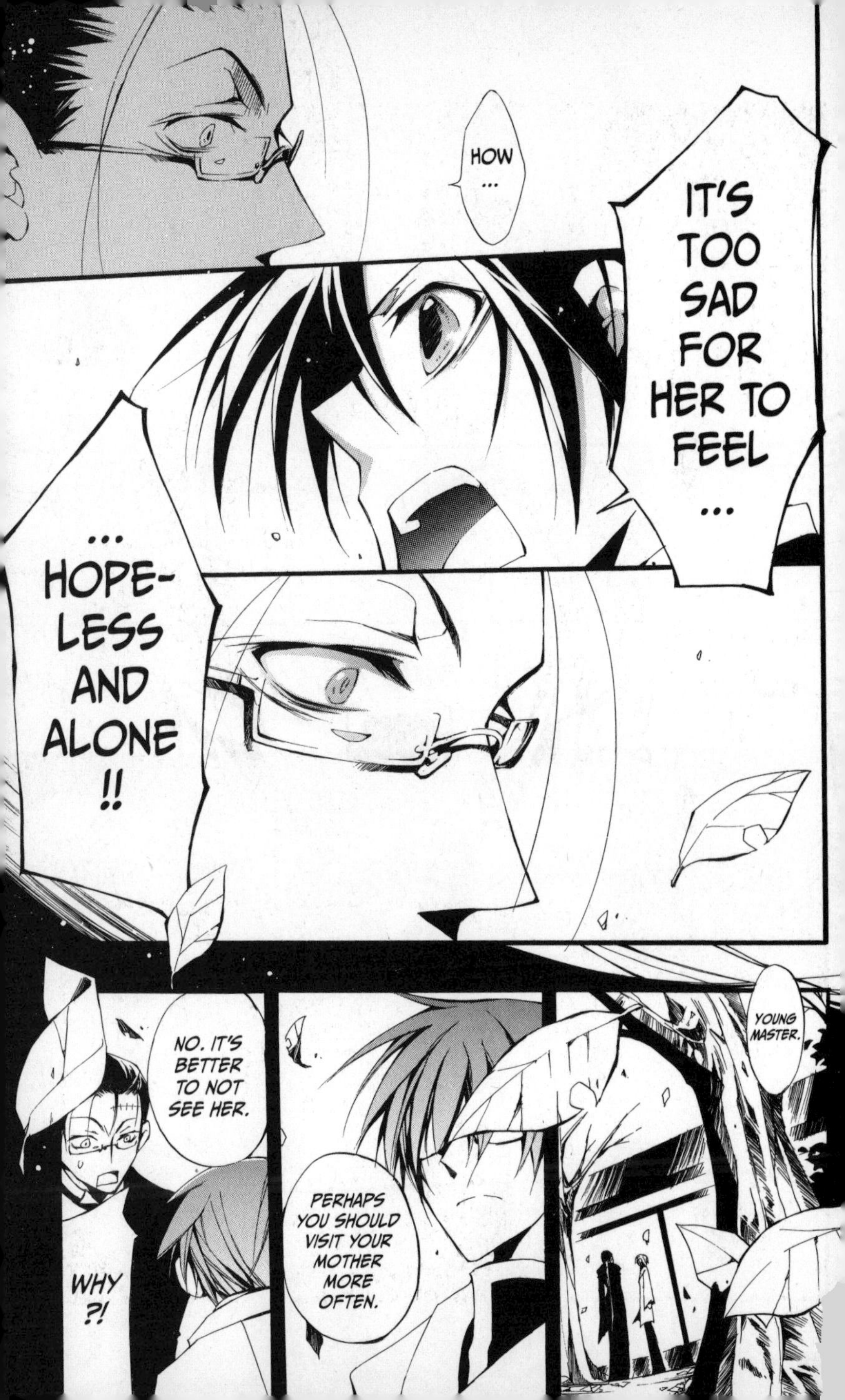
HOW ...
IT'S TOO SAD FOR HER TO FEEL ...
... HOPE-LESS AND ALONE !!
YOUNG MASTER.
PERHAPS YOU SHOULD VISIT YOUR MOTHER MORE OFTEN.
NO. IT'S BETTER TO NOT SEE HER.
WHY ?!

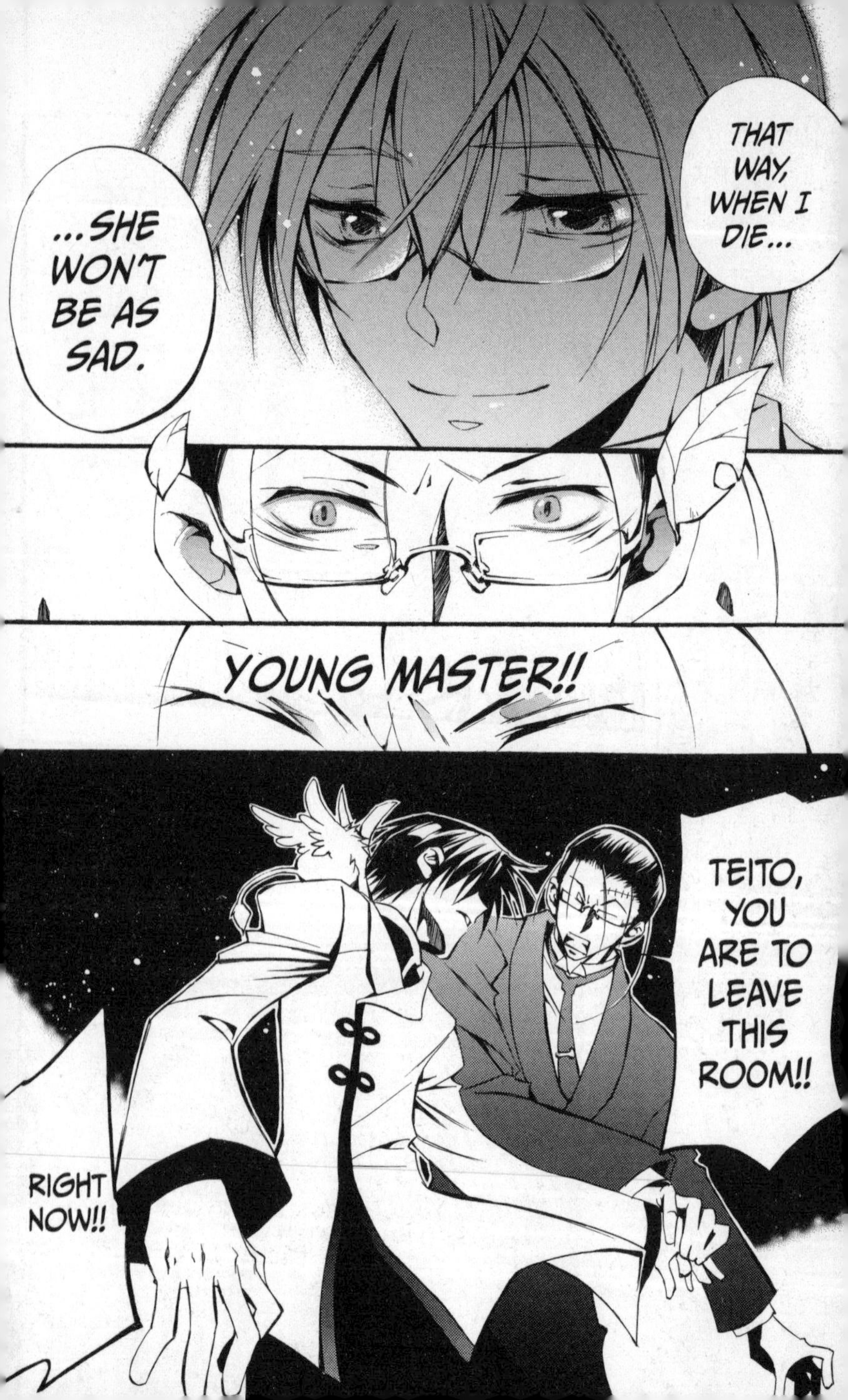
THAT WAY, WHEN I DIE...
...SHE WON'T BE AS SAD.
YOUNG MASTER!!
TEITO, YOU ARE TO LEAVE THIS ROOM!!
RIGHT NOW!!

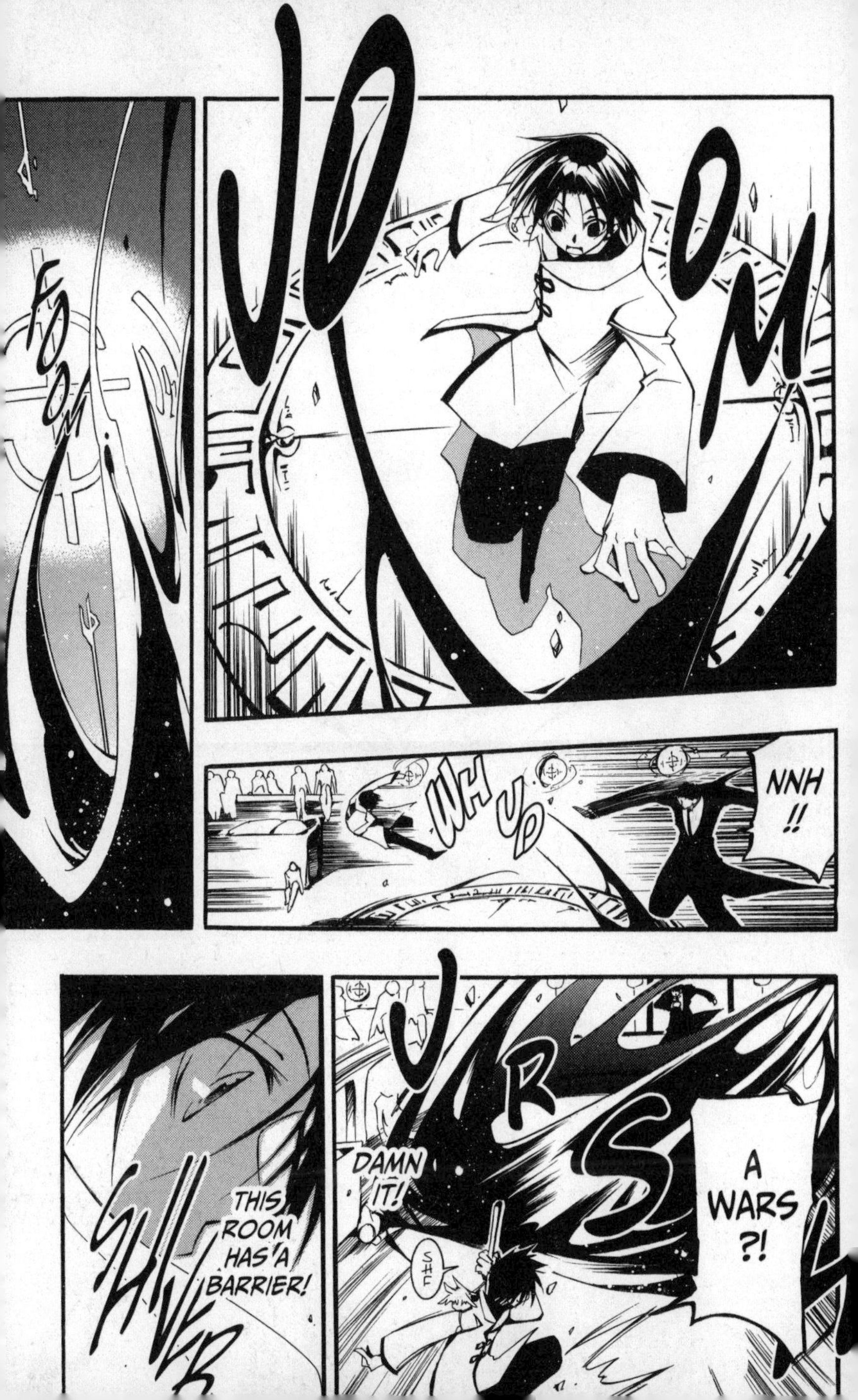
NNH !!
A WARS ?!
DAMN IT!
THIS ROOM HAS A BARRIER!

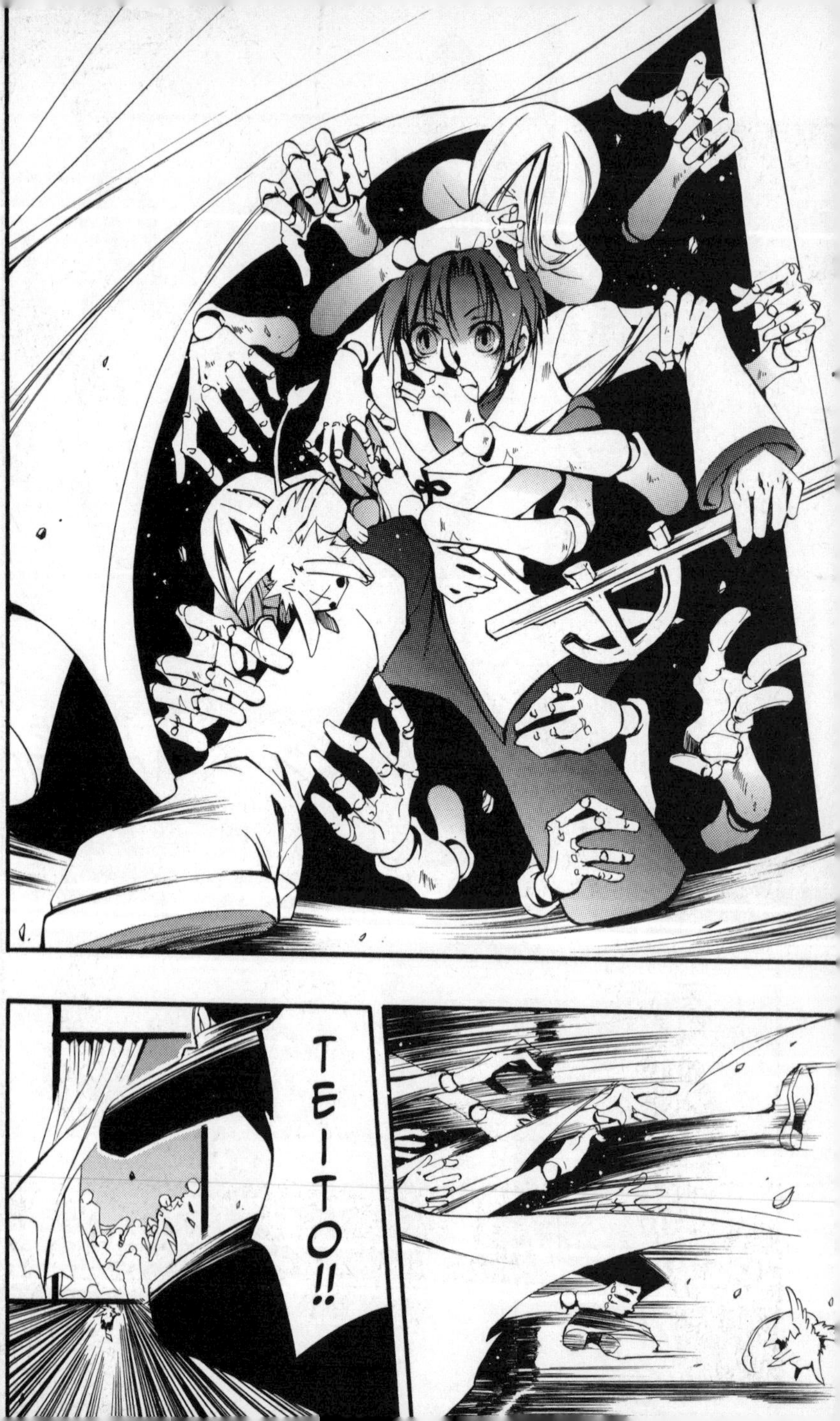
TEITO!!

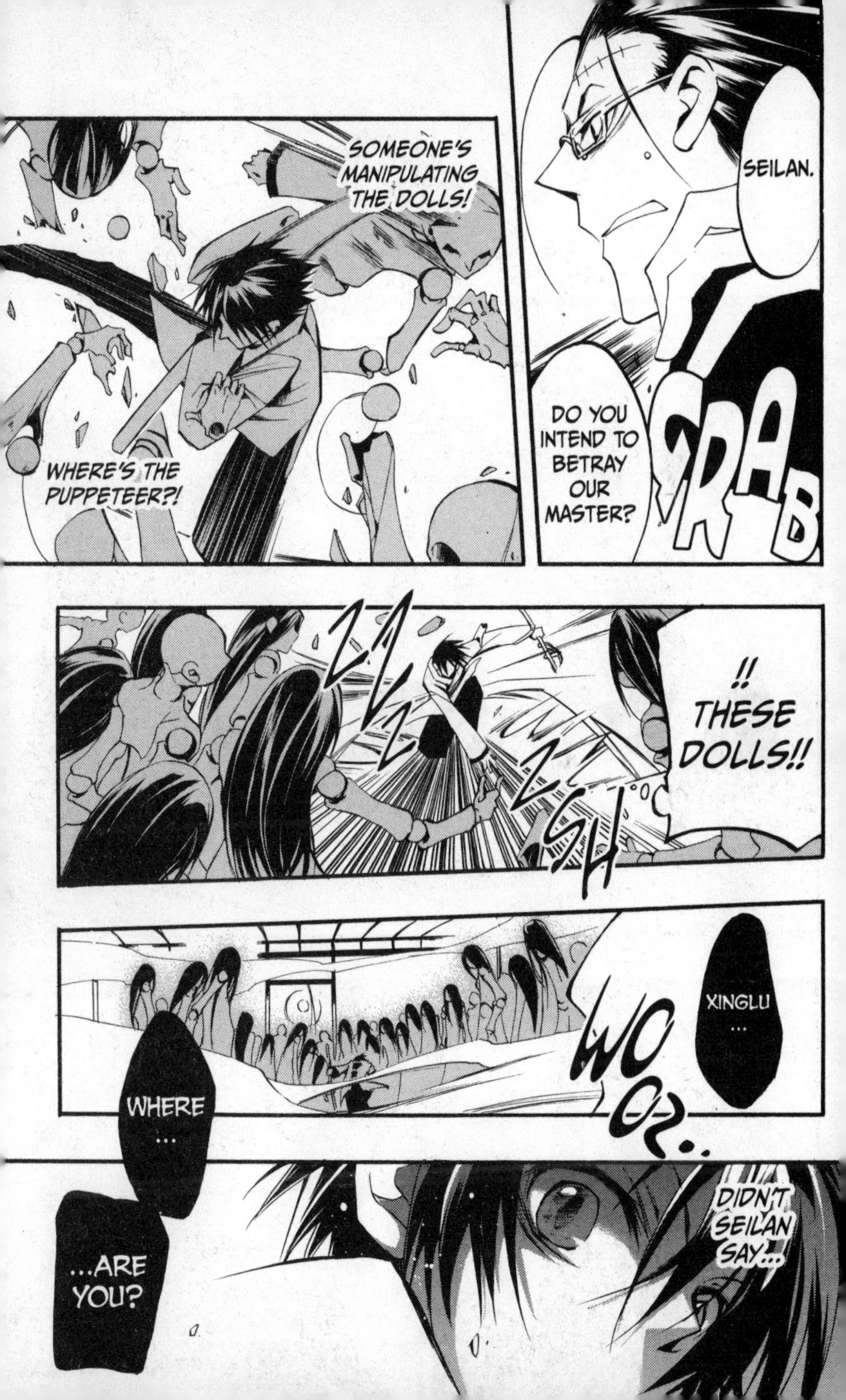
SEILAN.
DO YOU INTEND TO BETRAY OUR MASTER?
GRAB
SOMEONE'S MANIPULATING THE DOLLS!
WHERE'S THE PUPPETEER?!
!! THESE DOLLS!!
XINGLU ...
WOO..
WHERE ...
DIDN'T SEILAN SAY...
...ARE YOU?

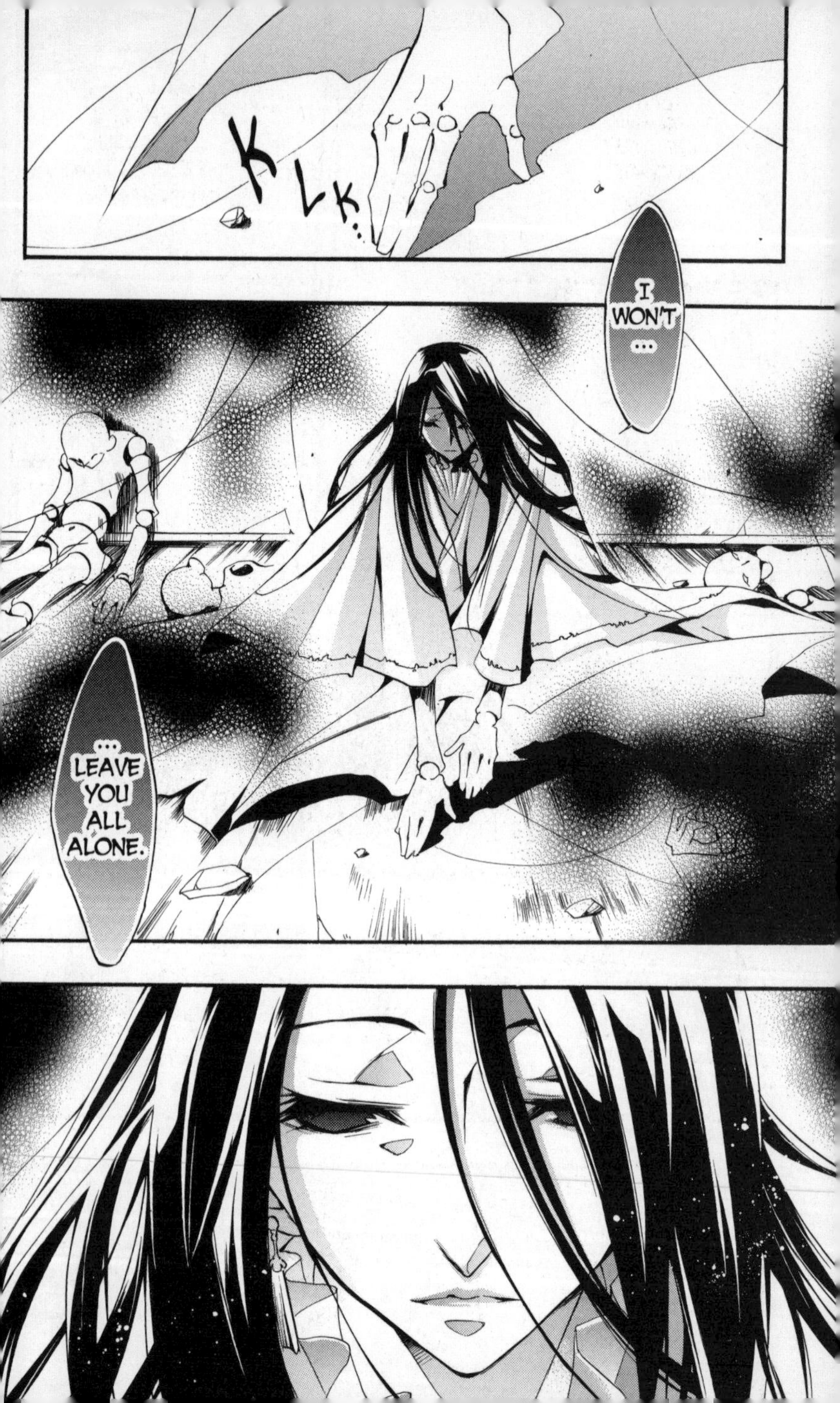
KLK...
I WON'T...
...LEAVE YOU ALL ALONE.

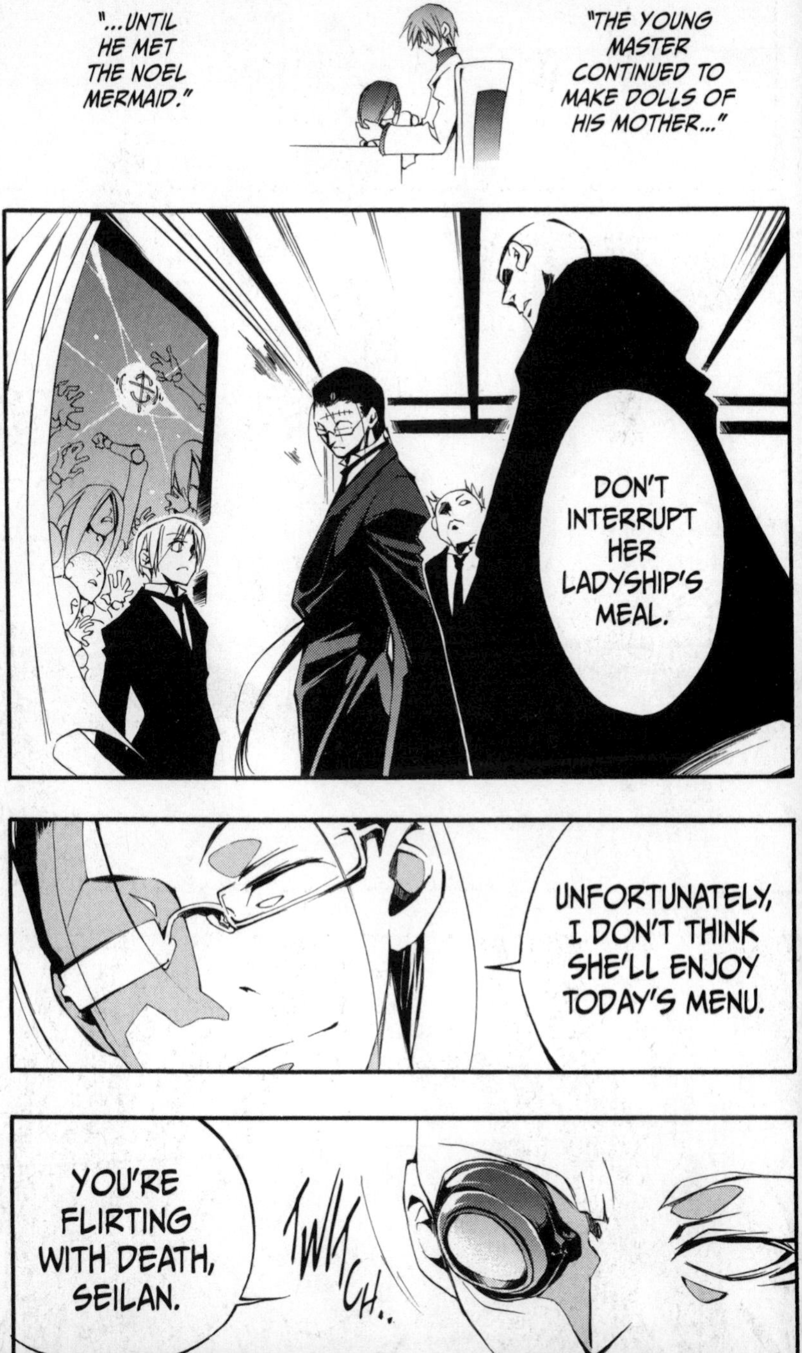
"THE YOUNG MASTER CONTINUED TO MAKE DOLLS OF HIS MOTHER..."
"...UNTIL HE MET THE NOEL MERMAID."
DON'T INTERRUPT HER LADYSHIP'S MEAL.
UNFORTUNATELY, I DON'T THINK SHE'LL ENJOY TODAY'S MENU.
TWITCH..
YOU'RE FLIRTING WITH DEATH, SEILAN.

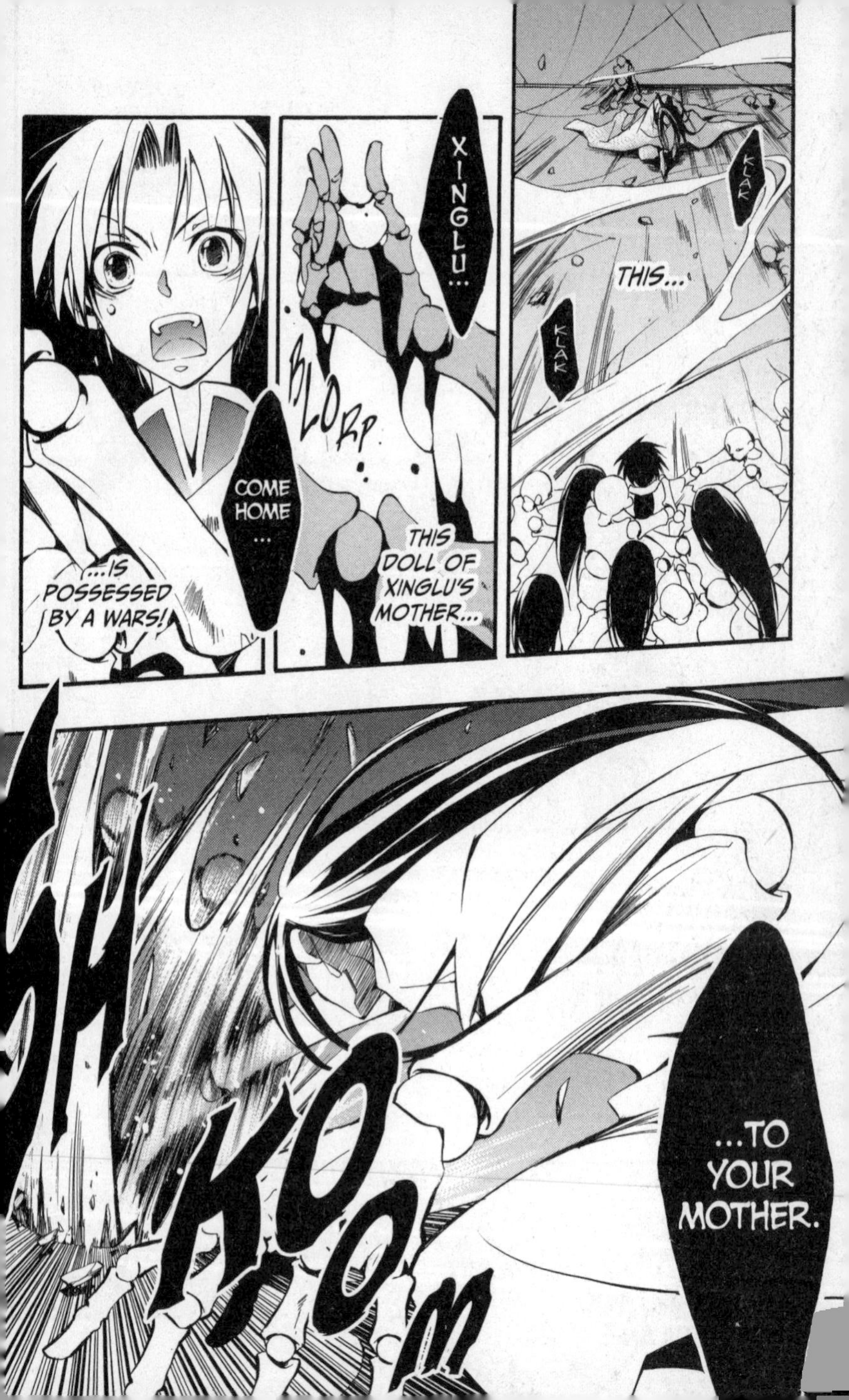
KLAK
THIS...
KLAK
XINGLU...
BLORP
THIS DOLL OF XINGLU'S MOTHER...
COME HOME ...
...IS POSSESSED BY A WARS!
...TO YOUR MOTHER.

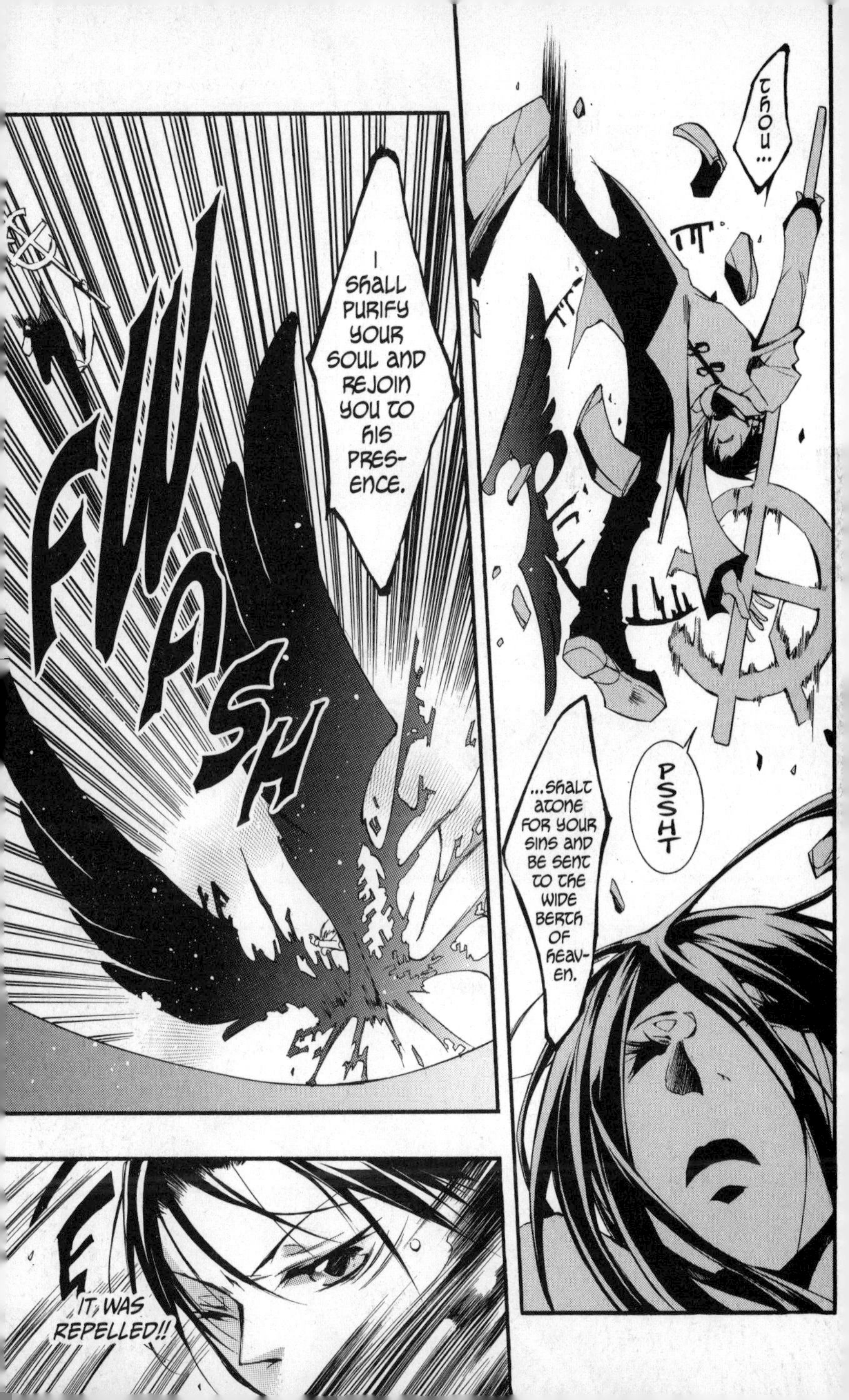
THOU...
PSSHT
...SHALT ATONE FOR YOUR SINS AND BE SENT TO THE WIDE BERTH OF HEAV-EN.
I SHALL PURIFY YOUR SOUL AND REJOIN YOU TO HIS PRES-ENCE.
FLASH
F
IT WAS REPELLED!!

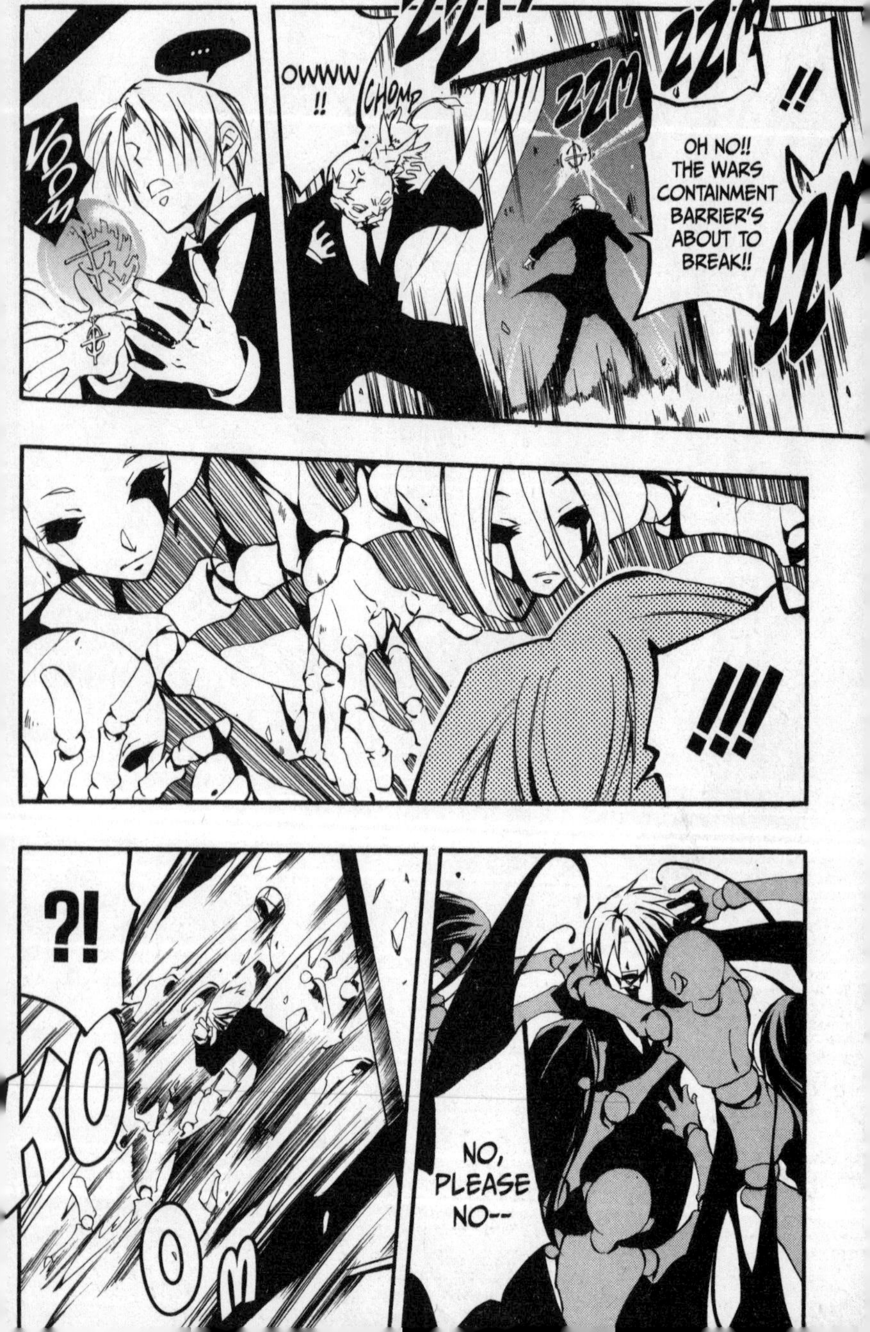
ZZM
ZZM
ZZM
!!
OH NO!! THE WARS CONTAINMENT BARRIER'S ABOUT TO BREAK!!
ZZM
OWWW!!
CHOMP
...
VOOM
!!!
NO, PLEASE NO--
?!
KOOOM

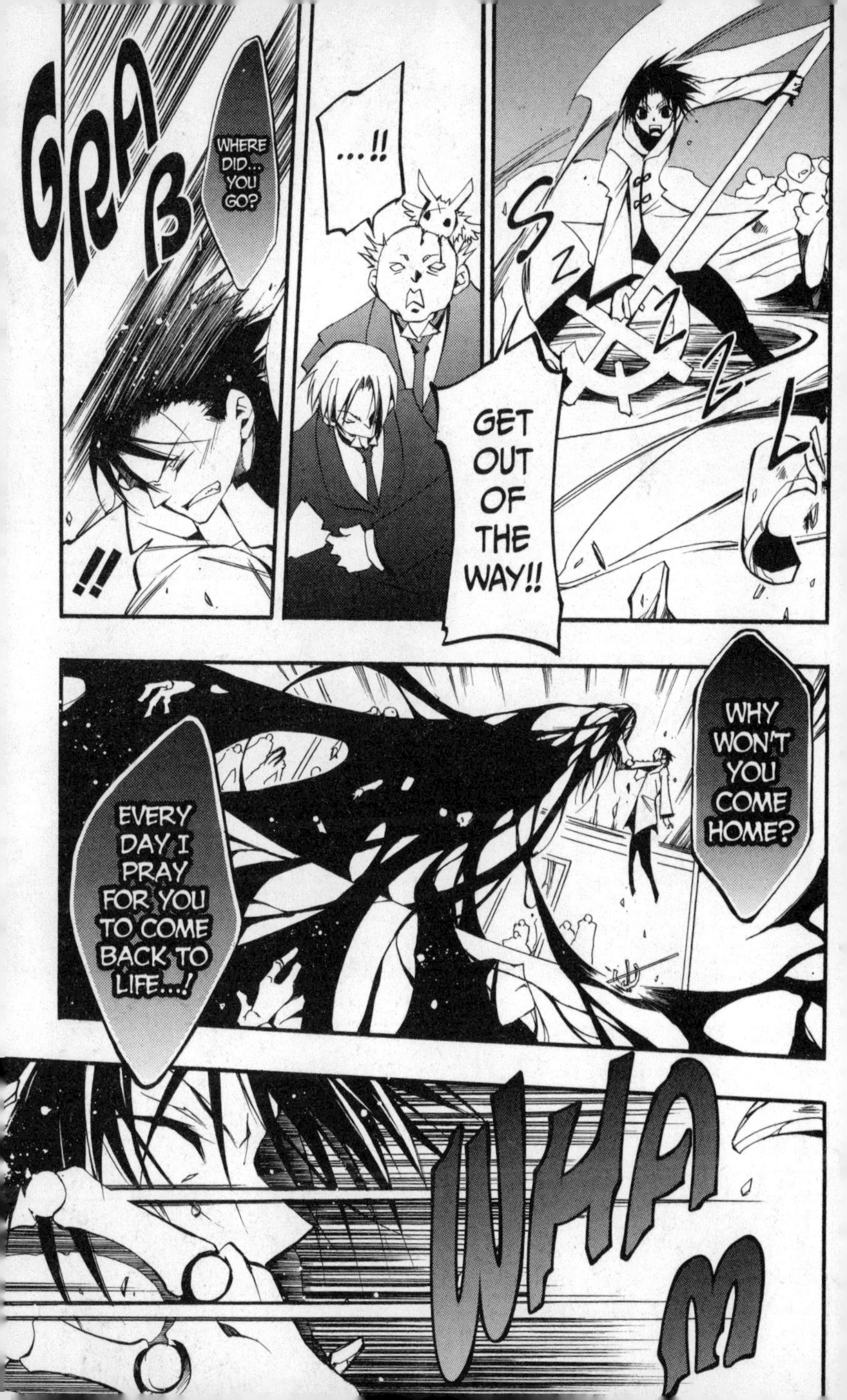
SZZZZL
GET OUT OF THE WAY!!
...!!
WHERE DID... YOU GO?
GRAB
!!
WHY WON'T YOU COME HOME?
EVERY DAY I PRAY FOR YOU TO COME BACK TO LIFE...!
WHAM

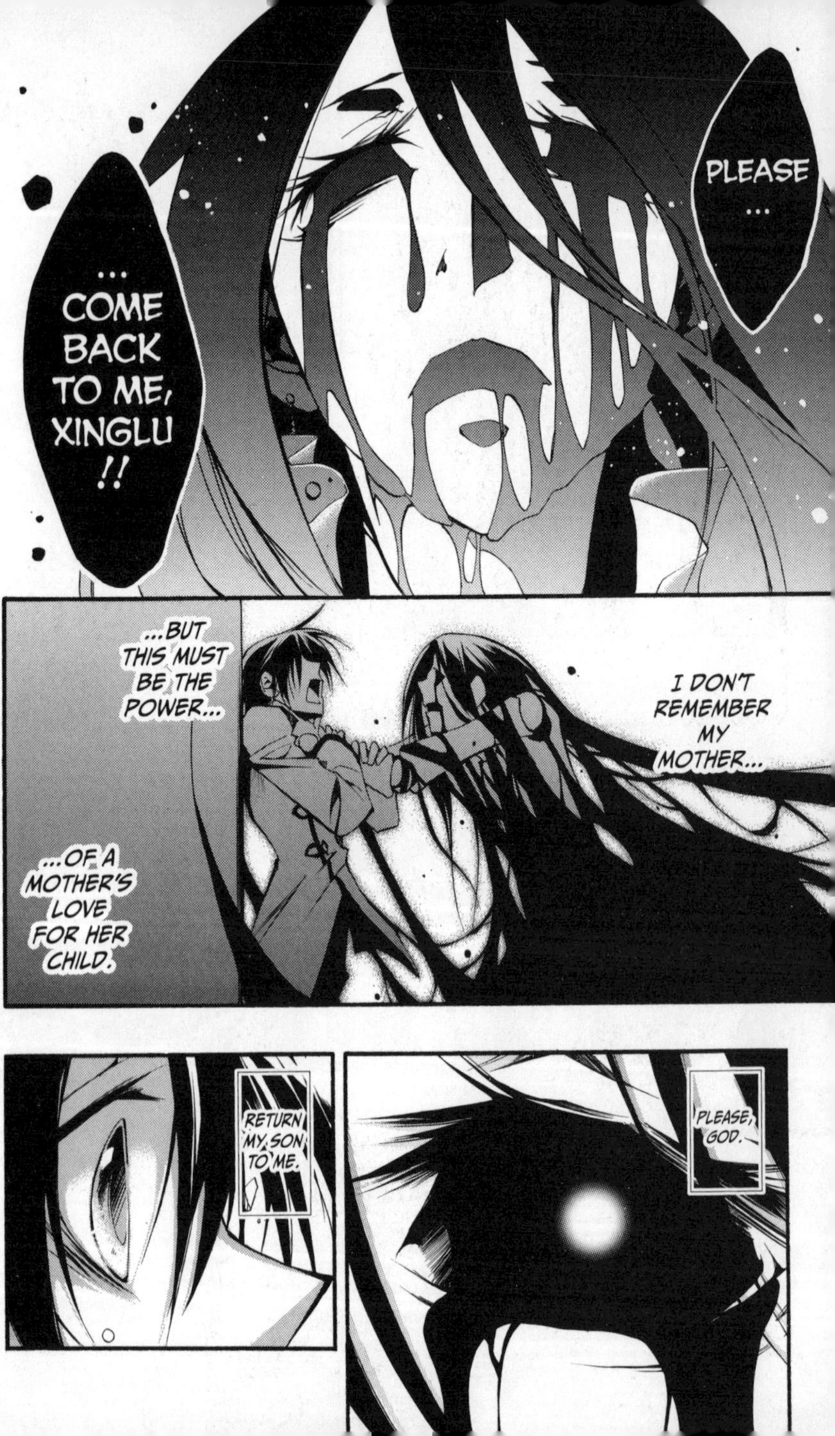
PLEASE ...
... COME BACK TO ME, XINGLU !!
I DON'T REMEMBER MY MOTHER...
...BUT THIS MUST BE THE POWER...
...OF A MOTHER'S LOVE FOR HER CHILD.
PLEASE, GOD.
RETURN MY SON TO ME.

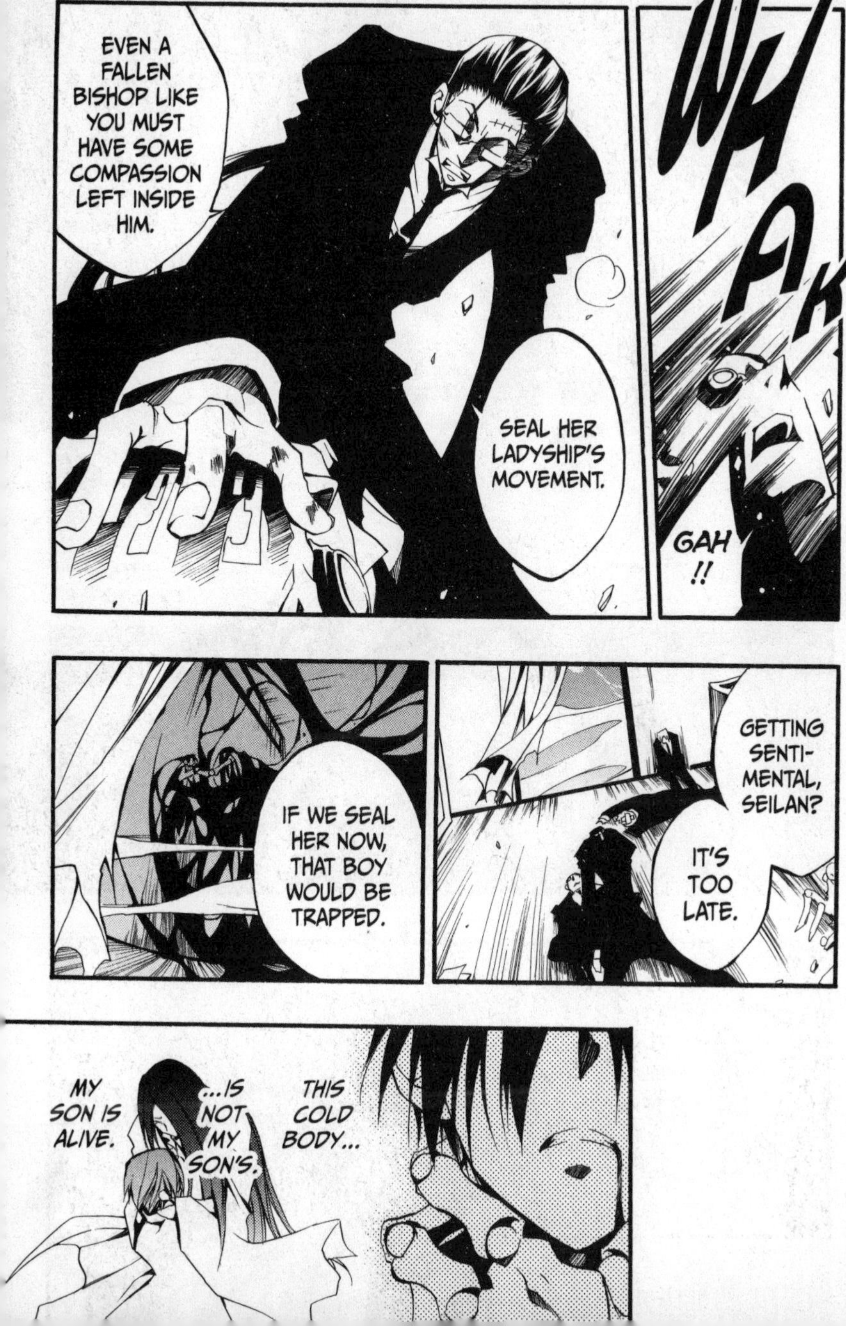
WHAK
GAH !!
EVEN A FALLEN BISHOP LIKE YOU MUST HAVE SOME COMPASSION LEFT INSIDE HIM.
SEAL HER LADYSHIP'S MOVEMENT.
GETTING SENTI-MENTAL, SEILAN?
IT'S TOO LATE.
IF WE SEAL HER NOW, THAT BOY WOULD BE TRAPPED.
THIS COLD BODY...
...IS NOT MY SON'S.
MY SON IS ALIVE.

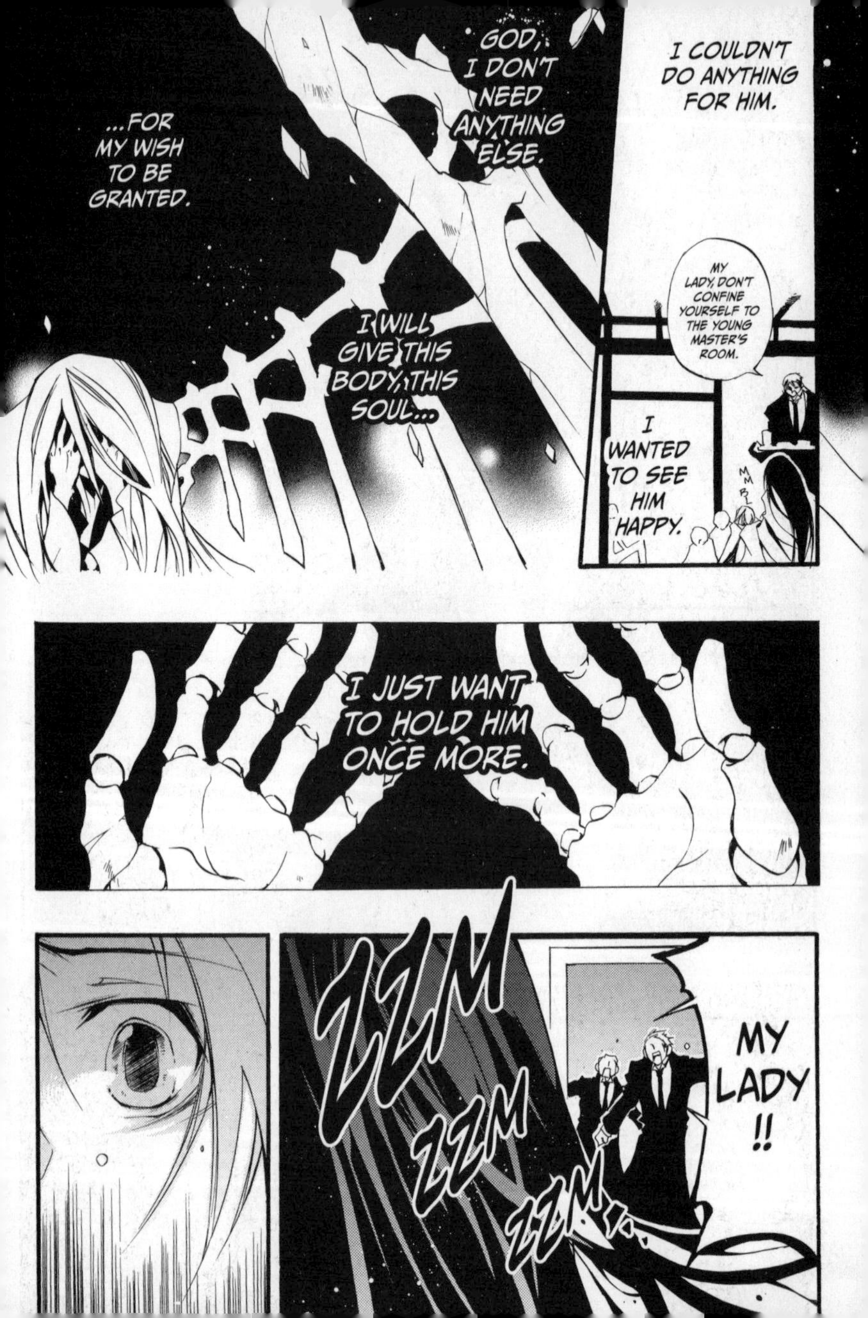
I COULDN'T DO ANYTHING FOR HIM.
MY LADY, DON'T CONFINE YOURSELF TO THE YOUNG MASTER'S ROOM.
I WANTED TO SEE HIM HAPPY.
MMBL
GOD, I DON'T NEED ANYTHING ELSE.
I WILL GIVE THIS BODY, THIS SOUL...
...FOR MY WISH TO BE GRANTED.
I JUST WANT TO HOLD HIM ONCE MORE.
MY LADY!!
ZZM
ZZM
ZZM

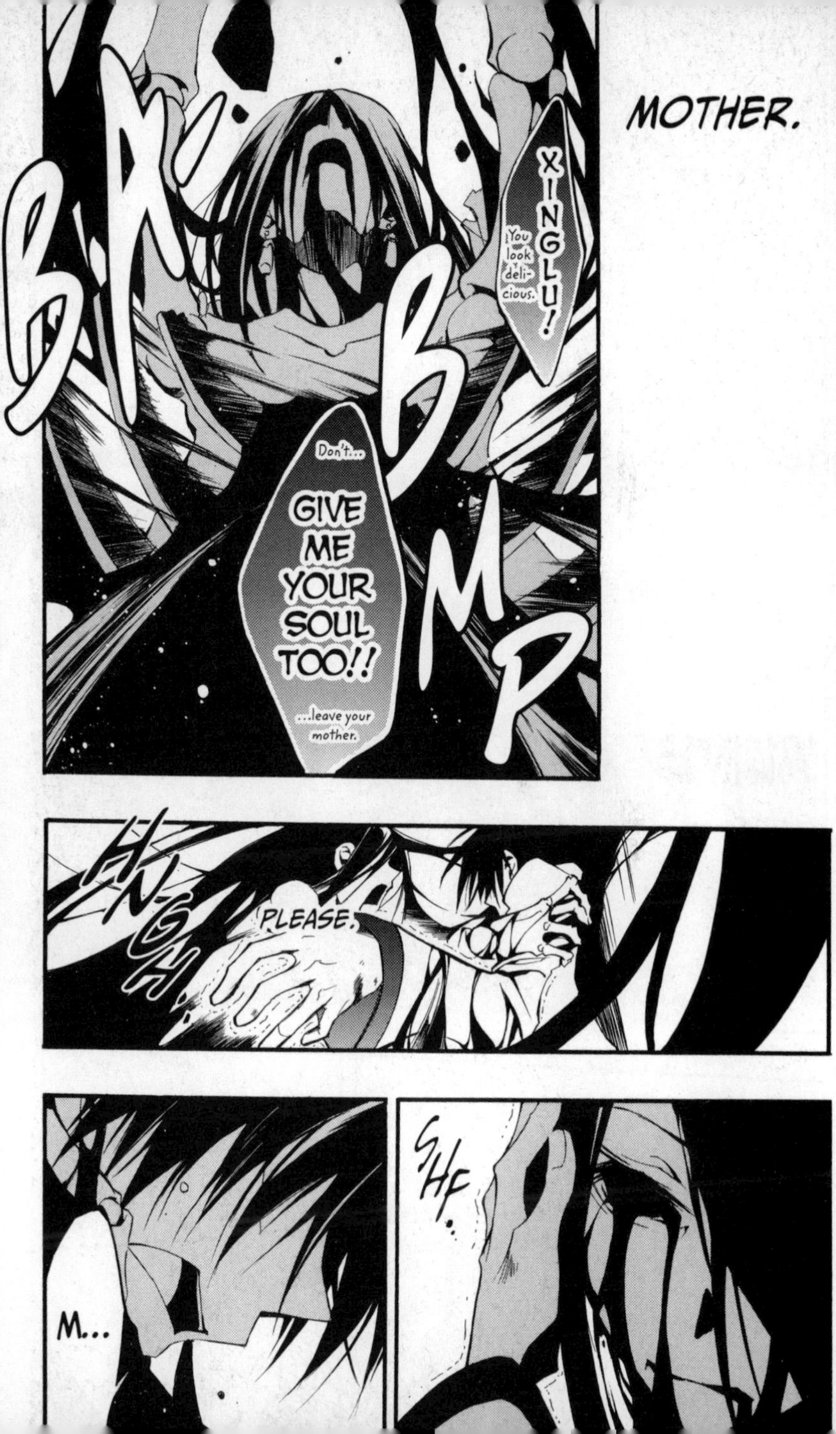
MOTHER.
XINGLU!
You look delicious.
BA-BUMP
Don't...
GIVE ME YOUR SOUL TOO!!
...leave your mother.
HNGH
PLEASE.
SHF
M...

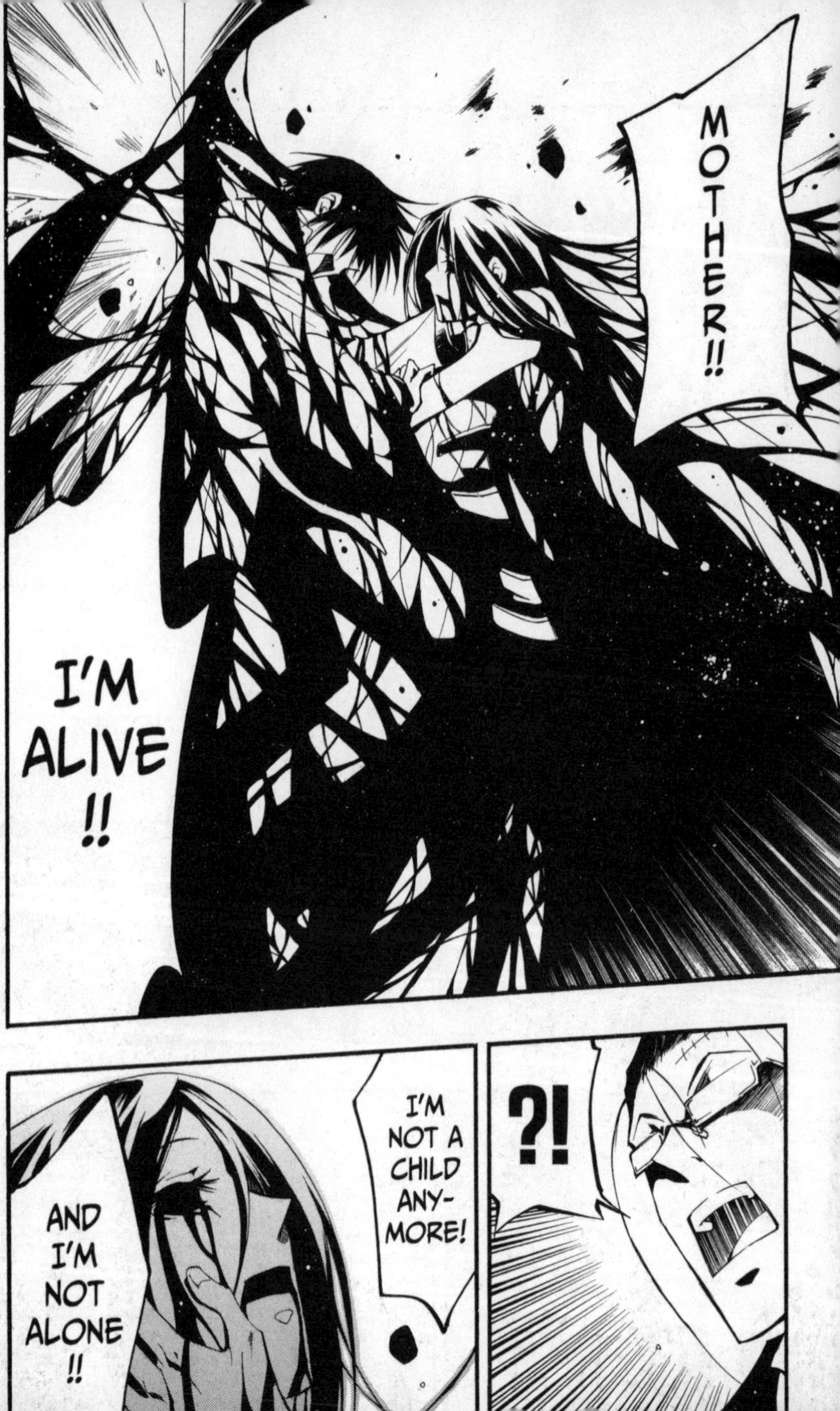
MOTHER!!
I'M ALIVE!!
?!
I'M NOT A CHILD ANYMORE!
AND I'M NOT ALONE!!

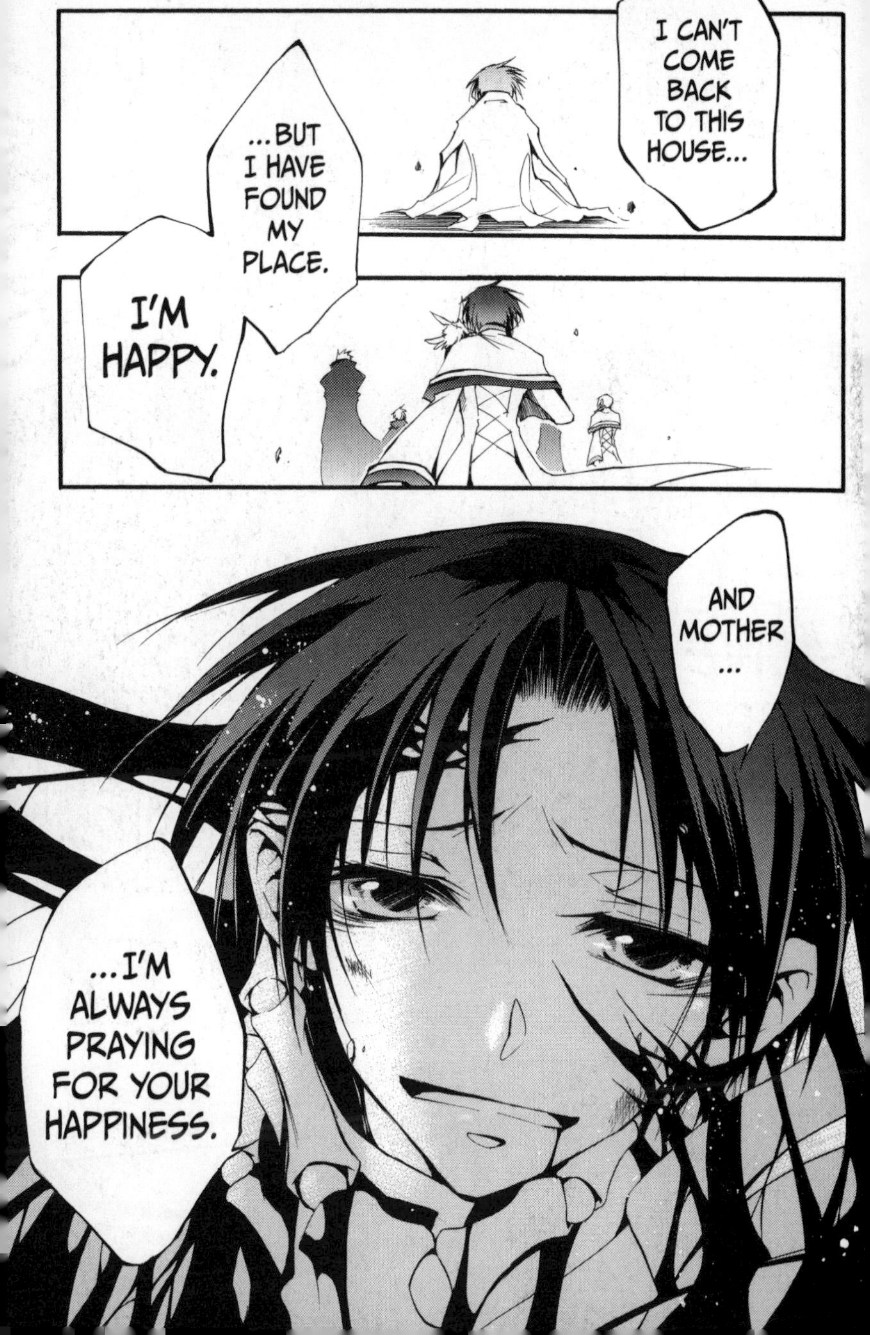
I CAN'T COME BACK TO THIS HOUSE...
...BUT I HAVE FOUND MY PLACE.
I'M HAPPY.
AND MOTHER ...
...I'M ALWAYS PRAYING FOR YOUR HAPPINESS.

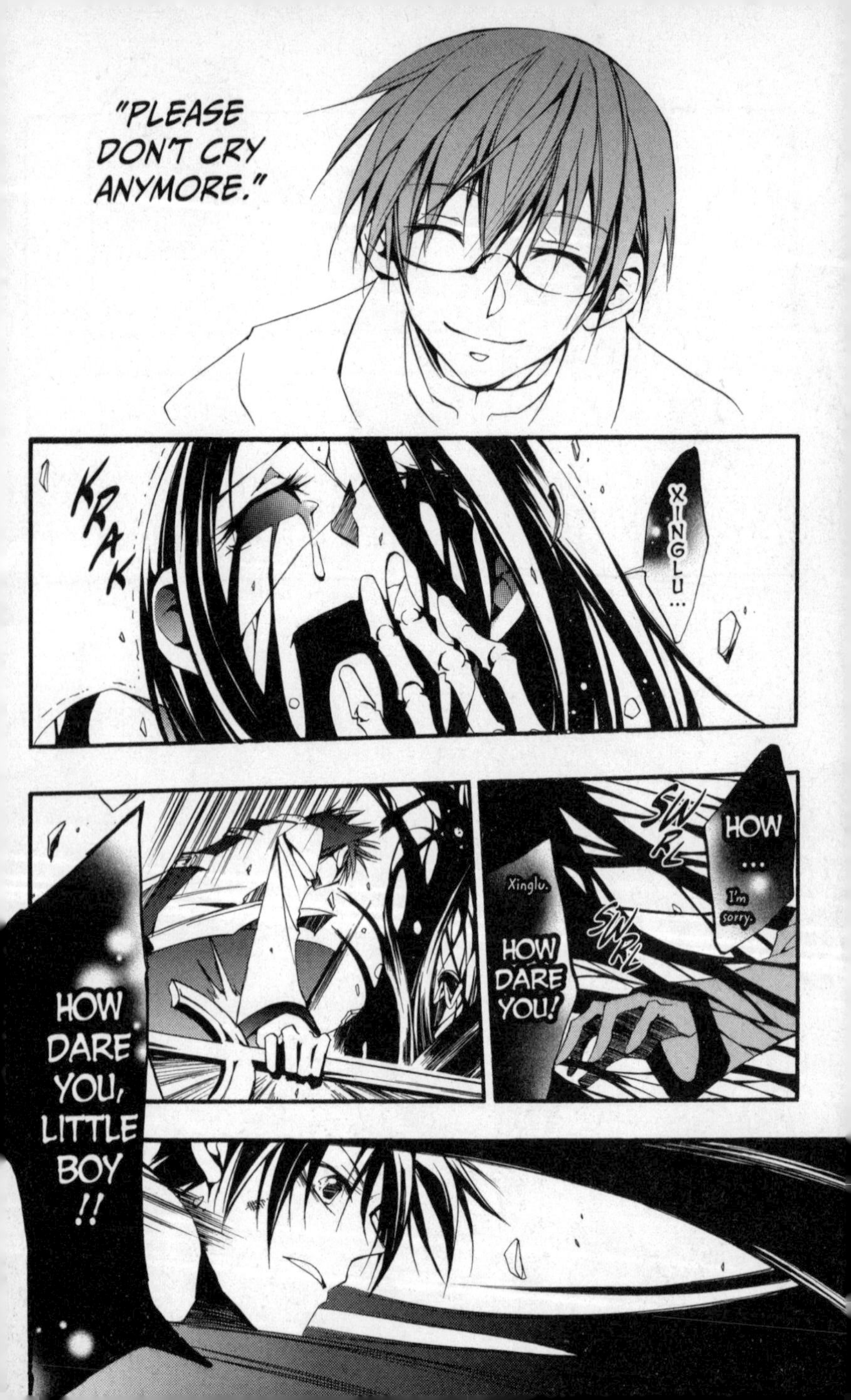
"PLEASE DON'T CRY ANYMORE."
XINGLU...
KRAK
SWRL
HOW ...
I'm sorry.
Xinglu.
SWRL
HOW DARE YOU!
HOW DARE YOU, LITTLE BOY!!

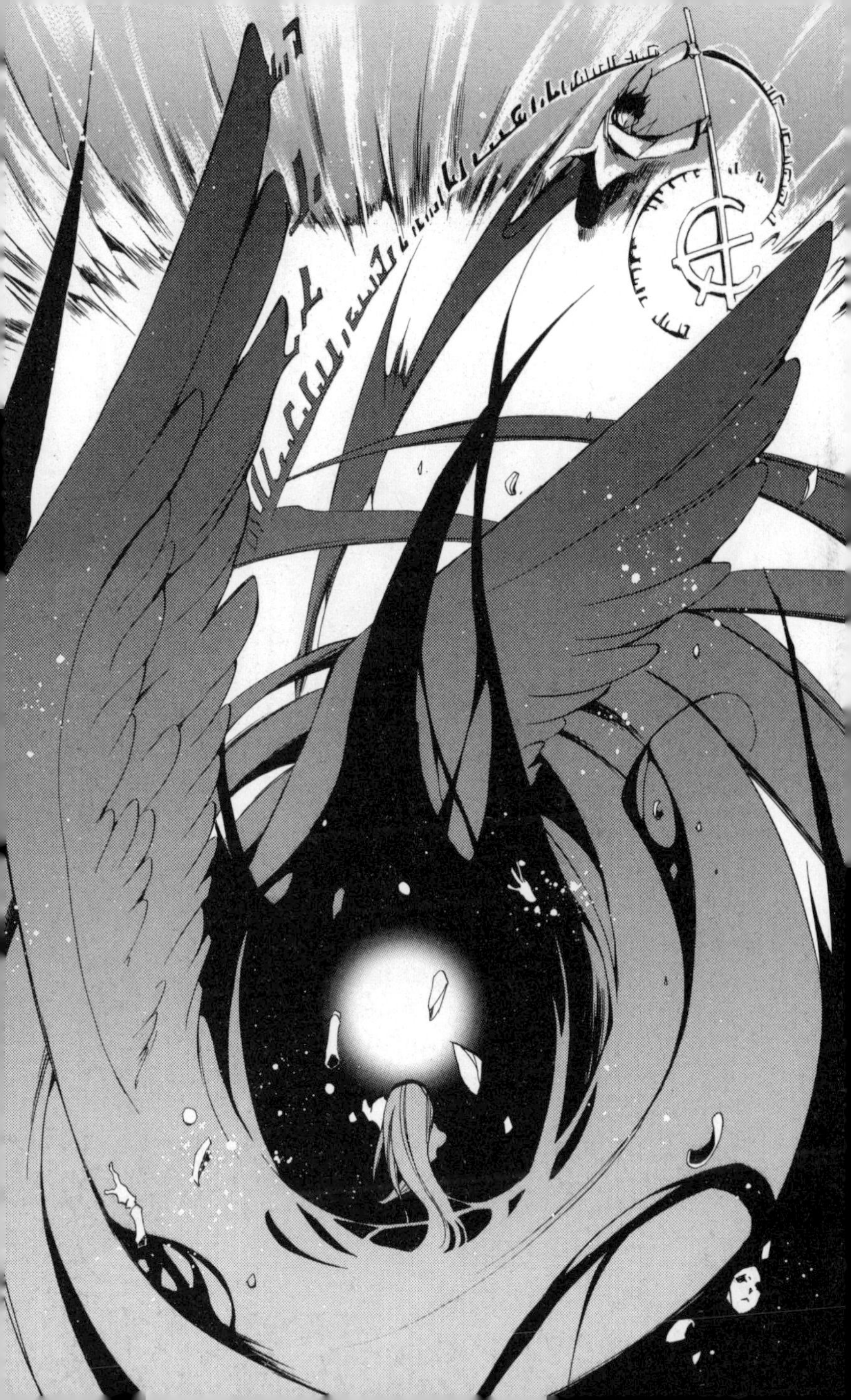

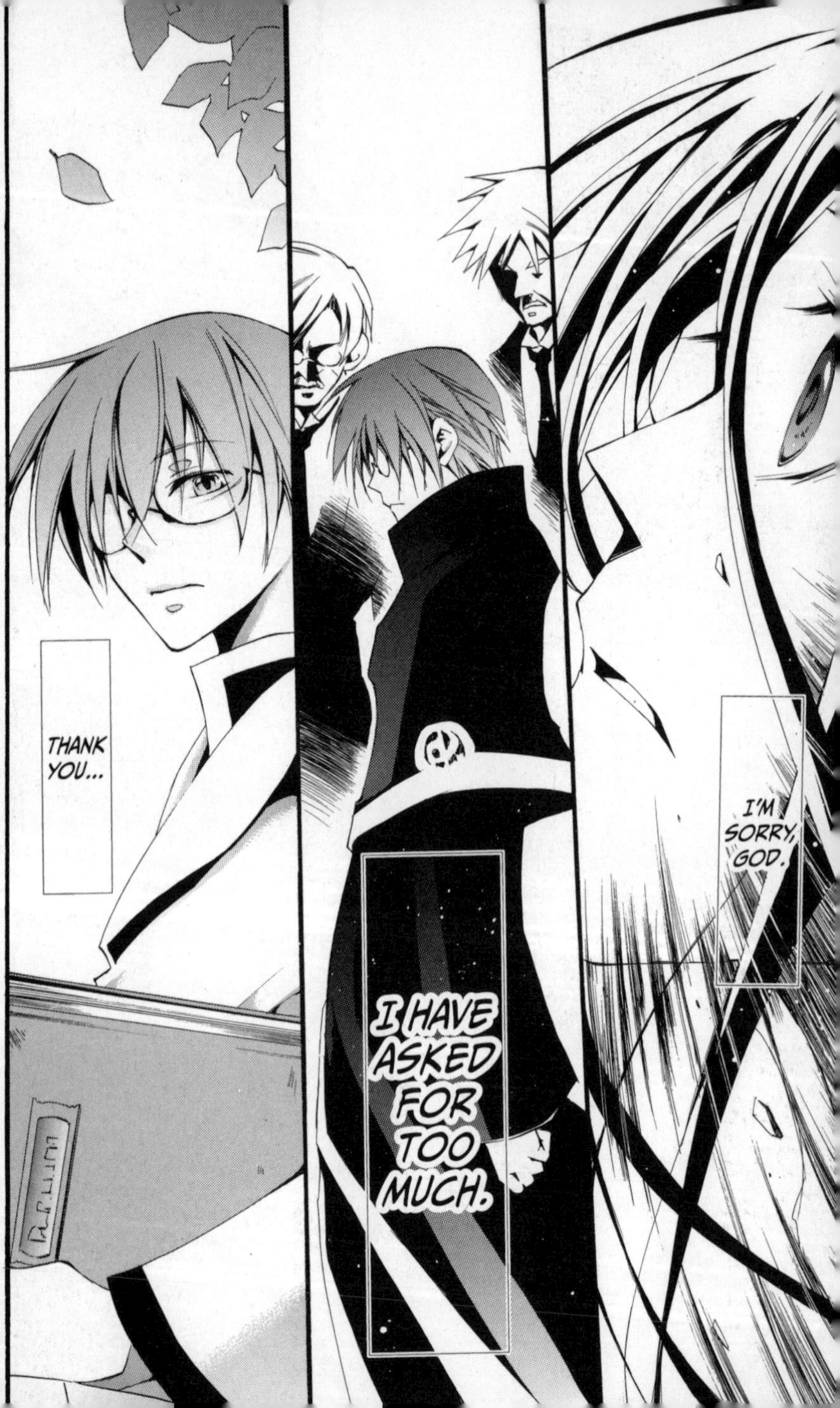
I'M SORRY, GOD.
I HAVE ASKED FOR TOO MUCH.
THANK YOU...

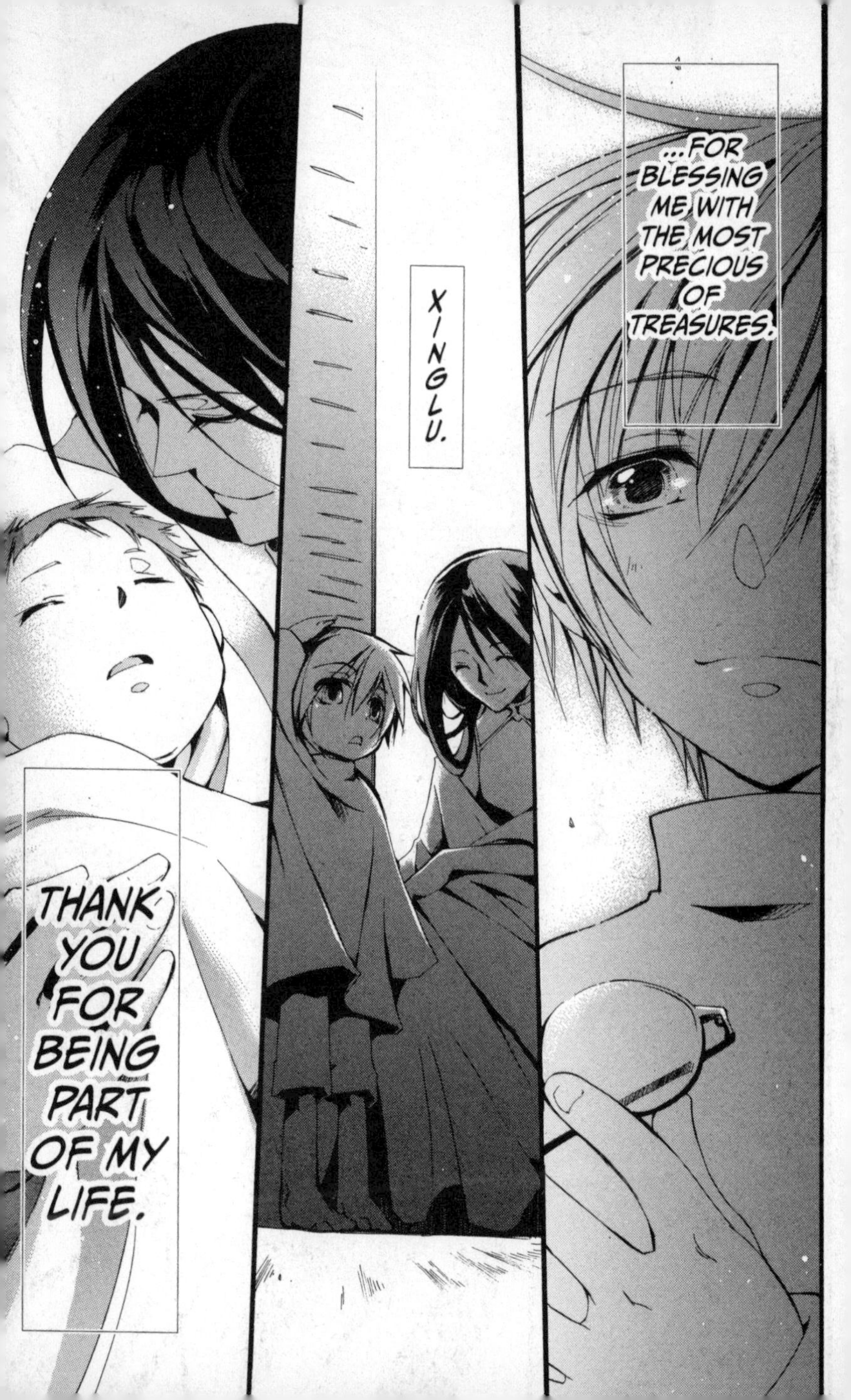
...FOR BLESSING ME WITH THE MOST PRECIOUS OF TREASURES.
XINGLU.
THANK YOU FOR BEING PART OF MY LIFE.

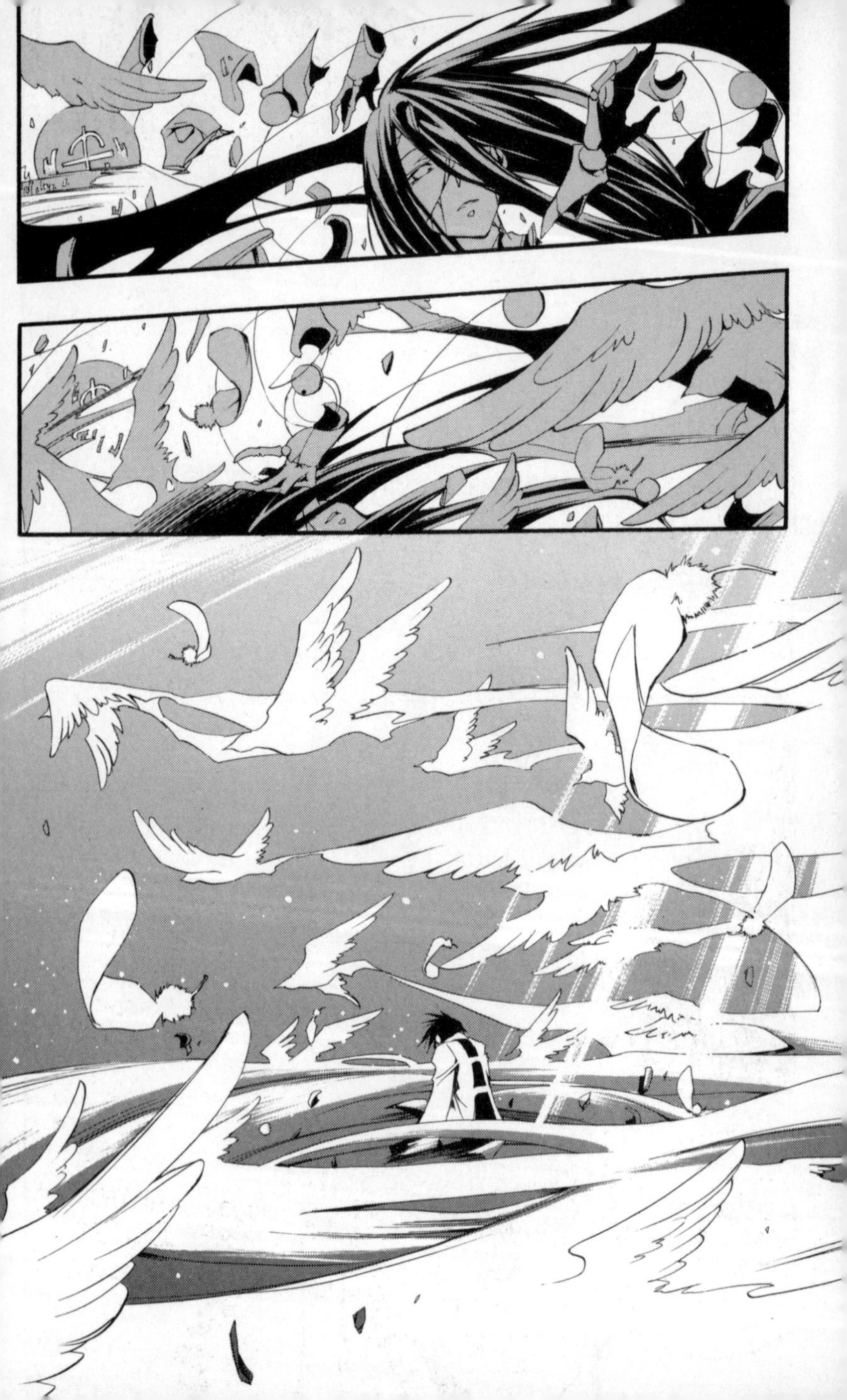

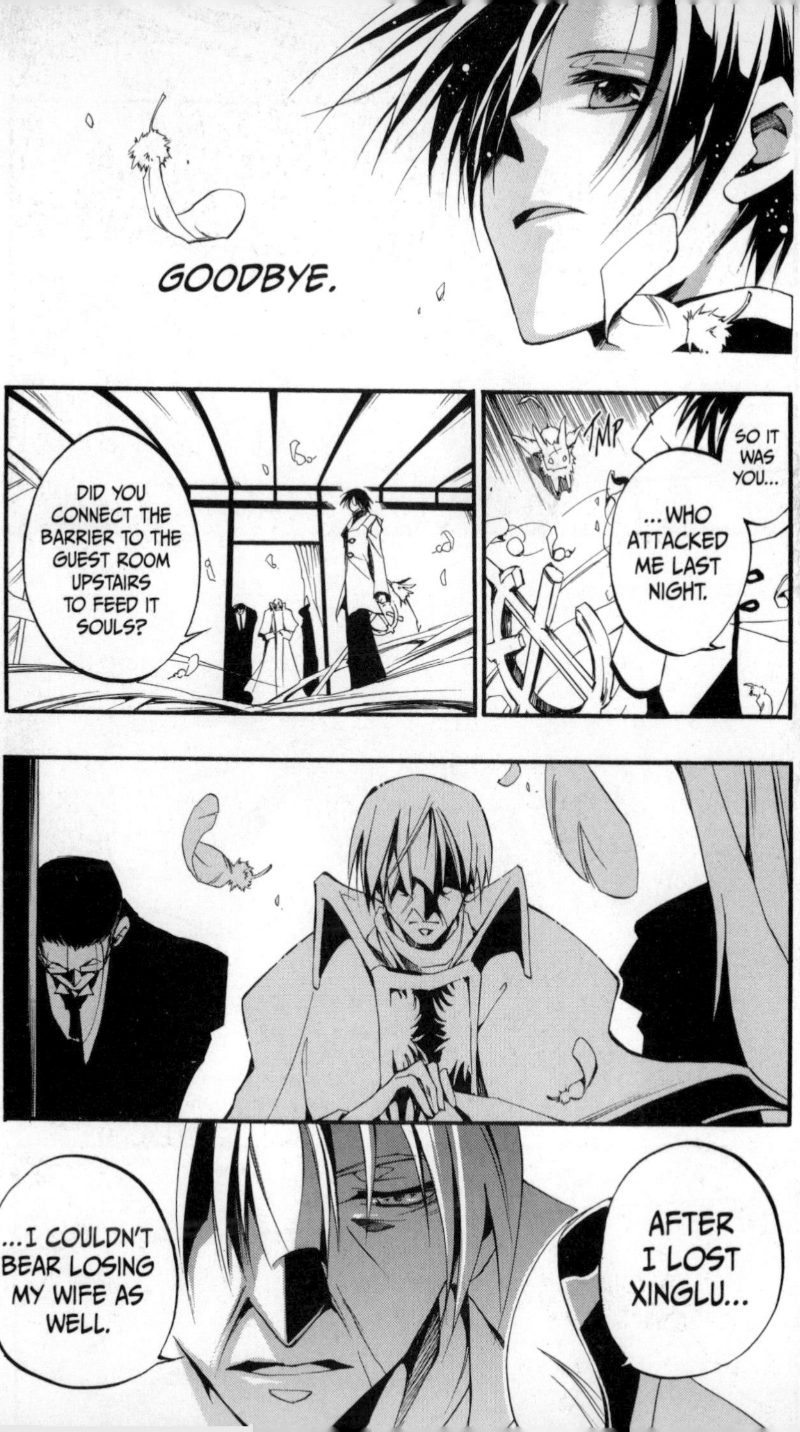
GOODBYE.
TMP
SO IT WAS YOU...
...WHO ATTACKED ME LAST NIGHT.
DID YOU CONNECT THE BARRIER TO THE GUEST ROOM UPSTAIRS TO FEED IT SOULS?
AFTER I LOST XINGLU...
...I COULDN'T BEAR LOSING MY WIFE AS WELL.

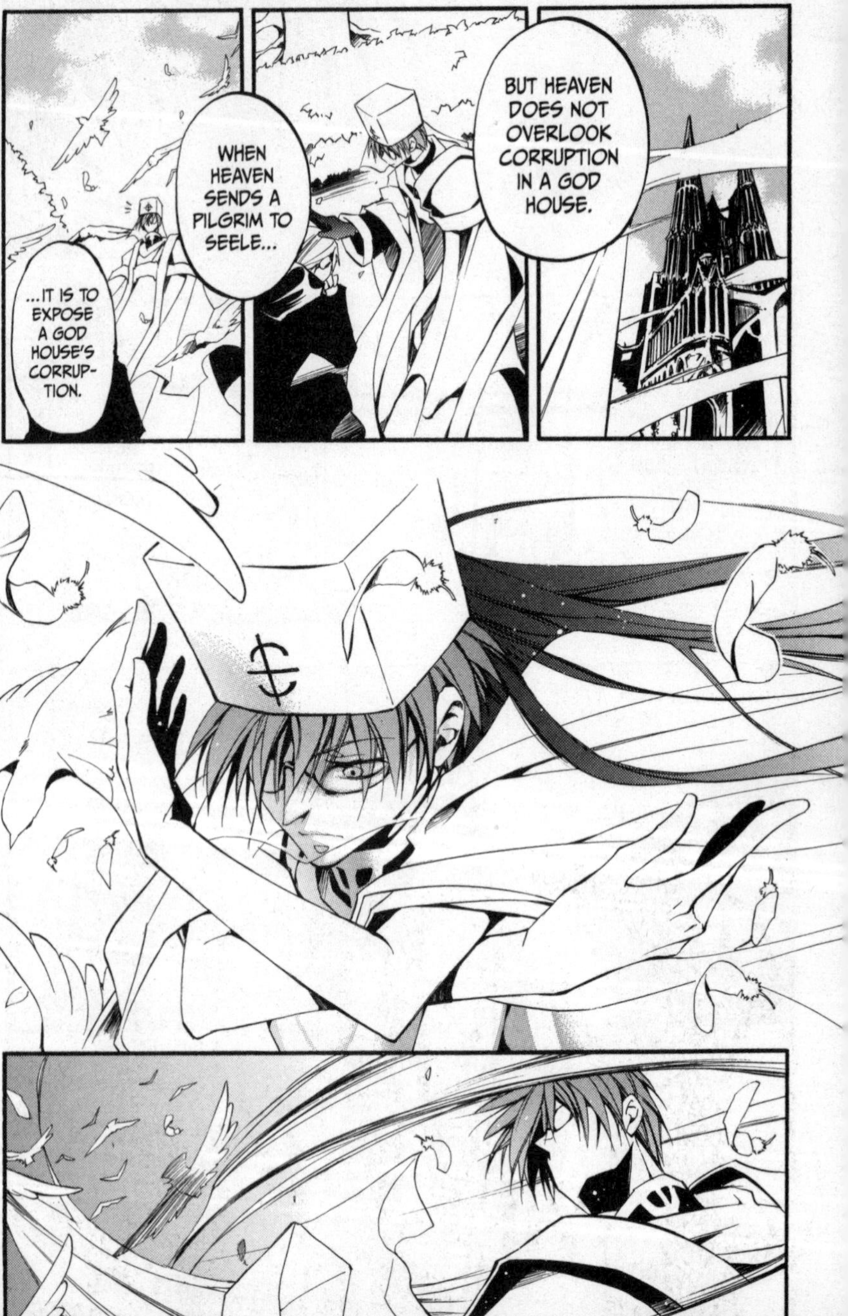
BUT HEAVEN DOES NOT OVERLOOK CORRUPTION IN A GOD HOUSE.
WHEN HEAVEN SENDS A PILGRIM TO SEELE...
...IT IS TO EXPOSE A GOD HOUSE'S CORRUP-TION.

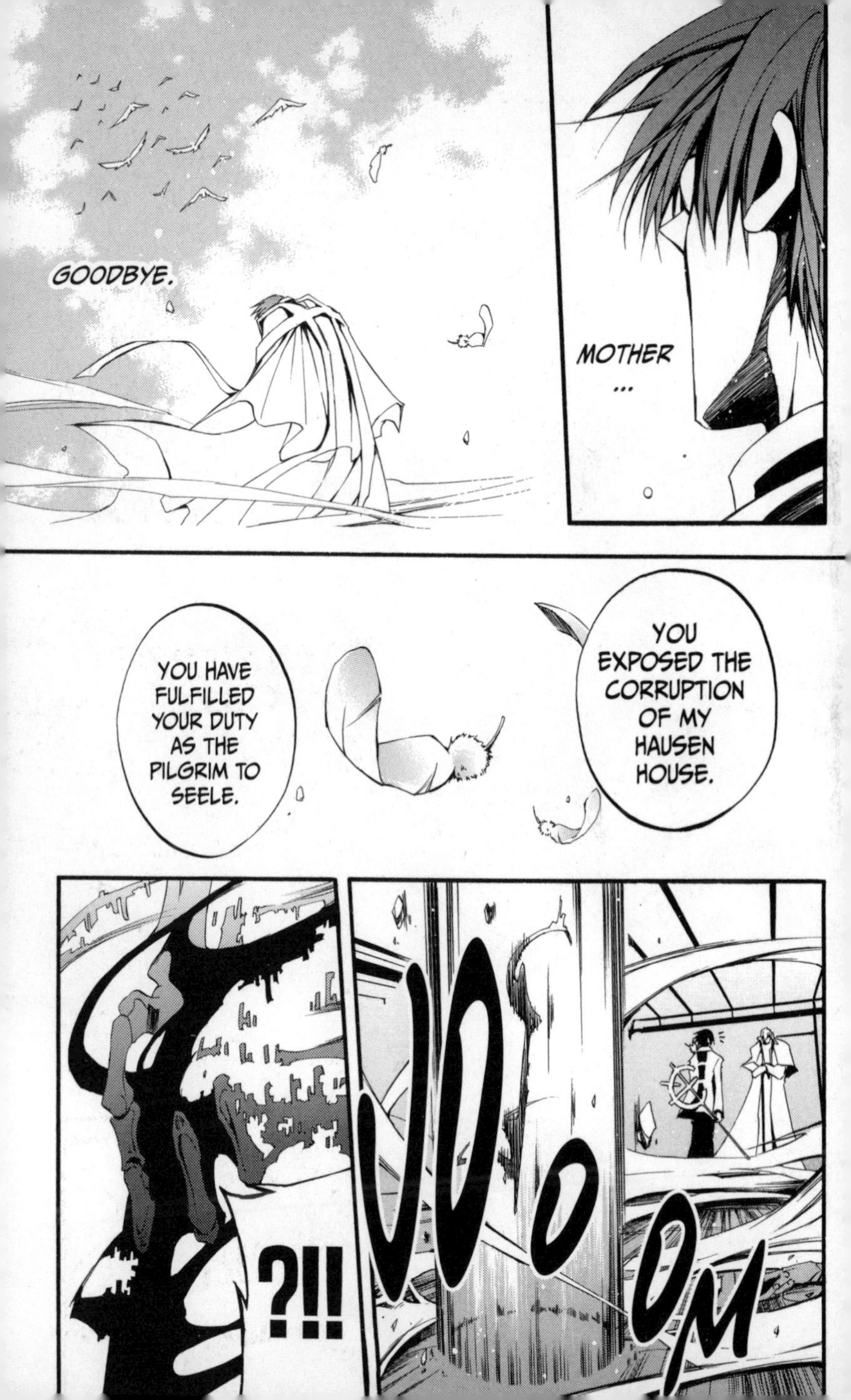
MOTHER...
GOODBYE.
YOU EXPOSED THE CORRUPTION OF MY HAUSEN HOUSE.
YOU HAVE FULFILLED YOUR DUTY AS THE PILGRIM TO SEELE.
VOOOM
?!!

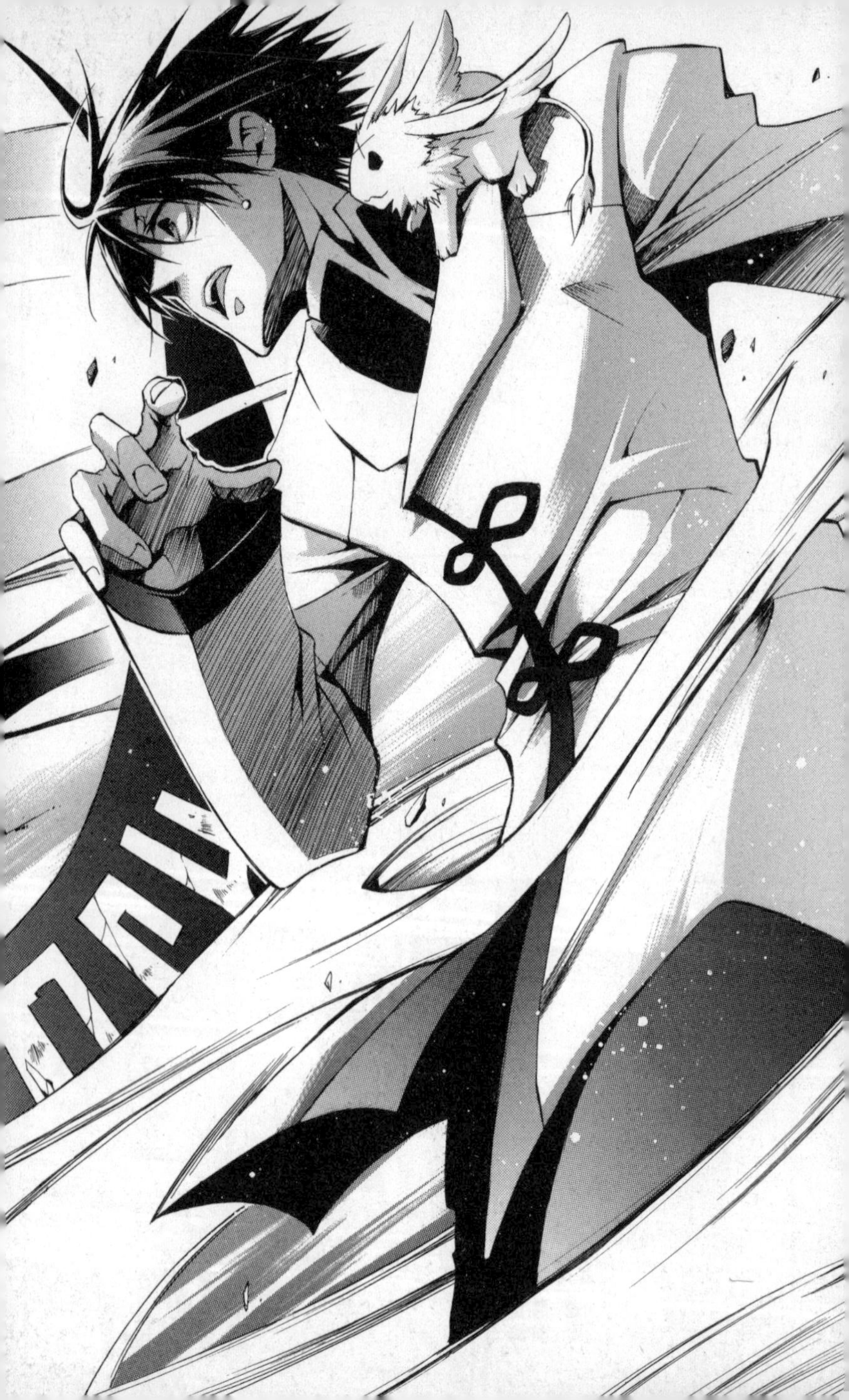

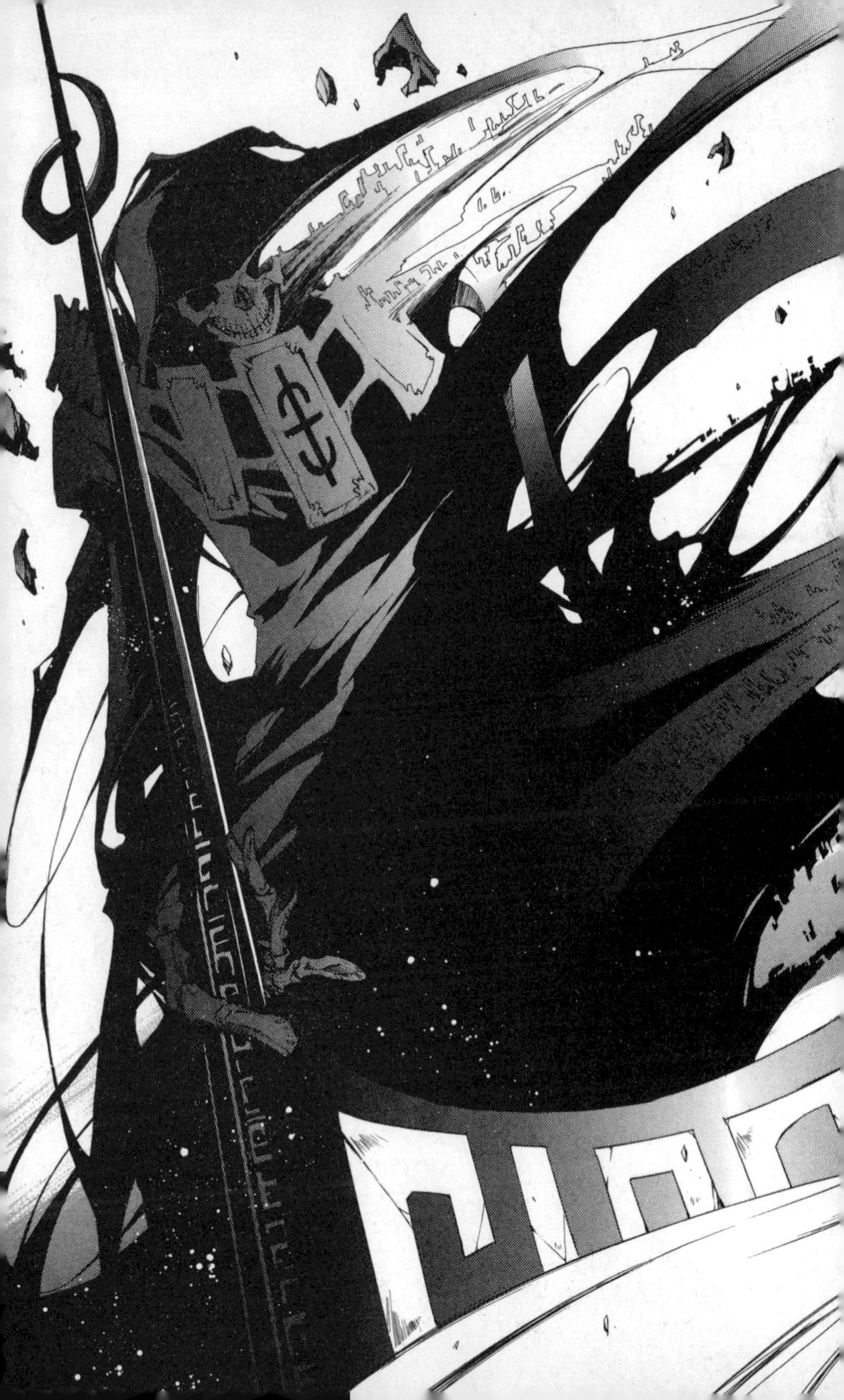

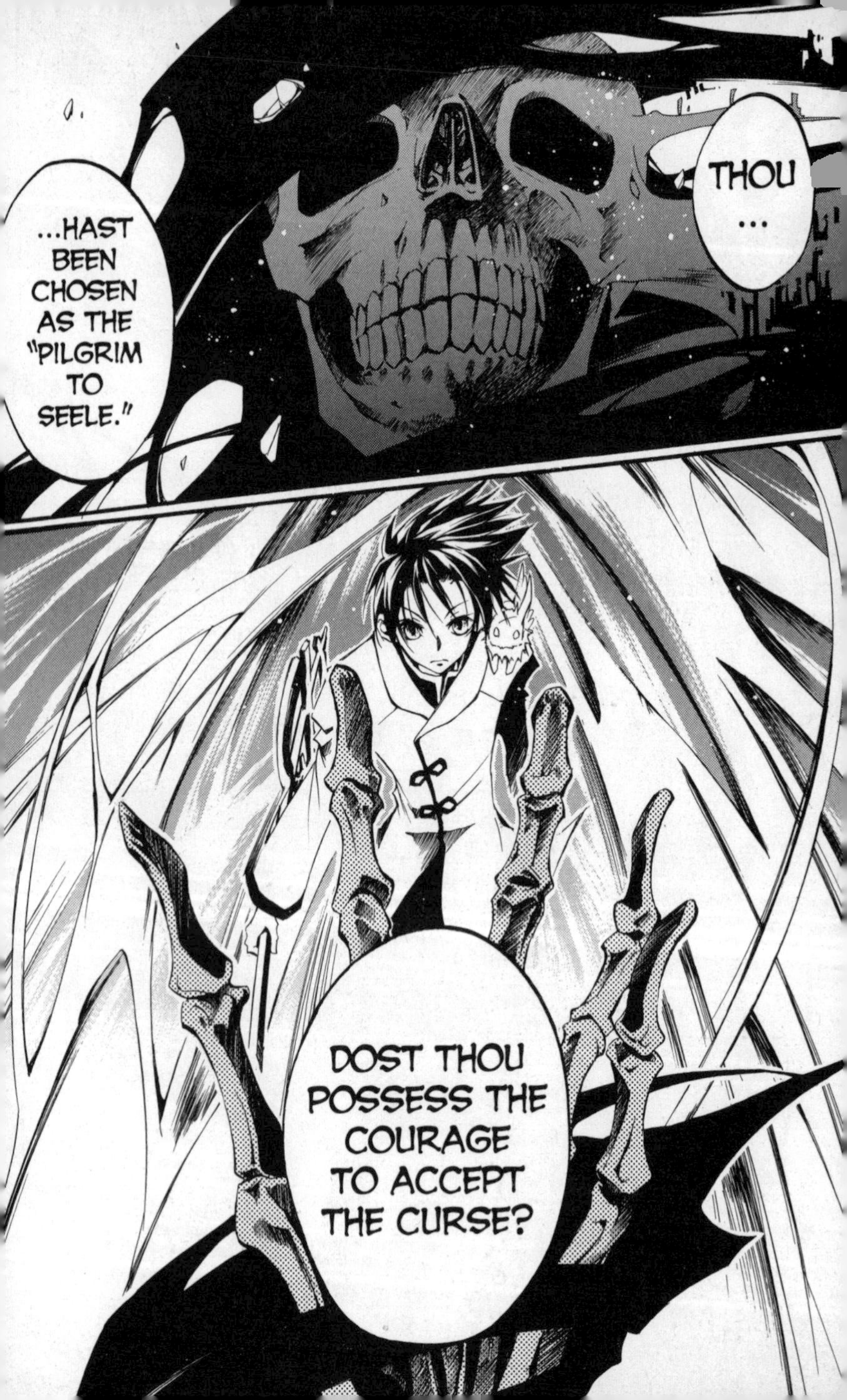
THOU...
...HAST BEEN CHOSEN AS THE "PILGRIM TO SEELE."
DOST THOU POSSESS THE COURAGE TO ACCEPT THE CURSE?

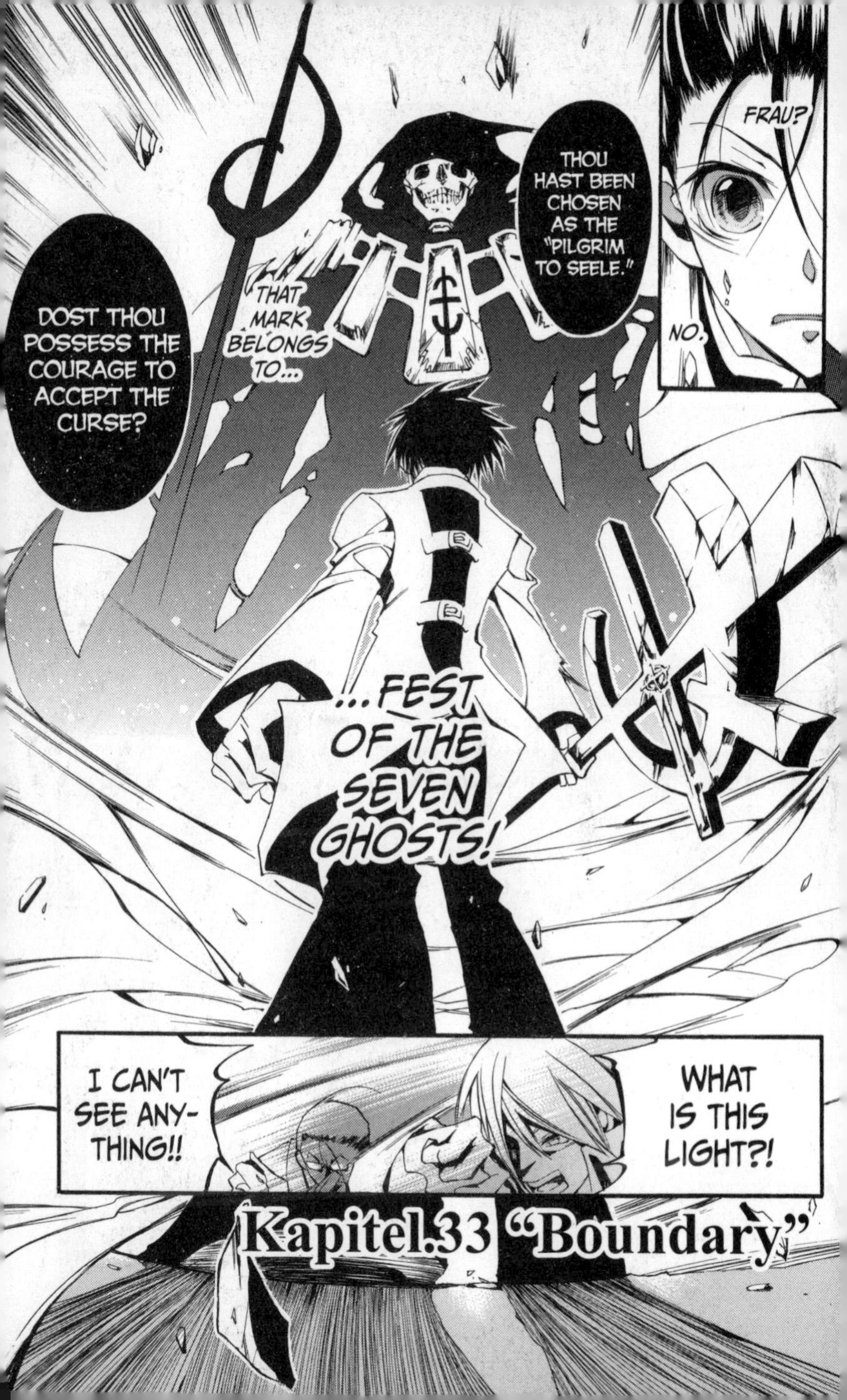
FRAU?
NO.
THOU HAST BEEN CHOSEN AS THE "PILGRIM TO SEELE."
THAT MARK BELONGS TO...
DOST THOU POSSESS THE COURAGE TO ACCEPT THE CURSE?
...FEST OF THE SEVEN GHOSTS!
WHAT IS THIS LIGHT?!
I CAN'T SEE ANY-THING!!

Kapitel.33 "Boundary"

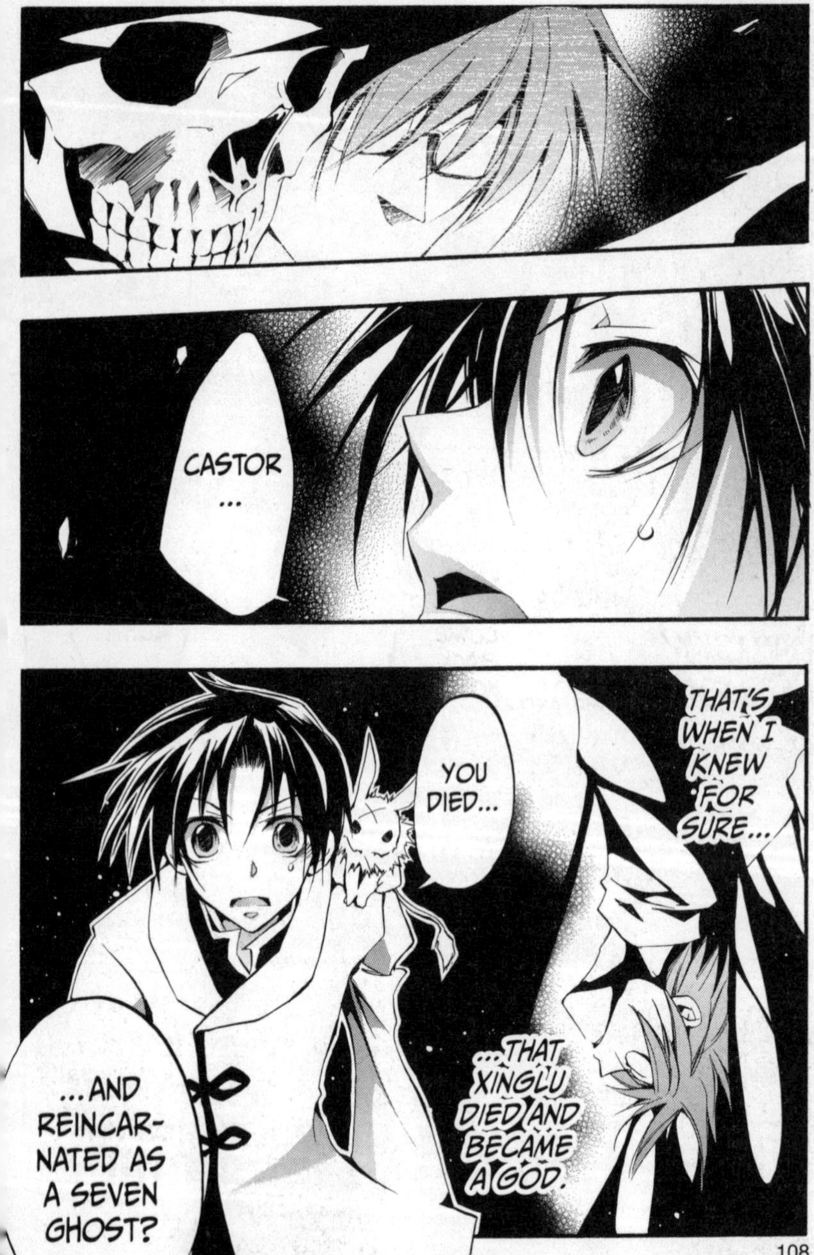
CASTOR ...
THAT'S WHEN I KNEW FOR SURE...
YOU DIED...
...THAT XINGLU DIED AND BECAME A GOD.
...AND REINCAR-NATED AS A SEVEN GHOST?

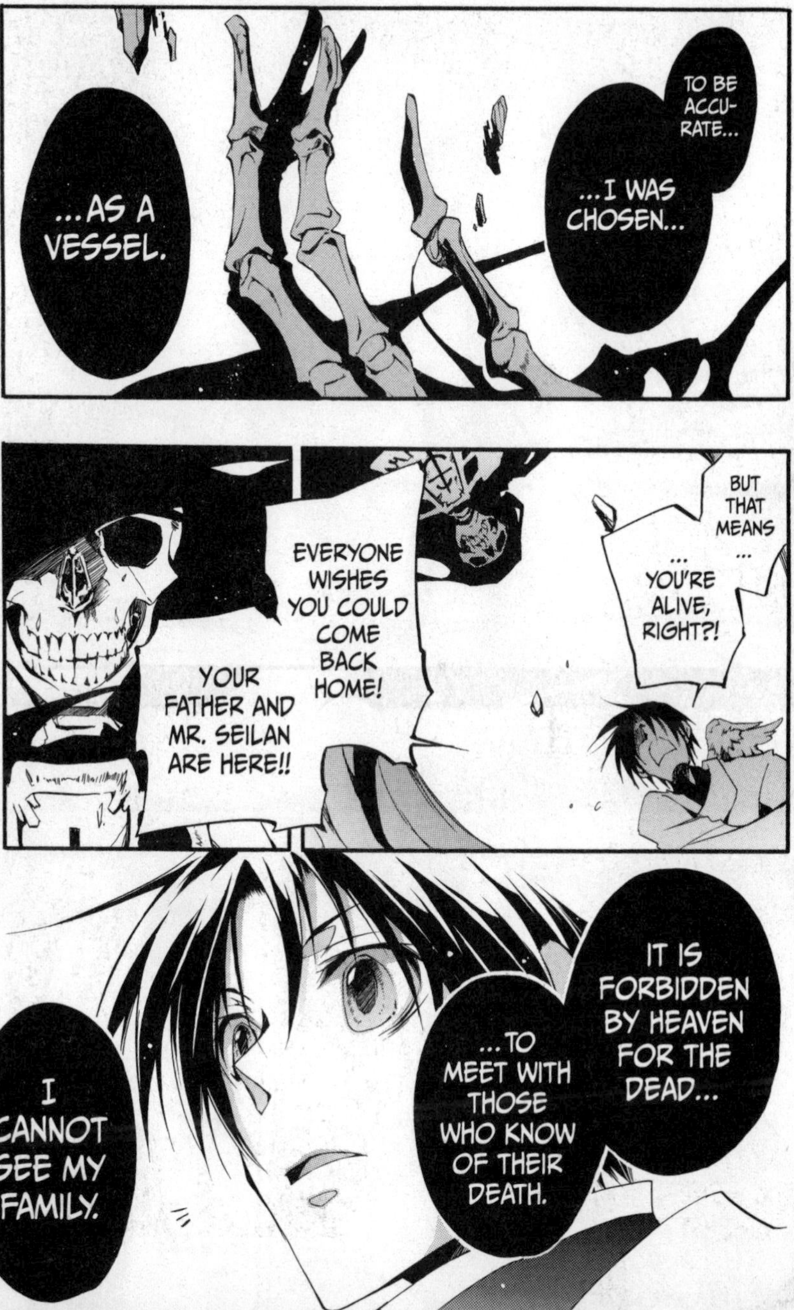
TO BE ACCURATE...
...I WAS CHOSEN...
...AS A VESSEL.
BUT THAT MEANS ... ... YOU'RE ALIVE, RIGHT?!
EVERYONE WISHES YOU COULD COME BACK HOME!
YOUR FATHER AND MR. SEILAN ARE HERE!!
IT IS FORBIDDEN BY HEAVEN FOR THE DEAD...
...TO MEET WITH THOSE WHO KNOW OF THEIR DEATH.
I CANNOT SEE MY FAMILY.

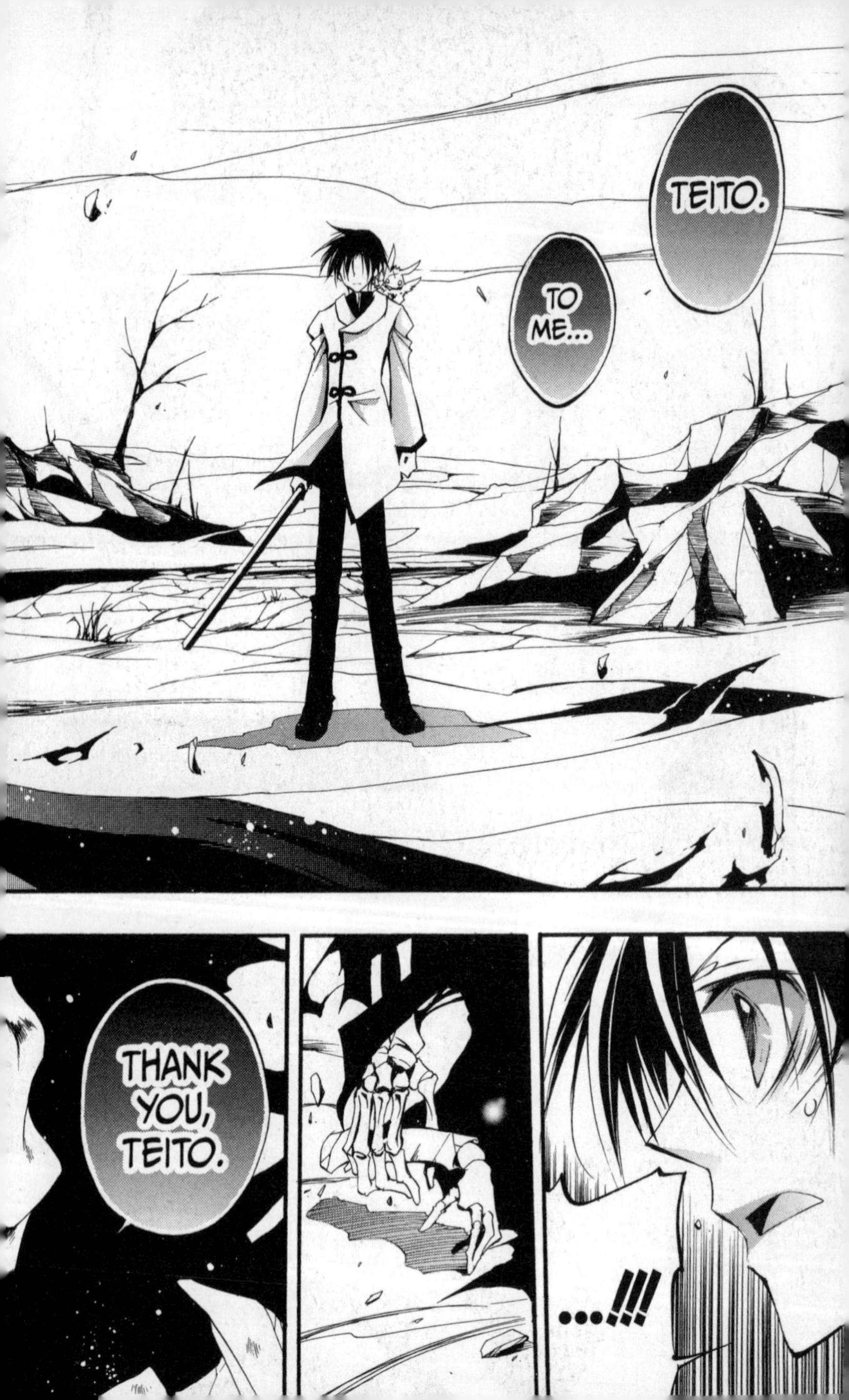
TEITO.
TO ME...
...!!!
THANK YOU, TEITO.

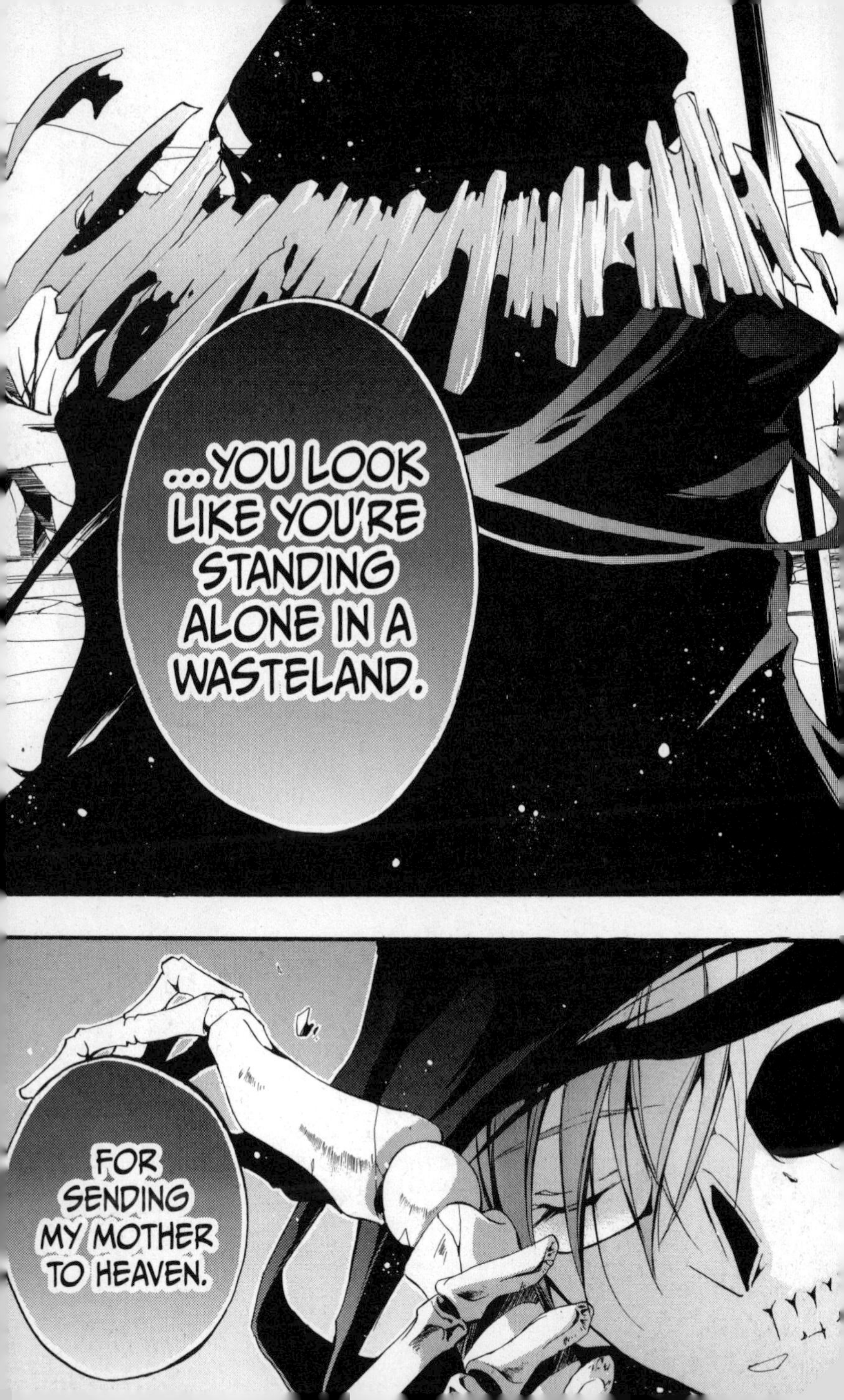
...YOU LOOK LIKE YOU'RE STANDING ALONE IN A WASTELAND.
FOR SENDING MY MOTHER TO HEAVEN.

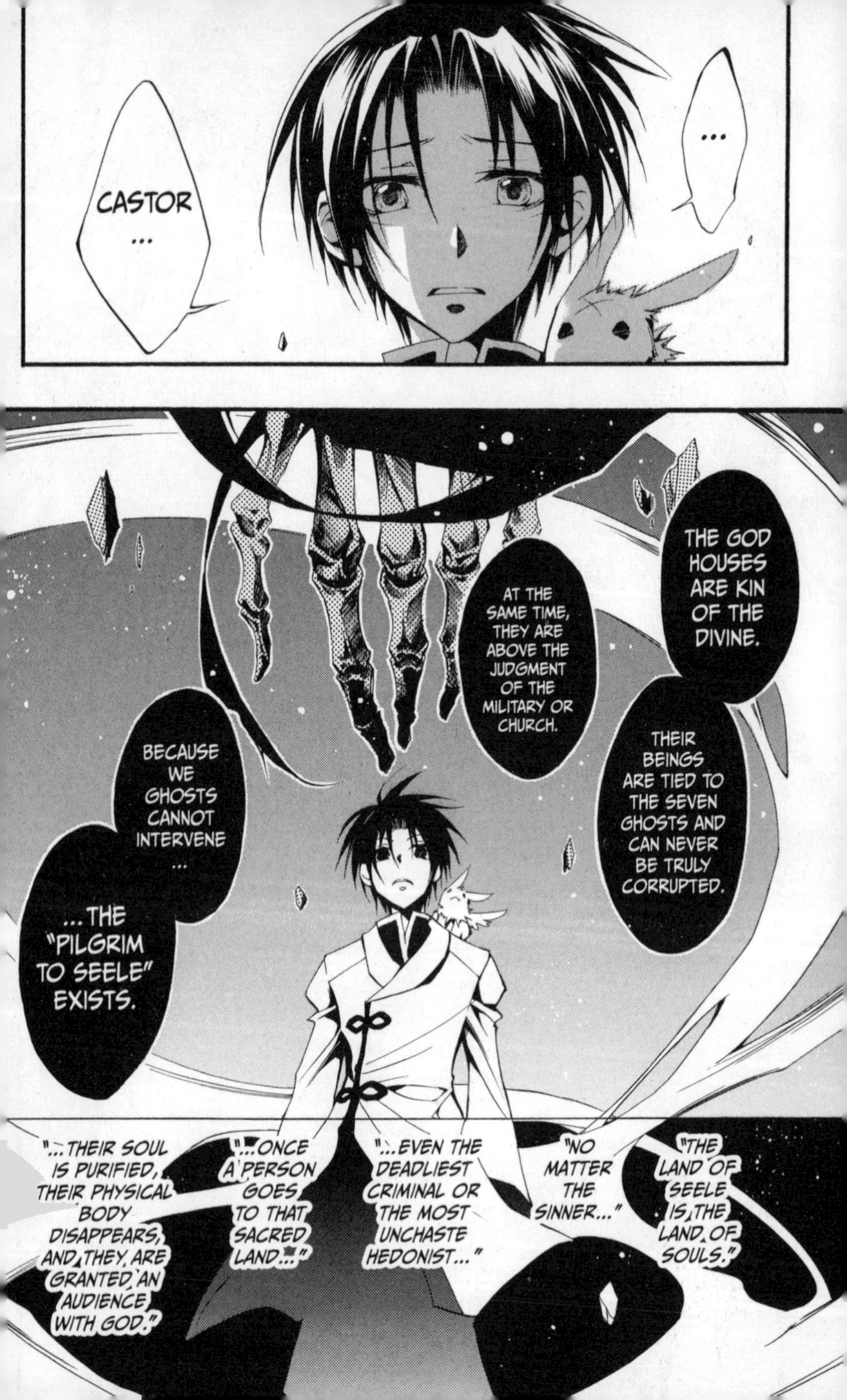
...
CASTOR ...
THE GOD HOUSES ARE KIN OF THE DIVINE.
AT THE SAME TIME, THEY ARE ABOVE THE JUDGMENT OF THE MILITARY OR CHURCH.
THEIR BEINGS ARE TIED TO THE SEVEN GHOSTS AND CAN NEVER BE TRULY CORRUPTED.
BECAUSE WE GHOSTS CANNOT INTERVENE ...
...THE "PILGRIM TO SEELE" EXISTS.
"THE LAND OF SEELE IS THE LAND OF SOULS."
"NO MATTER THE SINNER..."
"...EVEN THE DEADLIEST CRIMINAL OR THE MOST UNCHASTE HEDONIST..."
"...ONCE A PERSON GOES TO THAT SACRED LAND..."
"...THEIR SOUL IS PURIFIED, THEIR PHYSICAL BODY DISAPPEARS, AND THEY ARE GRANTED AN AUDIENCE WITH GOD."

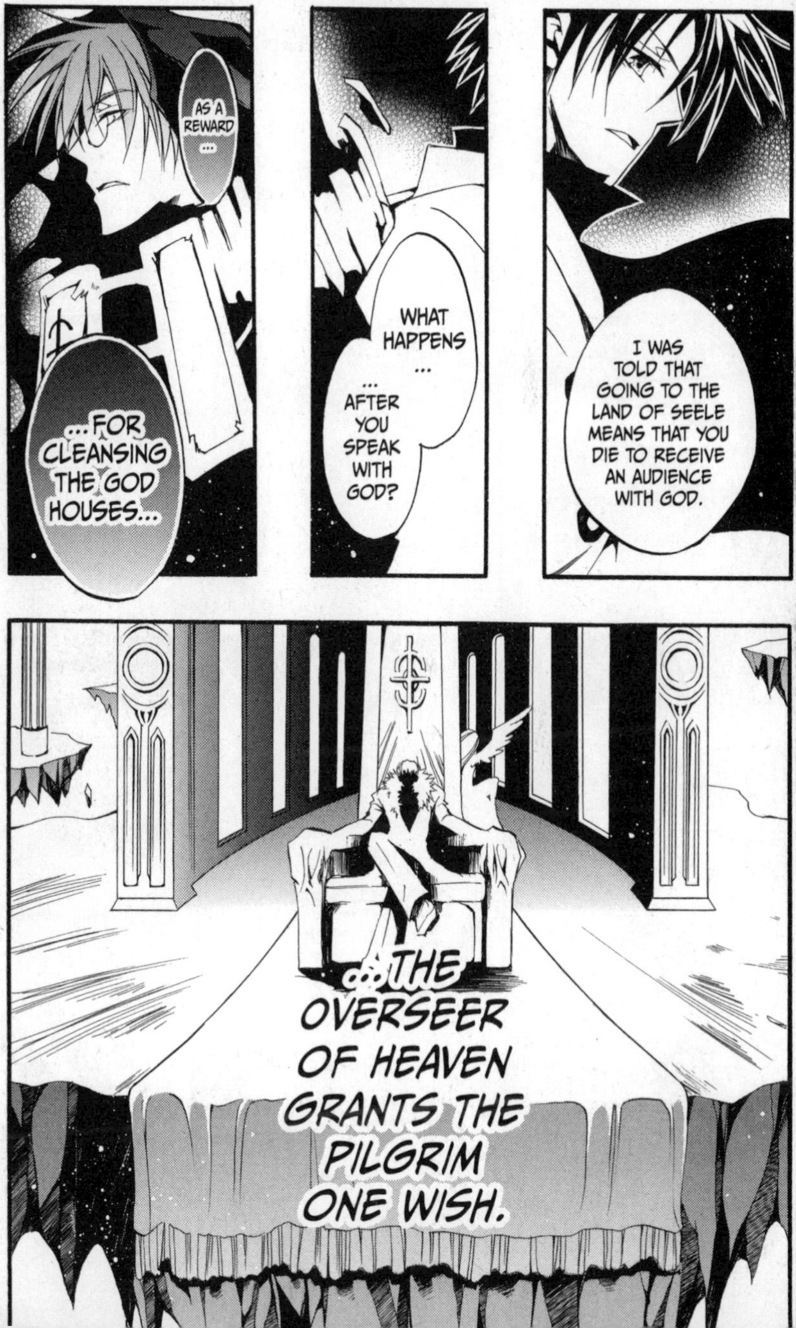
I WAS TOLD THAT GOING TO THE LAND OF SEELE MEANS THAT YOU DIE TO RECEIVE AN AUDIENCE WITH GOD.
WHAT HAPPENS ...
... AFTER YOU SPEAK WITH GOD?
AS A REWARD ...
...FOR CLEANSING THE GOD HOUSES...
...THE OVERSEER OF HEAVEN GRANTS THE PILGRIM ONE WISH.

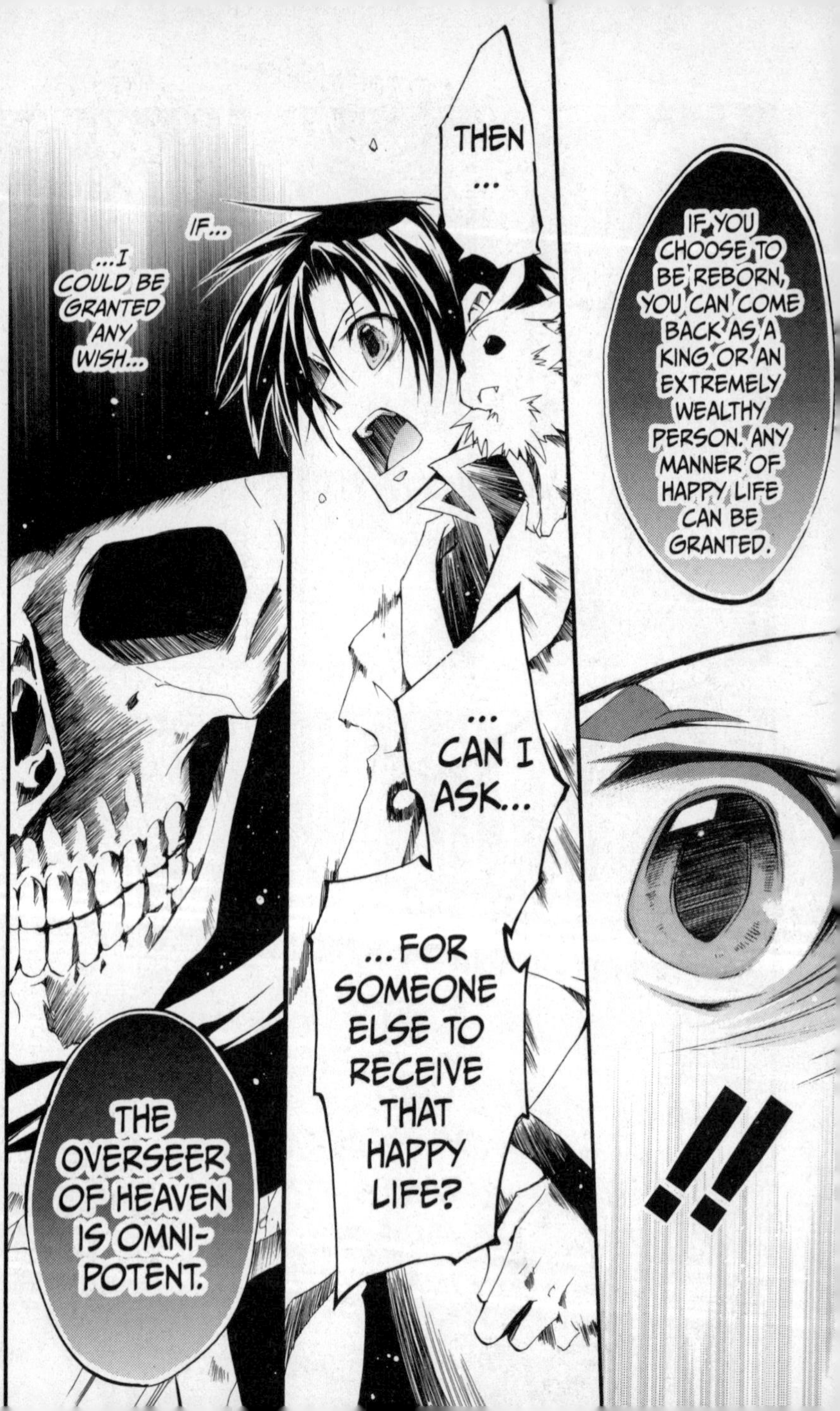
IF YOU CHOOSE TO BE REBORN, YOU CAN COME BACK AS A KING OR AN EXTREMELY WEALTHY PERSON. ANY MANNER OF HAPPY LIFE CAN BE GRANTED.
!!
THEN ...
... CAN I ASK...
...FOR SOMEONE ELSE TO RECEIVE THAT HAPPY LIFE?
IF...
...I COULD BE GRANTED ANY WISH...
THE OVERSEER OF HEAVEN IS OMNI-POTENT.

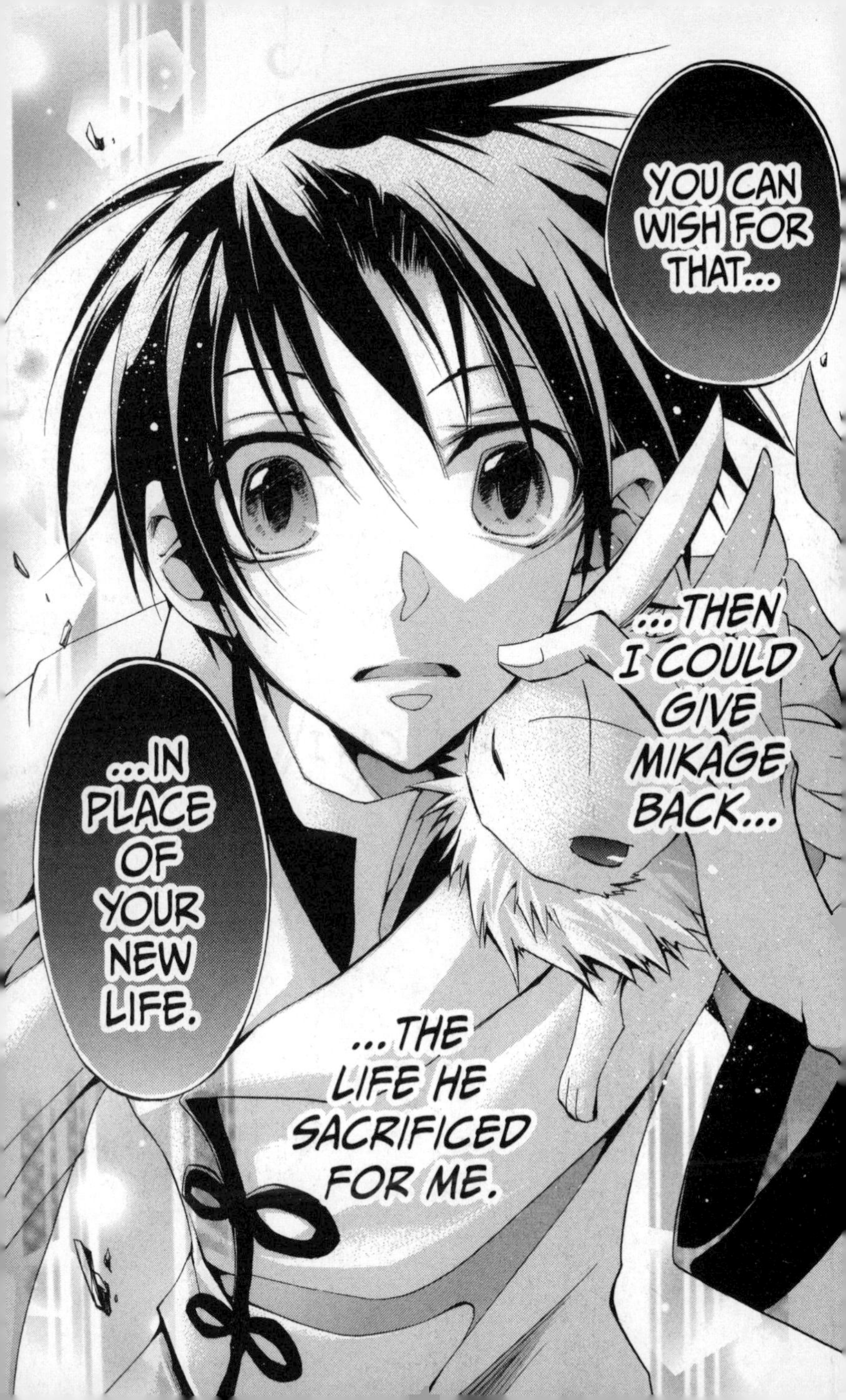
YOU CAN WISH FOR THAT...
...IN PLACE OF YOUR NEW LIFE.
...THEN I COULD GIVE MIKAGE BACK...
...THE LIFE HE SACRIFICED FOR ME.

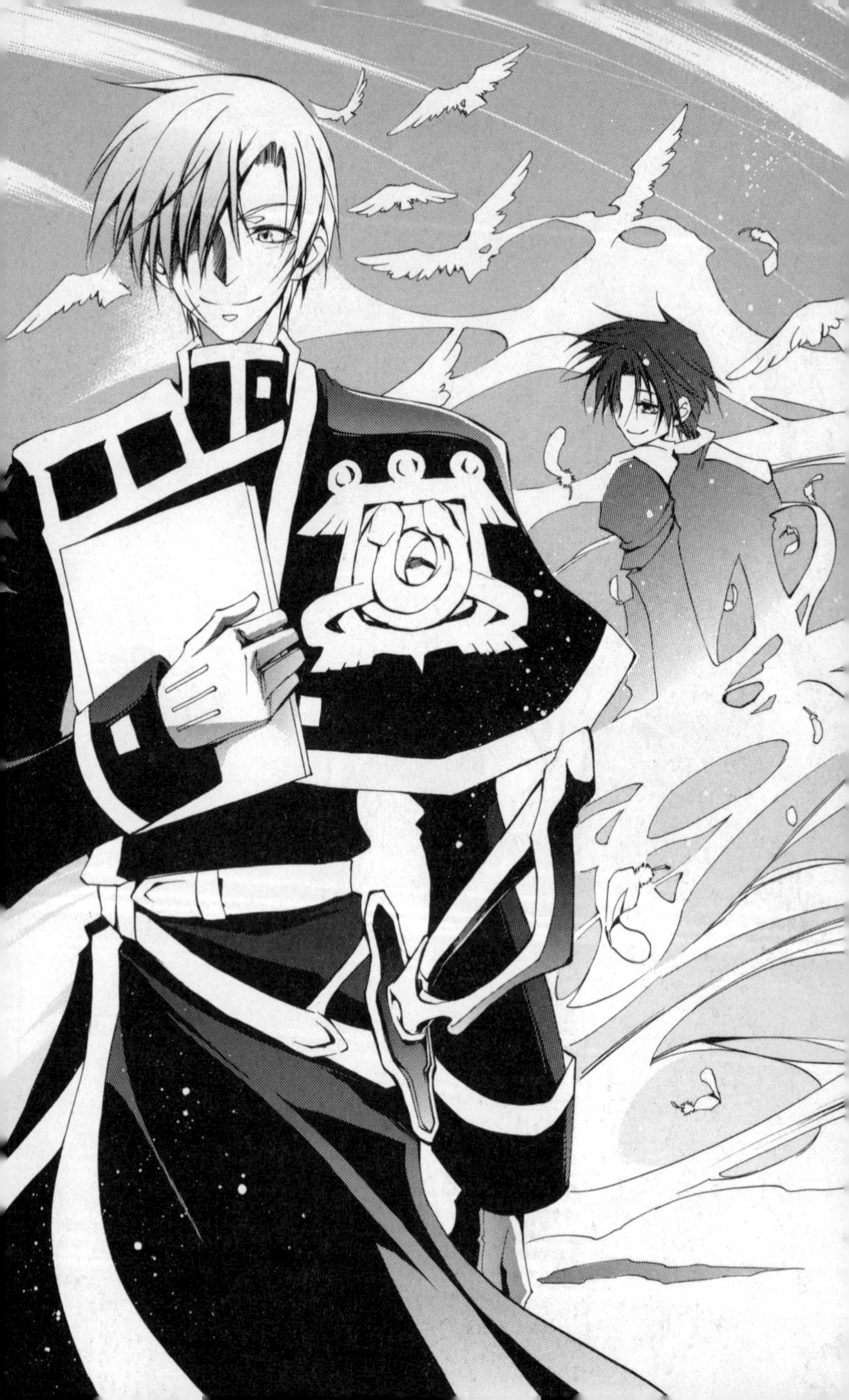

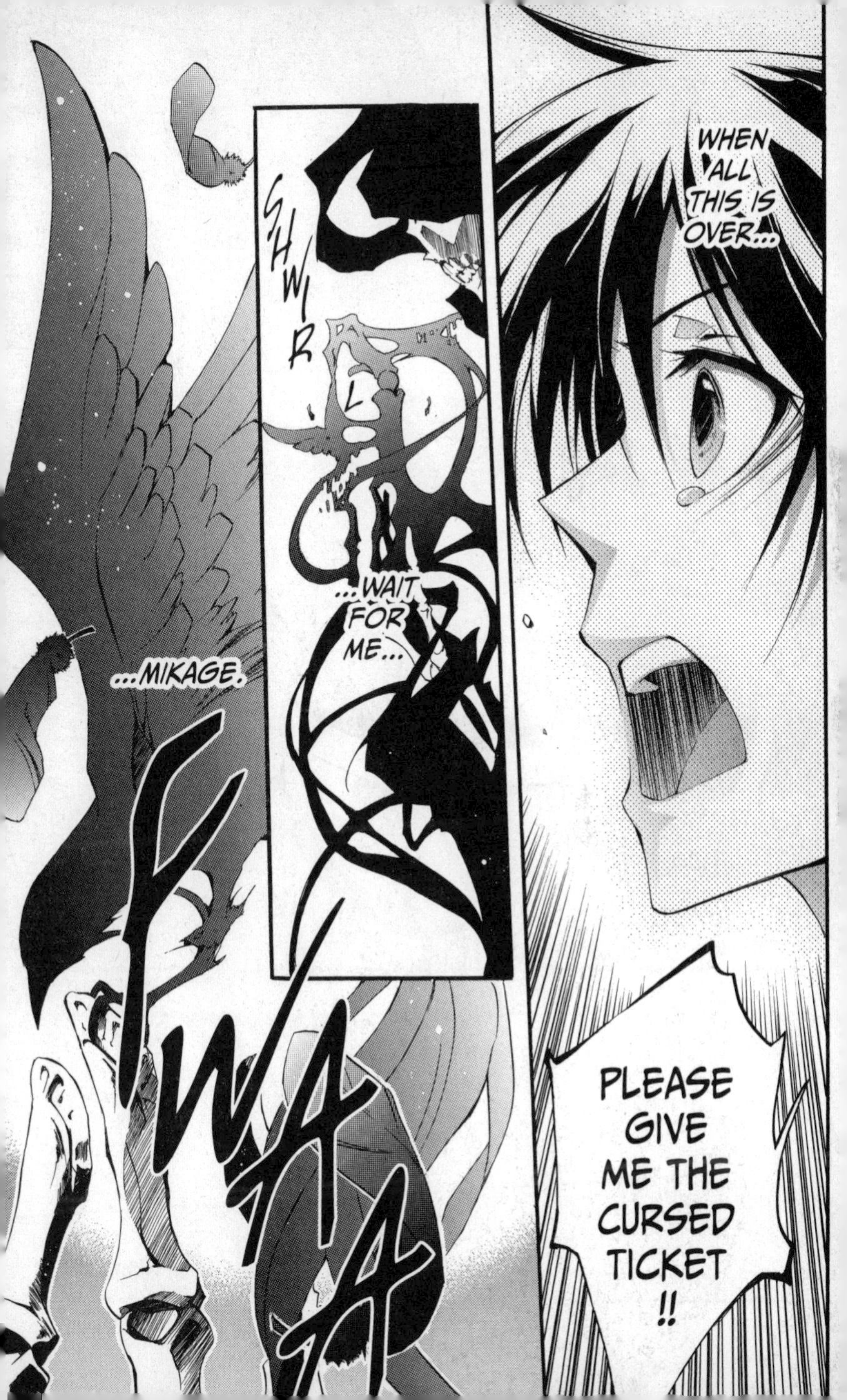
WHEN ALL THIS IS OVER...
PLEASE GIVE ME THE CURSED TICKET!!
SHWIRL
...WAIT FOR ME...
...MIKAGE.
FWAAA

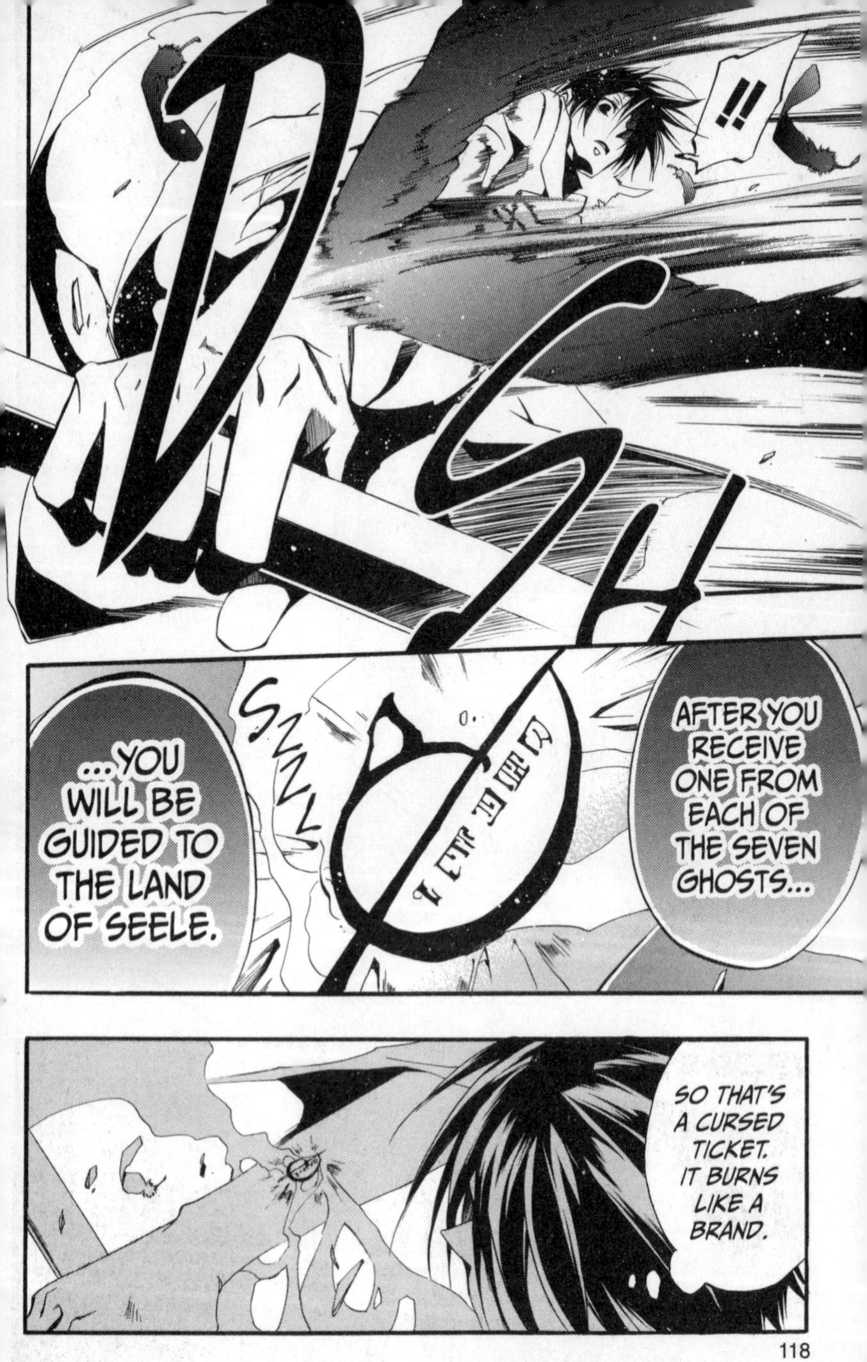
!!
AFTER YOU RECEIVE ONE FROM EACH OF THE SEVEN GHOSTS...
...YOU WILL BE GUIDED TO THE LAND OF SEELE.
SO THAT'S A CURSED TICKET. IT BURNS LIKE A BRAND.

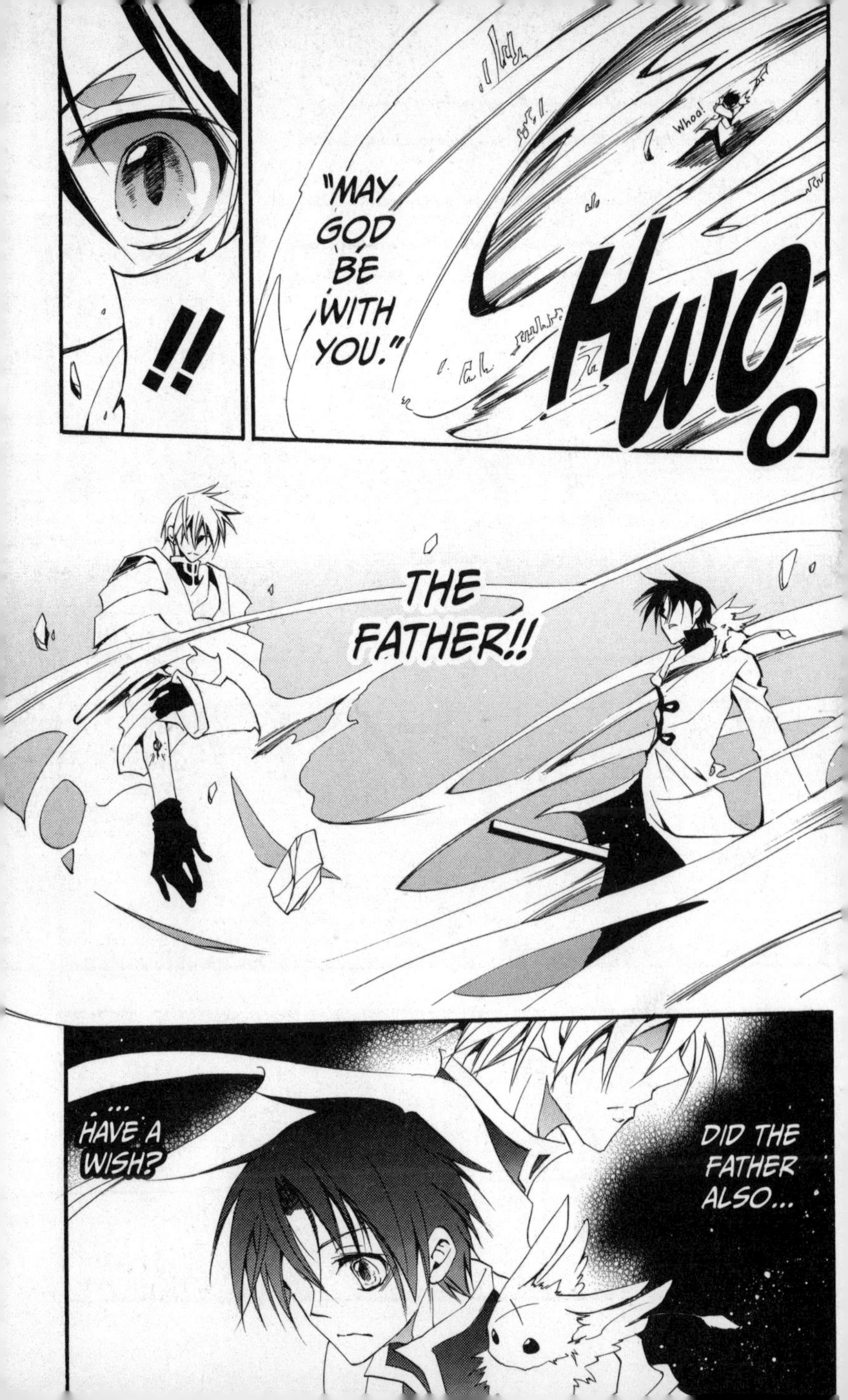
Whoa!
"MAY GOD BE WITH YOU."
HWOO
!!
THE FATHER!!
DID THE FATHER ALSO...
... HAVE A WISH?

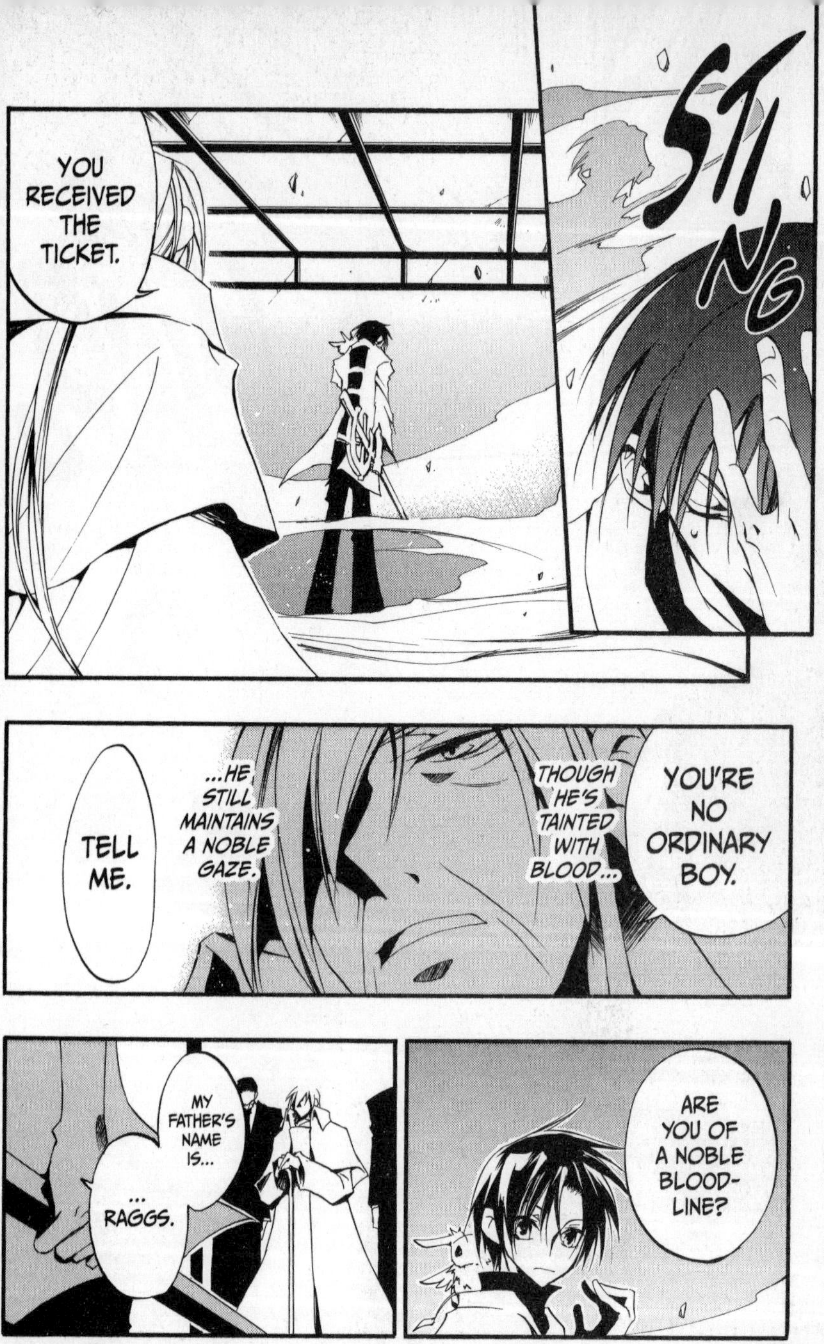
STING
YOU RECEIVED THE TICKET.
YOU'RE NO ORDINARY BOY.
THOUGH HE'S TAINTED WITH BLOOD...
...HE STILL MAINTAINS A NOBLE GAZE.
TELL ME.
ARE YOU OF A NOBLE BLOOD-LINE?
MY FATHER'S NAME IS...
...RAGGS.

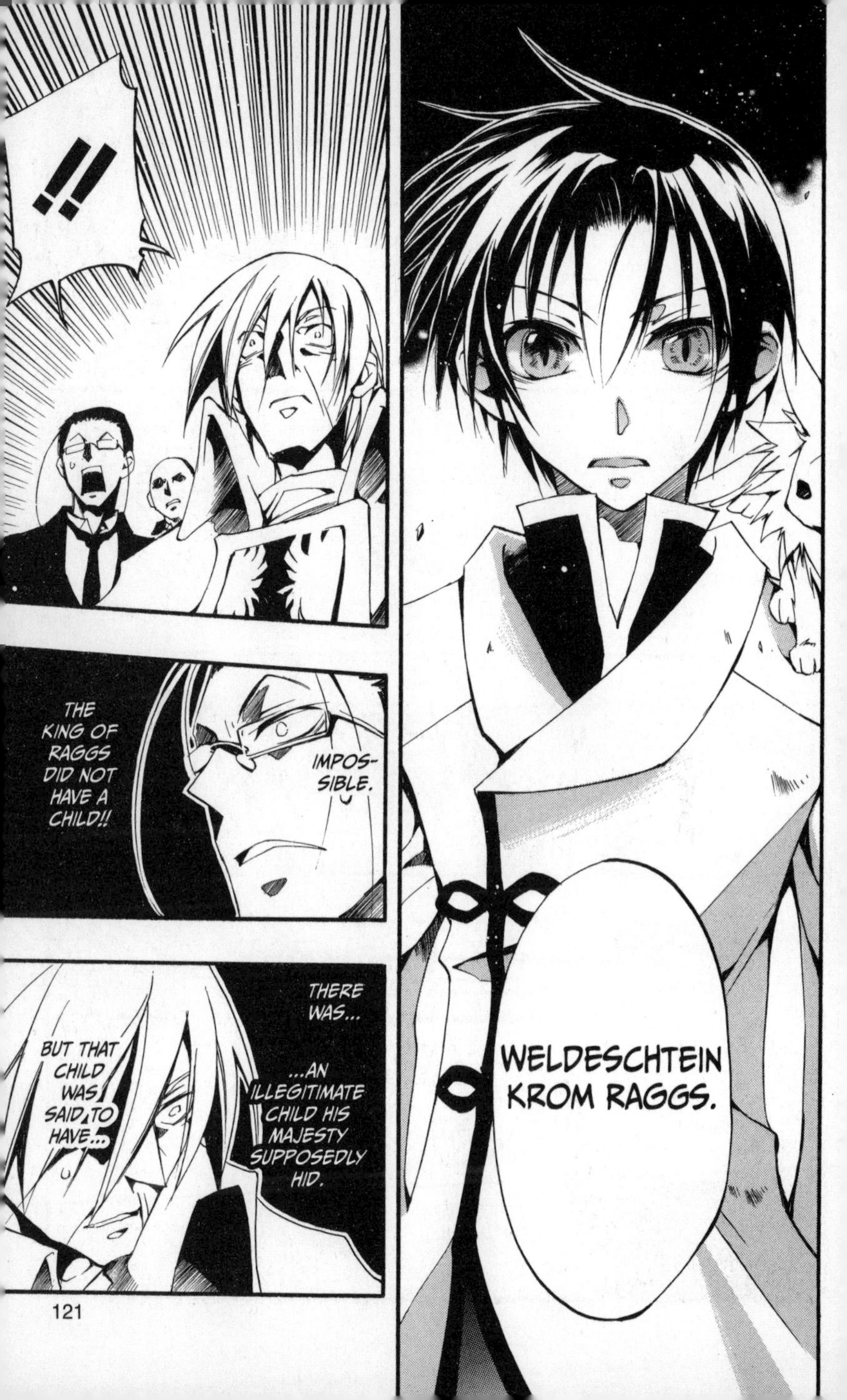
WELDESCHTEIN KROM RAGGS.
!!
IMPOSSIBLE.
THE KING OF RAGGS DID NOT HAVE A CHILD!!
THERE WAS...
...AN ILLEGITIMATE CHILD HIS MAJESTY SUPPOSEDLY HID.
BUT THAT CHILD WAS SAID TO HAVE...

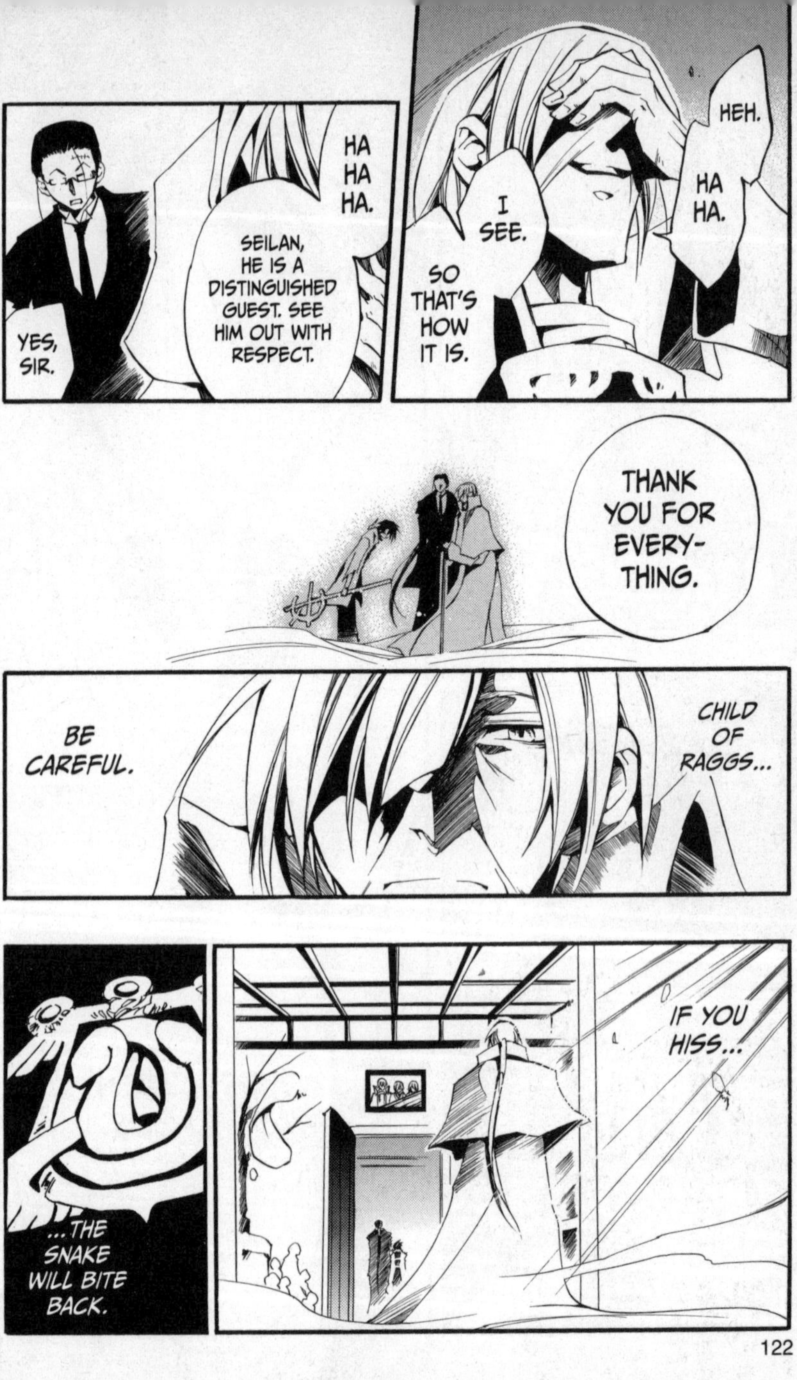
HEH.
HA HA.
I SEE.
SO THAT'S HOW IT IS.
HA HA HA.
SEILAN, HE IS A DISTINGUISHED GUEST. SEE HIM OUT WITH RESPECT.
YES, SIR.
THANK YOU FOR EVERY-THING.
CHILD OF RAGGS...
BE CAREFUL.
IF YOU HISS...
...THE SNAKE WILL BITE BACK.

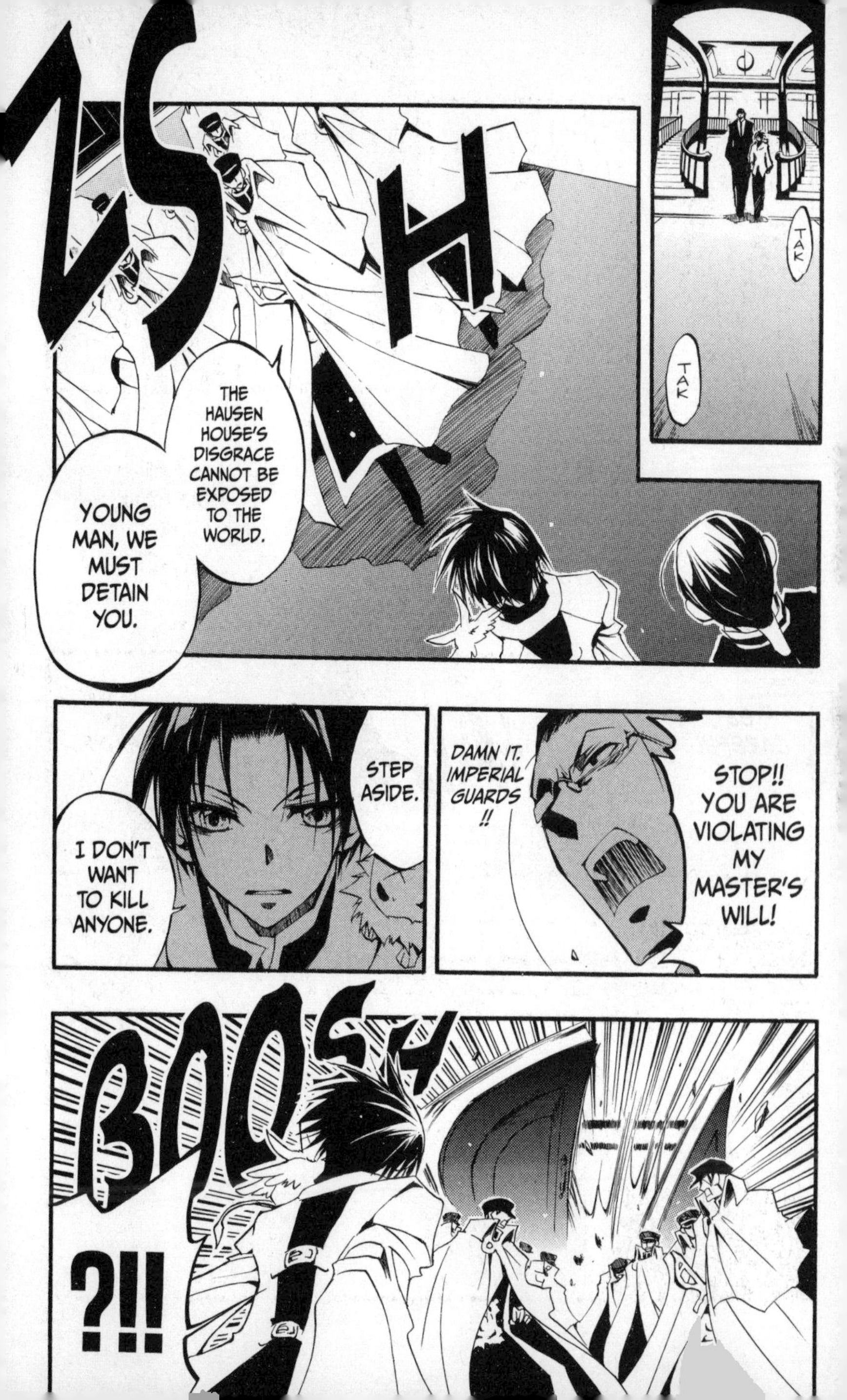
TAK
TAK
ZSH
THE HAUSEN HOUSE'S DISGRACE CANNOT BE EXPOSED TO THE WORLD.
YOUNG MAN, WE MUST DETAIN YOU.
STOP!! YOU ARE VIOLATING MY MASTER'S WILL!
DAMN IT. IMPERIAL GUARDS !!
STEP ASIDE.
I DON'T WANT TO KILL ANYONE.
BOOSH
?!!

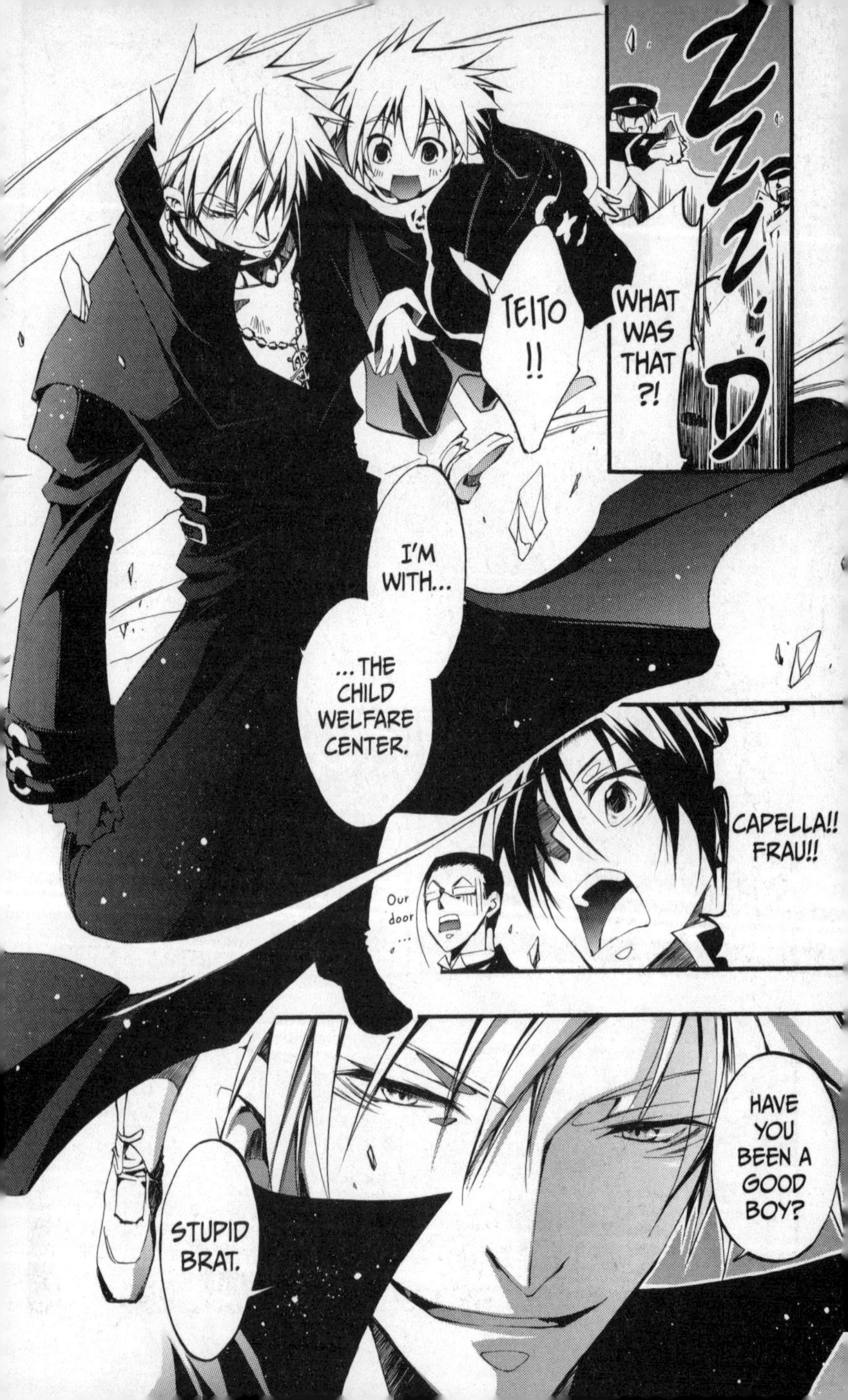
ZZZD
WHAT WAS THAT?!
TEITO!!
I'M WITH...
...THE CHILD WELFARE CENTER.
CAPELLA!! FRAU!!
Our door...
HAVE YOU BEEN A GOOD BOY?
STUPID BRAT.

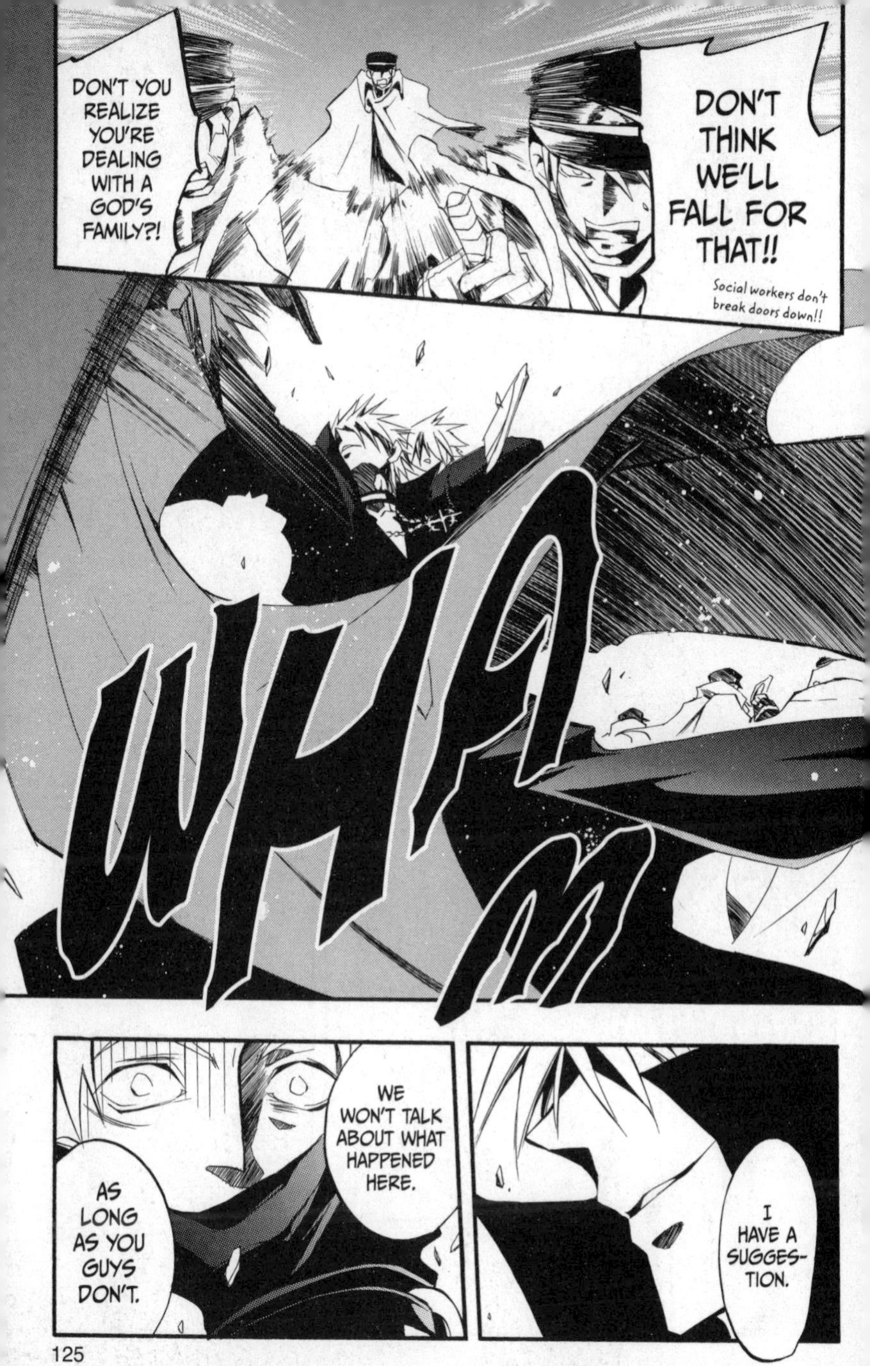
DON'T THINK WE'LL FALL FOR THAT!!
Social workers don't break doors down!!
DON'T YOU REALIZE YOU'RE DEALING WITH A GOD'S FAMILY?!
WHAM
I HAVE A SUGGES-TION.
WE WON'T TALK ABOUT WHAT HAPPENED HERE.
AS LONG AS YOU GUYS DON'T.

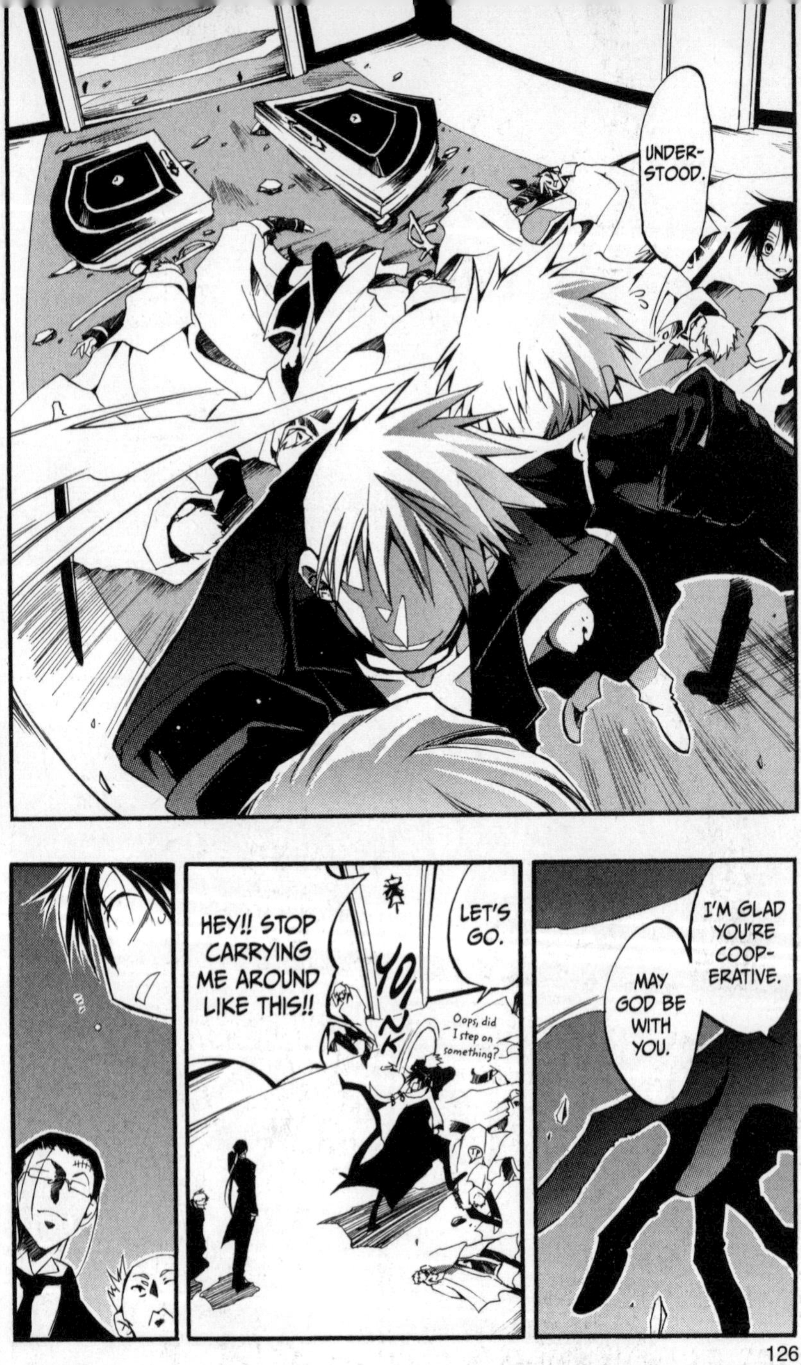
UNDER-STOOD.
I'M GLAD YOU'RE COOP-ERATIVE.
MAY GOD BE WITH YOU.
LET'S GO.
YOINK
Oops, did I step on something?
HEY!! STOP CARRYING ME AROUND LIKE THIS!!

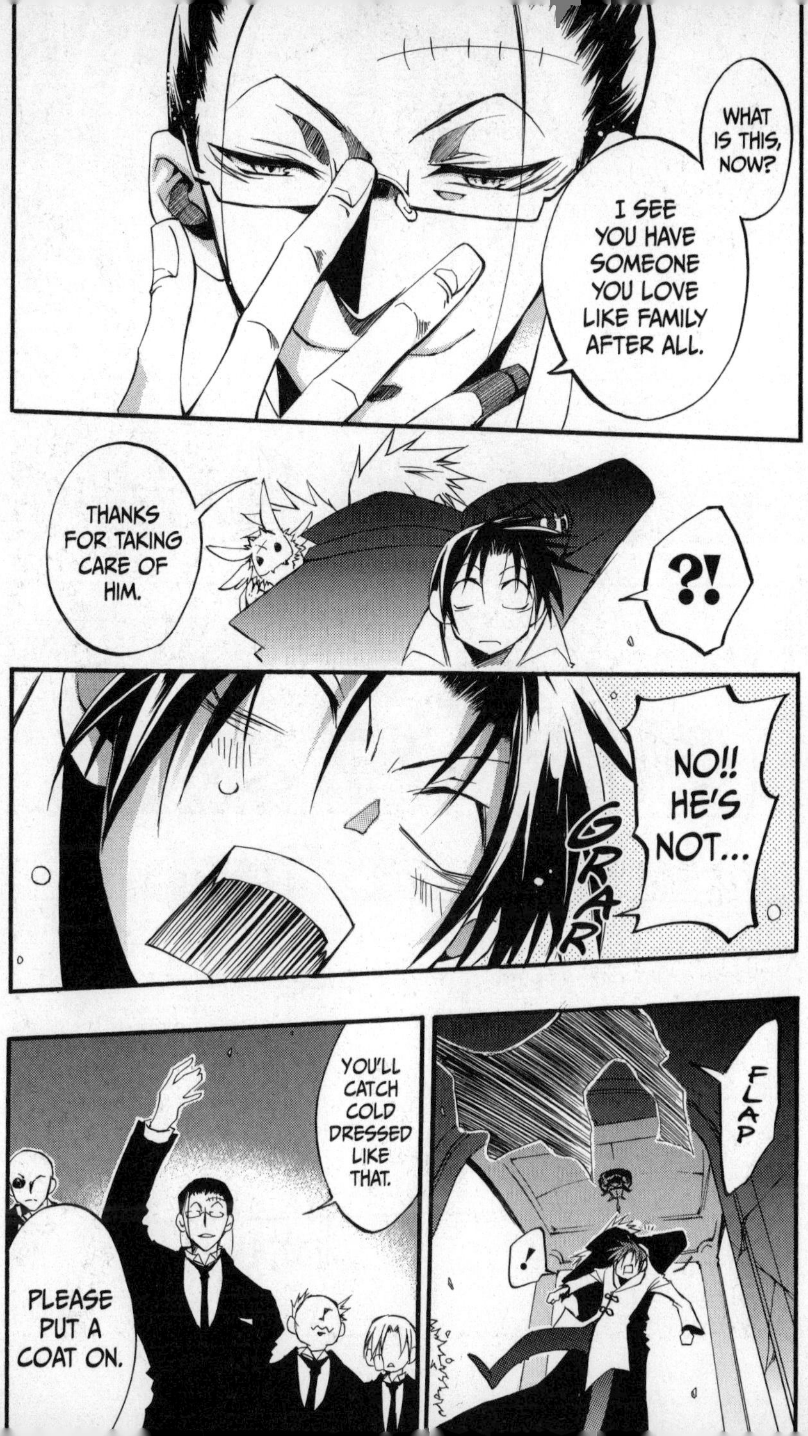
WHAT IS THIS, NOW?
I SEE YOU HAVE SOMEONE YOU LOVE LIKE FAMILY AFTER ALL.
THANKS FOR TAKING CARE OF HIM.
?!
NO!! HE'S NOT...
GRAR
FLAP
!
YOU'LL CATCH COLD DRESSED LIKE THAT.
PLEASE PUT A COAT ON.

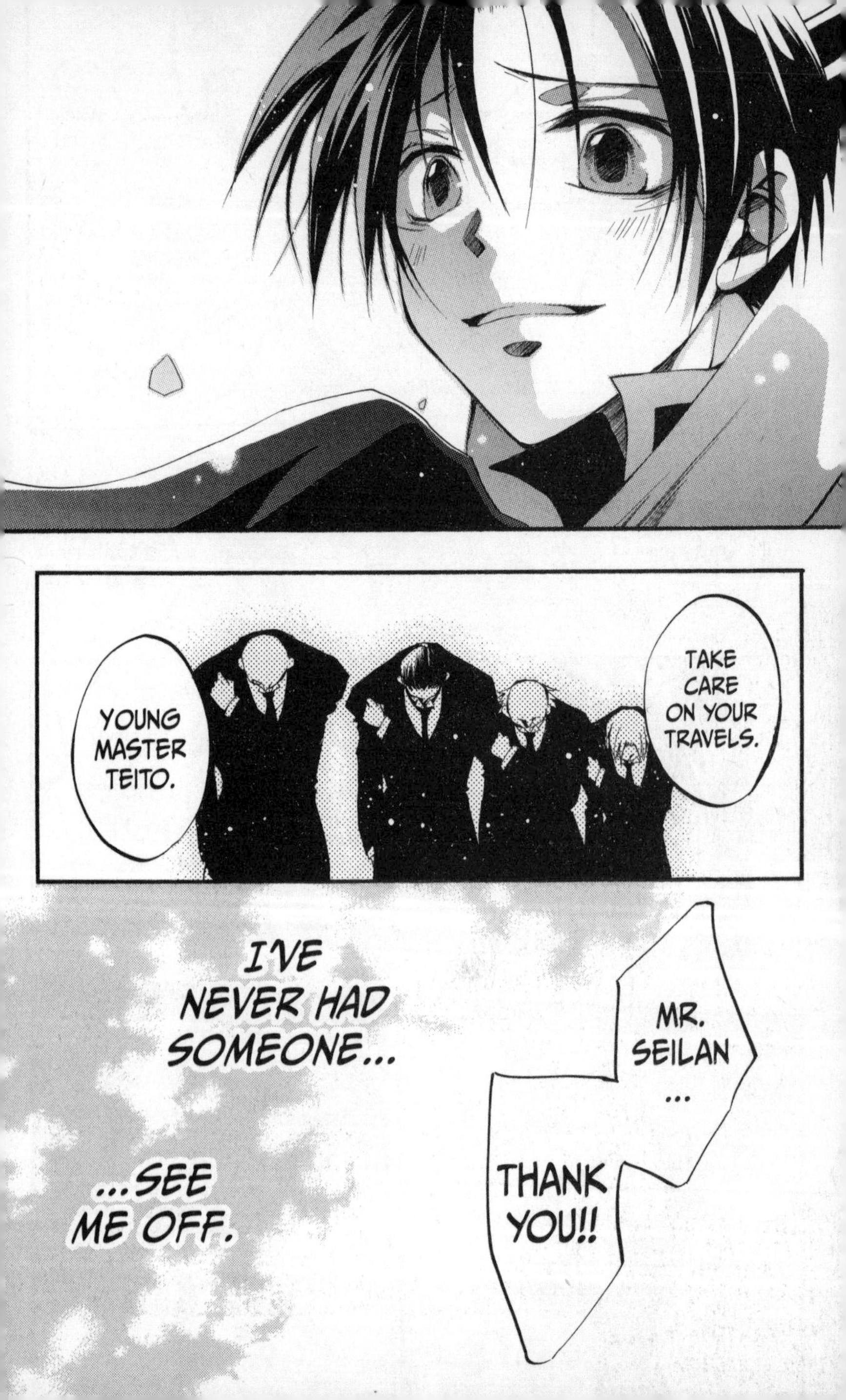
TAKE CARE ON YOUR TRAVELS.
YOUNG MASTER TEITO.
MR. SEILAN ... THANK YOU!!
I'VE NEVER HAD SOMEONE...
...SEE ME OFF.

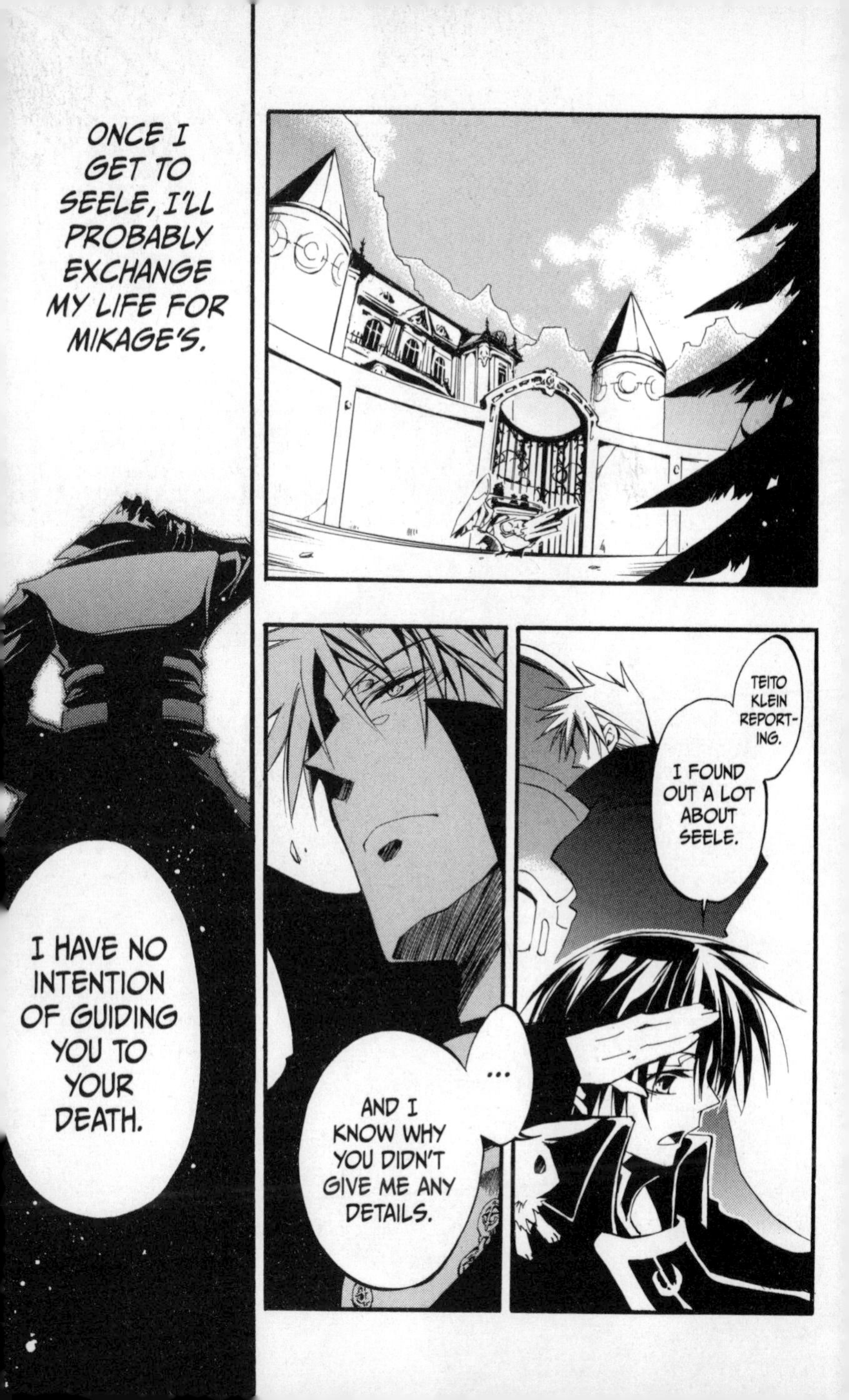
TEITO KLEIN REPORTING.
I FOUND OUT A LOT ABOUT SEELE.
...
AND I KNOW WHY YOU DIDN'T GIVE ME ANY DETAILS.
ONCE I GET TO SEELE, I'LL PROBABLY EXCHANGE MY LIFE FOR MIKAGE'S.
I HAVE NO INTENTION OF GUIDING YOU TO YOUR DEATH.

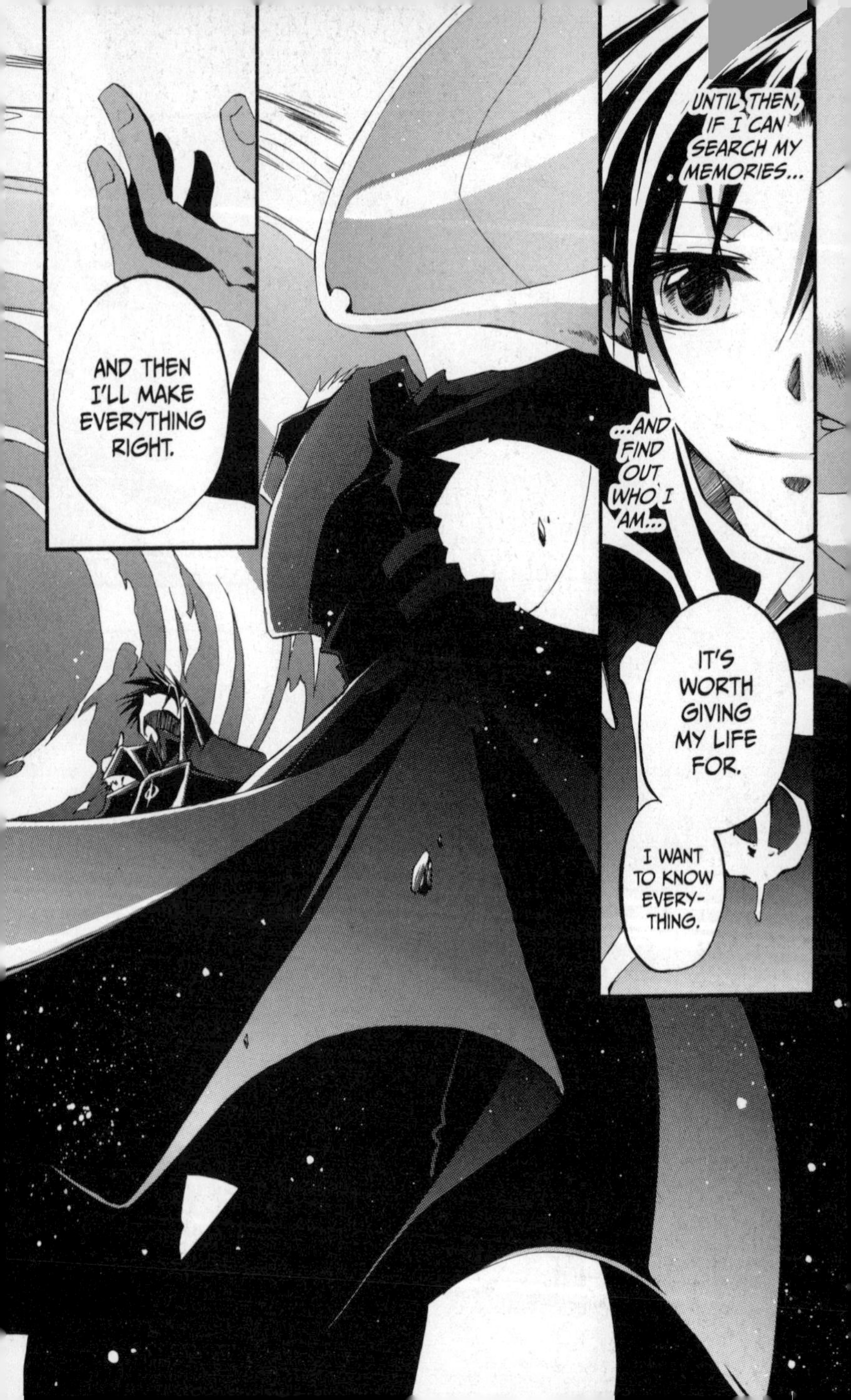
UNTIL THEN, IF I CAN SEARCH MY MEMORIES...
...AND FIND OUT WHO I AM...
IT'S WORTH GIVING MY LIFE FOR.
I WANT TO KNOW EVERY-THING.
AND THEN I'LL MAKE EVERYTHING RIGHT.

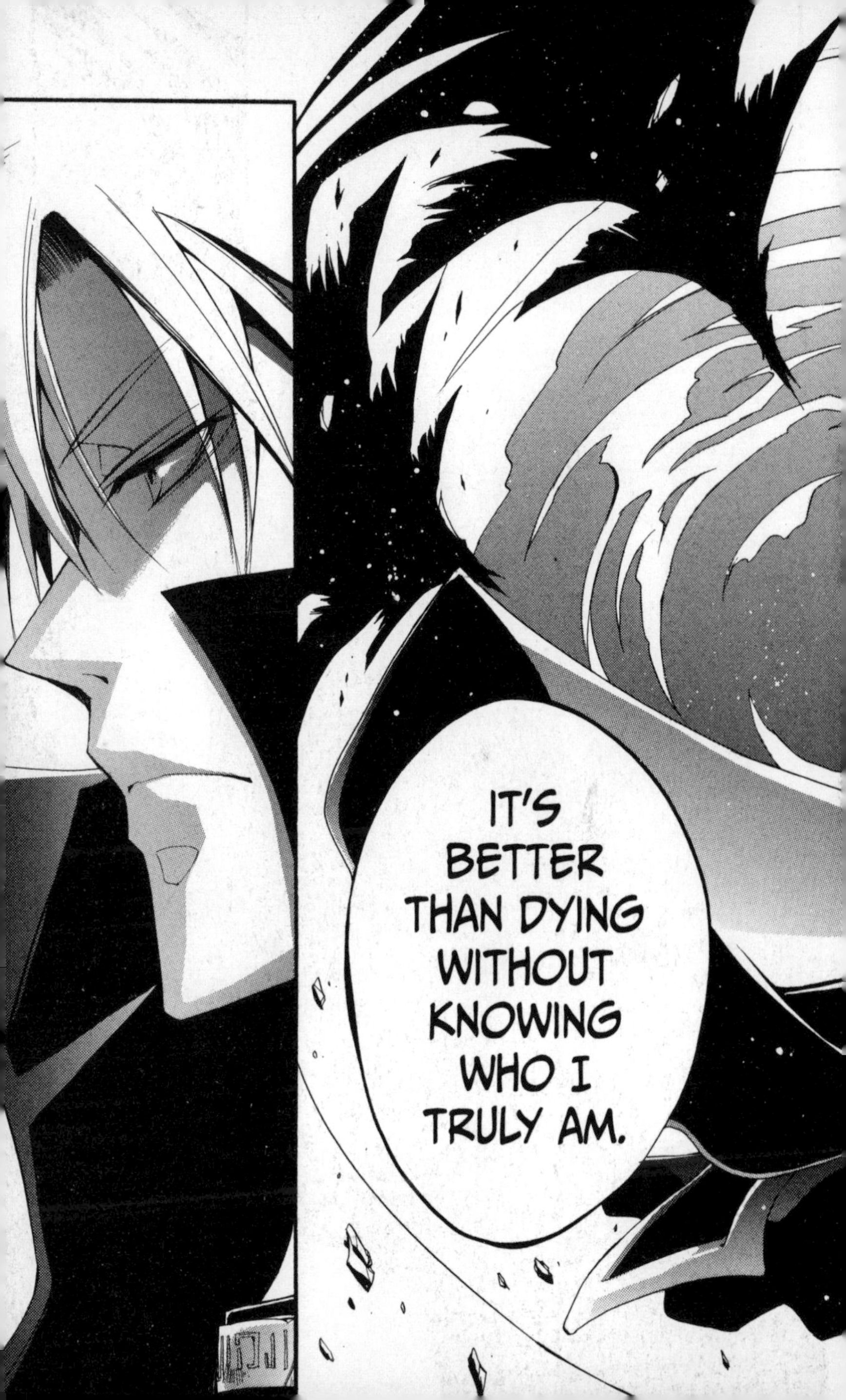
IT'S BETTER THAN DYING WITHOUT KNOWING WHO I TRULY AM.

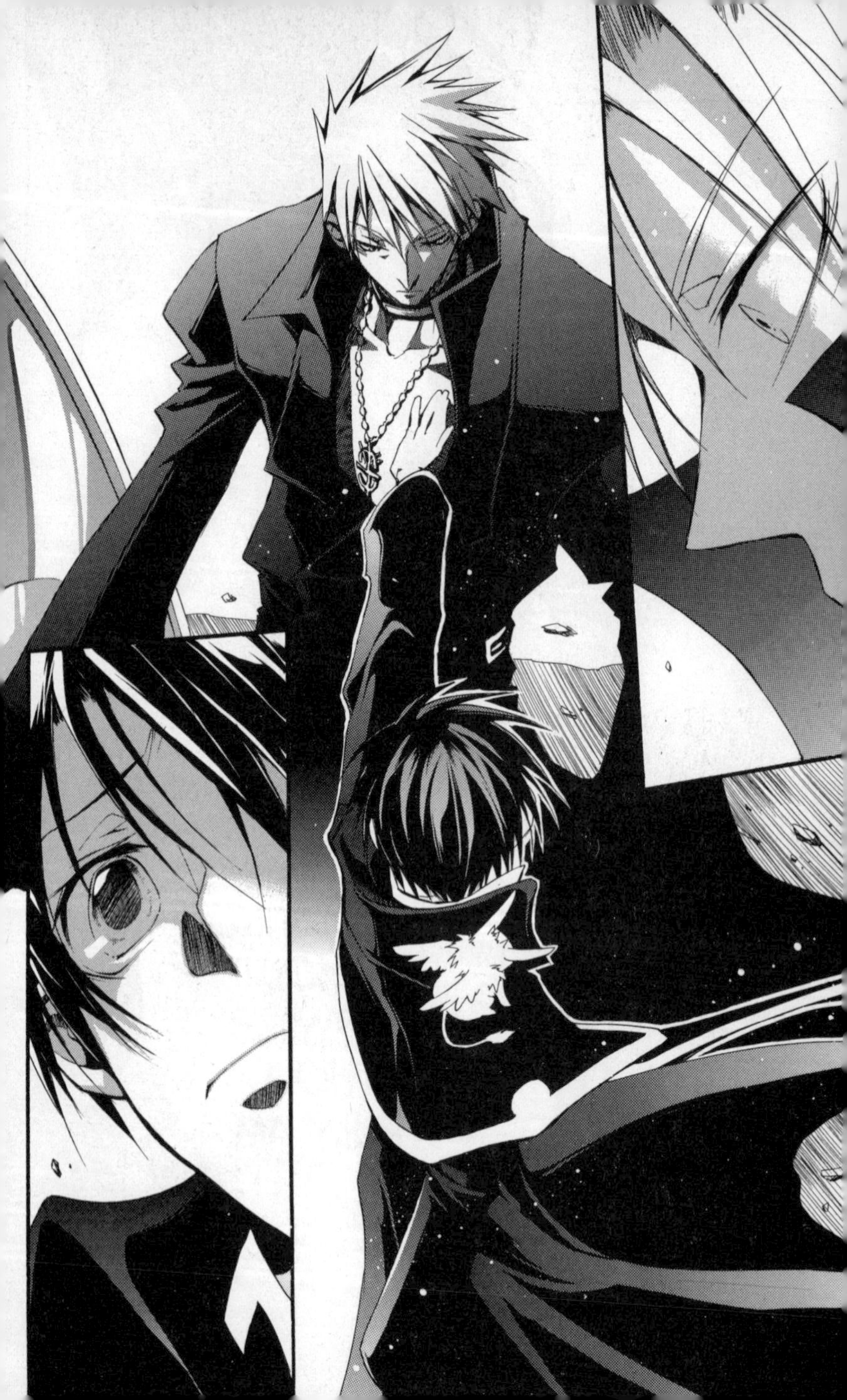

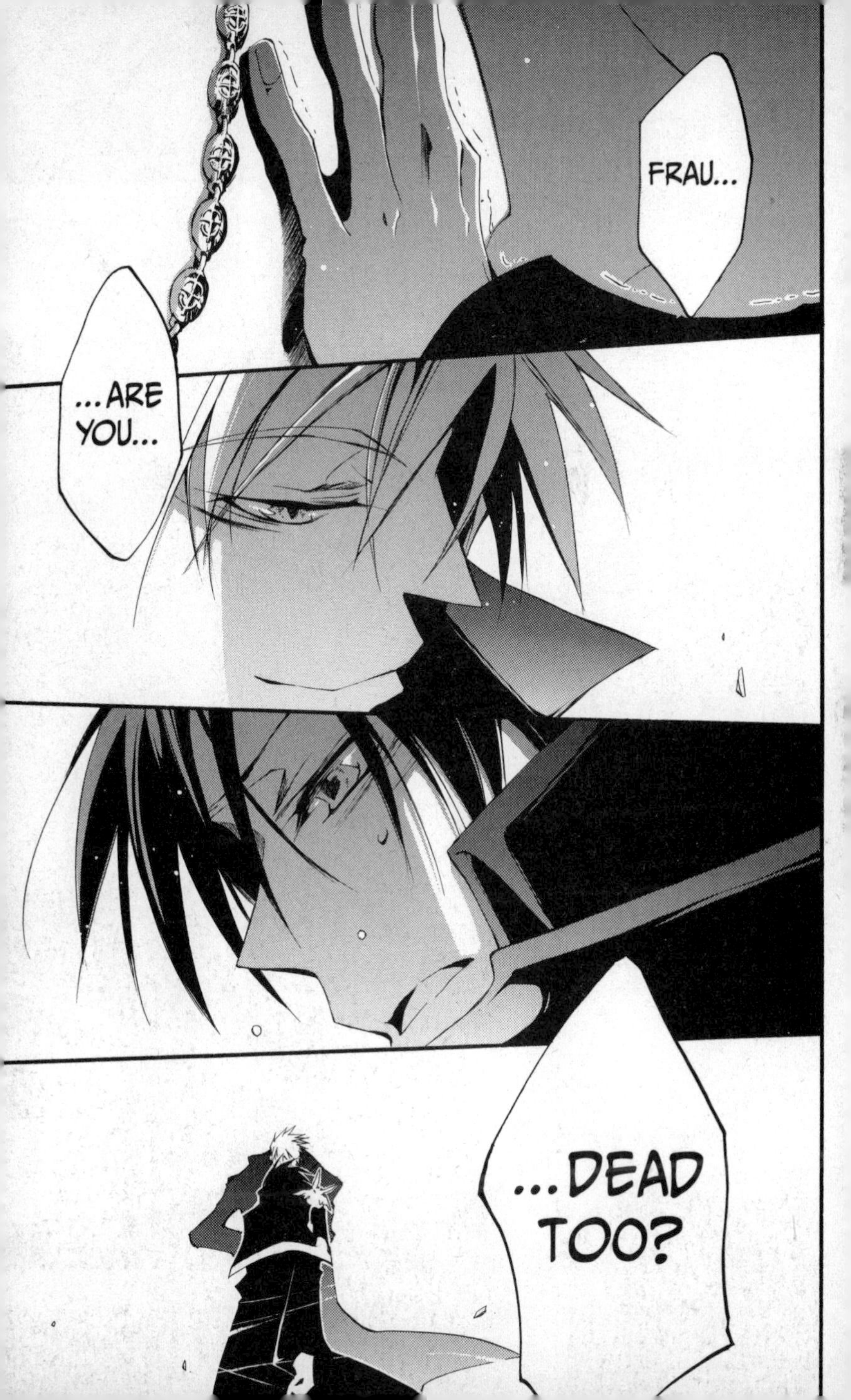
FRAU...
...ARE YOU...
...DEAD TOO?

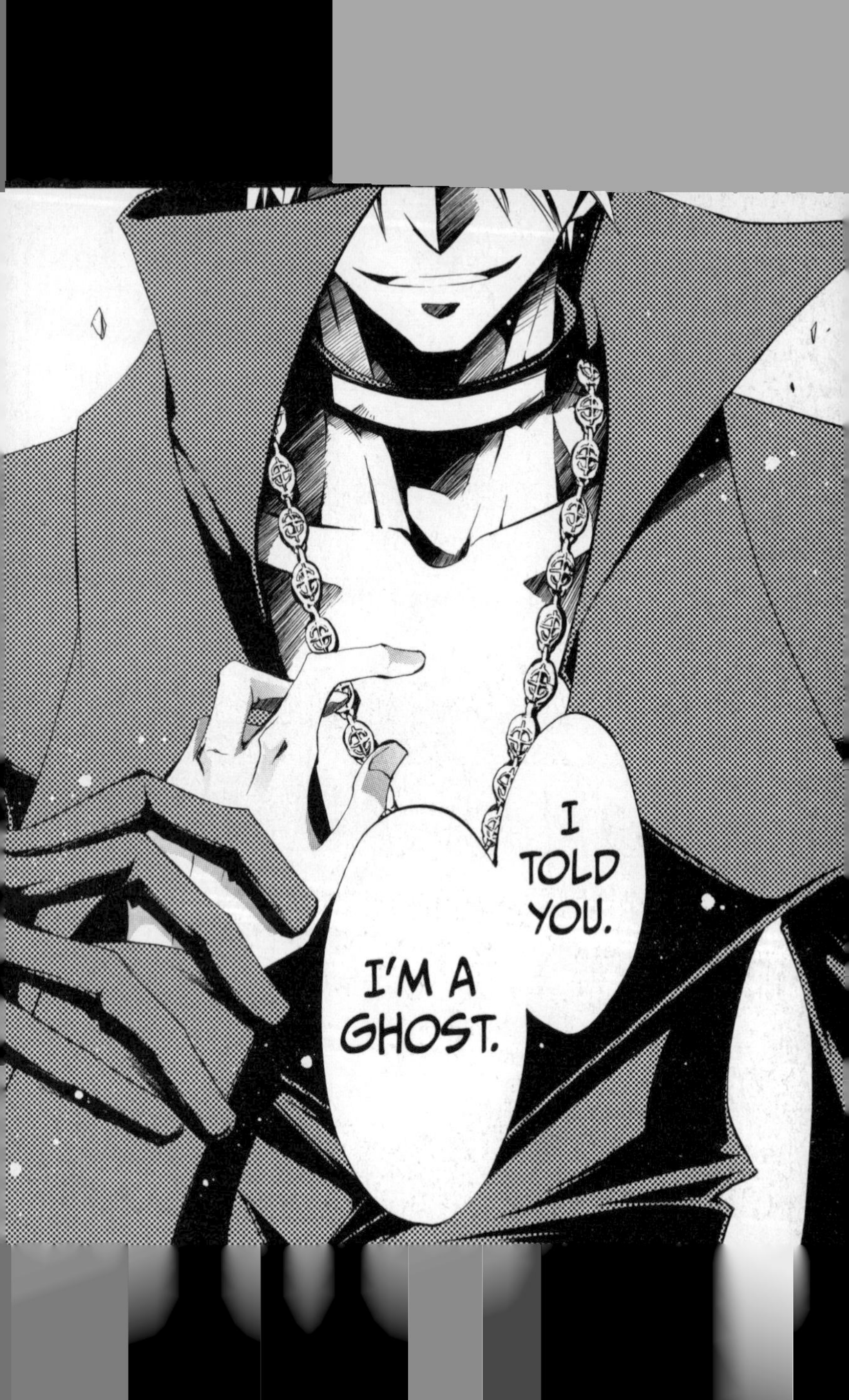
I TOLD YOU.
I'M A GHOST.

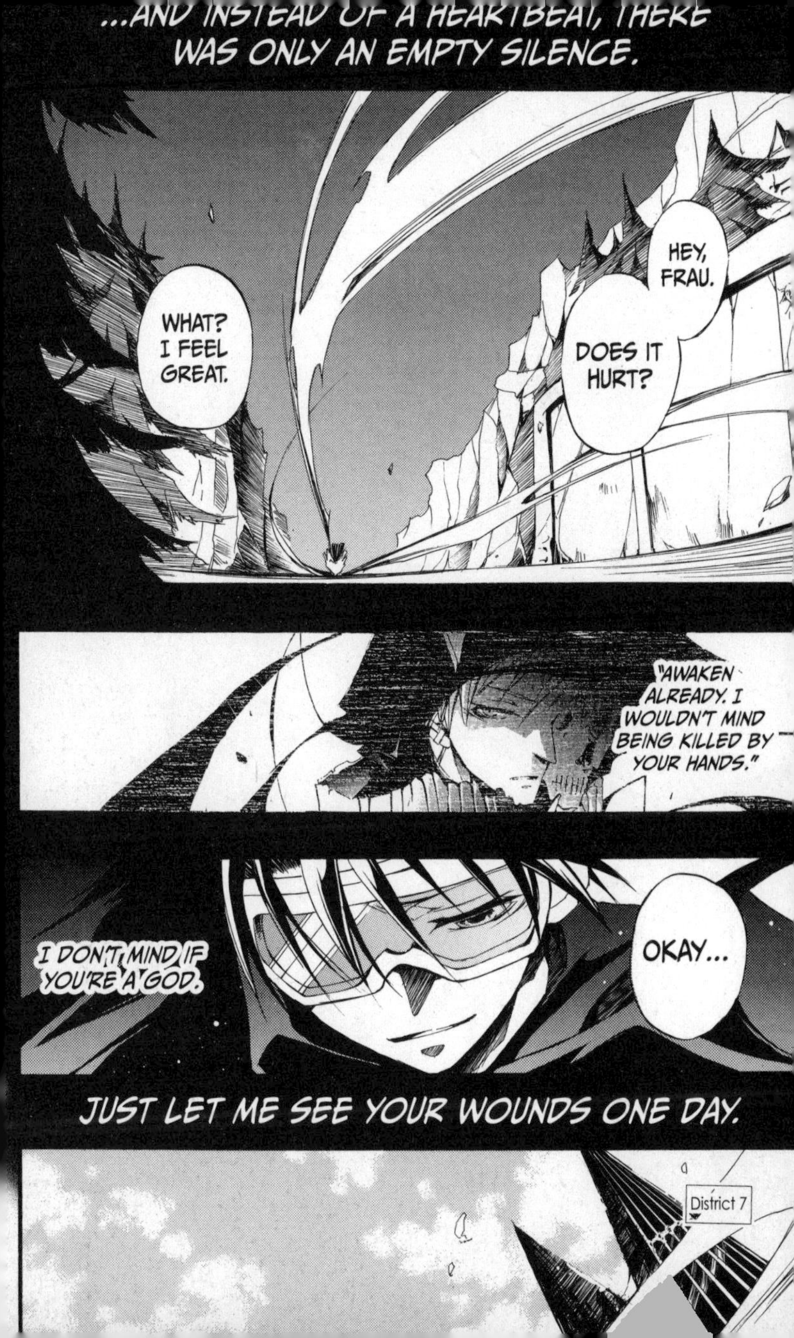
...AND INSTEAD OF A HEARTBEAT, THERE WAS ONLY AN EMPTY SILENCE.
HEY, FRAU.
DOES IT HURT?
WHAT? I FEEL GREAT.
"AWAKEN ALREADY. I WOULDN'T MIND BEING KILLED BY YOUR HANDS."
OKAY...
I DON'T MIND IF YOU'RE A GOD.
JUST LET ME SEE YOUR WOUNDS ONE DAY.
District 7

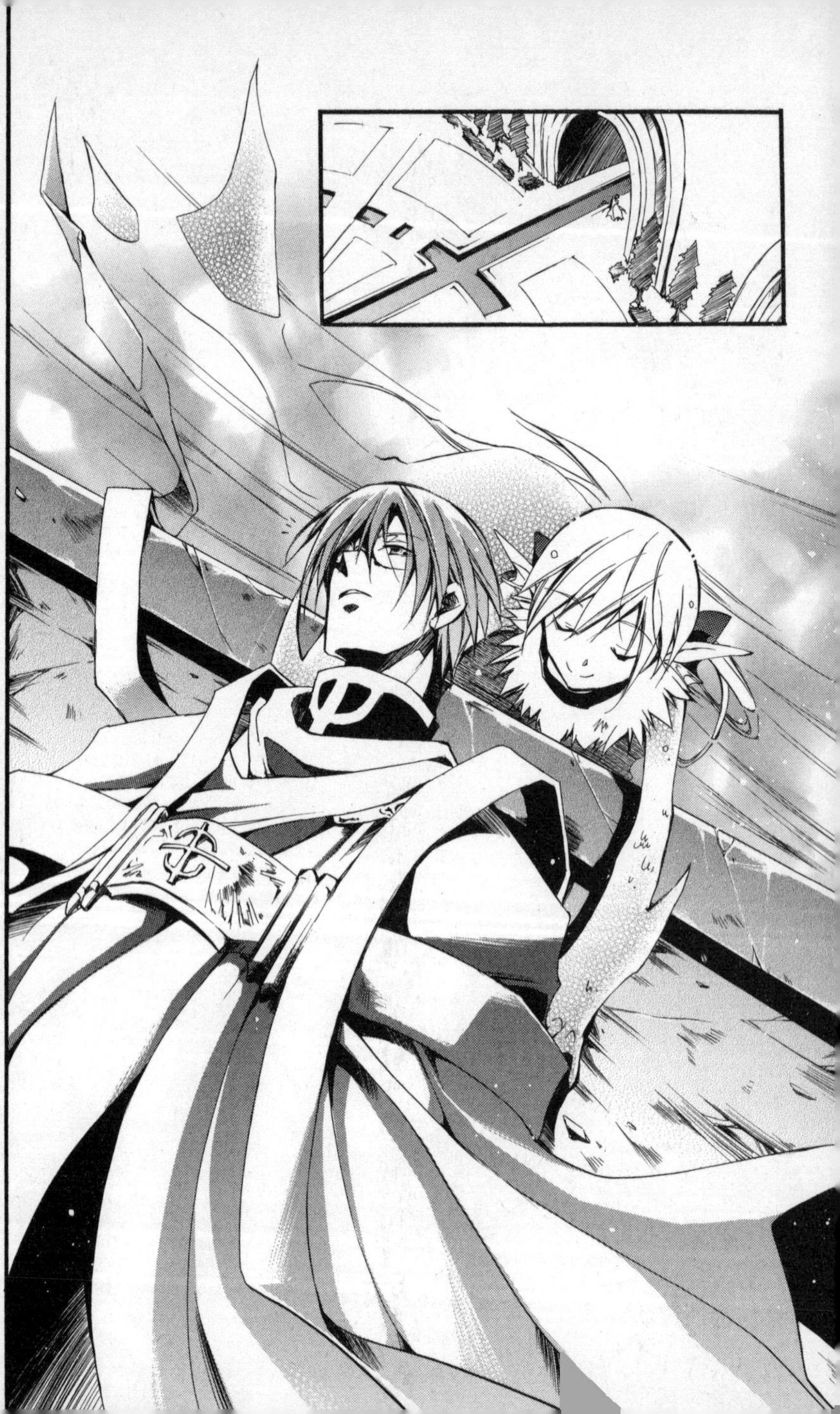

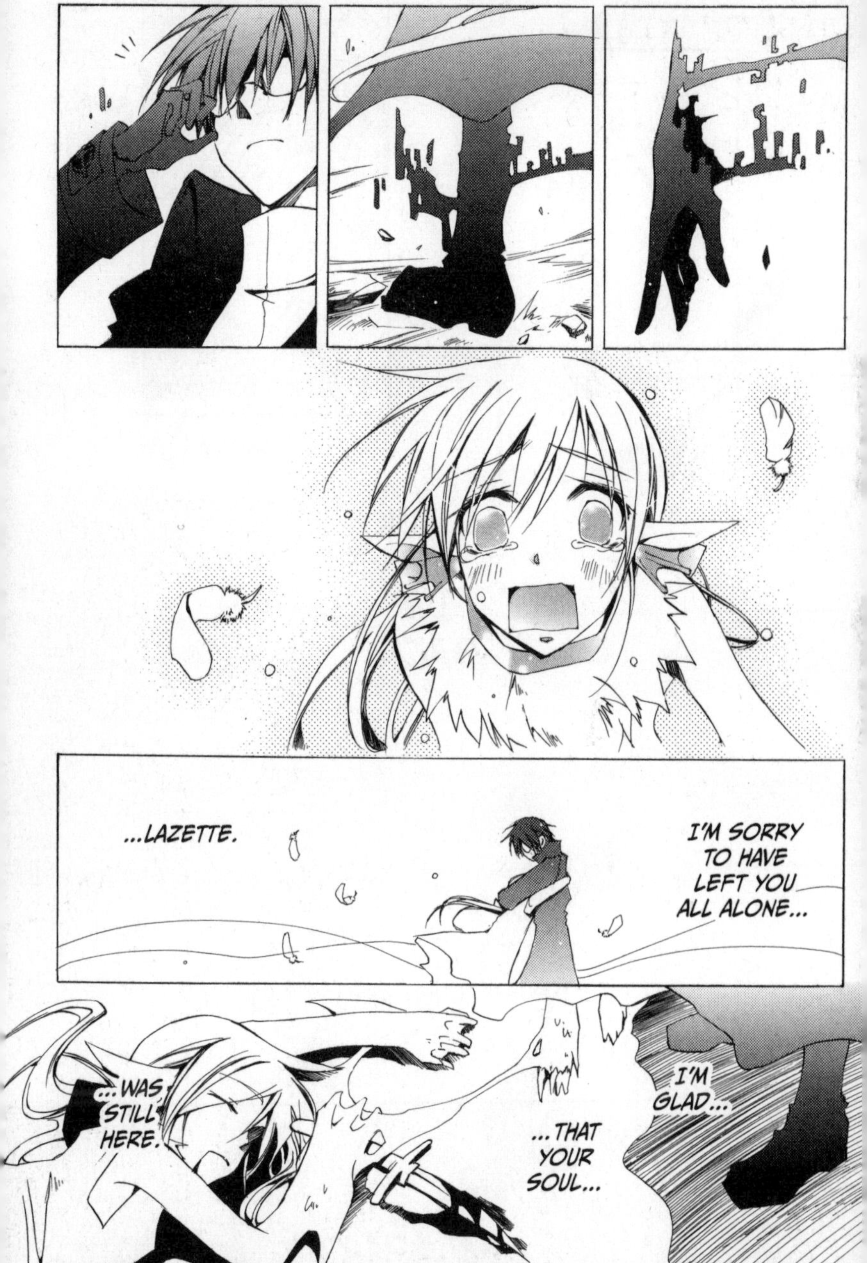
I'M SORRY TO HAVE LEFT YOU ALL ALONE...
...LAZETTE.
I'M GLAD...
...THAT YOUR SOUL...
...WAS STILL HERE.

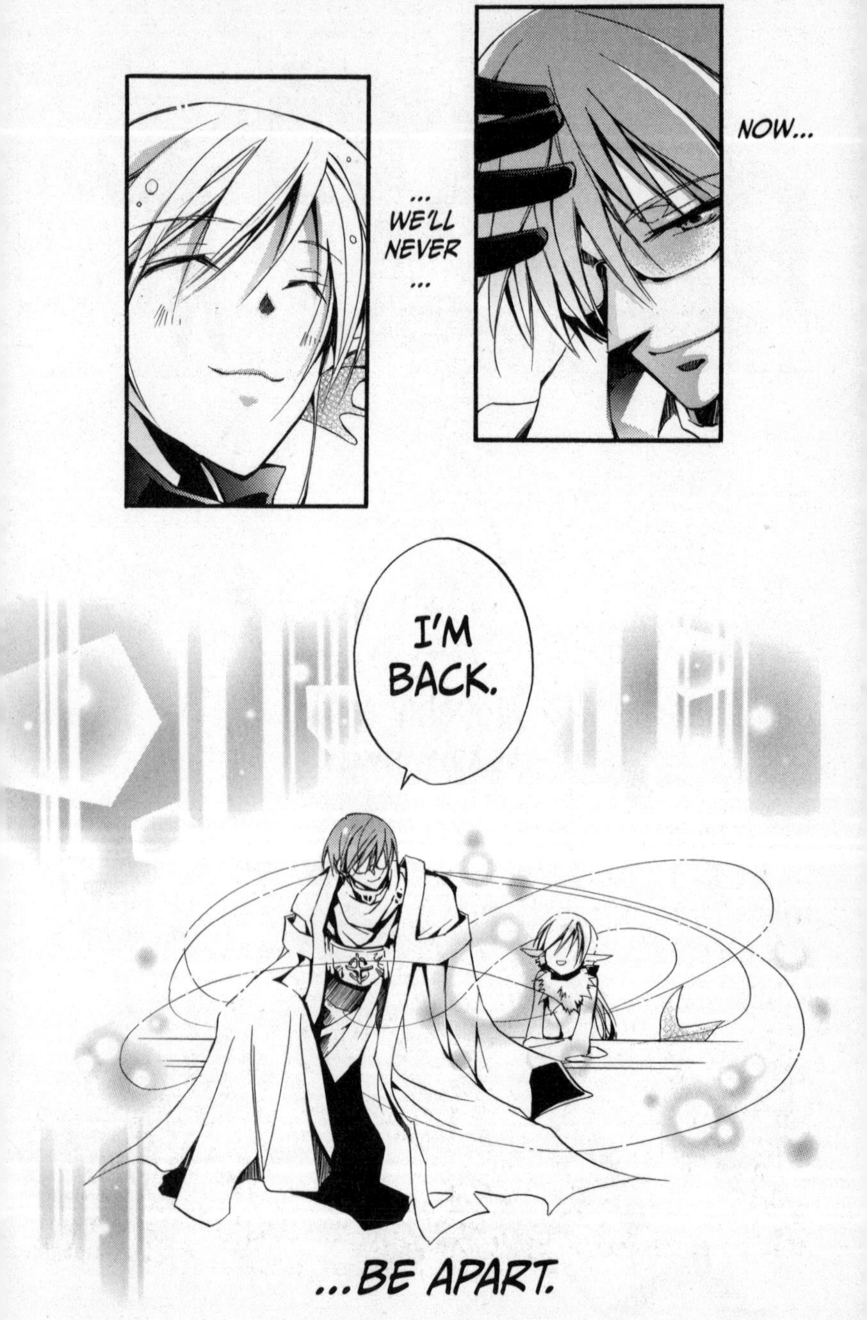
NOW...
...WE'LL NEVER...
I'M BACK.
...BE APART.

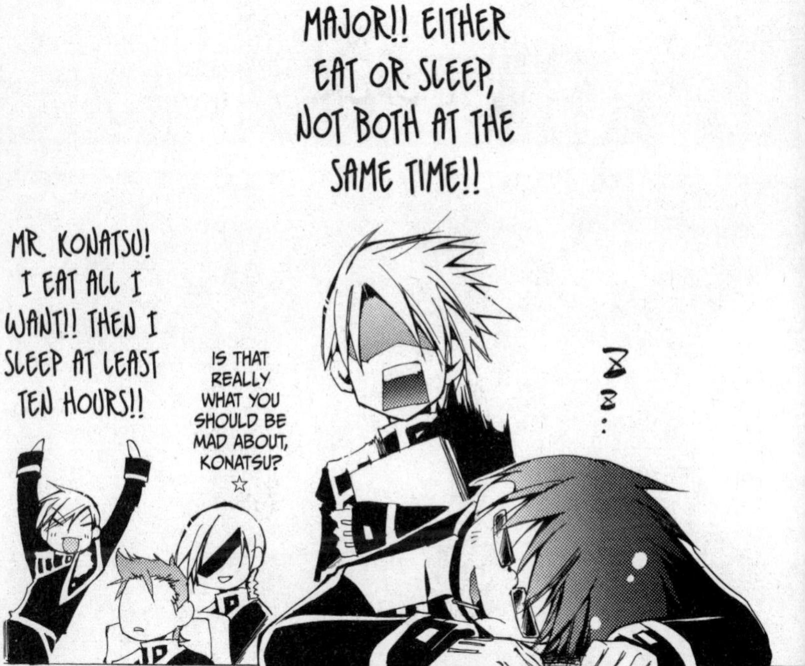
MAJOR!! EITHER EAT OR SLEEP, NOT BOTH AT THE SAME TIME!!
MR. KONATSU! I EAT ALL I WANT!! THEN I SLEEP AT LEAST TEN HOURS!!
IS THAT REALLY WHAT YOU SHOULD BE MAD ABOUT, KONATSU? ☆

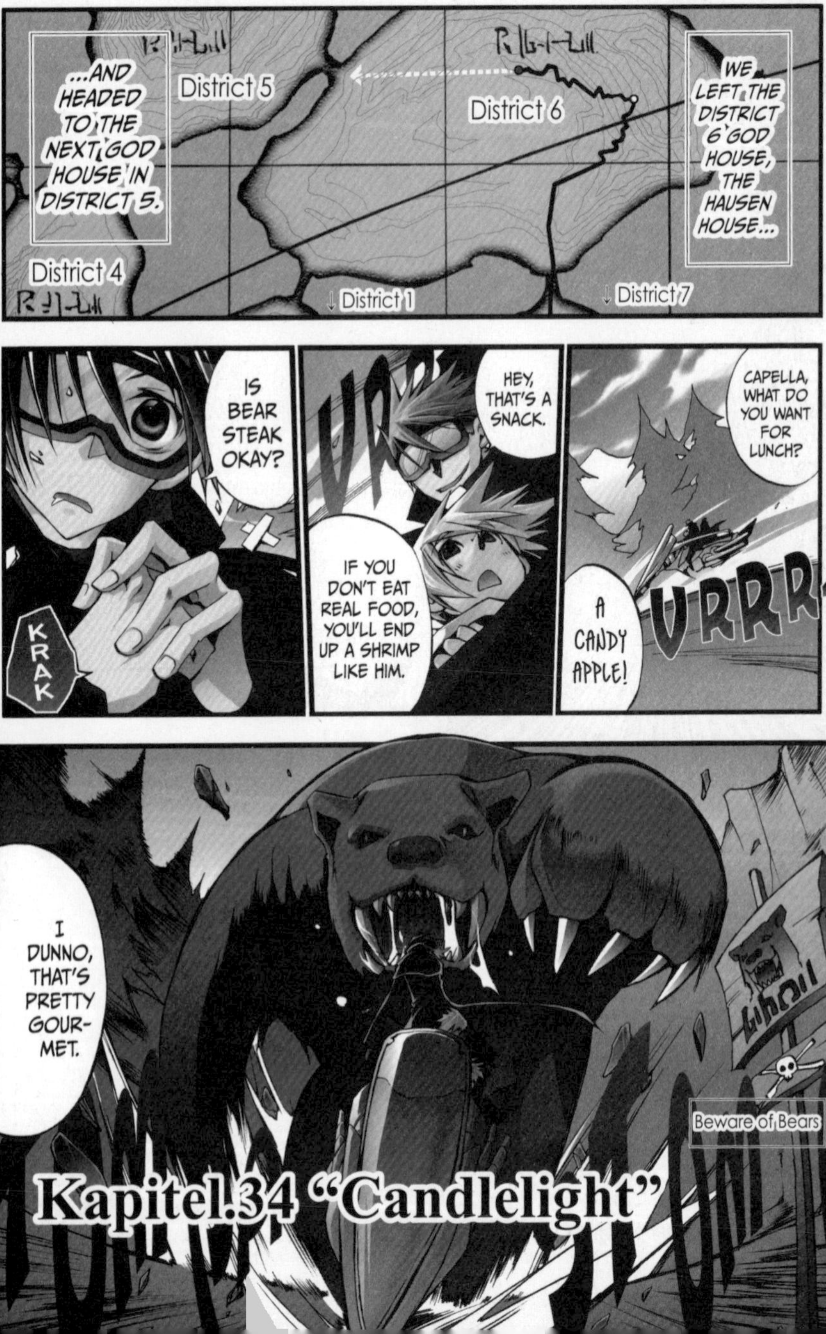
WE LEFT THE DISTRICT 6 GOD HOUSE, THE HAUSEN HOUSE...
District 6
District 5
...AND HEADED TO THE NEXT GOD HOUSE IN DISTRICT 5.
District 4
↓ District 1
↓ District 7
CAPELLA, WHAT DO YOU WANT FOR LUNCH?
A CANDY APPLE!
VRRR..
HEY, THAT'S A SNACK.
IF YOU DON'T EAT REAL FOOD, YOU'LL END UP A SHRIMP LIKE HIM.
IS BEAR STEAK OKAY?
KRAK
I DUNNO, THAT'S PRETTY GOURMET.
Beware of Bears
Kapitel.34 "Candlelight"

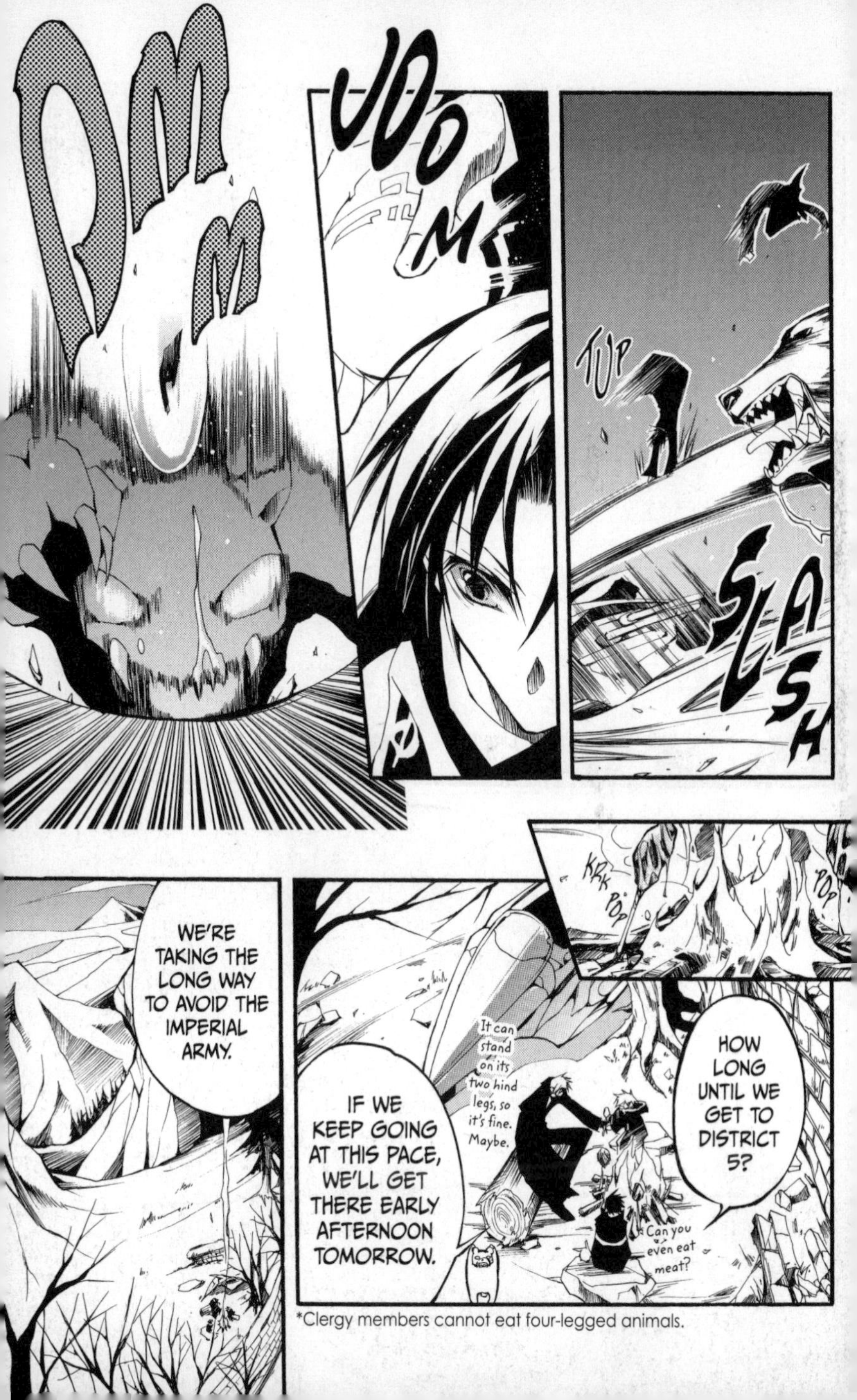
TUP
SLASH
JOOM
DMM
KRK
POP
POP
HOW LONG UNTIL WE GET TO DISTRICT 5?
Can you even eat meat?
It can stand on its two hind legs, so it's fine. Maybe.
IF WE KEEP GOING AT THIS PACE, WE'LL GET THERE EARLY AFTERNOON TOMORROW.
WE'RE TAKING THE LONG WAY TO AVOID THE IMPERIAL ARMY.
*Clergy members cannot eat four-legged animals.

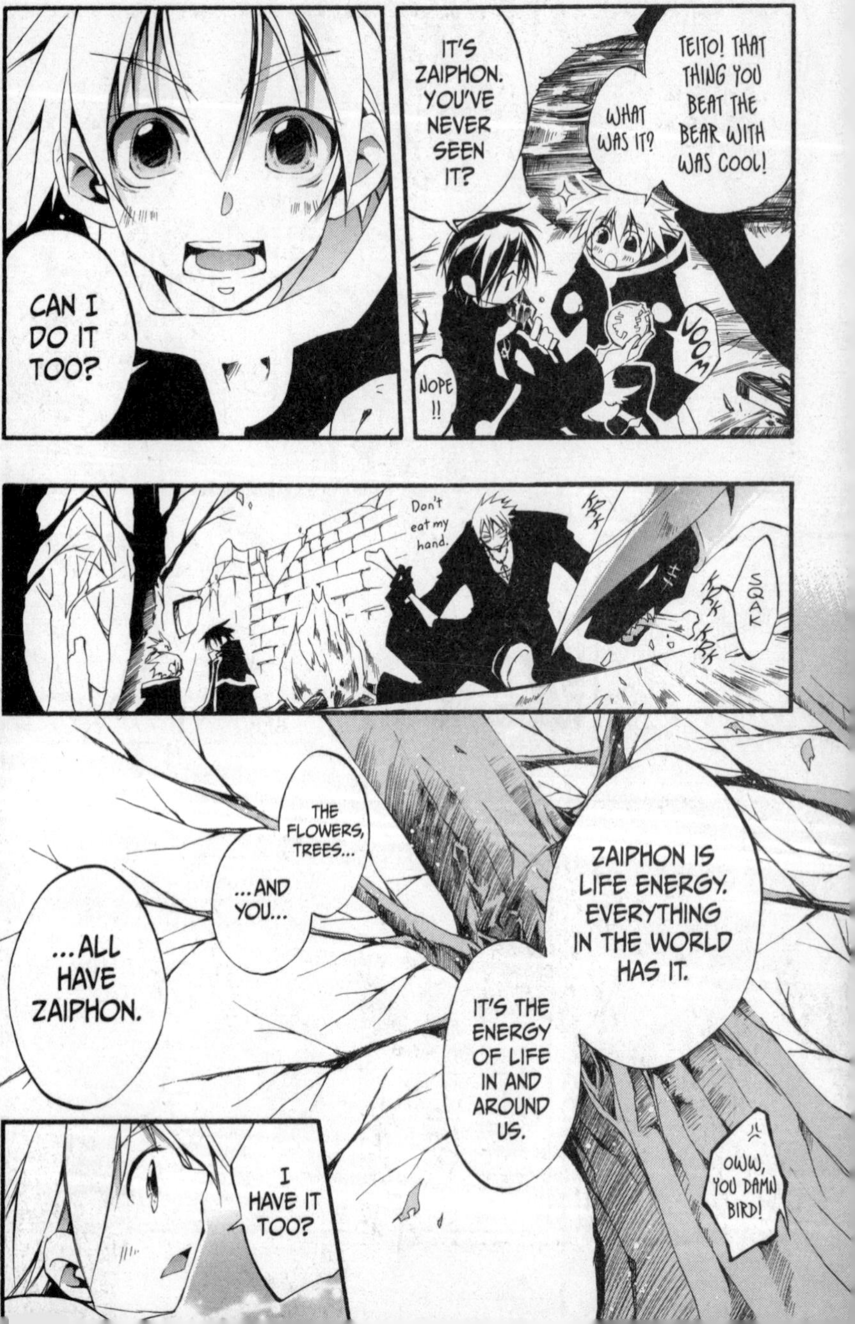
TEITO! THAT THING YOU BEAT THE BEAR WITH WAS COOL!
WHAT WAS IT?
IT'S ZAIPHON. YOU'VE NEVER SEEN IT?
VOOM
NOPE !!
CAN I DO IT TOO?
KRK
SQAK
KRK KRK KRK
Don't eat my hand.
ZAIPHON IS LIFE ENERGY. EVERYTHING IN THE WORLD HAS IT.
IT'S THE ENERGY OF LIFE IN AND AROUND US.
THE FLOWERS, TREES...
...AND YOU...
...ALL HAVE ZAIPHON.
OWW, YOU DAMN BIRD!
I HAVE IT TOO?

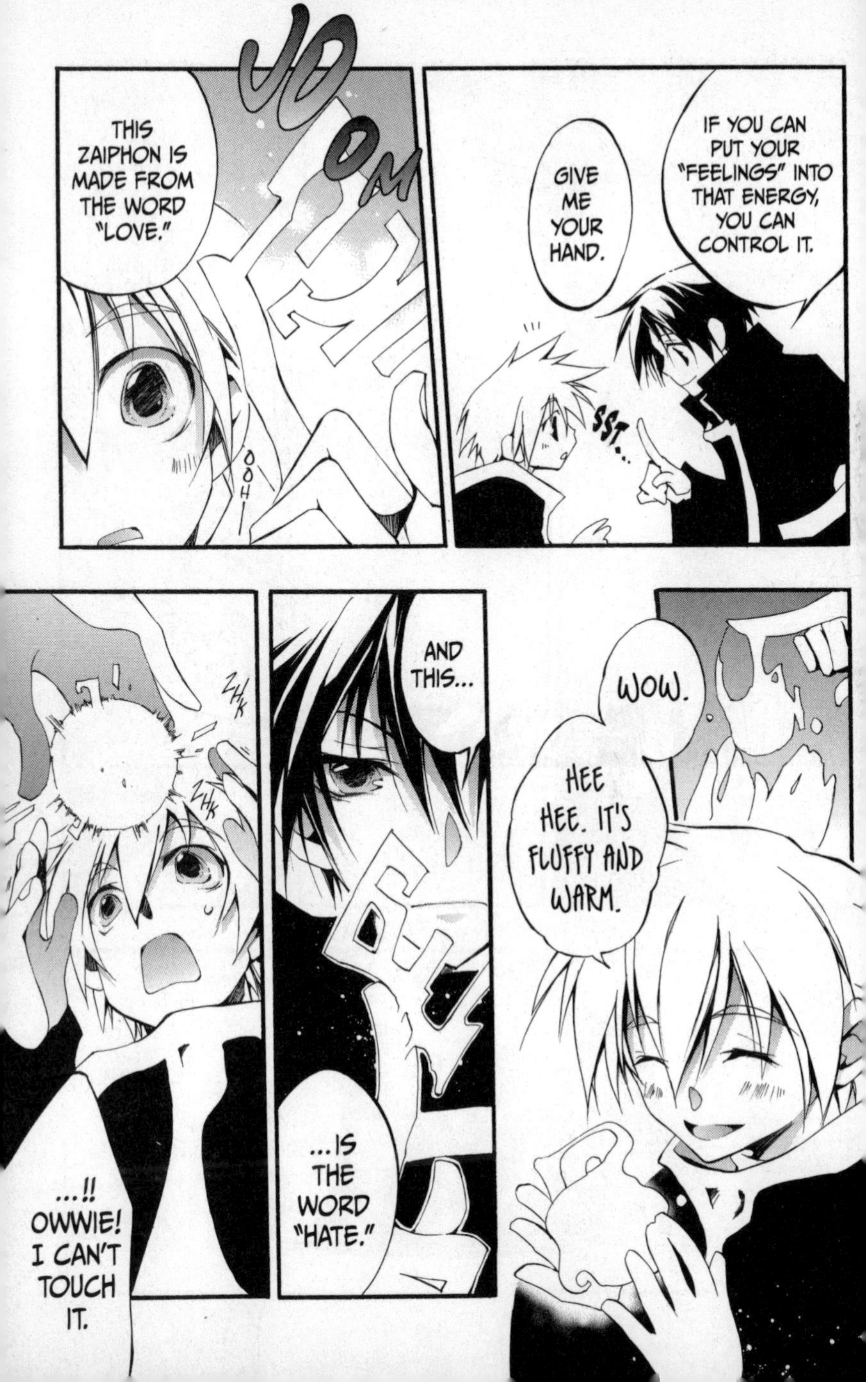
IF YOU CAN PUT YOUR "FEELINGS" INTO THAT ENERGY, YOU CAN CONTROL IT.
GIVE ME YOUR HAND.
SST...
JOOM
THIS ZAIPHON IS MADE FROM THE WORD "LOVE."
OOH!
WOW.
HEE HEE. IT'S FLUFFY AND WARM.
AND THIS...
...IS THE WORD "HATE."
ZHK
ZHK
...!! OWWIE! I CAN'T TOUCH IT.

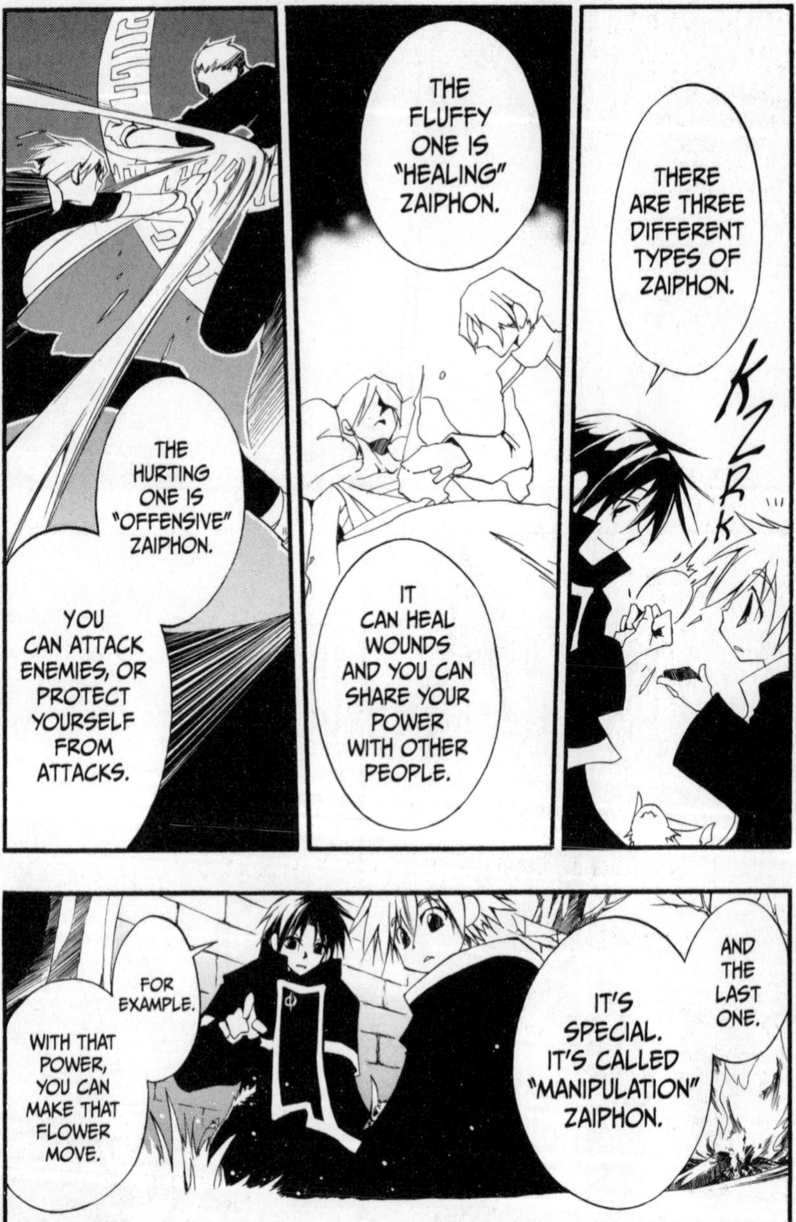
THERE ARE THREE DIFFERENT TYPES OF ZAIPHON.
KZRK
THE FLUFFY ONE IS "HEALING" ZAIPHON.
IT CAN HEAL WOUNDS AND YOU CAN SHARE YOUR POWER WITH OTHER PEOPLE.
THE HURTING ONE IS "OFFENSIVE" ZAIPHON.
YOU CAN ATTACK ENEMIES, OR PROTECT YOURSELF FROM ATTACKS.
AND THE LAST ONE.
IT'S SPECIAL. IT'S CALLED "MANIPULATION" ZAIPHON.
FOR EXAMPLE.
WITH THAT POWER, YOU CAN MAKE THAT FLOWER MOVE.

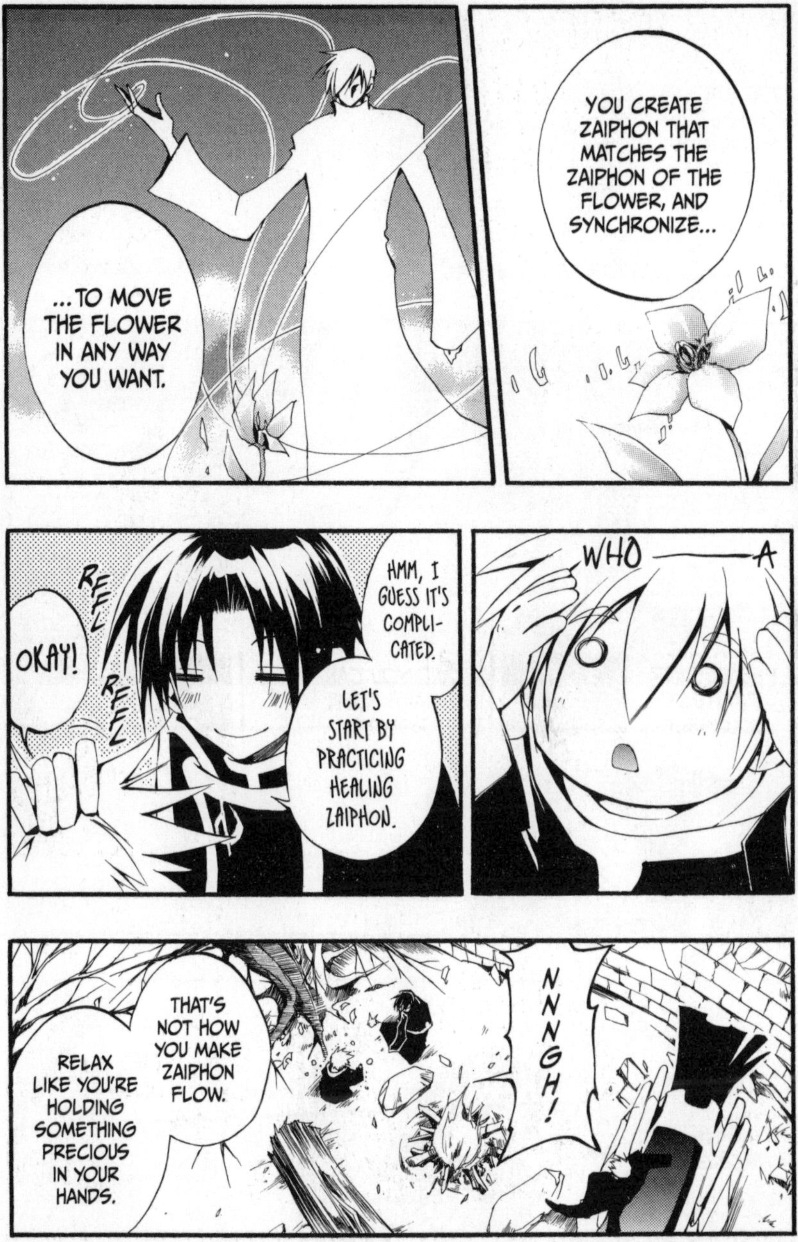
YOU CREATE ZAIPHON THAT MATCHES THE ZAIPHON OF THE FLOWER, AND SYNCHRONIZE...
...TO MOVE THE FLOWER IN ANY WAY YOU WANT.
WHO—A
HMM, I GUESS IT'S COMPLICATED.
LET'S START BY PRACTICING HEALING ZAIPHON.
RFFL RFFL
OKAY!
NNNGH!
THAT'S NOT HOW YOU MAKE ZAIPHON FLOW.
RELAX LIKE YOU'RE HOLDING SOMETHING PRECIOUS IN YOUR HANDS.

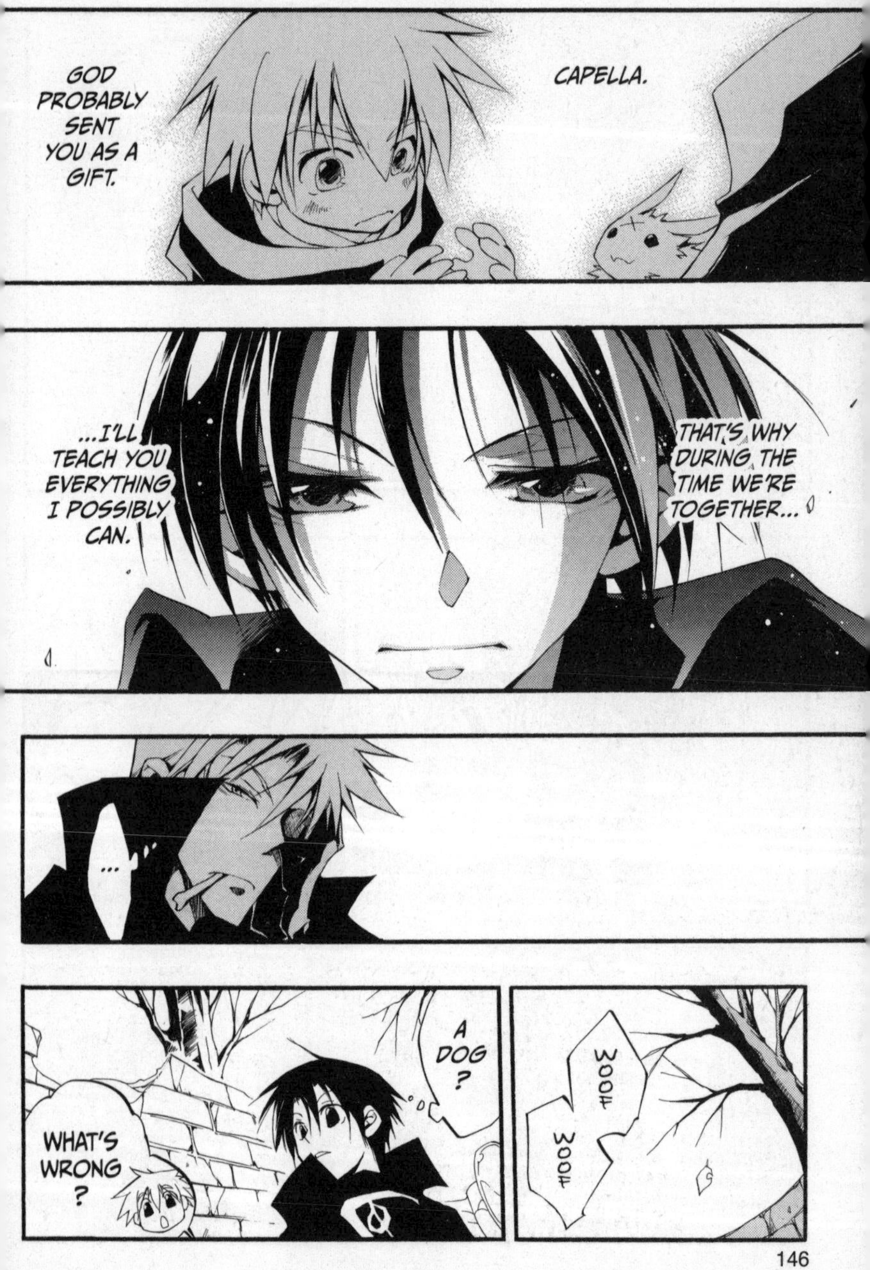
CAPELLA.
GOD PROBABLY SENT YOU AS A GIFT.
THAT'S WHY DURING THE TIME WE'RE TOGETHER...
...I'LL TEACH YOU EVERYTHING I POSSIBLY CAN.
...
WOOF WOOF
A DOG?
WHAT'S WRONG?

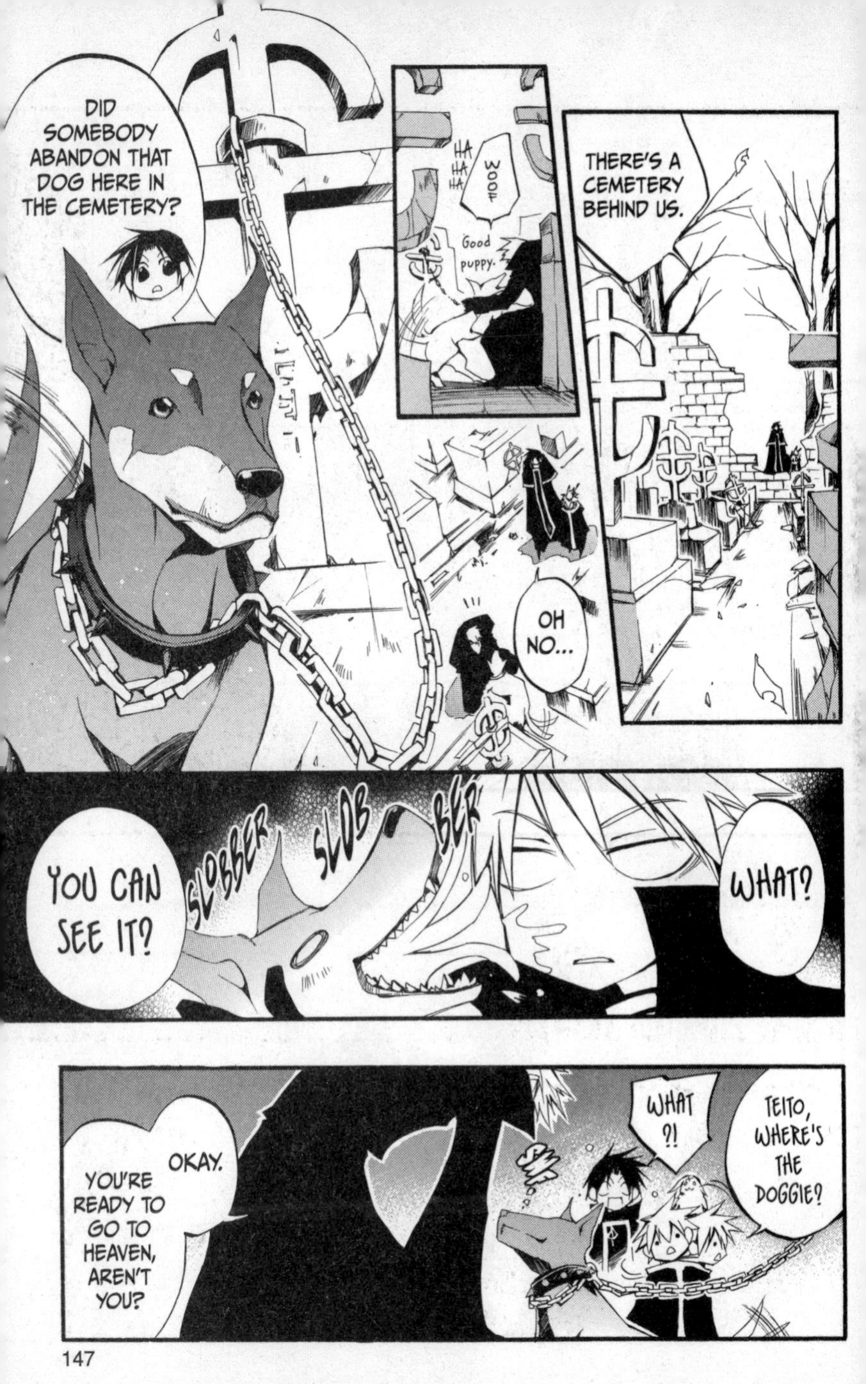
THERE'S A CEMETERY BEHIND US.
WOOF
HA HA HA
Good puppy.
DID SOMEBODY ABANDON THAT DOG HERE IN THE CEMETERY?
OH NO...
WHAT?
SLOBBER SLOB BER
YOU CAN SEE IT?
TEITO, WHERE'S THE DOGGIE?
WHAT?!
OKAY.
YOU'RE READY TO GO TO HEAVEN, AREN'T YOU?

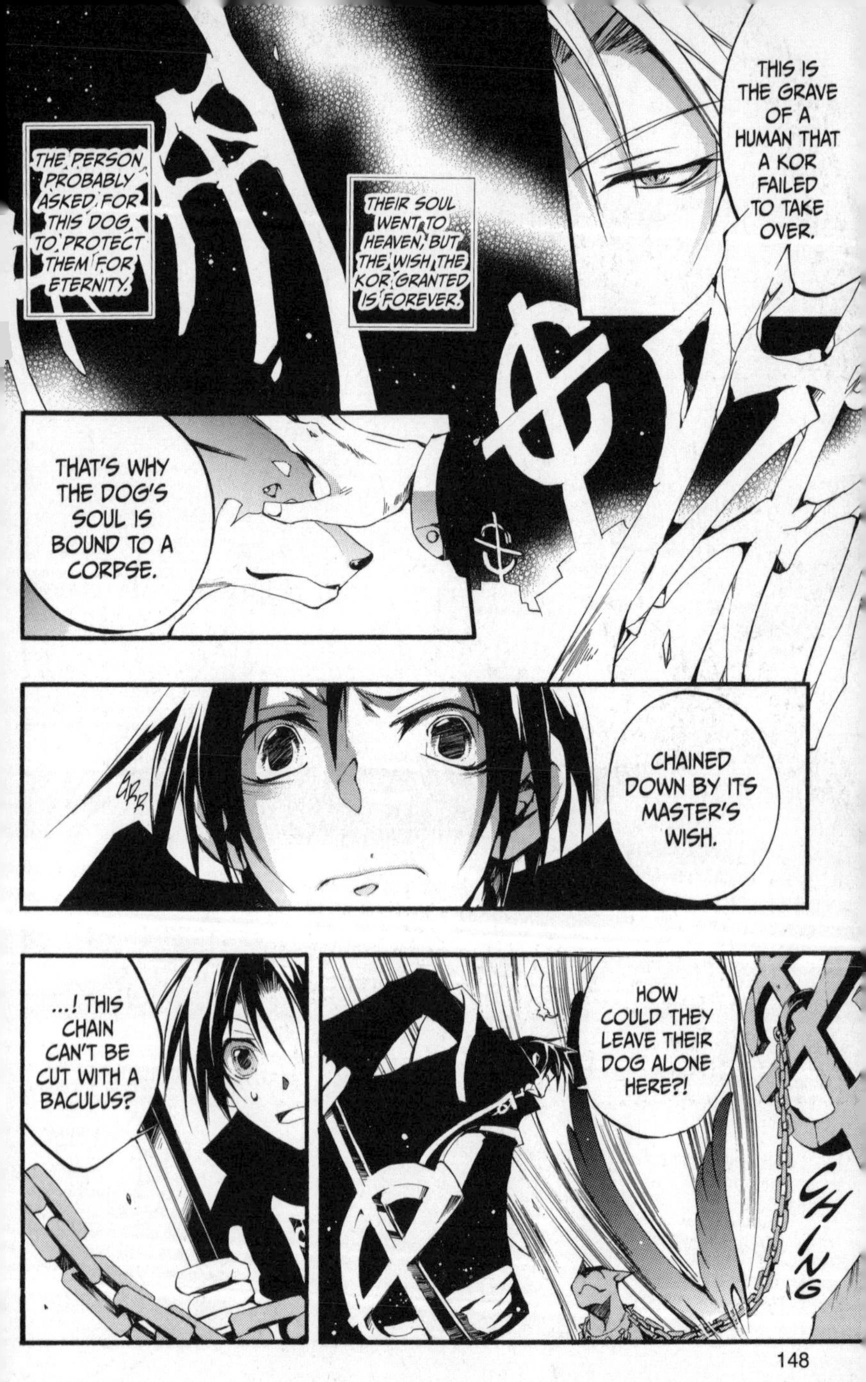
THIS IS THE GRAVE OF A HUMAN THAT A KOR FAILED TO TAKE OVER.
THEIR SOUL WENT TO HEAVEN, BUT THE WISH THE KOR GRANTED IS FOREVER.
THE PERSON PROBABLY ASKED FOR THIS DOG TO PROTECT THEM FOR ETERNITY.
THAT'S WHY THE DOG'S SOUL IS BOUND TO A CORPSE.
CHAINED DOWN BY ITS MASTER'S WISH.
HOW COULD THEY LEAVE THEIR DOG ALONE HERE?!
CHING
...! THIS CHAIN CAN'T BE CUT WITH A BACULUS?

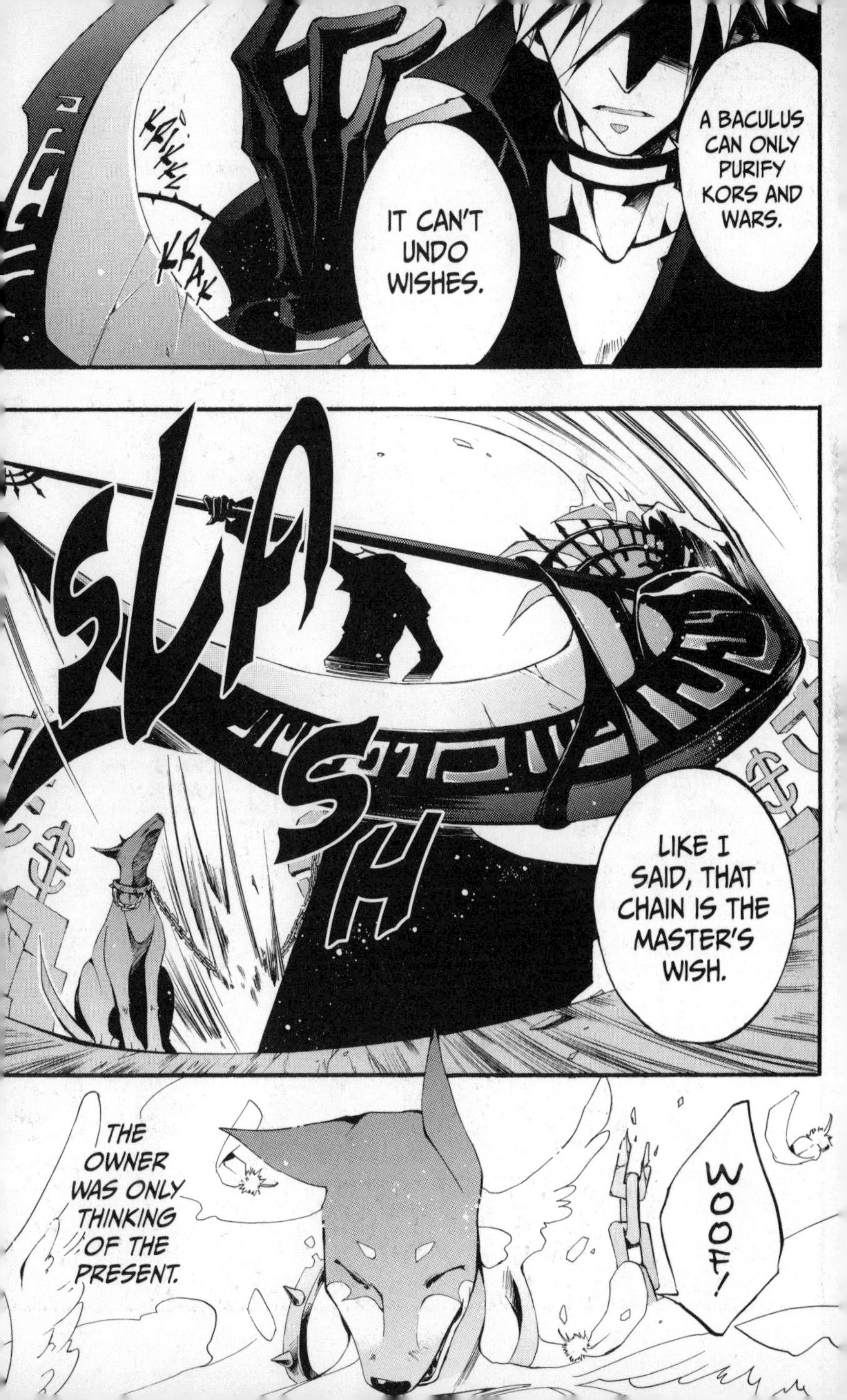
A BACULUS CAN ONLY PURIFY KORS AND WARS.
IT CAN'T UNDO WISHES.
KRIKKK
KRAK
SLASH
LIKE I SAID, THAT CHAIN IS THE MASTER'S WISH.
WOOF!
THE OWNER WAS ONLY THINKING OF THE PRESENT.

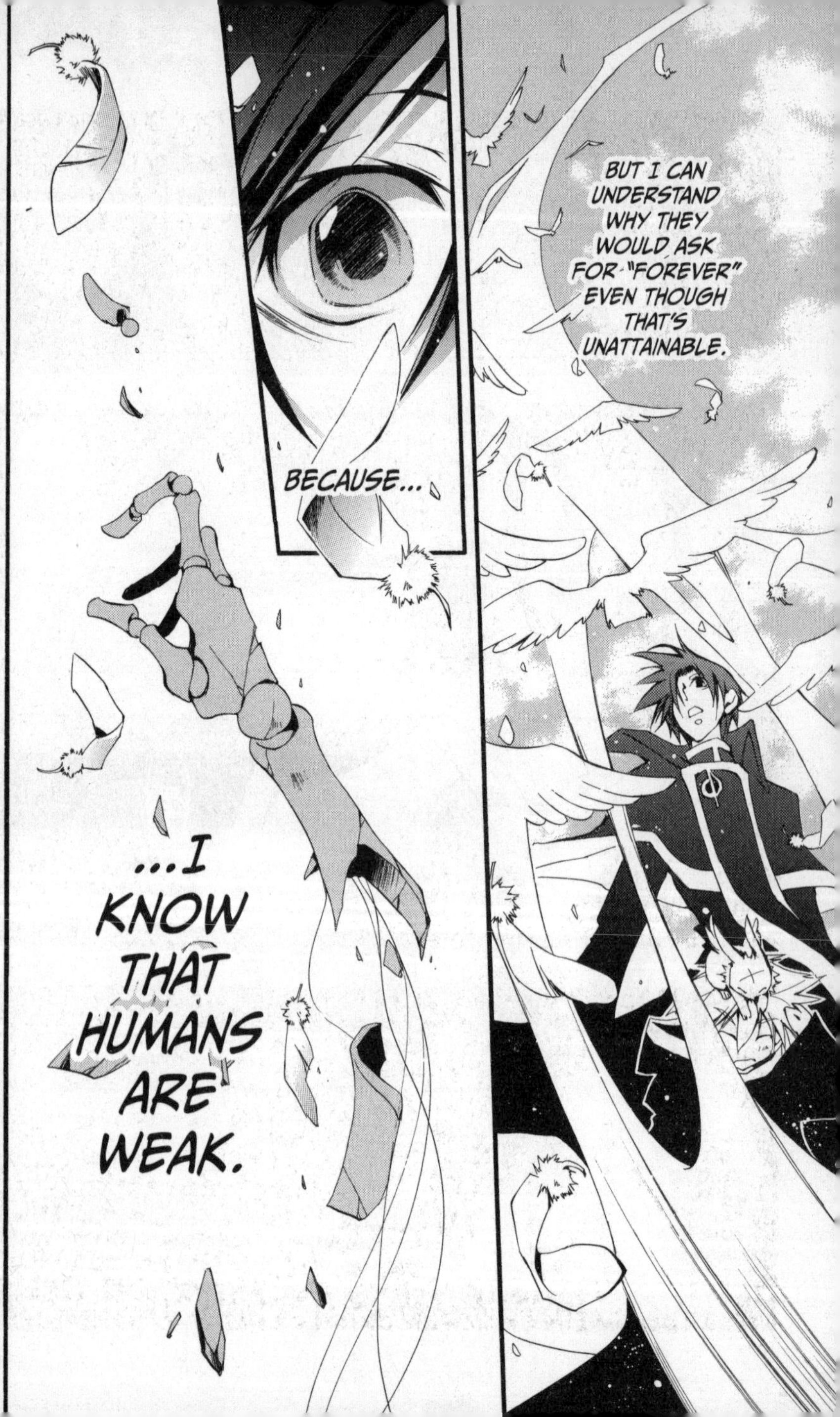
BUT I CAN UNDERSTAND WHY THEY WOULD ASK FOR "FOREVER" EVEN THOUGH THAT'S UNATTAINABLE.
BECAUSE...
...I KNOW THAT HUMANS ARE WEAK.

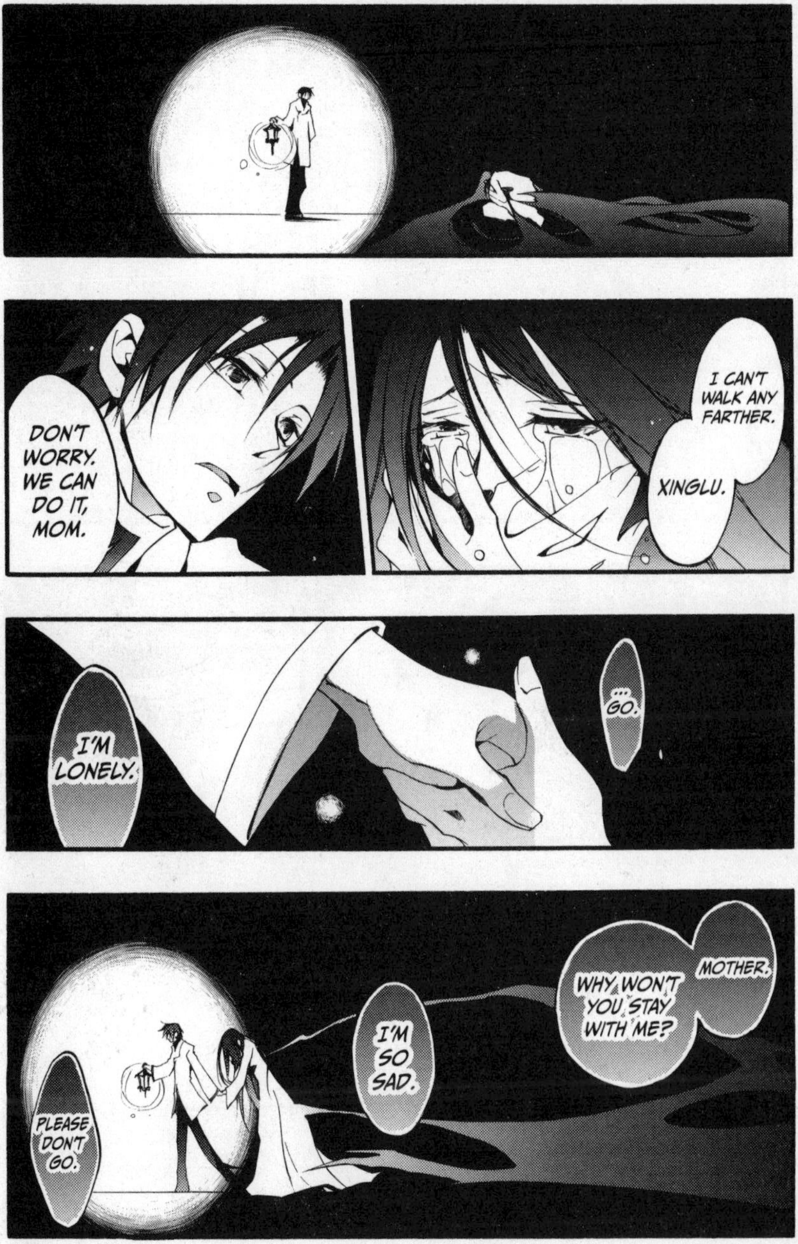
I CAN'T WALK ANY FARTHER.
XINGLU.
DON'T WORRY. WE CAN DO IT, MOM.
...GO.
I'M LONELY.
MOTHER.
WHY WON'T YOU STAY WITH ME?
I'M SO SAD.
PLEASE DON'T GO.

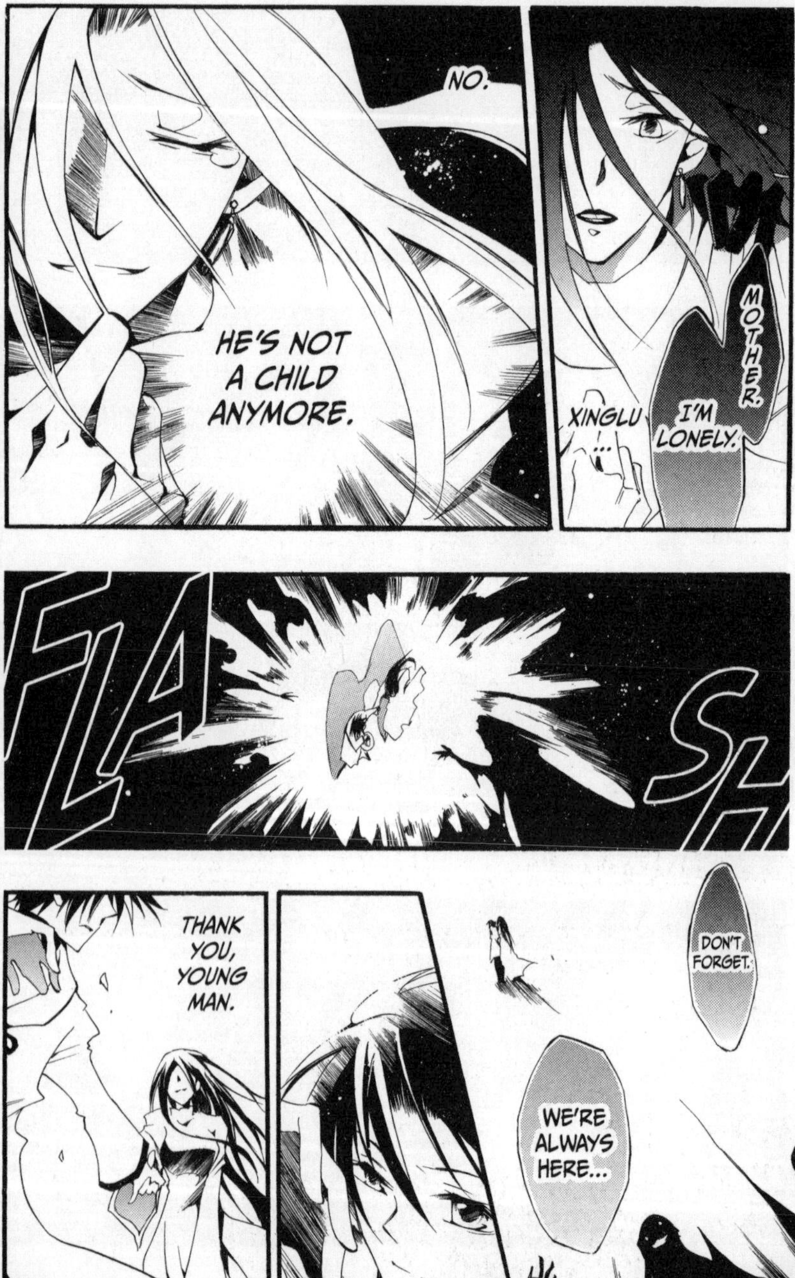
MOTHER.
I'M LONELY.
XINGLU...
NO.
HE'S NOT A CHILD ANYMORE.
FLASH
DON'T FORGET.
WE'RE ALWAYS HERE...
THANK YOU, YOUNG MAN.

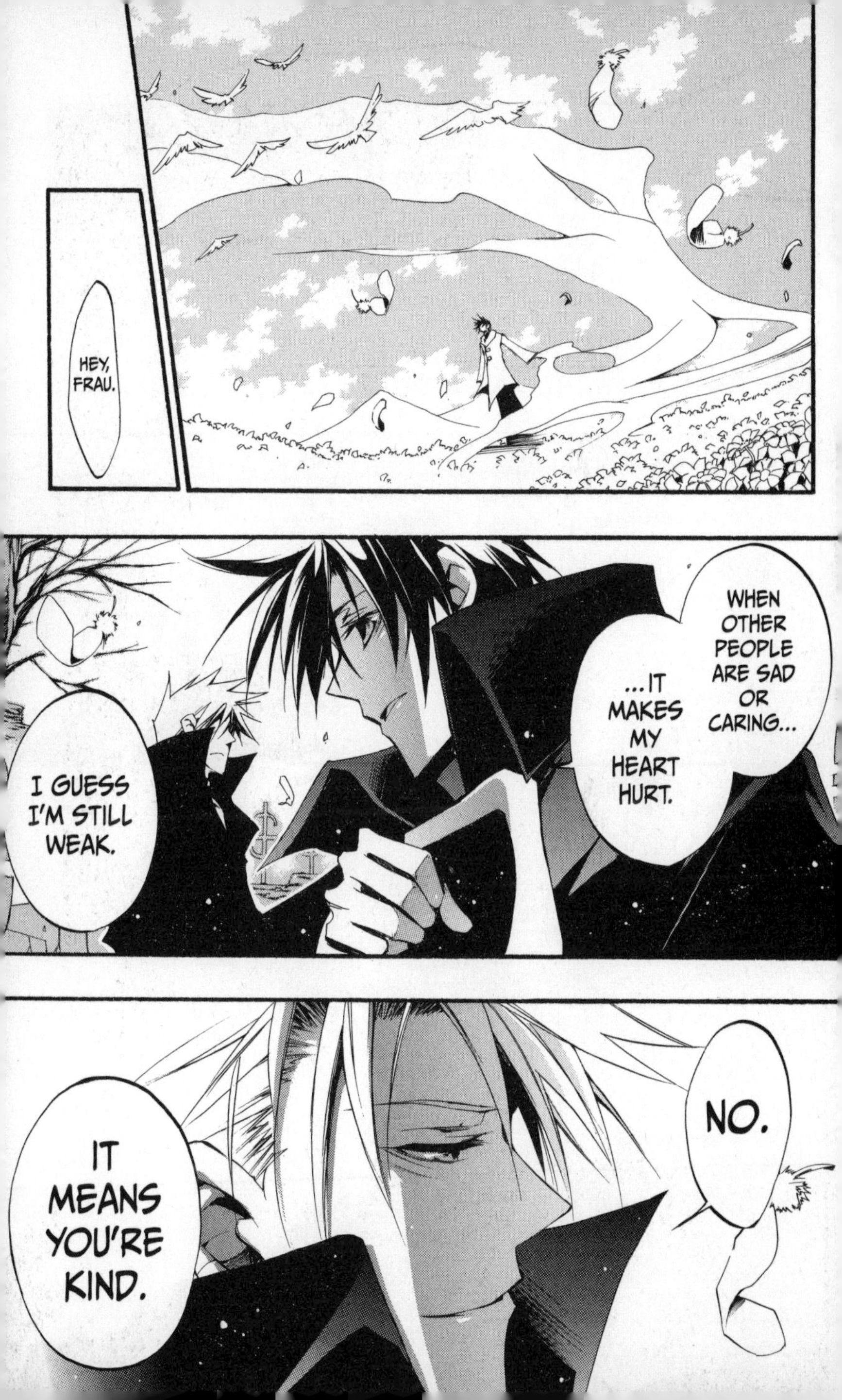
HEY, FRAU.
WHEN OTHER PEOPLE ARE SAD OR CARING...
...IT MAKES MY HEART HURT.
I GUESS I'M STILL WEAK.
NO.
IT MEANS YOU'RE KIND.

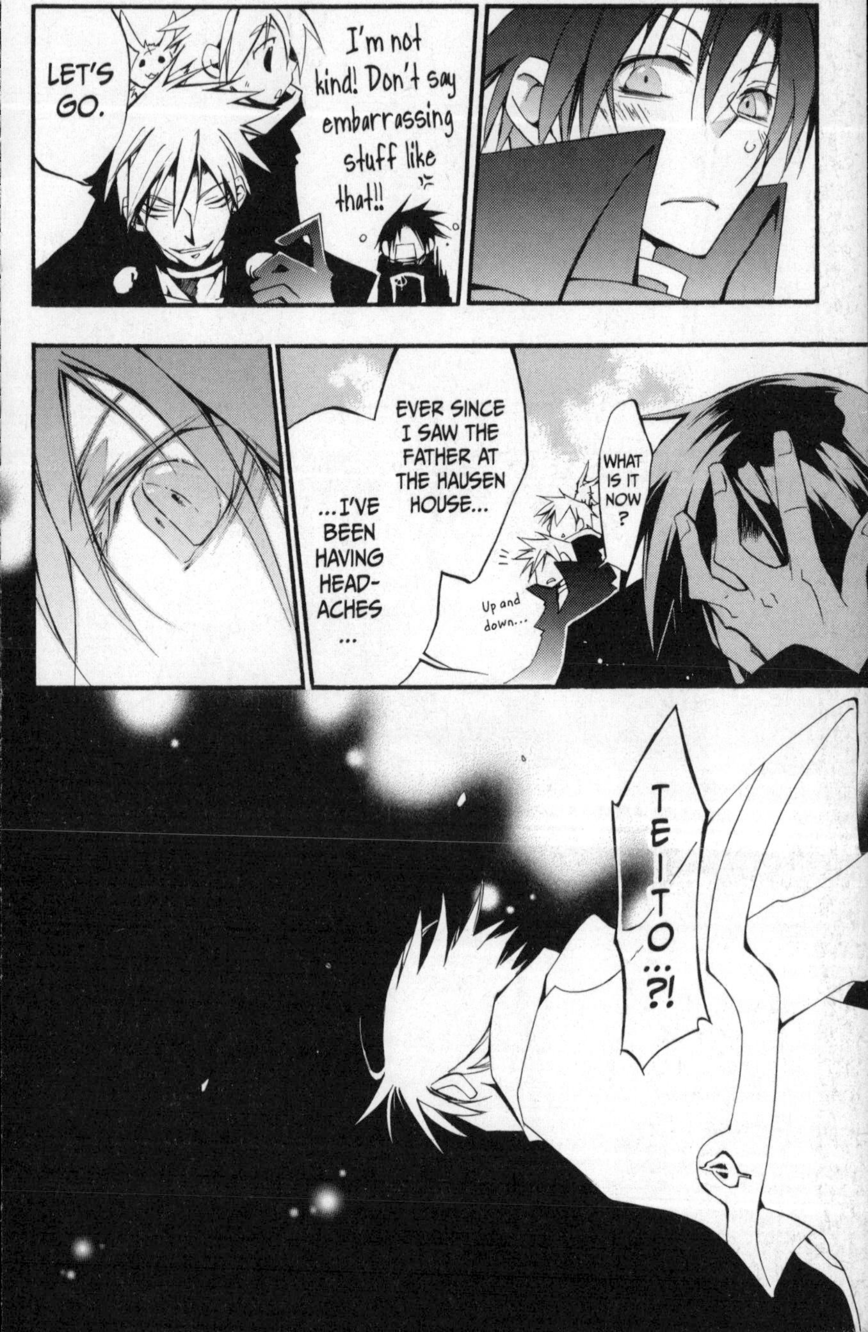
I'm not kind! Don't say embarrassing stuff like that!!
LET'S GO.
WHAT IS IT NOW?
EVER SINCE I SAW THE FATHER AT THE HAUSEN HOUSE...
...I'VE BEEN HAVING HEAD-ACHES...
Up and down...
TEITO...?!

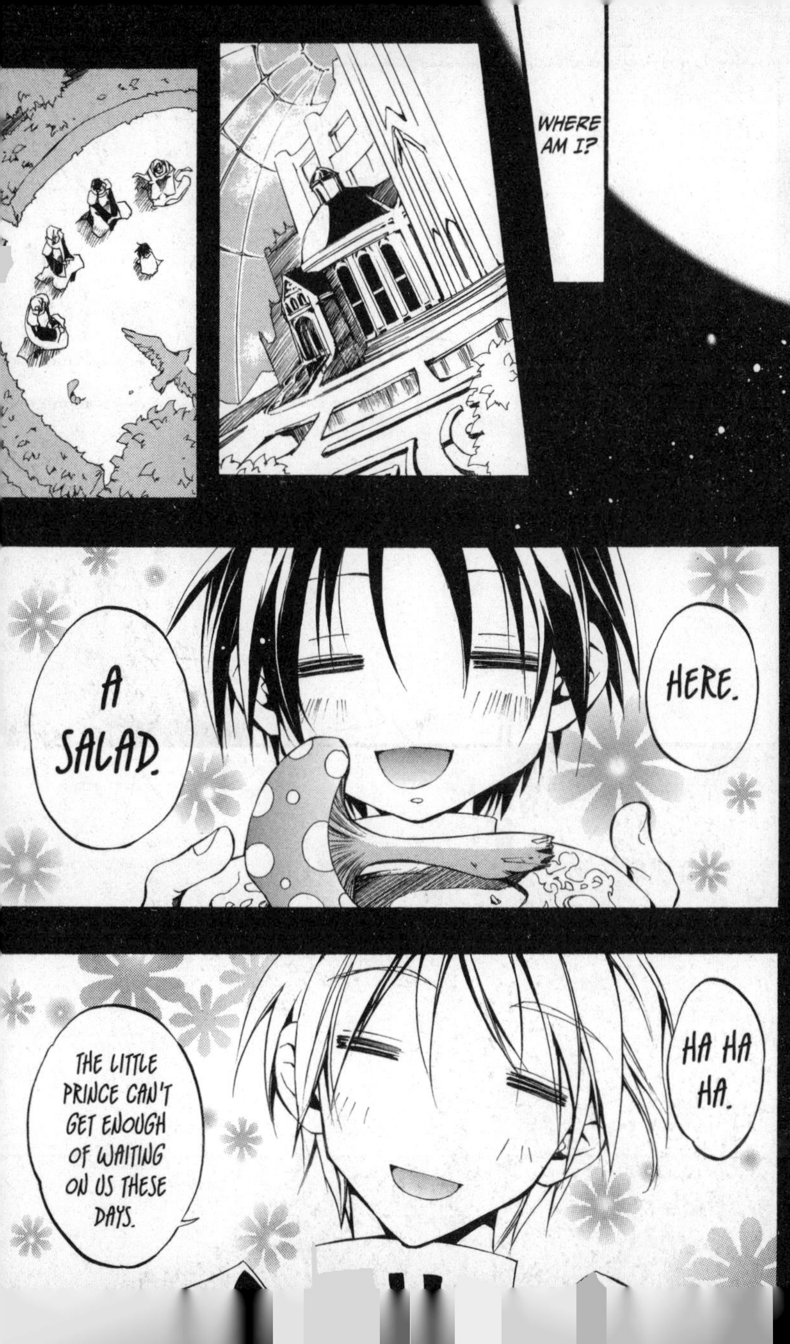
WHERE AM I?
HERE.
A SALAD.
HA HA HA.
THE LITTLE PRINCE CAN'T GET ENOUGH OF WAITING ON US THESE DAYS.

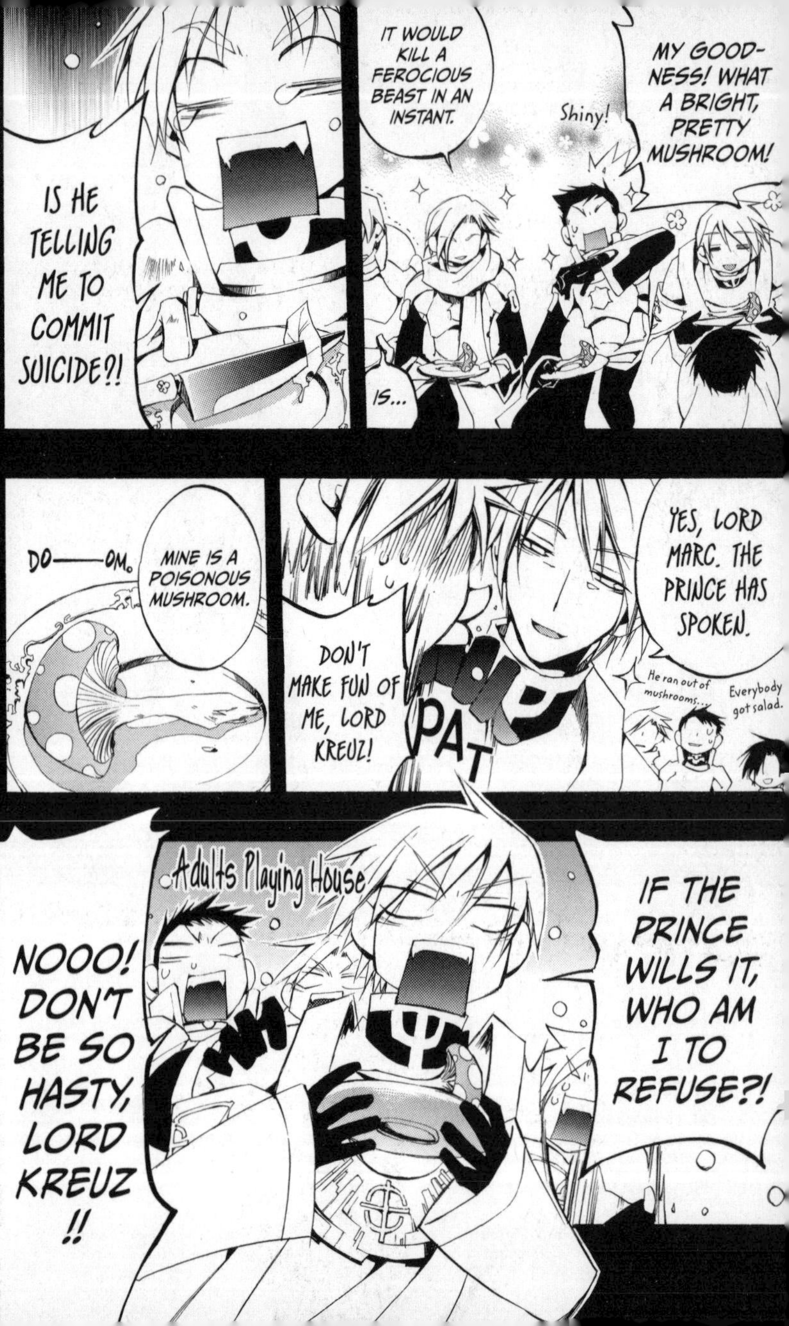
MY GOODNESS! WHAT A BRIGHT, PRETTY MUSHROOM!
Shiny!
IT WOULD KILL A FEROCIOUS BEAST IN AN INSTANT.
IS...
IS HE TELLING ME TO COMMIT SUICIDE?!
YES, LORD MARC. THE PRINCE HAS SPOKEN.
He ran out of mushrooms...
Everybody got salad.
DON'T MAKE FUN OF ME, LORD KREUZ!
PAT
MINE IS A POISONOUS MUSHROOM.
DO——OM.
IF THE PRINCE WILLS IT, WHO AM I TO REFUSE?!
Adults Playing House
NOOO! DON'T BE SO HASTY, LORD KREUZ!!

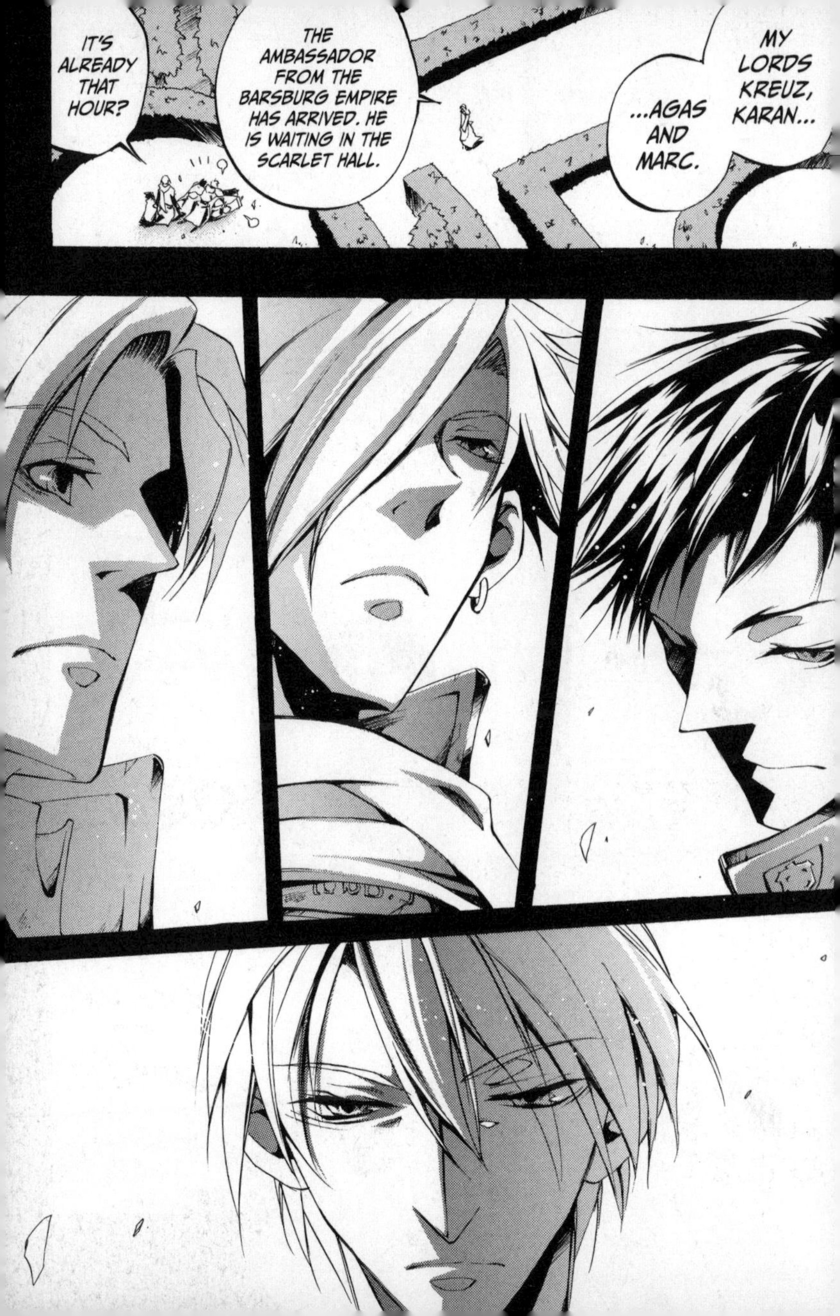
MY LORDS KREUZ, KARAN...
...AGAS AND MARC.
THE AMBASSADOR FROM THE BARSBURG EMPIRE HAS ARRIVED. HE IS WAITING IN THE SCARLET HALL.
IT'S ALREADY THAT HOUR?

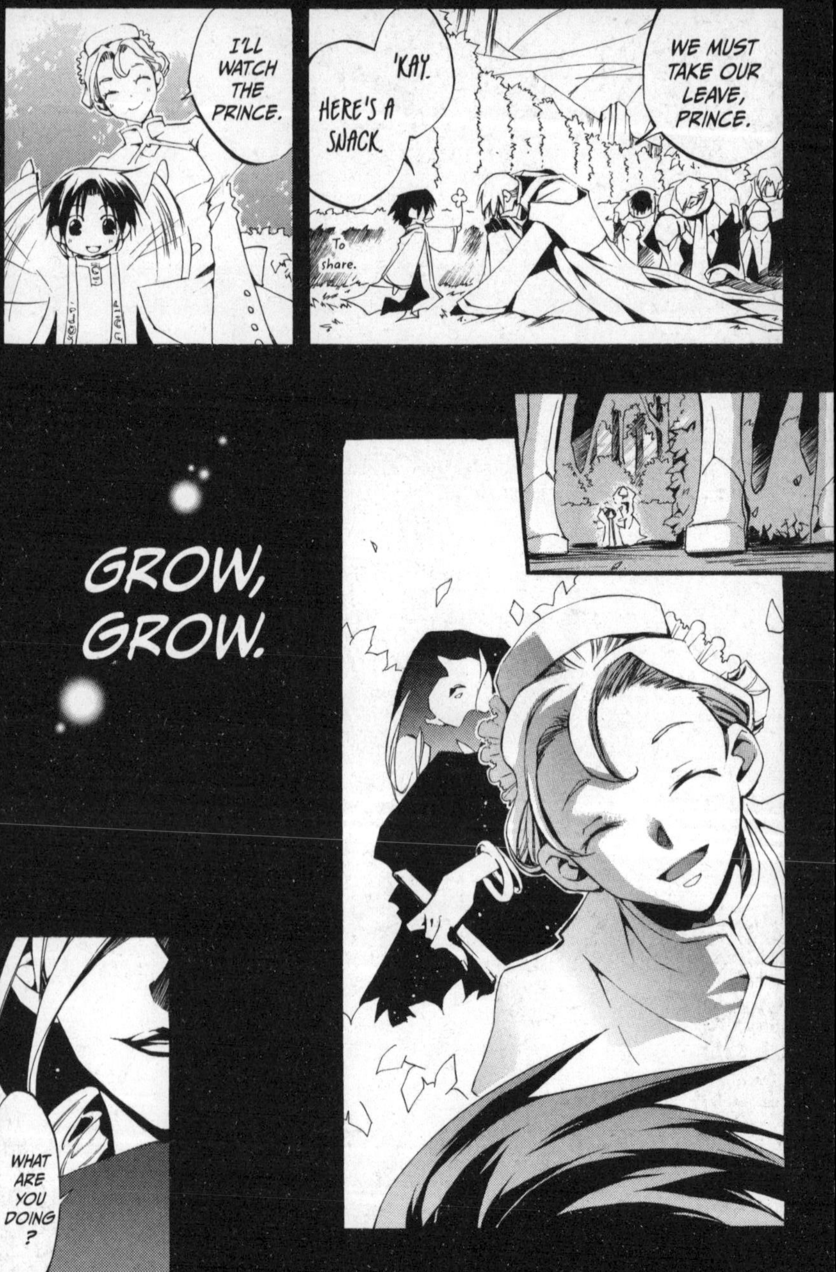
WE MUST TAKE OUR LEAVE, PRINCE.
'KAY.
HERE'S A SNACK.
To share.
I'LL WATCH THE PRINCE.
GROW, GROW.
WHAT ARE YOU DOING?

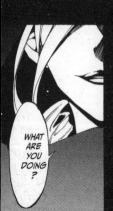

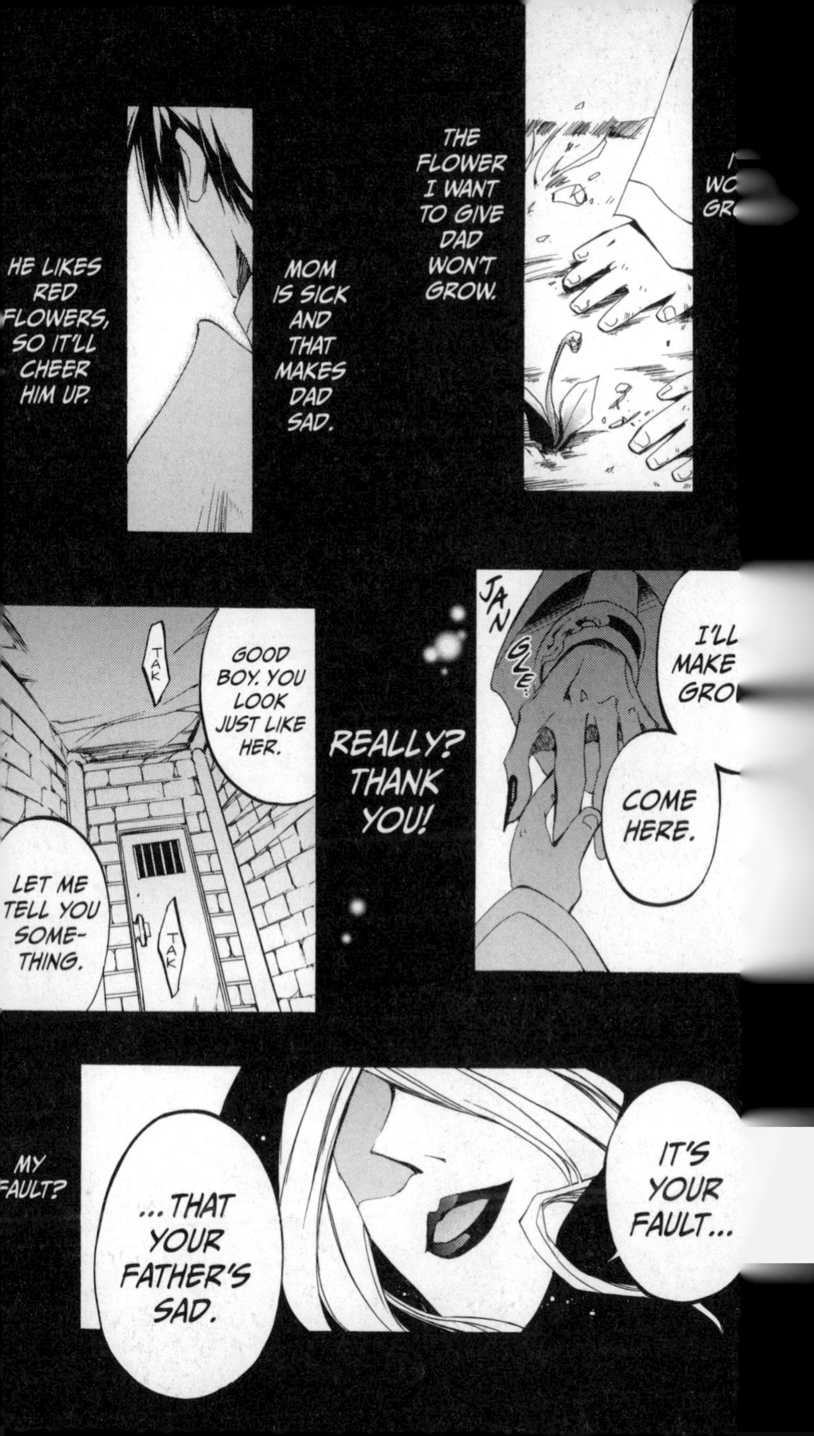
THE FLOWER I WANT TO GIVE DAD WON'T GROW.
MOM IS SICK AND THAT MAKES DAD SAD.
HE LIKES RED FLOWERS, SO IT'LL CHEER HIM UP.
JANGLE
I'LL MAKE
COME HERE.
REALLY? THANK YOU!
TAK
GOOD BOY. YOU LOOK JUST LIKE HER.
TAK
LET ME TELL YOU SOMETHING.
IT'S YOUR FAULT...
...THAT YOUR FATHER'S SAD.
MY FAULT?

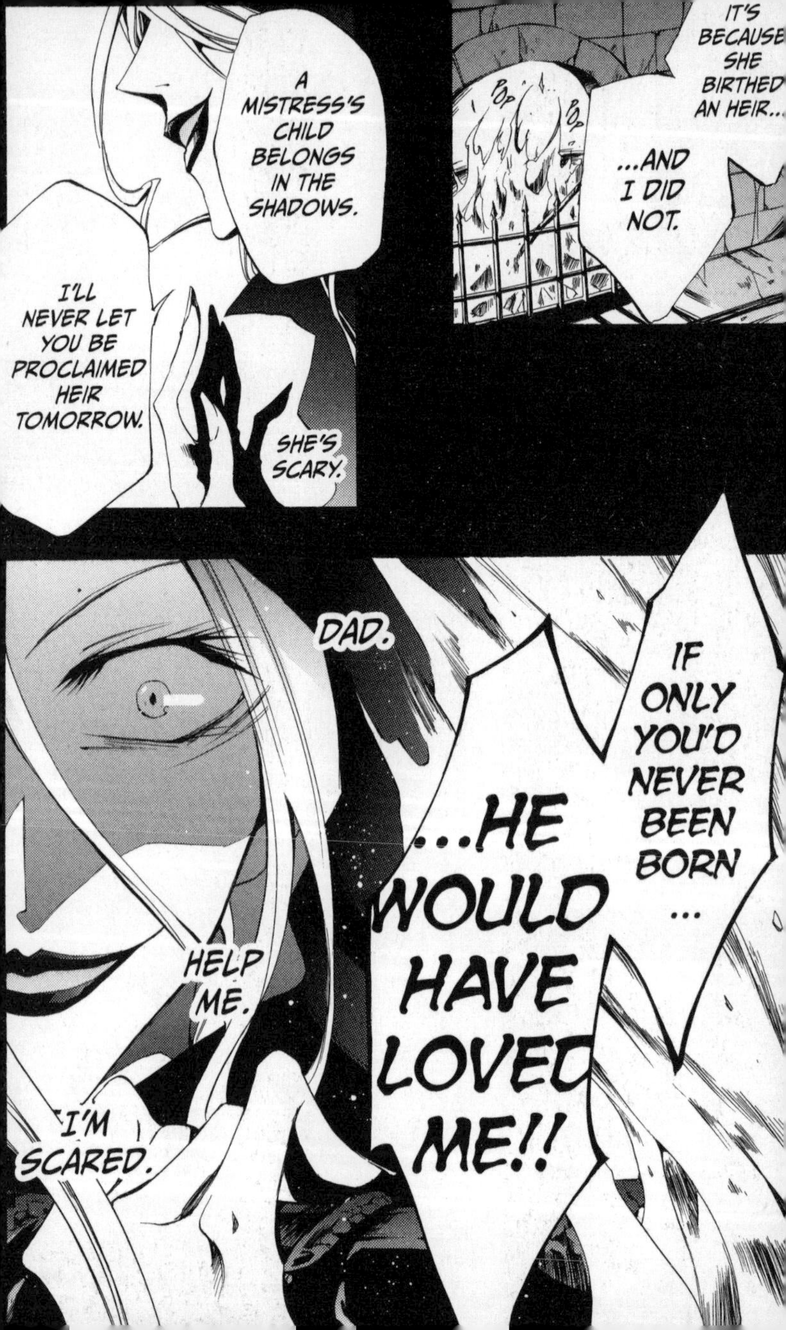
IT'S BECAUSE SHE BIRTHED AN HEIR...
...AND I DID NOT.
A MISTRESS'S CHILD BELONGS IN THE SHADOWS.
I'LL NEVER LET YOU BE PROCLAIMED HEIR TOMORROW.
SHE'S SCARY.
IF ONLY YOU'D NEVER BEEN BORN...
...HE WOULD HAVE LOVED ME!!
DAD.
HELP ME.
I'M SCARED.

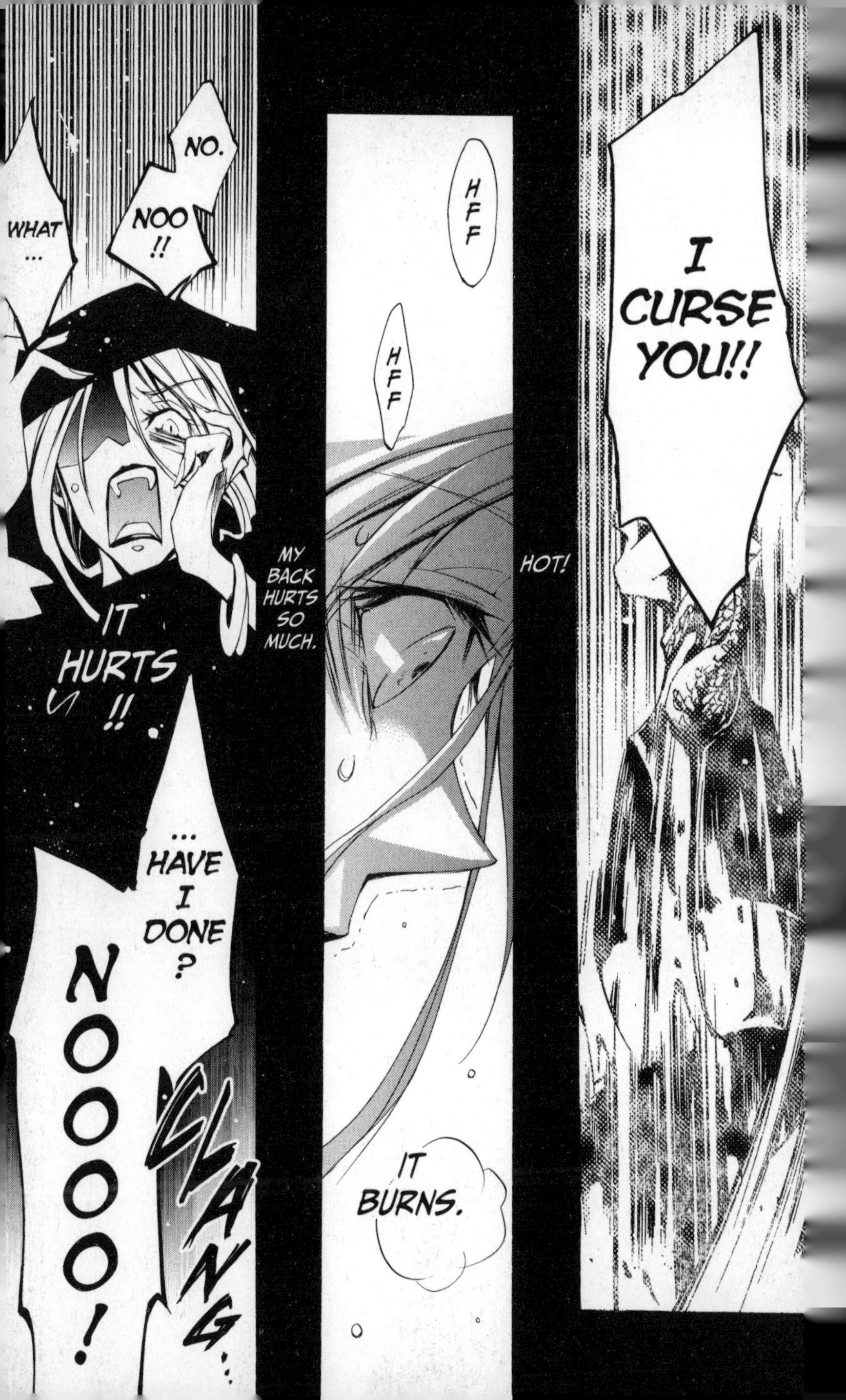
I CURSE YOU!!
HOT!
HFF
HFF
MY BACK HURTS SO MUCH.
IT BURNS.
NO.
NOO!!
WHAT ...
IT HURTS!!
... HAVE I DONE?
NOOOOO!
CLANG...

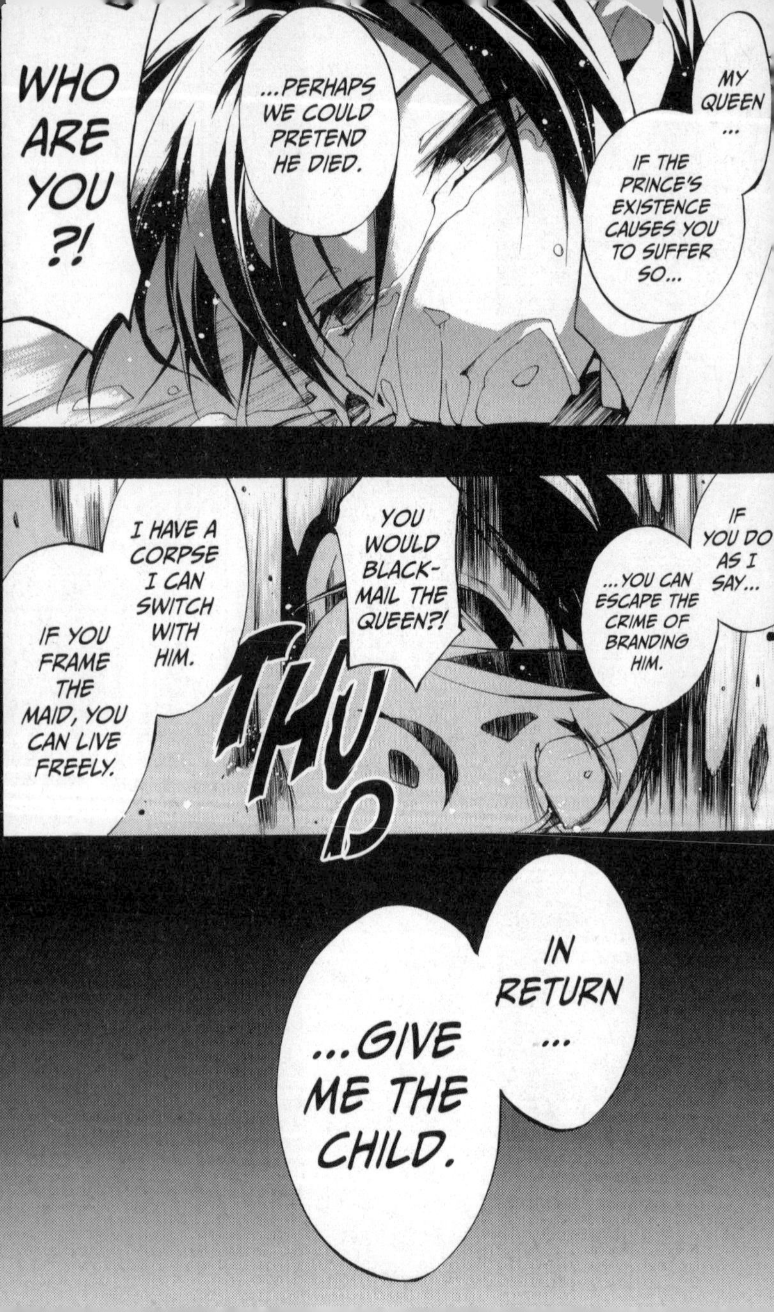
MY QUEEN ...
IF THE PRINCE'S EXISTENCE CAUSES YOU TO SUFFER SO...
...PERHAPS WE COULD PRETEND HE DIED.
WHO ARE YOU?!
IF YOU DO AS I SAY...
...YOU CAN ESCAPE THE CRIME OF BRANDING HIM.
YOU WOULD BLACK-MAIL THE QUEEN?!
THUD
I HAVE A CORPSE I CAN SWITCH WITH HIM.
IF YOU FRAME THE MAID, YOU CAN LIVE FREELY.
IN RETURN ...
...GIVE ME THE CHILD.

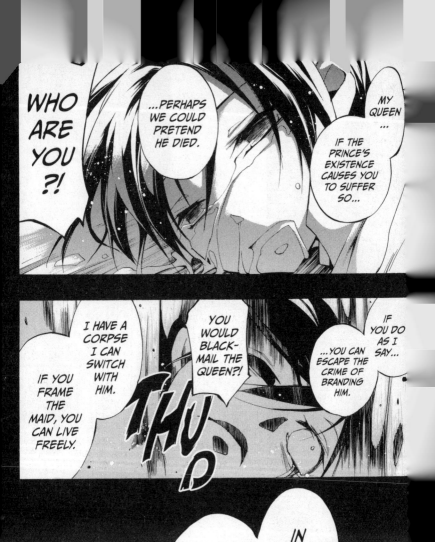

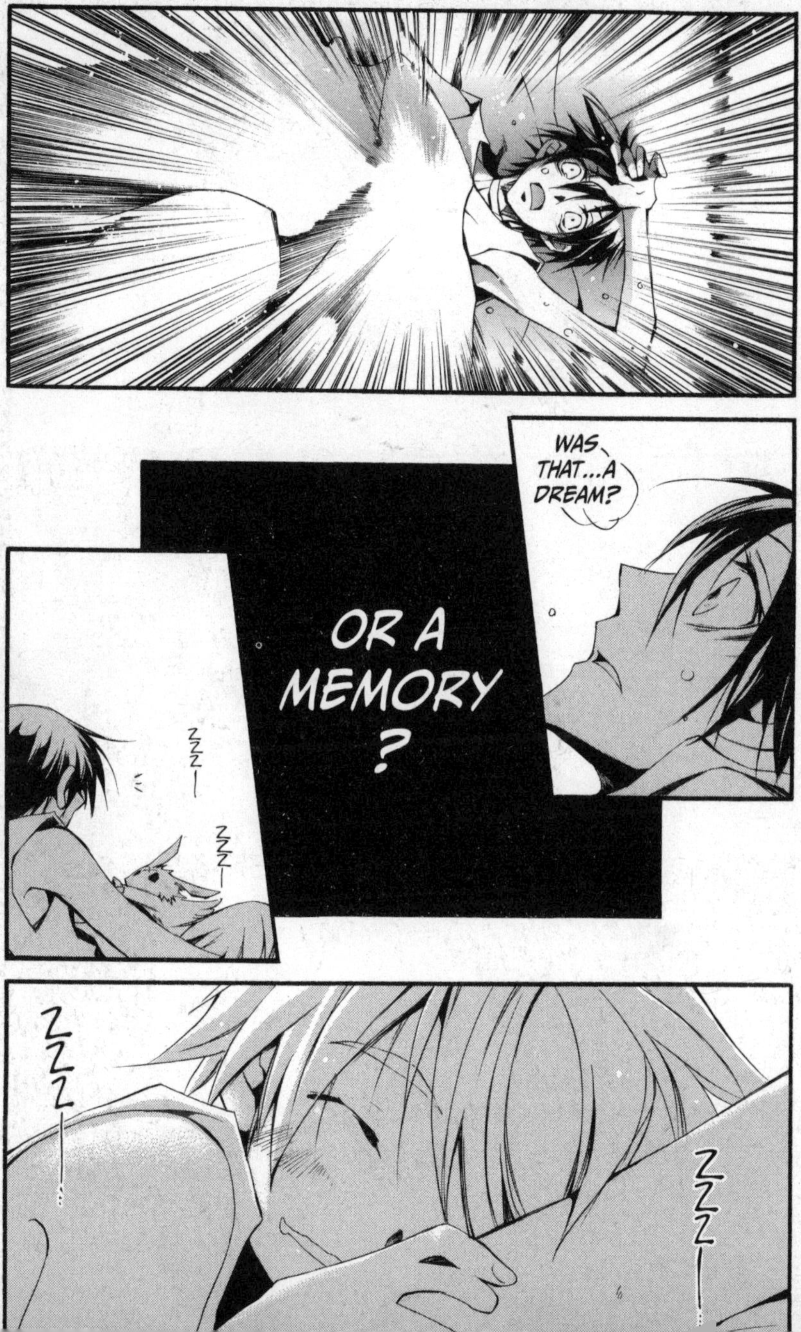
WAS THAT...A DREAM?
OR A MEMORY?
ZZZ—
ZZZ—
ZZZ—...
ZZZ—...

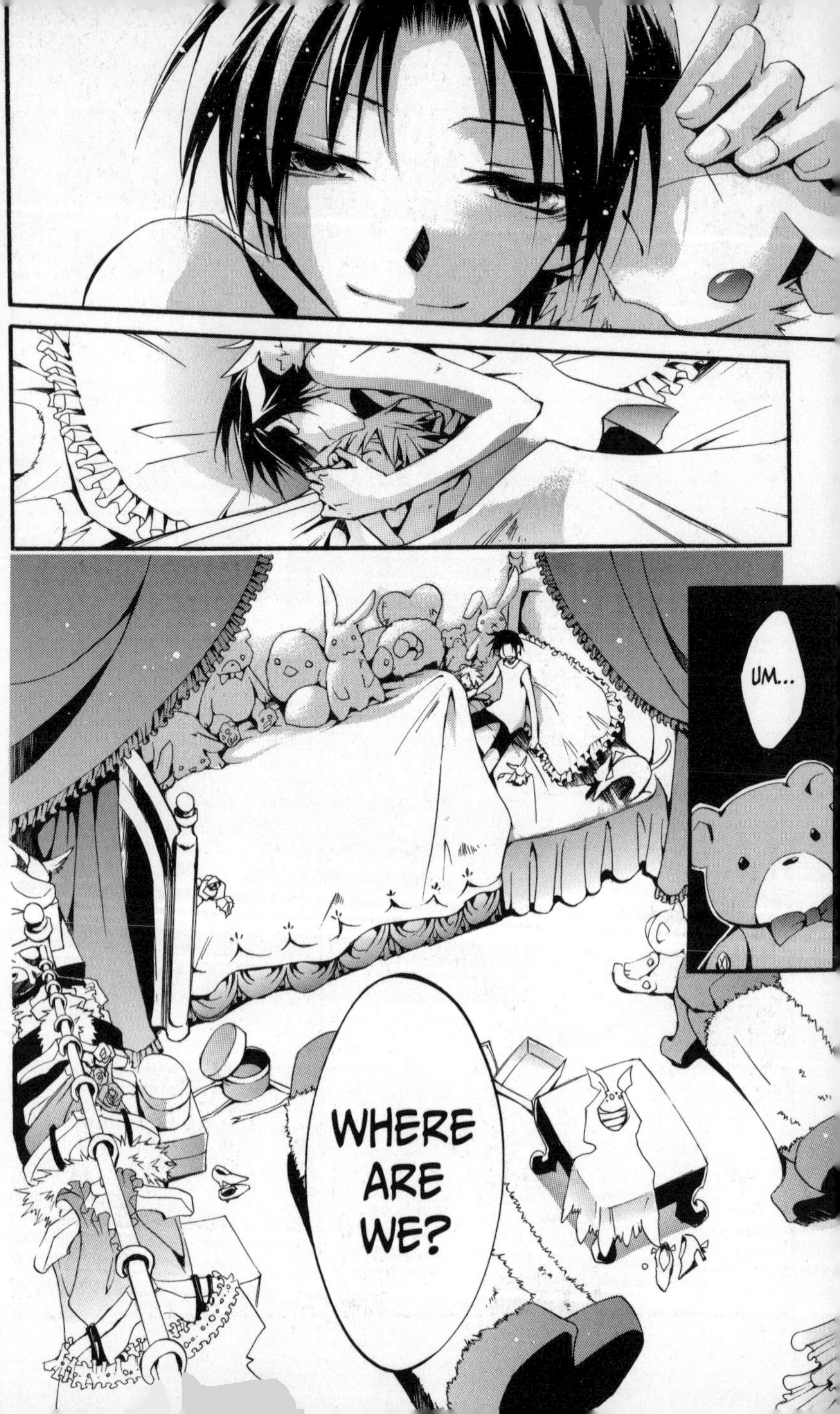
UM...
WHERE ARE WE?

Kapitel.35 "The Hated One"

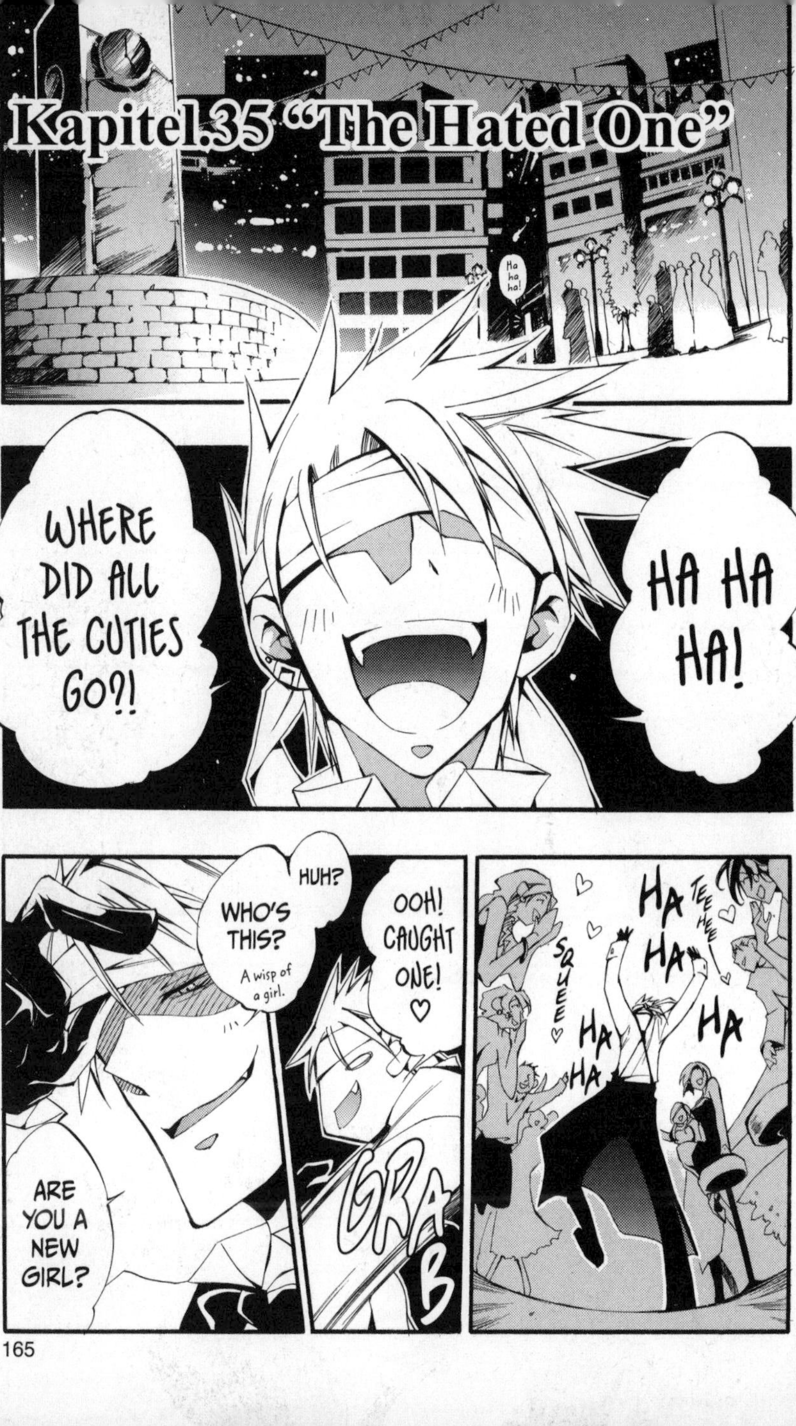

Ha ha ha!
HA HA HA!
WHERE DID ALL THE CUTIES GO?!
HA HA HA HA HA HA
TEE HEE
SQUEEE ♡
OOH! CAUGHT ONE! ♡
GRAB
HUH? WHO'S THIS?
A wisp of a girl.
ARE YOU A NEW GIRL?

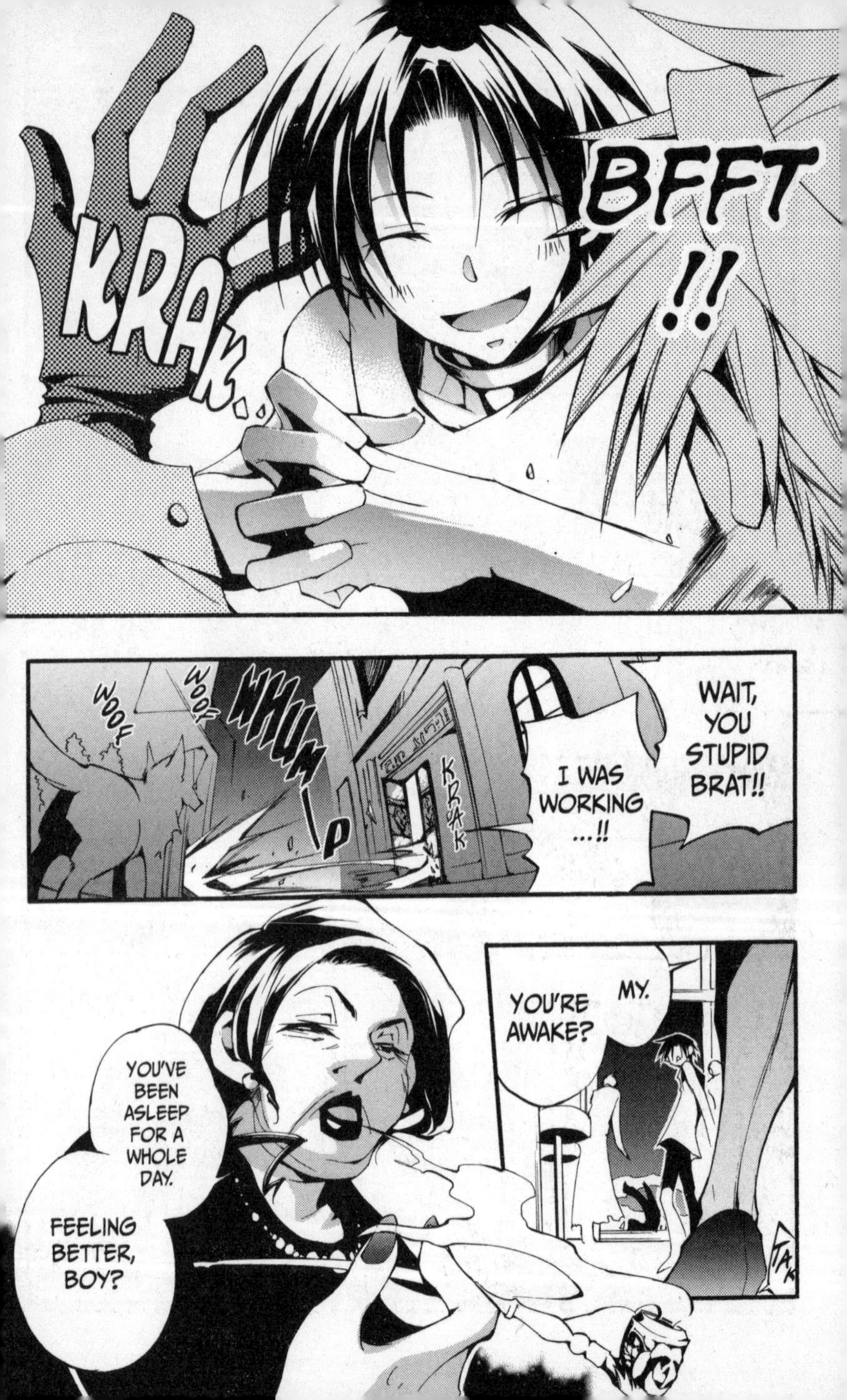
BFFT!!
KRAK..
WAIT, YOU STUPID BRAT!!
I WAS WORKING ...!!
KRAK
WHUMP
WOOF
WOOF
MY.
YOU'RE AWAKE?
TAK
YOU'VE BEEN ASLEEP FOR A WHOLE DAY.
FEELING BETTER, BOY?

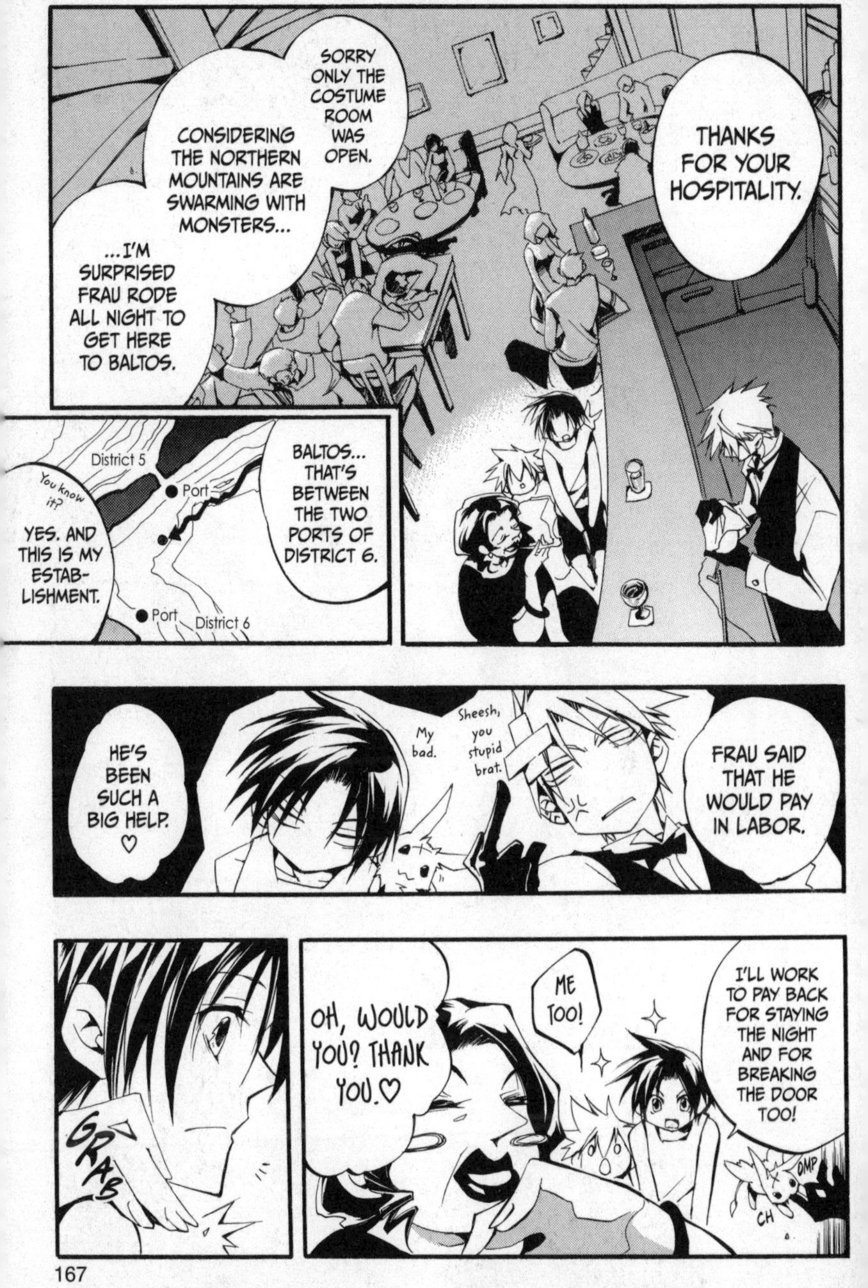
THANKS FOR YOUR HOSPITALITY.
SORRY ONLY THE COSTUME ROOM WAS OPEN.
CONSIDERING THE NORTHERN MOUNTAINS ARE SWARMING WITH MONSTERS...
...I'M SURPRISED FRAU RODE ALL NIGHT TO GET HERE TO BALTOS.
BALTOS... THAT'S BETWEEN THE TWO PORTS OF DISTRICT 6.
District 5
Port
Port
District 6
You know it?
YES. AND THIS IS MY ESTAB-LISHMENT.
FRAU SAID THAT HE WOULD PAY IN LABOR.
Sheesh, you stupid brat.
My bad.
HE'S BEEN SUCH A BIG HELP. ♡
I'LL WORK TO PAY BACK FOR STAYING THE NIGHT AND FOR BREAKING THE DOOR TOO!
ME TOO!
OMP
CH
OH, WOULD YOU? THANK YOU. ♡
GRAB

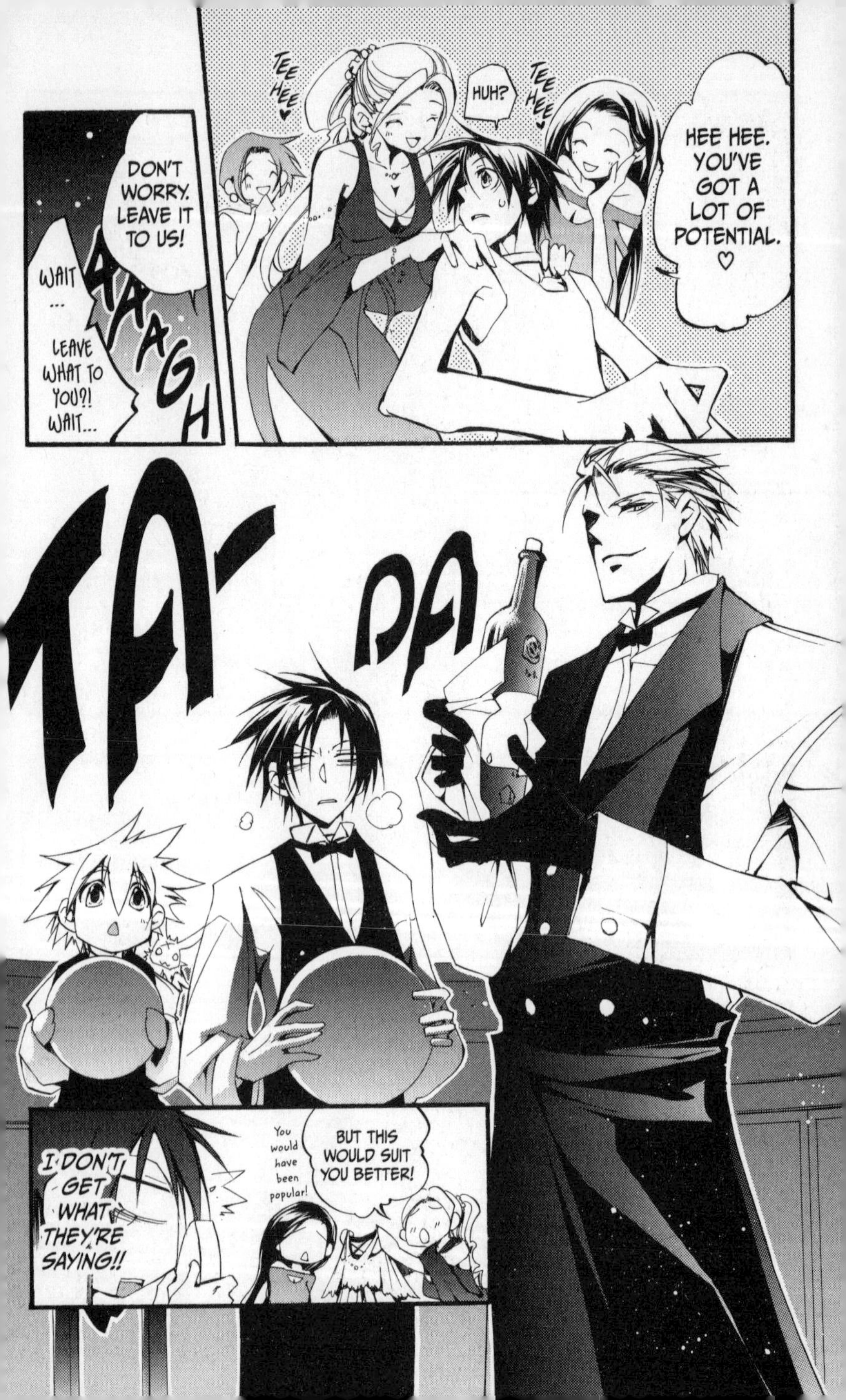

HEE HEE. YOU'VE GOT A LOT OF POTENTIAL. ♡
TEE HEE ♥
HUH?
TEE HEE ♥
DON'T WORRY. LEAVE IT TO US!
BRAAGH
WAIT... LEAVE WHAT TO YOU?! WAIT...
TA-DA
BUT THIS WOULD SUIT YOU BETTER!
You would have been popular!
I DON'T GET WHAT THEY'RE SAYING!!

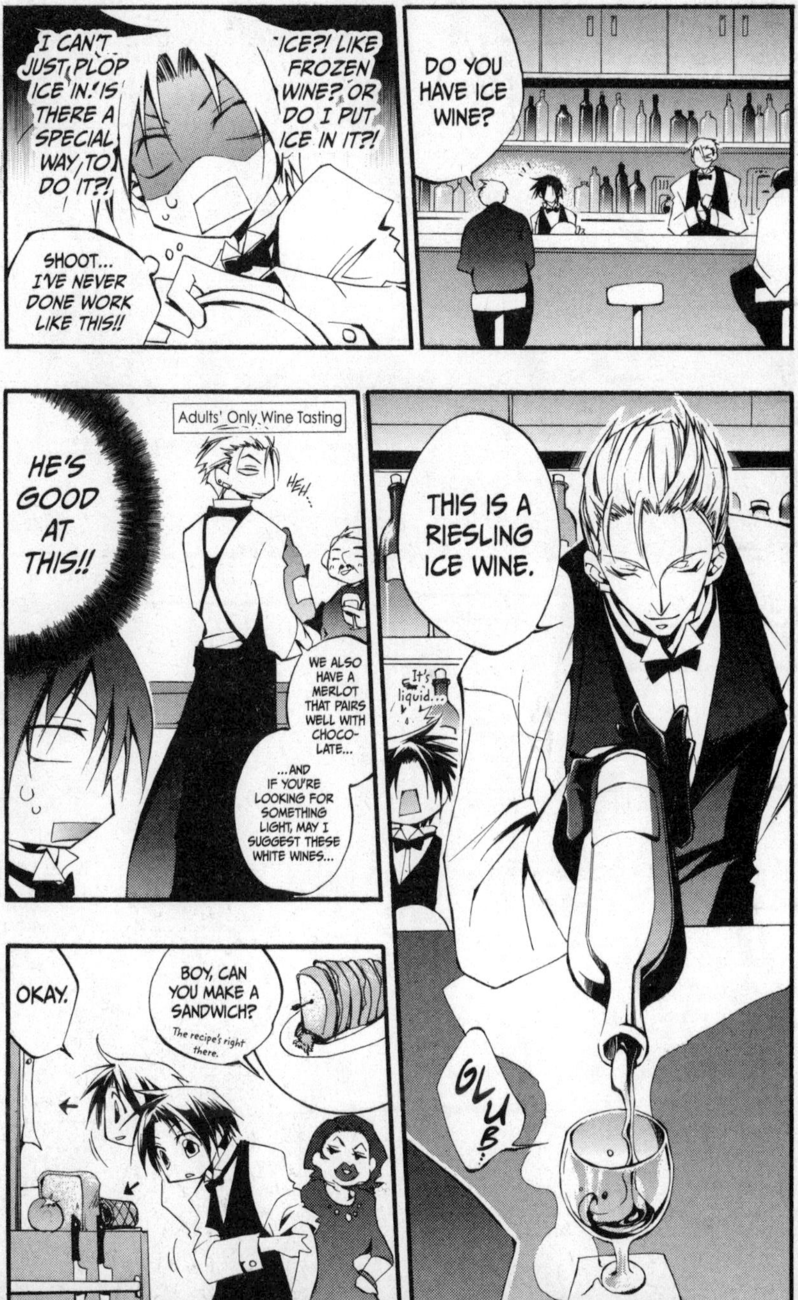
DO YOU HAVE ICE WINE?
ICE?! LIKE FROZEN WINE? OR DO I PUT ICE IN IT?!
I CAN'T JUST PLOP ICE IN! IS THERE A SPECIAL WAY TO DO IT?!
SHOOT... I'VE NEVER DONE WORK LIKE THIS!!
THIS IS A RIESLING ICE WINE.
It's liquid...
GLUB...
Adults' Only Wine Tasting
HEH...
HE'S GOOD AT THIS!!
WE ALSO HAVE A MERLOT THAT PAIRS WELL WITH CHOCO-LATE...
...AND IF YOU'RE LOOKING FOR SOMETHING LIGHT, MAY I SUGGEST THESE WHITE WINES...
BOY, CAN YOU MAKE A SANDWICH?
The recipe's right there.
OKAY.

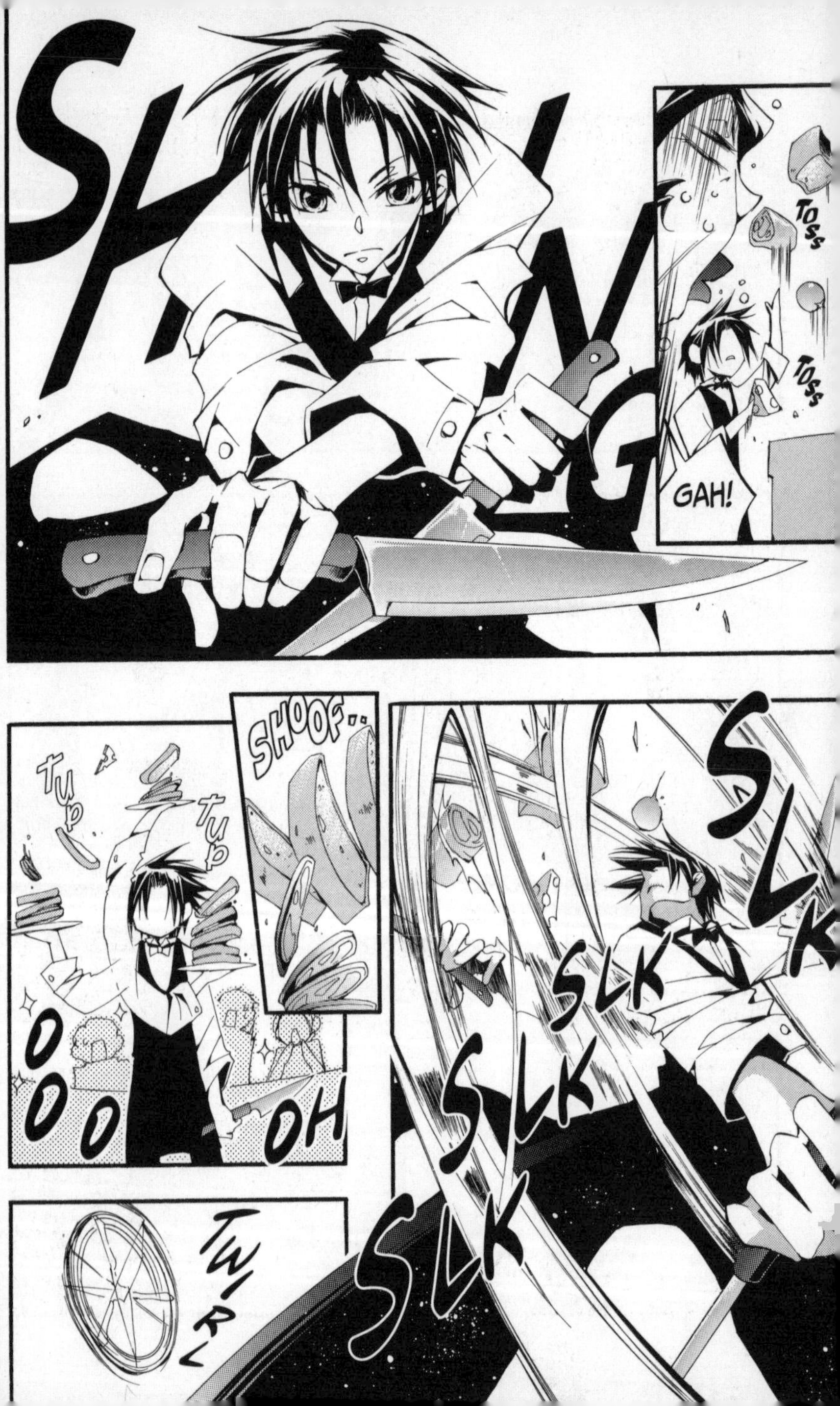
TOSS
TOSS
GAH!
SHING
SLK
SLK
SLK
SLK
SLK
SHOOF..
TUP
TUP
OOOOH
TWIRL

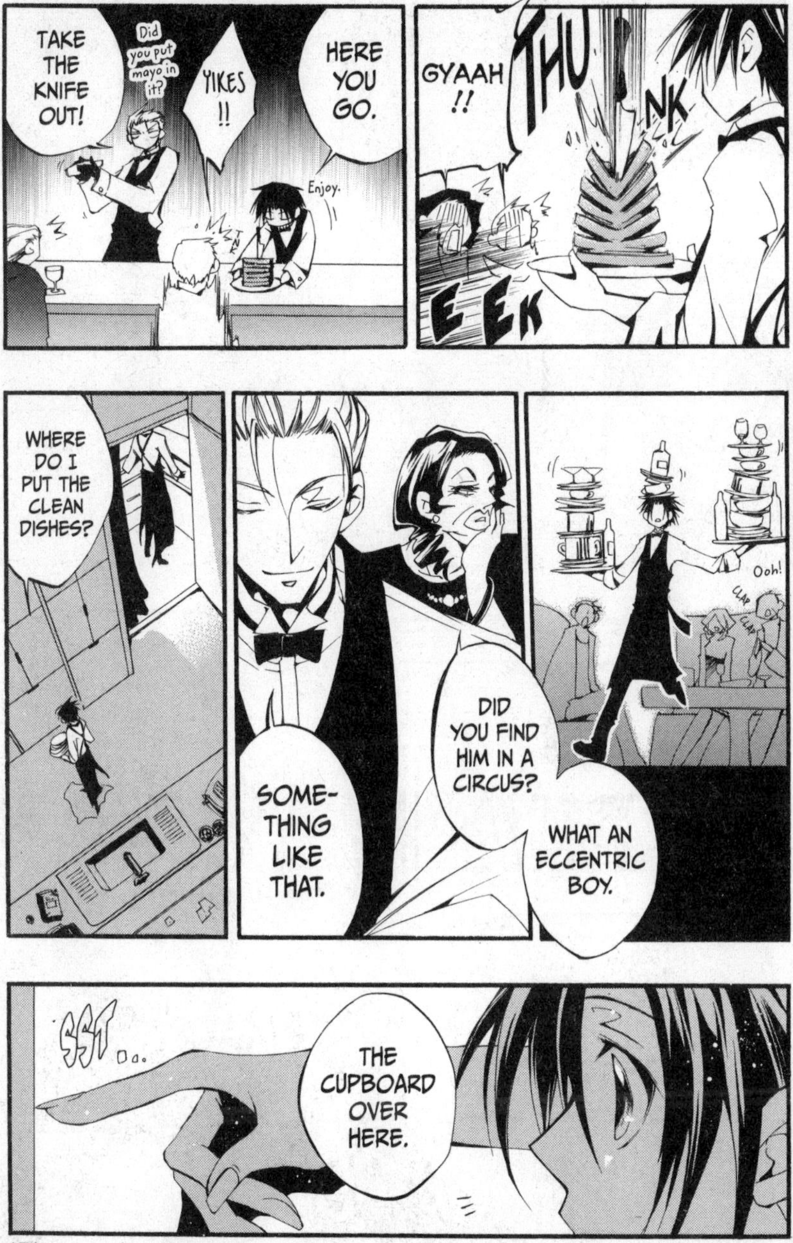
GYAAH!!
THUNK
EEK
HERE YOU GO.
YIKES!!
Did you put mayo in it?
TAKE THE KNIFE OUT!
Enjoy.
TNK
Ooh!
CLAP CLAP
DID YOU FIND HIM IN A CIRCUS?
WHAT AN ECCENTRIC BOY.
SOME-THING LIKE THAT.
WHERE DO I PUT THE CLEAN DISHES?
THE CUPBOARD OVER HERE.
SST

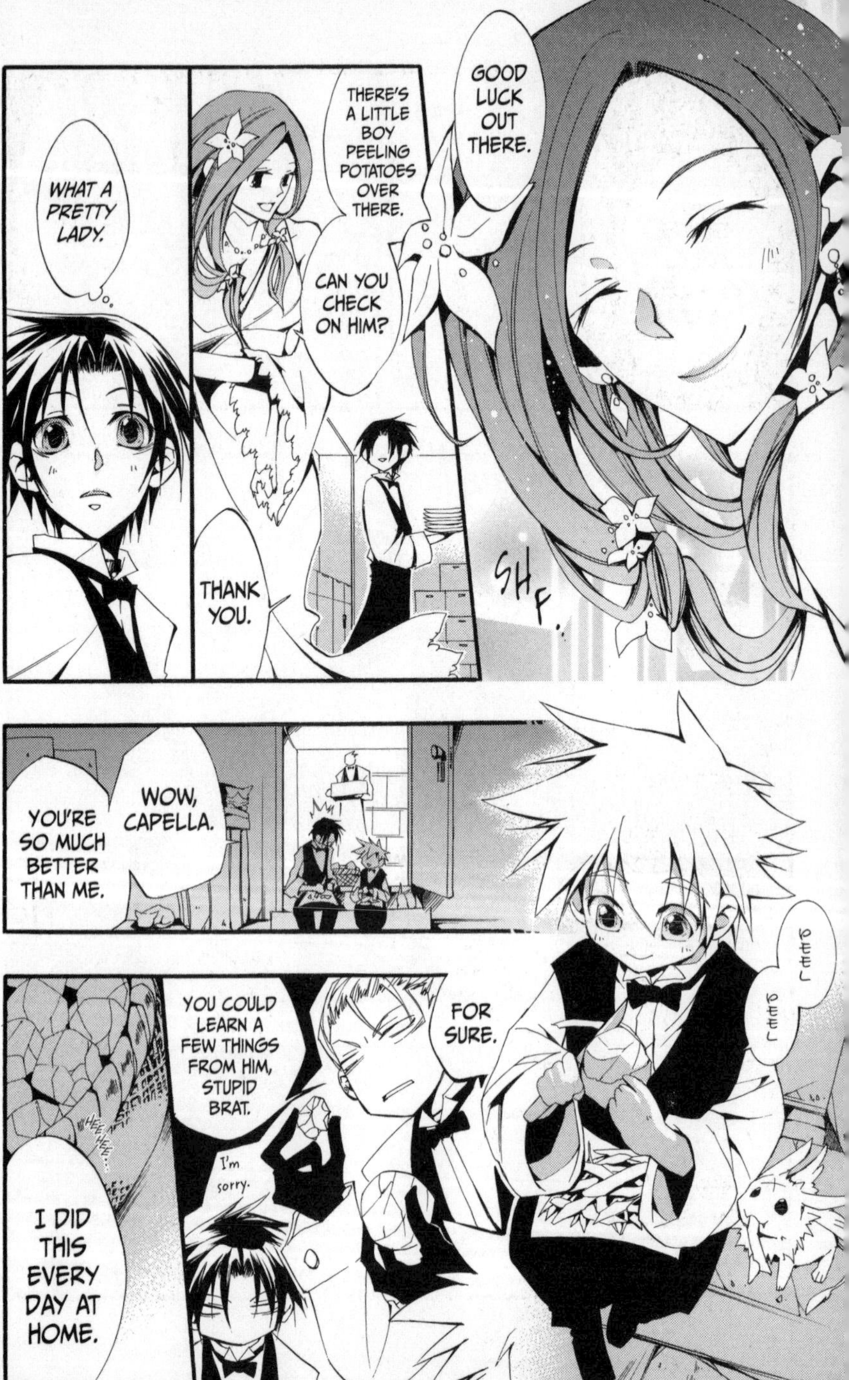
GOOD LUCK OUT THERE.
SHF.
THERE'S A LITTLE BOY PEELING POTATOES OVER THERE.
CAN YOU CHECK ON HIM?
THANK YOU.
WHAT A PRETTY LADY.
WOW, CAPELLA.
YOU'RE SO MUCH BETTER THAN ME.
FOR SURE.
YOU COULD LEARN A FEW THINGS FROM HIM, STUPID BRAT.
I'm sorry.
HEE HEE...
I DID THIS EVERY DAY AT HOME.

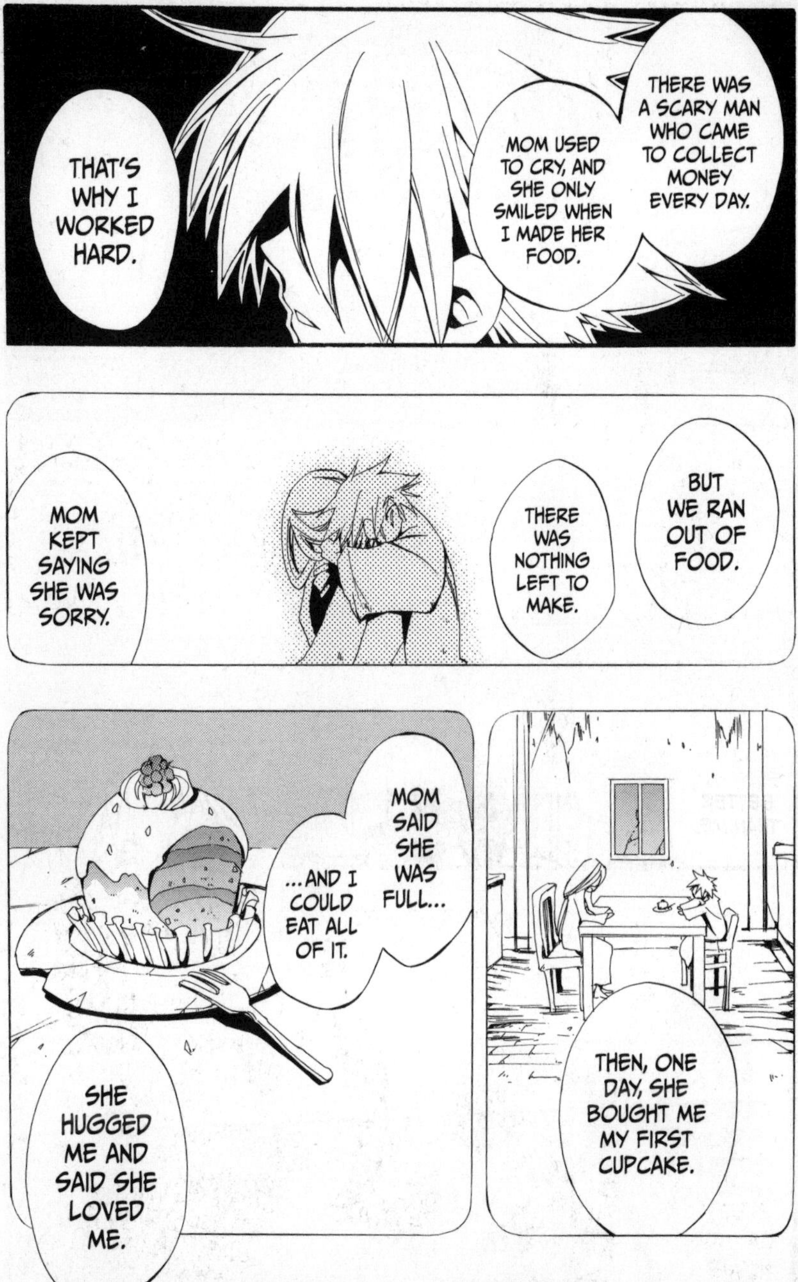
THERE WAS A SCARY MAN WHO CAME TO COLLECT MONEY EVERY DAY.
MOM USED TO CRY, AND SHE ONLY SMILED WHEN I MADE HER FOOD.
THAT'S WHY I WORKED HARD.
BUT WE RAN OUT OF FOOD.
THERE WAS NOTHING LEFT TO MAKE.
MOM KEPT SAYING SHE WAS SORRY.
THEN, ONE DAY, SHE BOUGHT ME MY FIRST CUPCAKE.
MOM SAID SHE WAS FULL...
...AND I COULD EAT ALL OF IT.
SHE HUGGED ME AND SAID SHE LOVED ME.

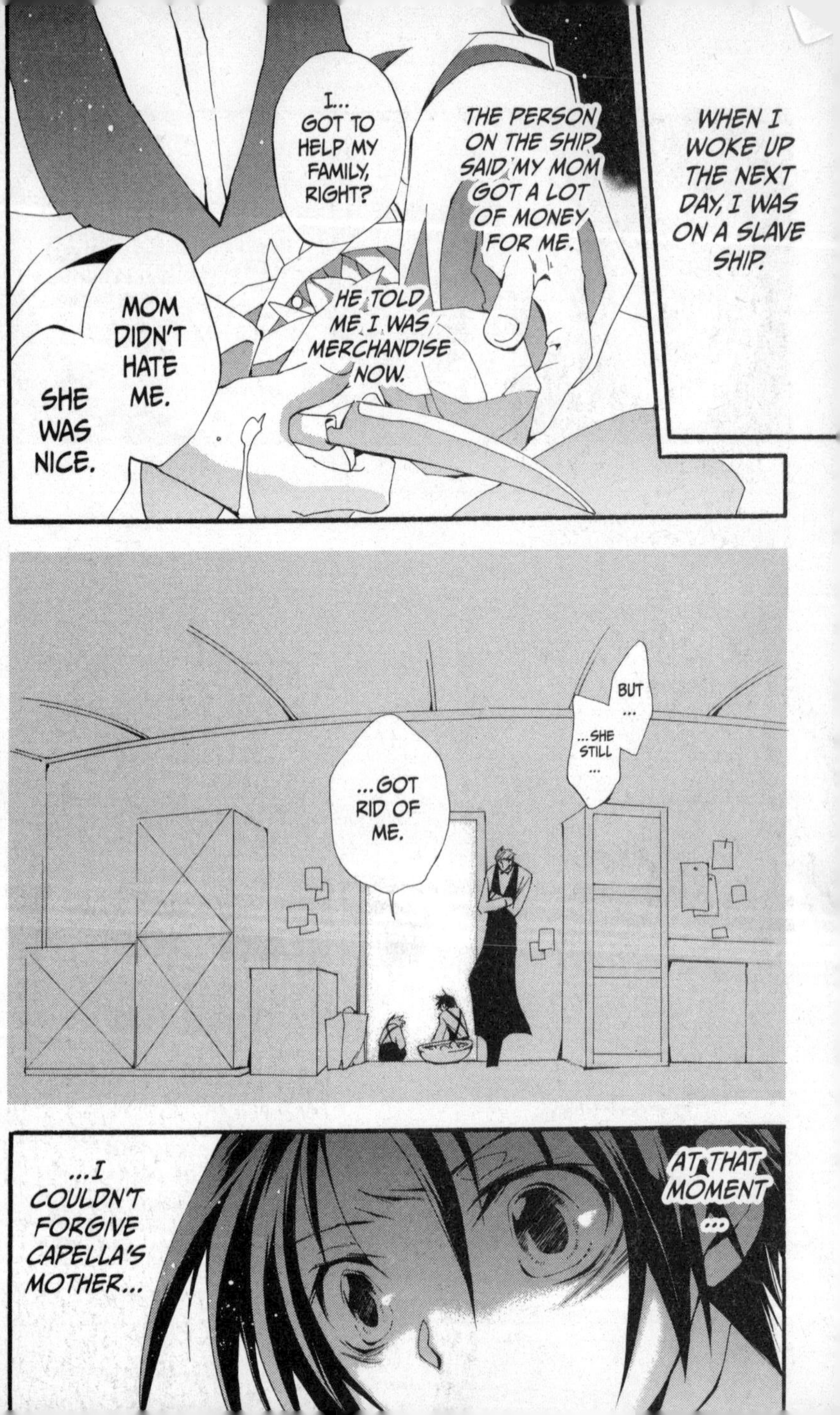
WHEN I WOKE UP THE NEXT DAY, I WAS ON A SLAVE SHIP.
THE PERSON ON THE SHIP SAID MY MOM GOT A LOT OF MONEY FOR ME.
I... GOT TO HELP MY FAMILY, RIGHT?
HE TOLD ME I WAS MERCHANDISE NOW.
MOM DIDN'T HATE ME.
SHE WAS NICE.
BUT ...
...SHE STILL ...
...GOT RID OF ME.
AT THAT MOMENT ...
...I COULDN'T FORGIVE CAPELLA'S MOTHER...

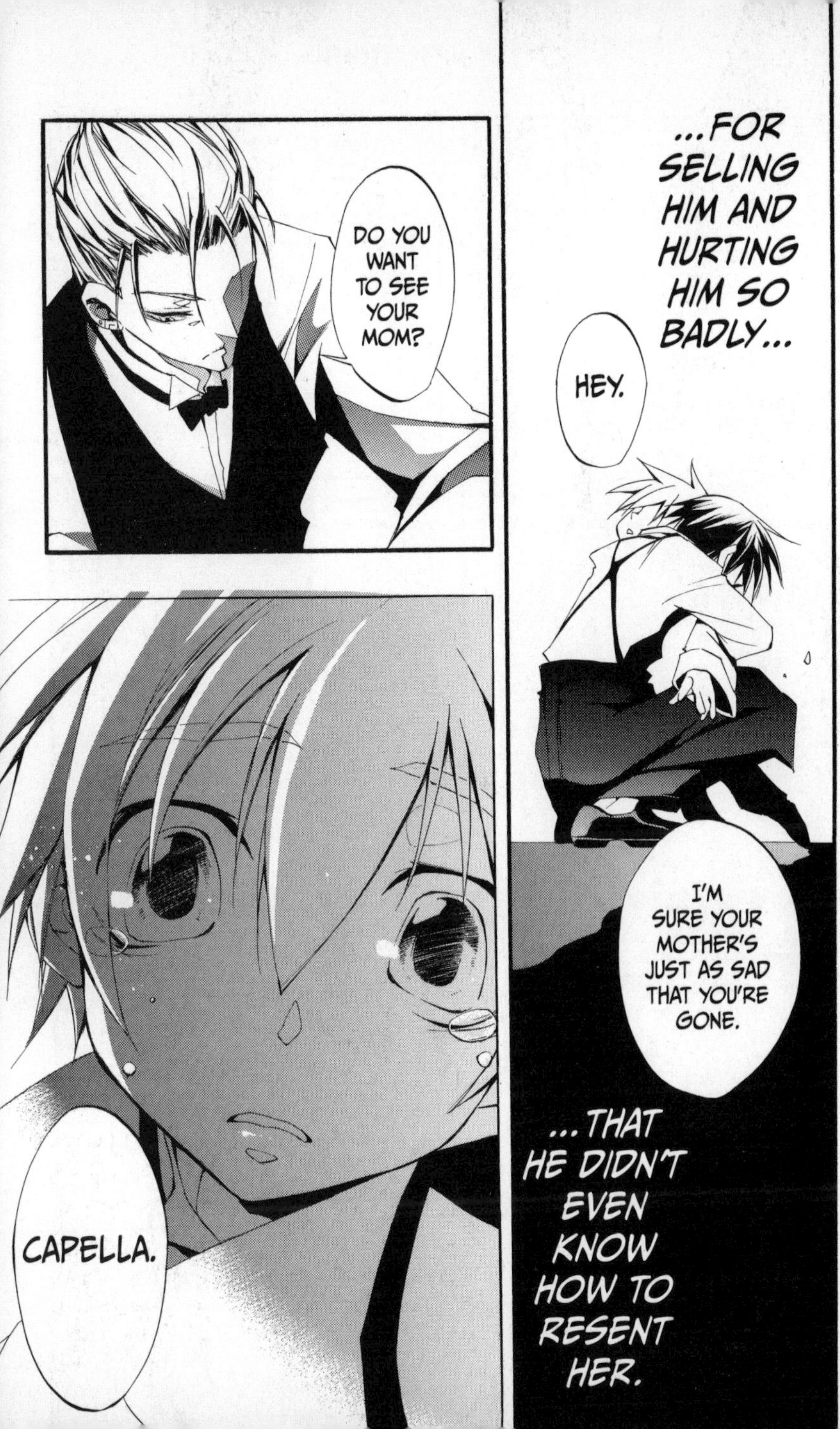
...FOR SELLING HIM AND HURTING HIM SO BADLY...
HEY.
I'M SURE YOUR MOTHER'S JUST AS SAD THAT YOU'RE GONE.
...THAT HE DIDN'T EVEN KNOW HOW TO RESENT HER.
DO YOU WANT TO SEE YOUR MOM?
CAPELLA.

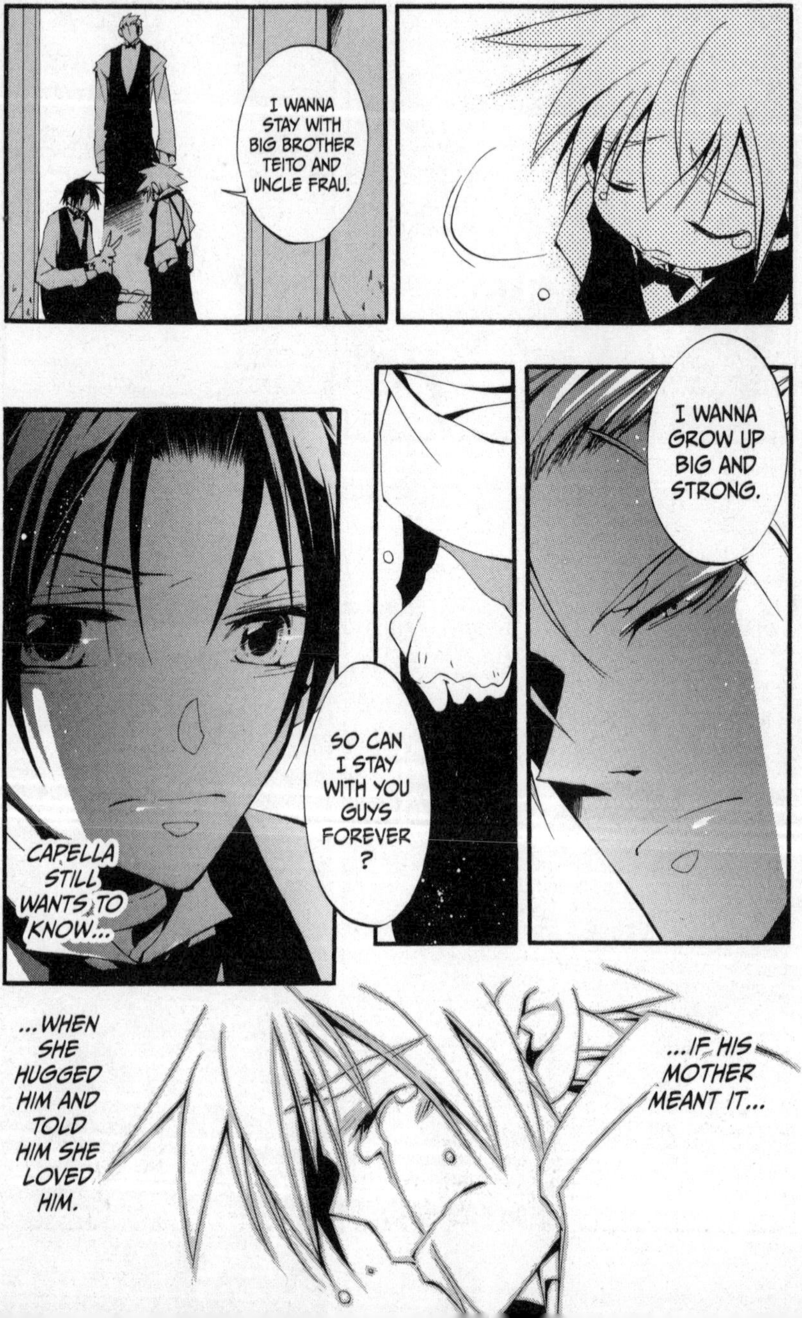
I WANNA STAY WITH BIG BROTHER TEITO AND UNCLE FRAU.
I WANNA GROW UP BIG AND STRONG.
SO CAN I STAY WITH YOU GUYS FOREVER?
CAPELLA STILL WANTS TO KNOW...
...IF HIS MOTHER MEANT IT...
...WHEN SHE HUGGED HIM AND TOLD HIM SHE LOVED HIM.

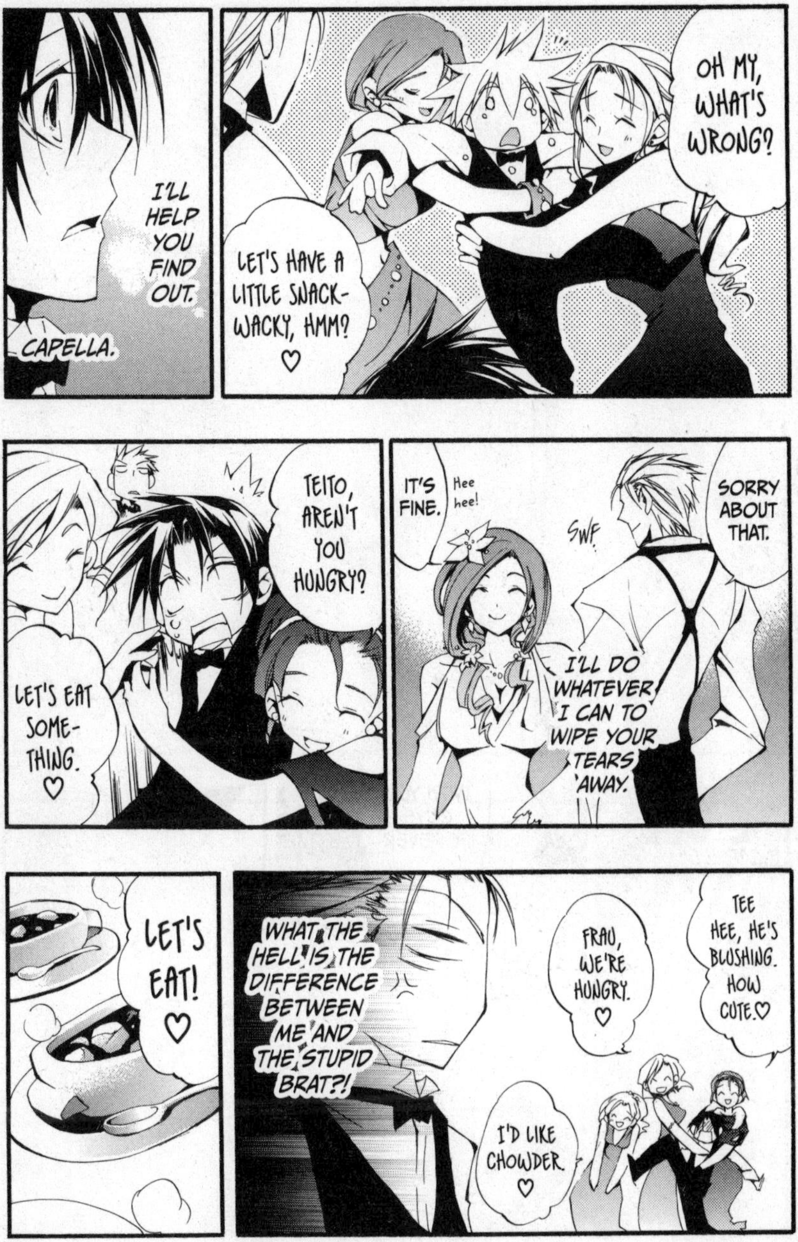
OH MY, WHAT'S WRONG?
LET'S HAVE A LITTLE SNACK-WACKY, HMM? ♡
I'LL HELP YOU FIND OUT.
CAPELLA.
SORRY ABOUT THAT.
SWF
IT'S FINE.
Hee hee!
I'LL DO WHATEVER I CAN TO WIPE YOUR TEARS AWAY.
TEITO, AREN'T YOU HUNGRY?
LET'S EAT SOMETHING. ♡
TEE HEE, HE'S BLUSHING. HOW CUTE.♡
FRAU, WE'RE HUNGRY. ♡
WHAT THE HELL IS THE DIFFERENCE BETWEEN ME AND THE STUPID BRAT?!
I'D LIKE CHOWDER. ♡
LET'S EAT! ♡

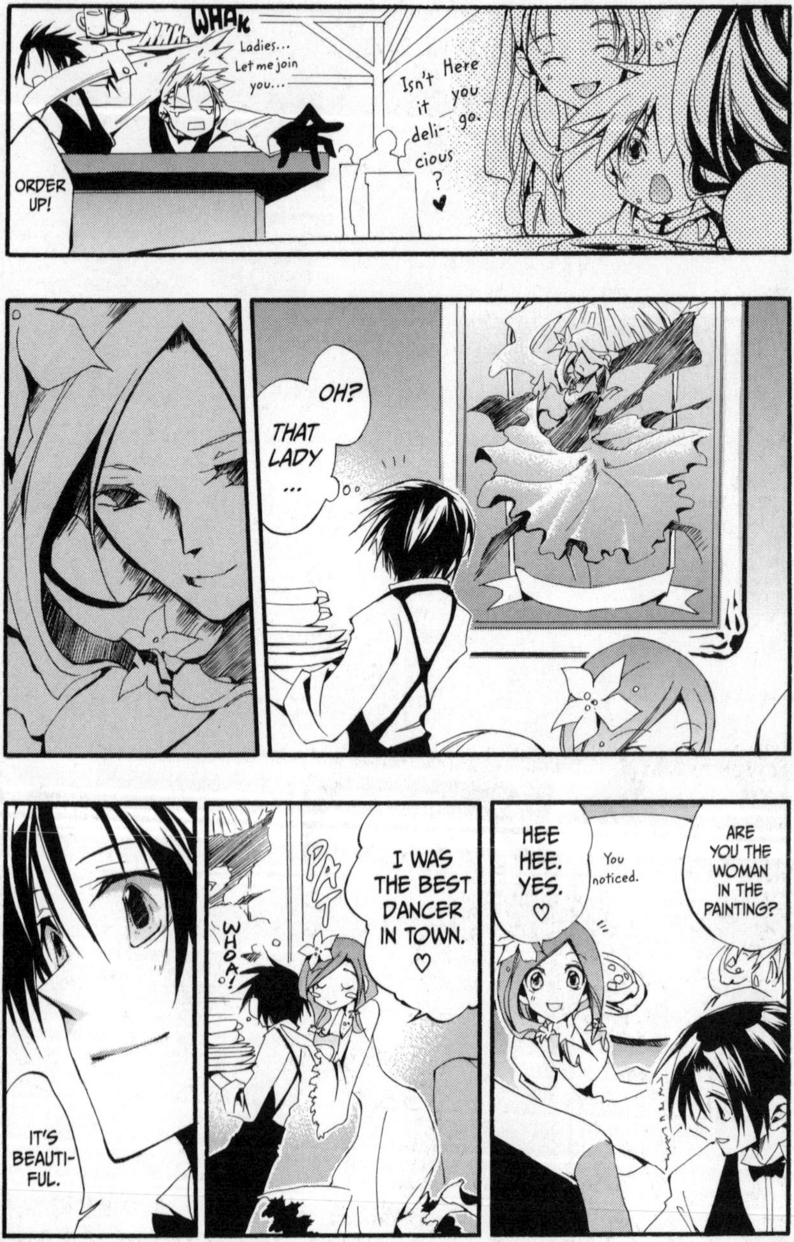
Here you go.
Isn't it delicious? ♥
WHAK
Ladies... Let me join you...
ORDER UP!
OH? THAT LADY ...
ARE YOU THE WOMAN IN THE PAINTING?
You noticed.
HEE HEE. YES. ♡
I WAS THE BEST DANCER IN TOWN. ♡
PAT
WHOA!
IT'S BEAUTI-FUL.

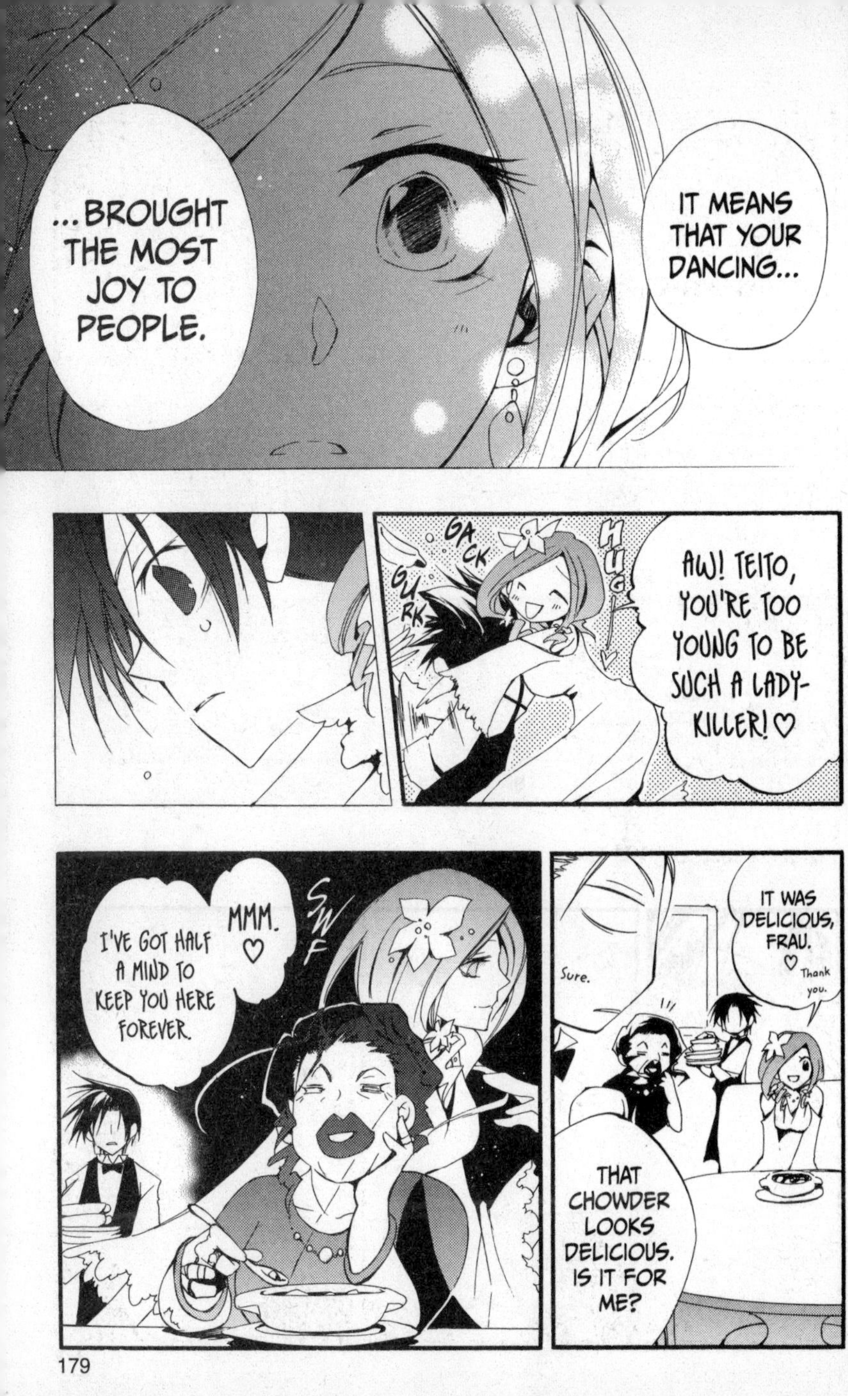
IT MEANS THAT YOUR DANCING...
...BROUGHT THE MOST JOY TO PEOPLE.
HUG
GACK
GURK
AW! TEITO, YOU'RE TOO YOUNG TO BE SUCH A LADY-KILLER! ♡
IT WAS DELICIOUS, FRAU. ♡
Thank you.
Sure.
THAT CHOWDER LOOKS DELICIOUS. IS IT FOR ME?
SWF
MMM. ♡
I'VE GOT HALF A MIND TO KEEP YOU HERE FOREVER.

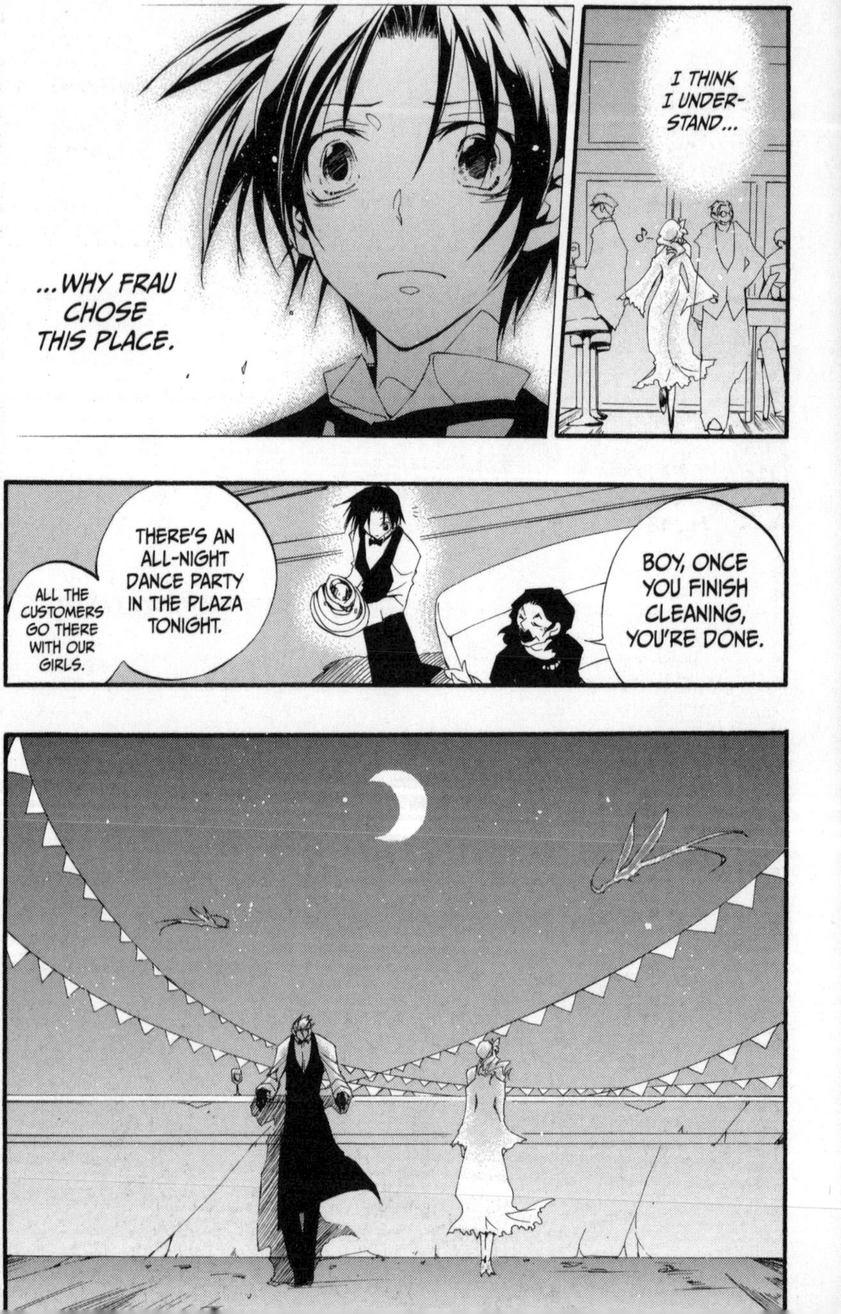
I THINK I UNDER-STAND...
...WHY FRAU CHOSE THIS PLACE.
BOY, ONCE YOU FINISH CLEANING, YOU'RE DONE.
THERE'S AN ALL-NIGHT DANCE PARTY IN THE PLAZA TONIGHT.
ALL THE CUSTOMERS GO THERE WITH OUR GIRLS.

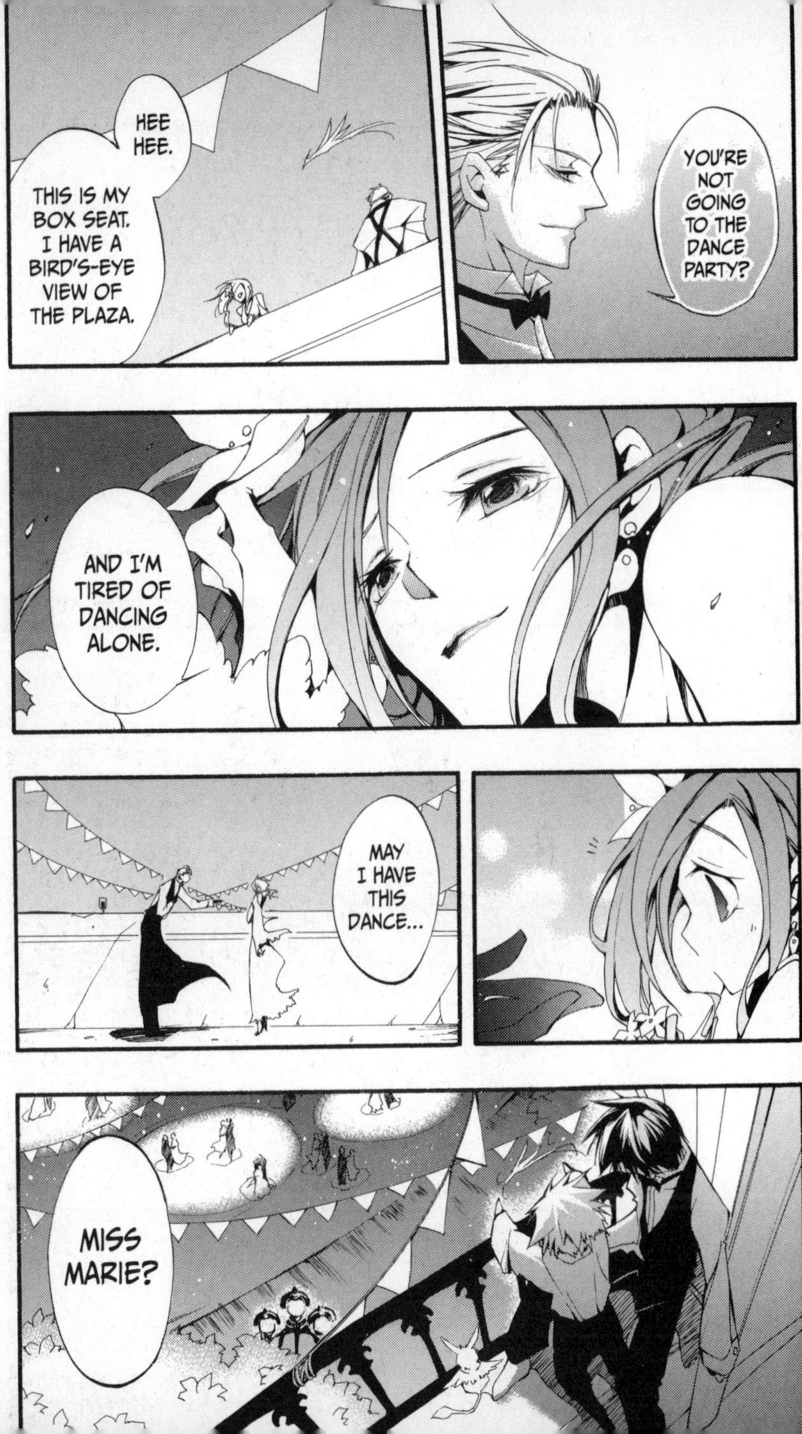
YOU'RE NOT GOING TO THE DANCE PARTY?
HEE HEE.
THIS IS MY BOX SEAT. I HAVE A BIRD'S-EYE VIEW OF THE PLAZA.
AND I'M TIRED OF DANCING ALONE.
MAY I HAVE THIS DANCE...
MISS MARIE?

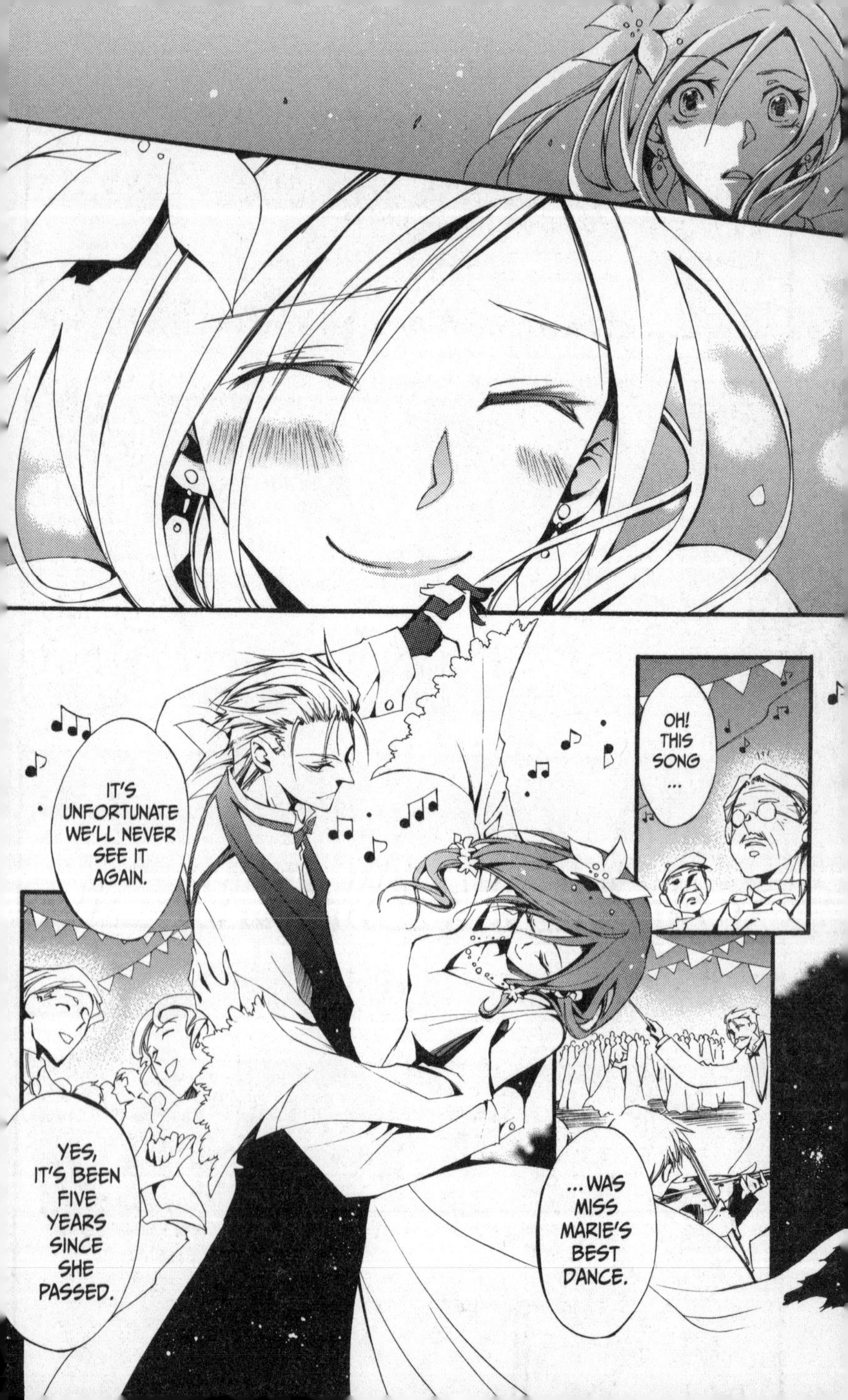
OH! THIS SONG ...
...WAS MISS MARIE'S BEST DANCE.
YES, IT'S BEEN FIVE YEARS SINCE SHE PASSED.
IT'S UNFORTUNATE WE'LL NEVER SEE IT AGAIN.

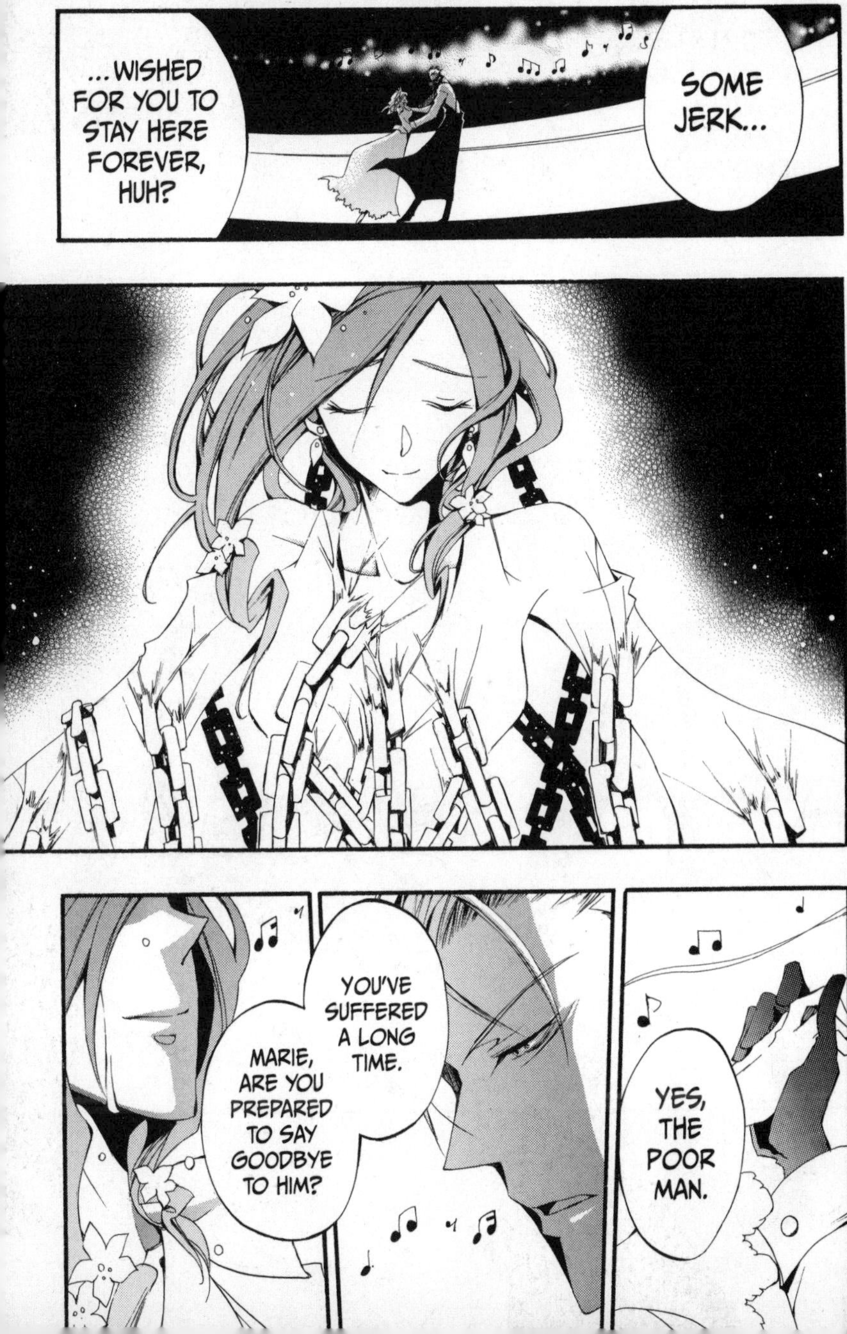
SOME JERK...
...WISHED FOR YOU TO STAY HERE FOREVER, HUH?
YES, THE POOR MAN.
YOU'VE SUFFERED A LONG TIME.
MARIE, ARE YOU PREPARED TO SAY GOODBYE TO HIM?

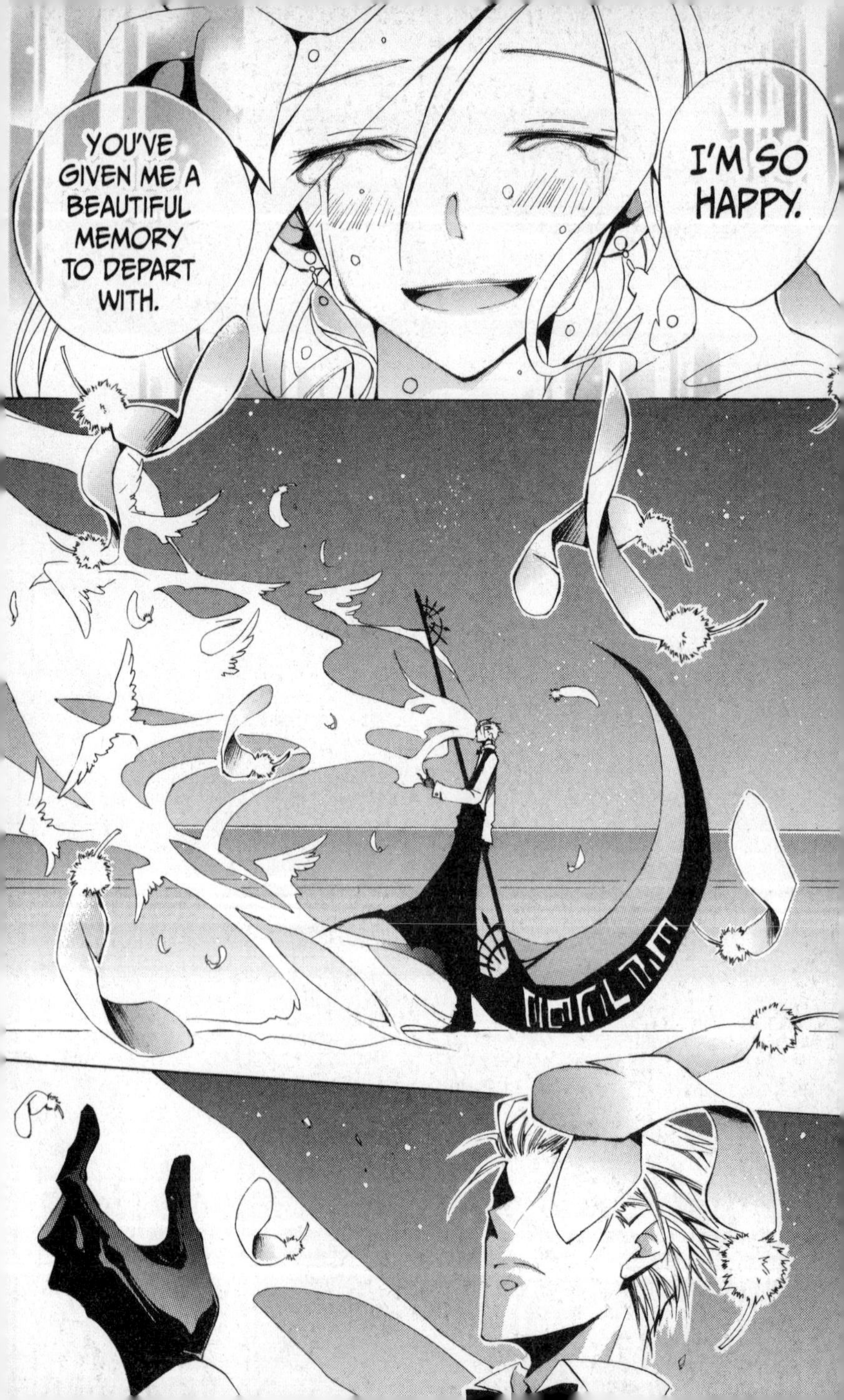
I'M SO HAPPY.
YOU'VE GIVEN ME A BEAUTIFUL MEMORY TO DEPART WITH.

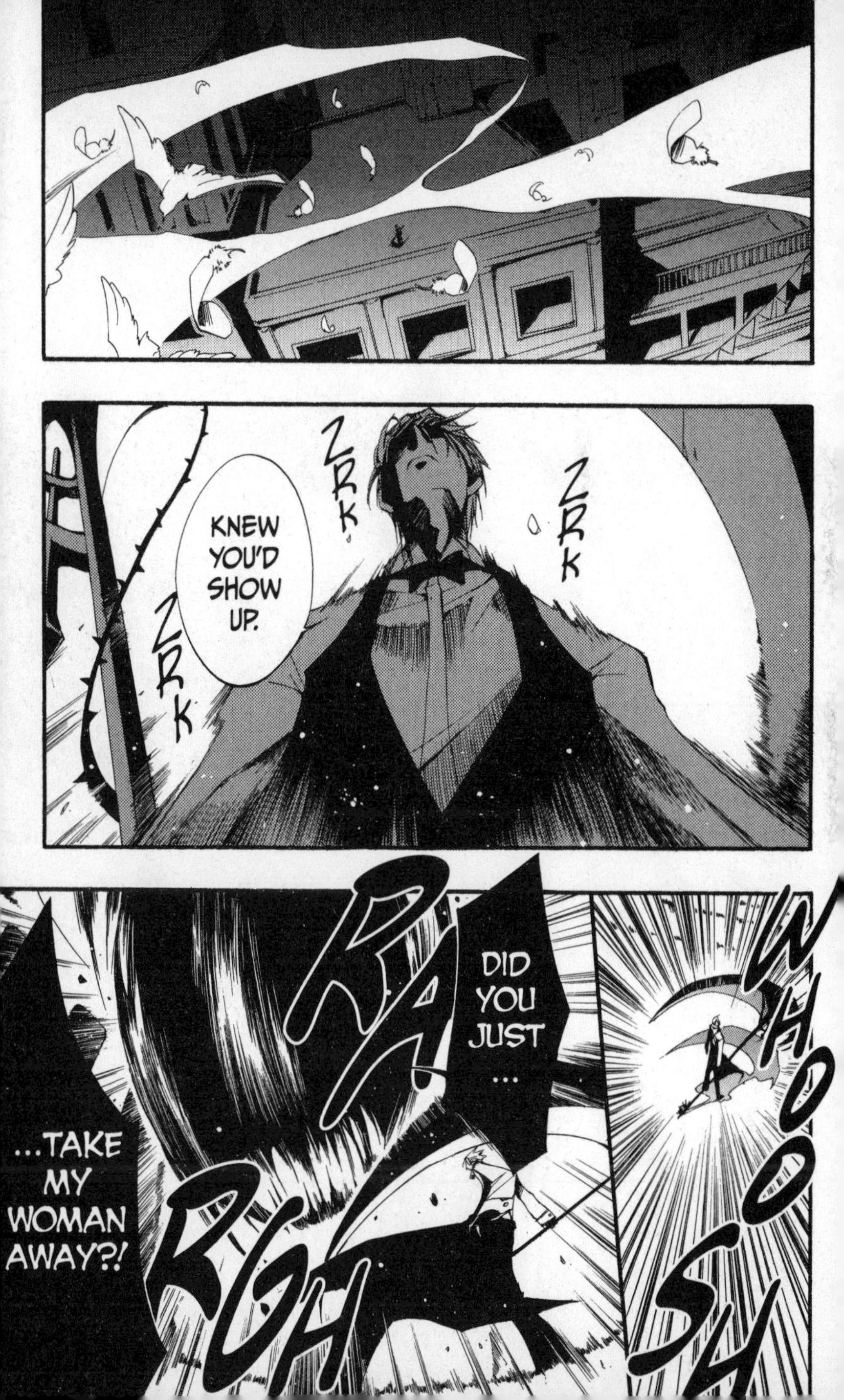
ZRK
ZRK
KNEW YOU'D SHOW UP.
ZRK
WHOOOSH
DID YOU JUST...
...TAKE MY WOMAN AWAY?!

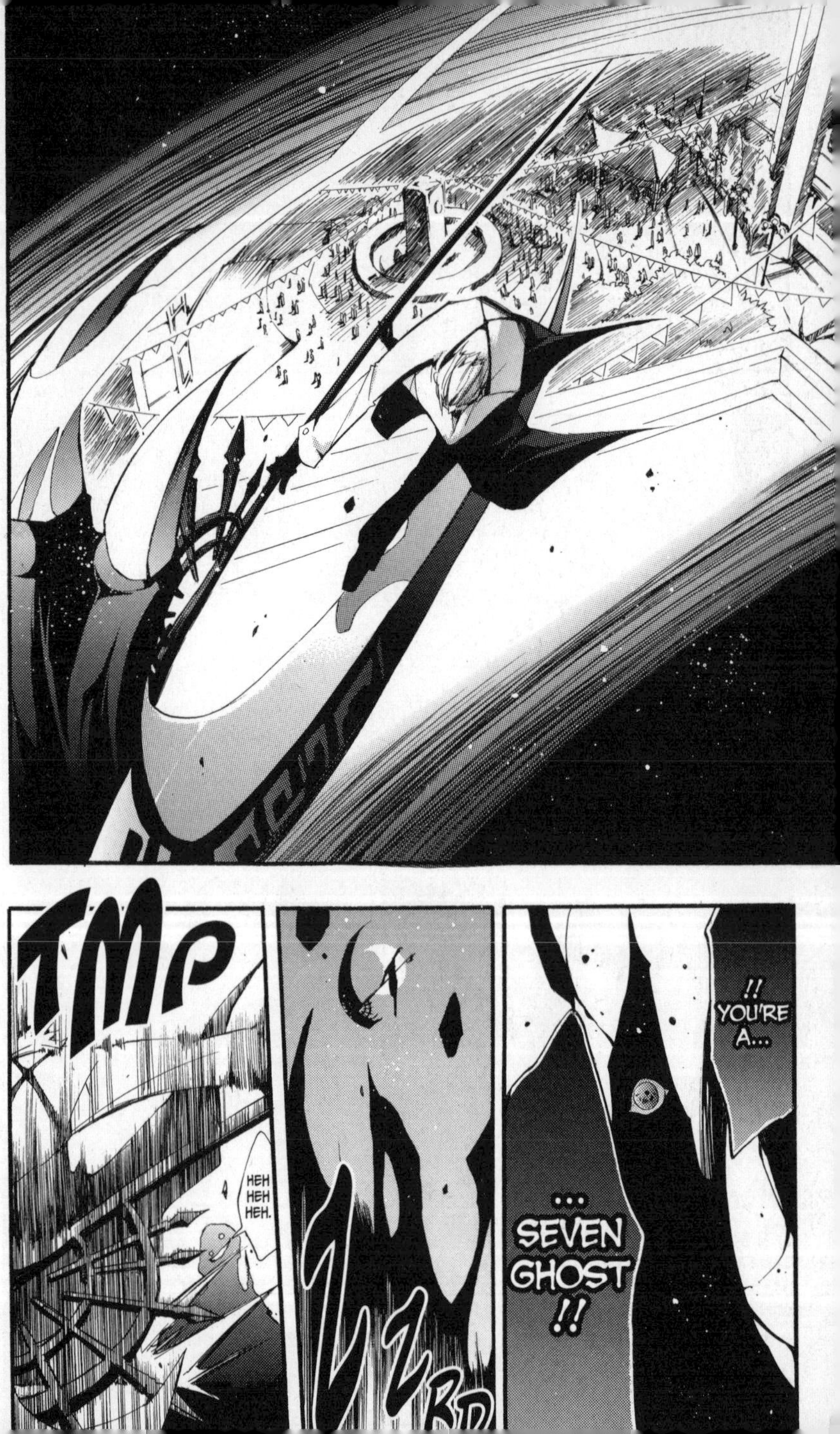
!! YOU'RE A...
...SEVEN GHOST !!
TMP
HEH HEH HEH.

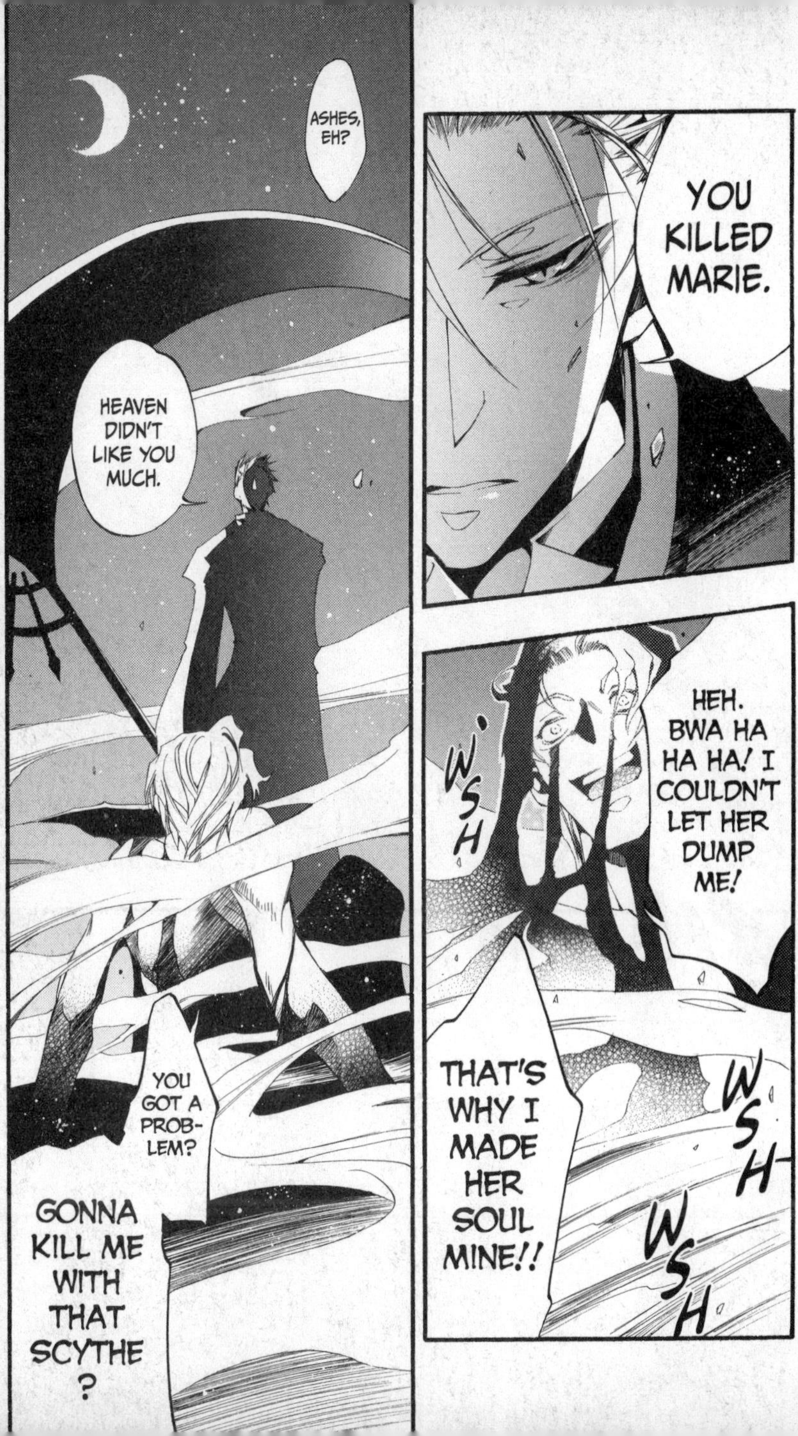
YOU KILLED MARIE.
HEH. BWA HA HA HA! I COULDN'T LET HER DUMP ME!
WSH
THAT'S WHY I MADE HER SOUL MINE!!
WSH
WSH
ASHES, EH?
HEAVEN DIDN'T LIKE YOU MUCH.
YOU GOT A PROB-LEM?
GONNA KILL ME WITH THAT SCYTHE?

THOSE WHO HEAVEN HAS FORGIVEN RECEIVE WINGS, BUT THOSE UNWORTHY ONLY MEET ONE END.

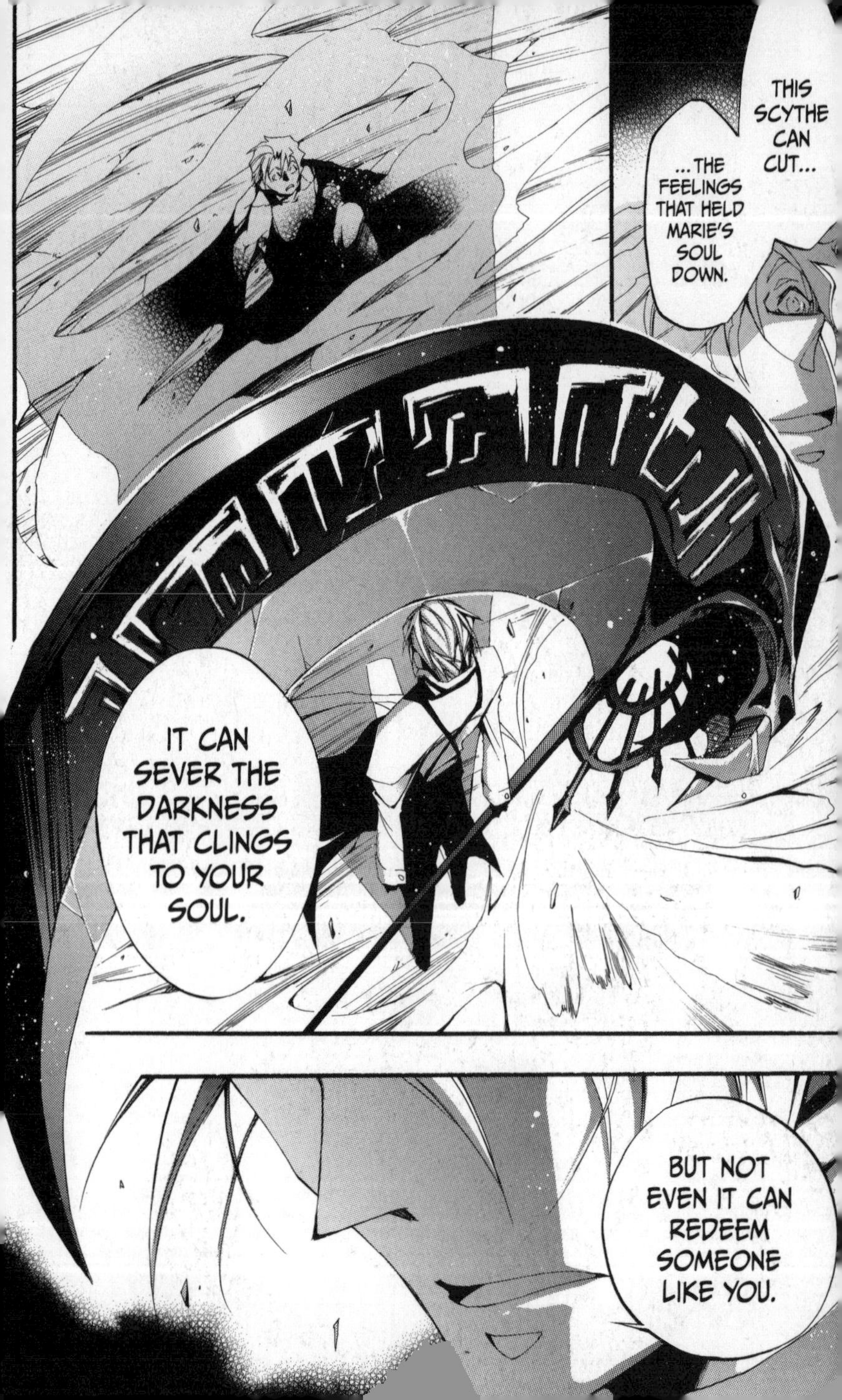
THIS SCYTHE CAN CUT...
...THE FEELINGS THAT HELD MARIE'S SOUL DOWN.
IT CAN SEVER THE DARKNESS THAT CLINGS TO YOUR SOUL.
BUT NOT EVEN IT CAN REDEEM SOMEONE LIKE YOU.

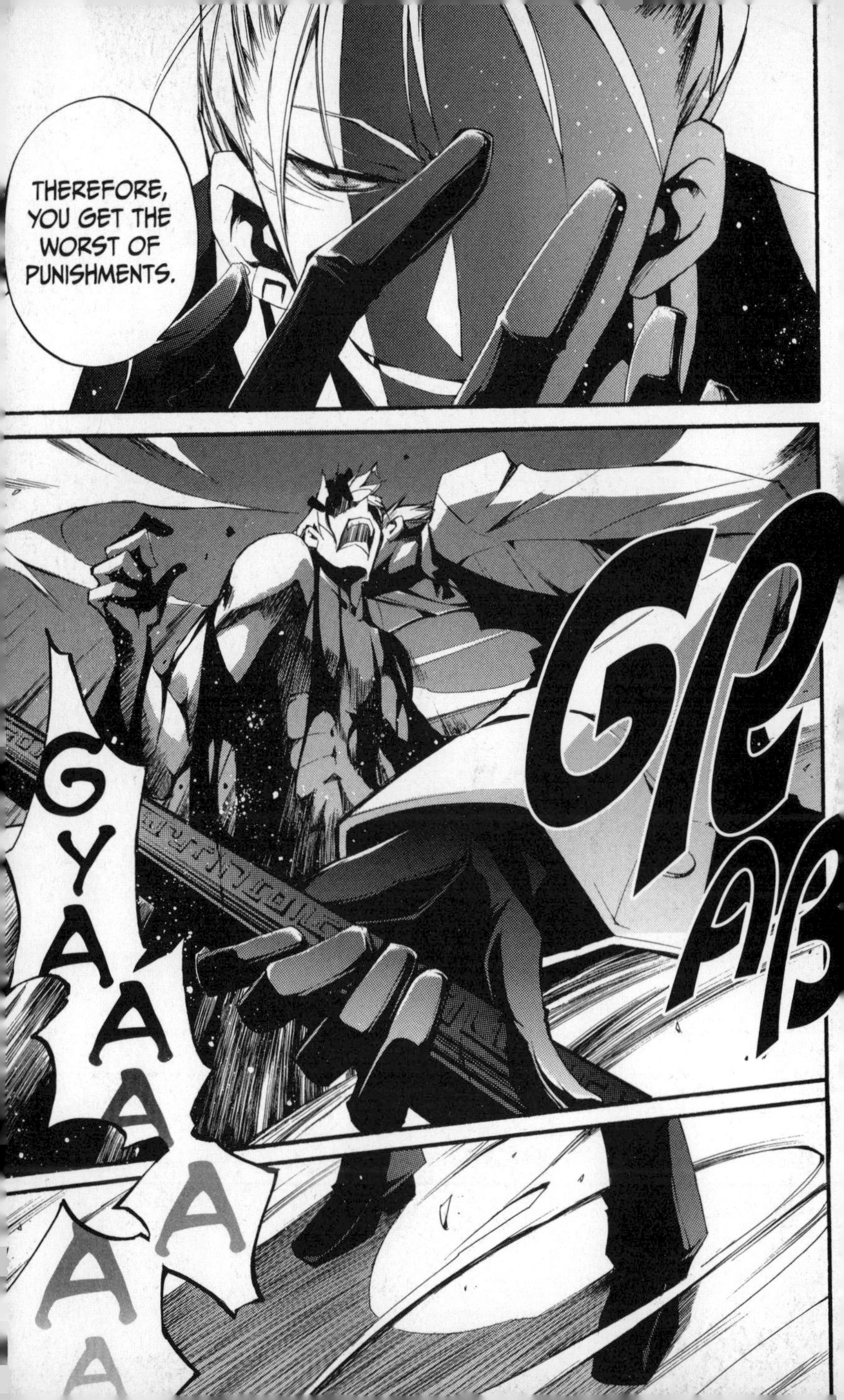
THEREFORE, YOU GET THE WORST OF PUNISHMENTS.
GYAAAAAAA

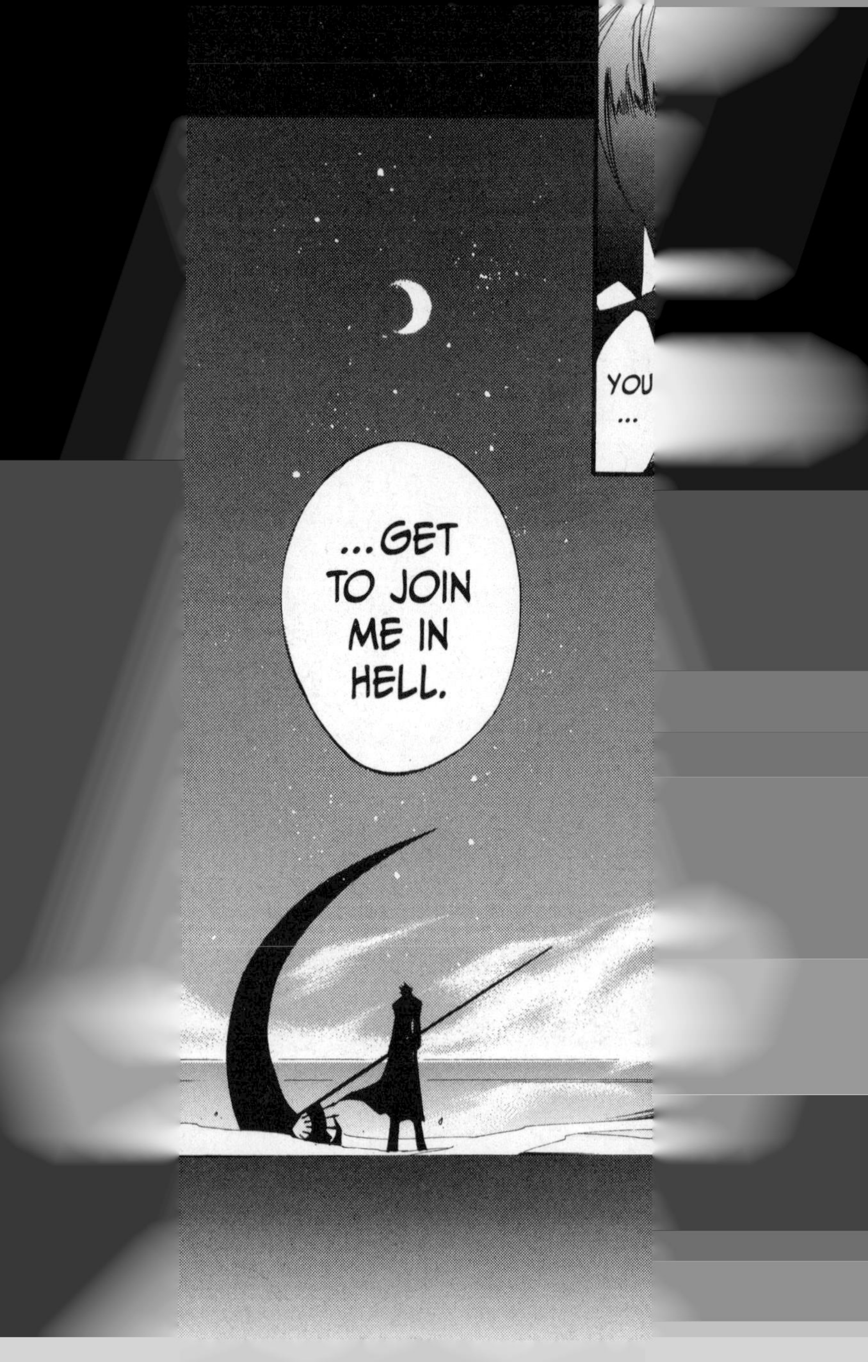
YOU ...
...GET TO JOIN ME IN HELL.

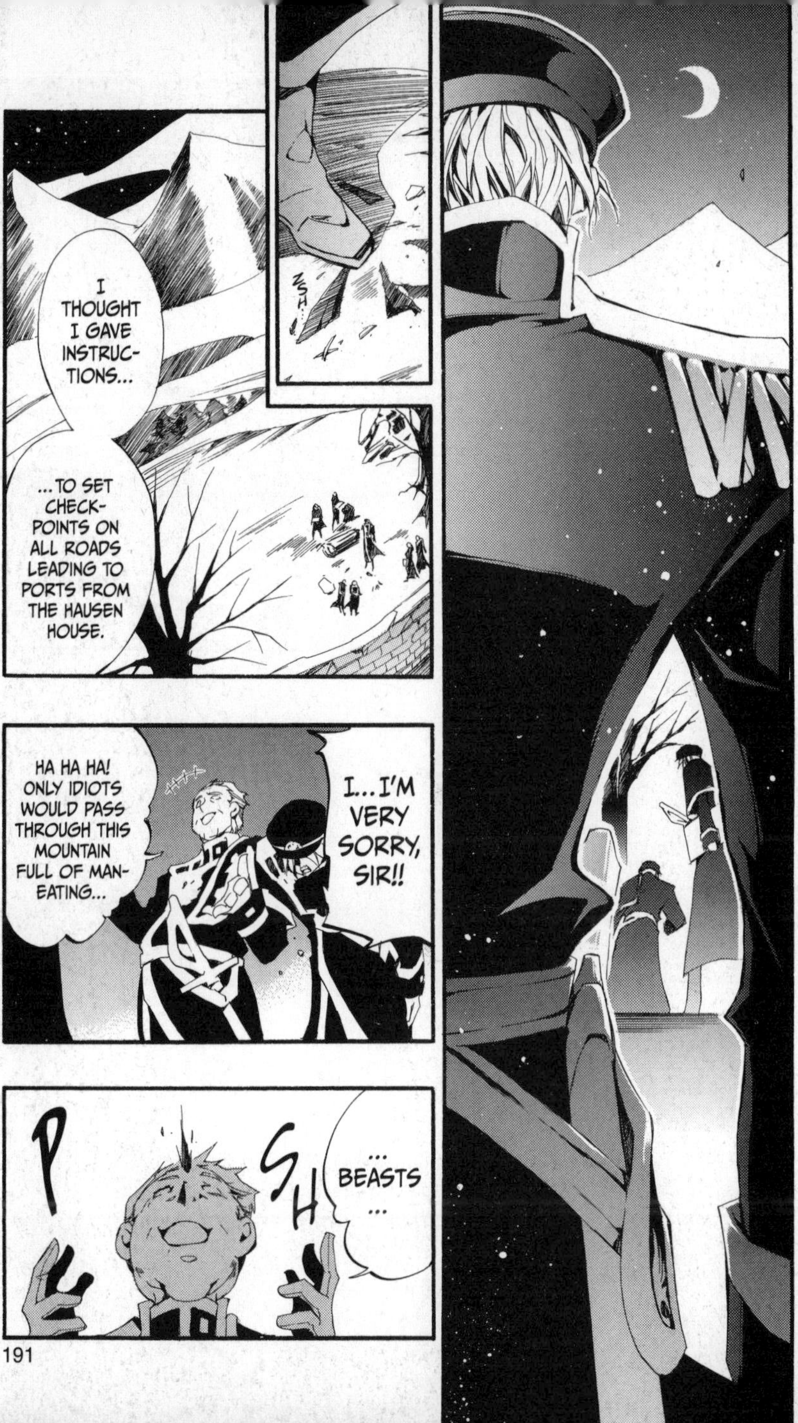
ZSH...
I THOUGHT I GAVE INSTRUC-TIONS...
...TO SET CHECK-POINTS ON ALL ROADS LEADING TO PORTS FROM THE HAUSEN HOUSE.
I...I'M VERY SORRY, SIR!!
HA HA HA! ONLY IDIOTS WOULD PASS THROUGH THIS MOUNTAIN FULL OF MAN-EATING...
... BEASTS ...
PSH

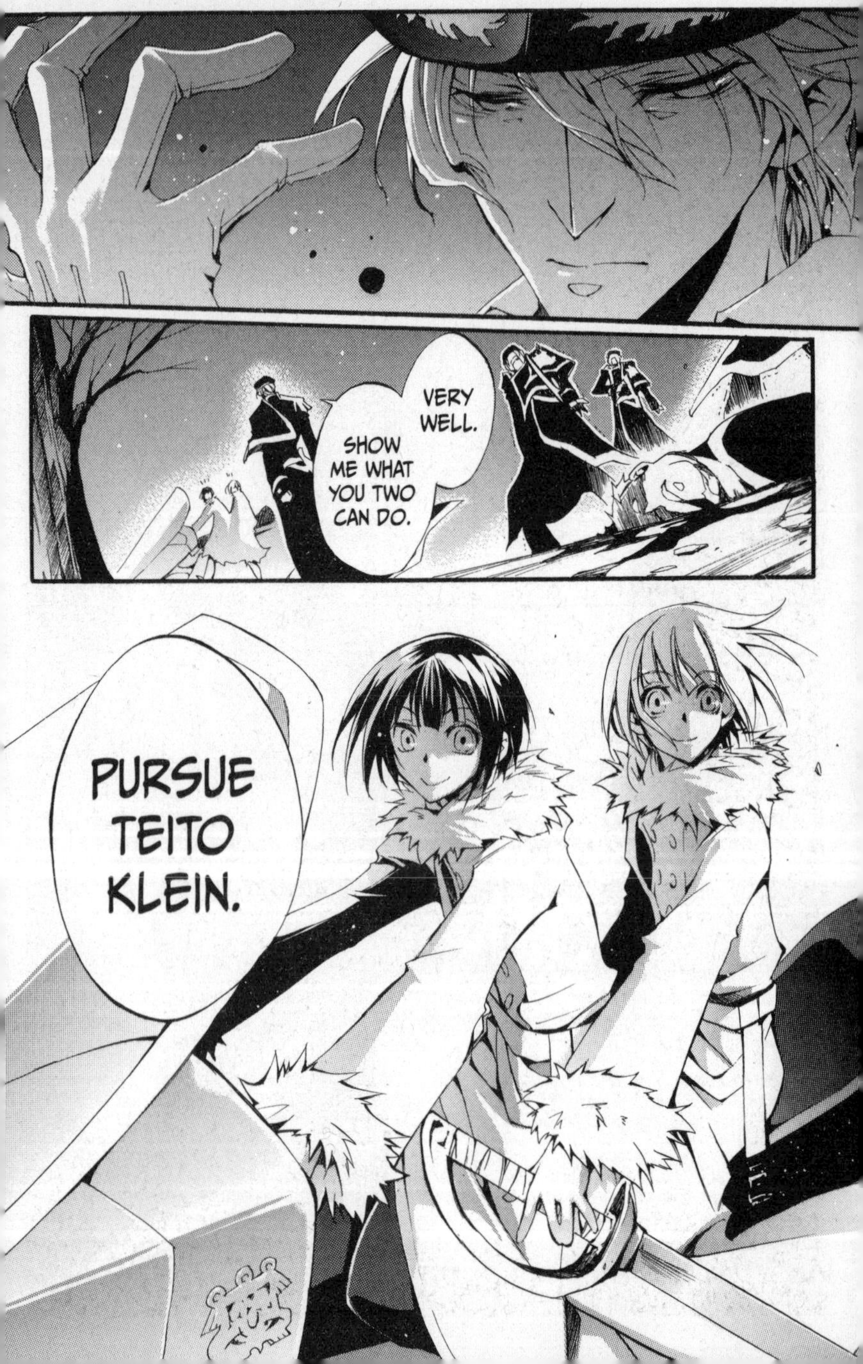
VERY WELL.
SHOW ME WHAT YOU TWO CAN DO.
PURSUE TEITO KLEIN.

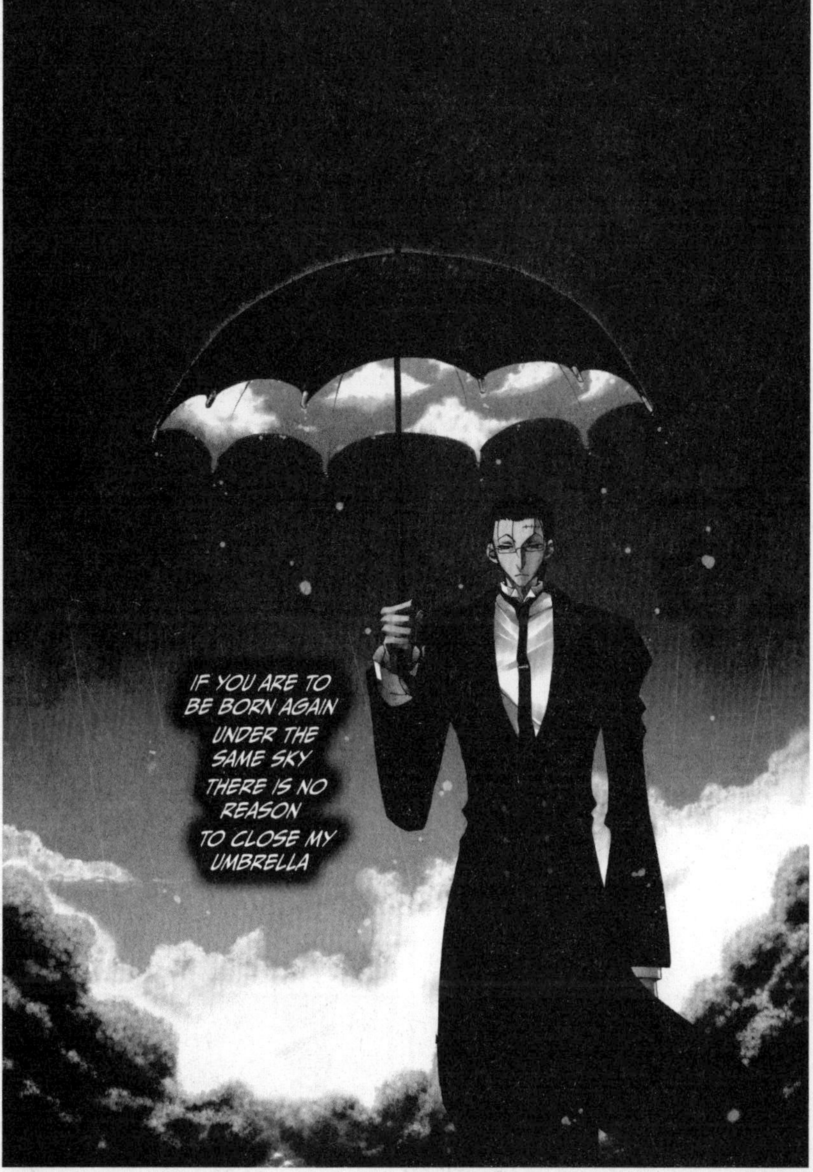
IF YOU ARE TO BE BORN AGAIN UNDER THE SAME SKY THERE IS NO REASON TO CLOSE MY UMBRELLA

↓ Capella

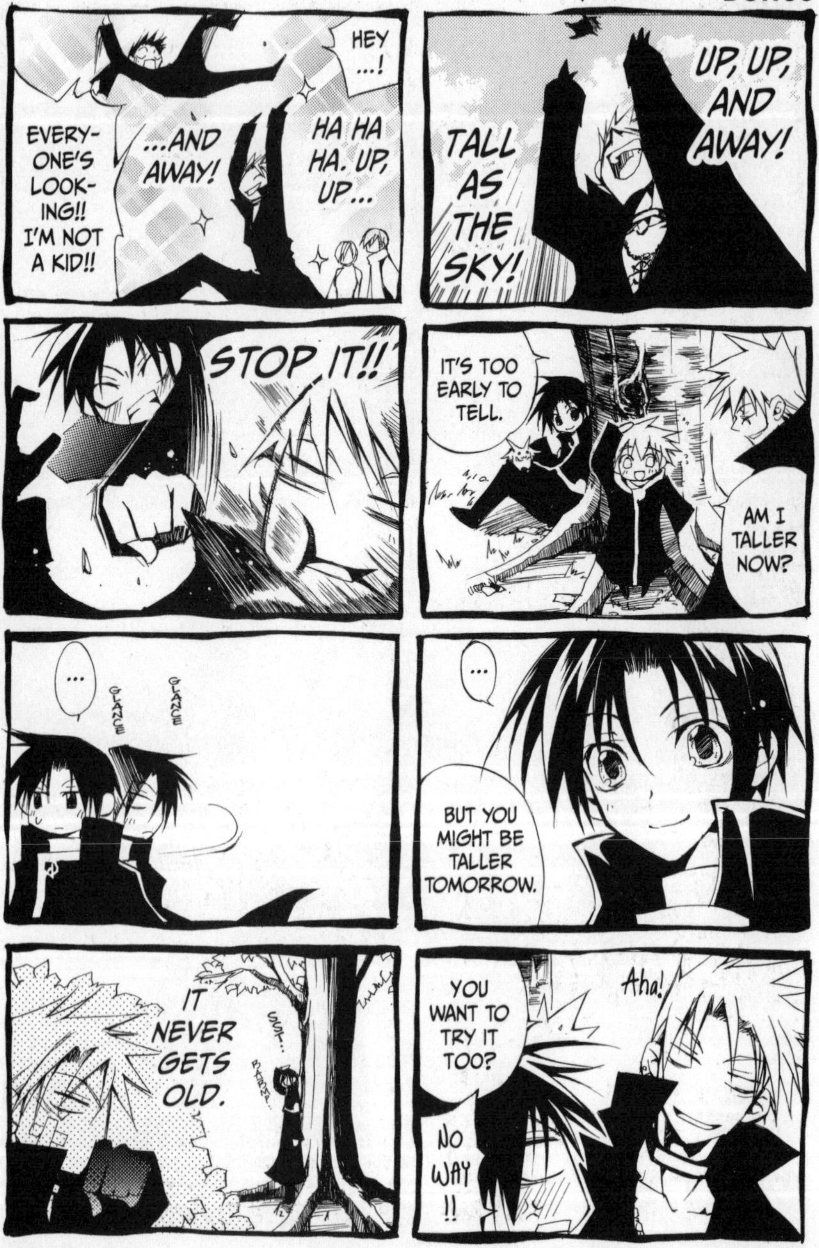
UP, UP, AND AWAY!
TALL AS THE SKY!
HEY ...!
HA HA HA. UP, UP...
...AND AWAY!
EVERYONE'S LOOKING!! I'M NOT A KID!!
AM I TALLER NOW?
IT'S TOO EARLY TO TELL.
STOP IT!!
...
BUT YOU MIGHT BE TALLER TOMORROW.
...
GLANCE
GLANCE
Aha!
YOU WANT TO TRY IT TOO?
NO WAY!!
IT NEVER GETS OLD.
SST...

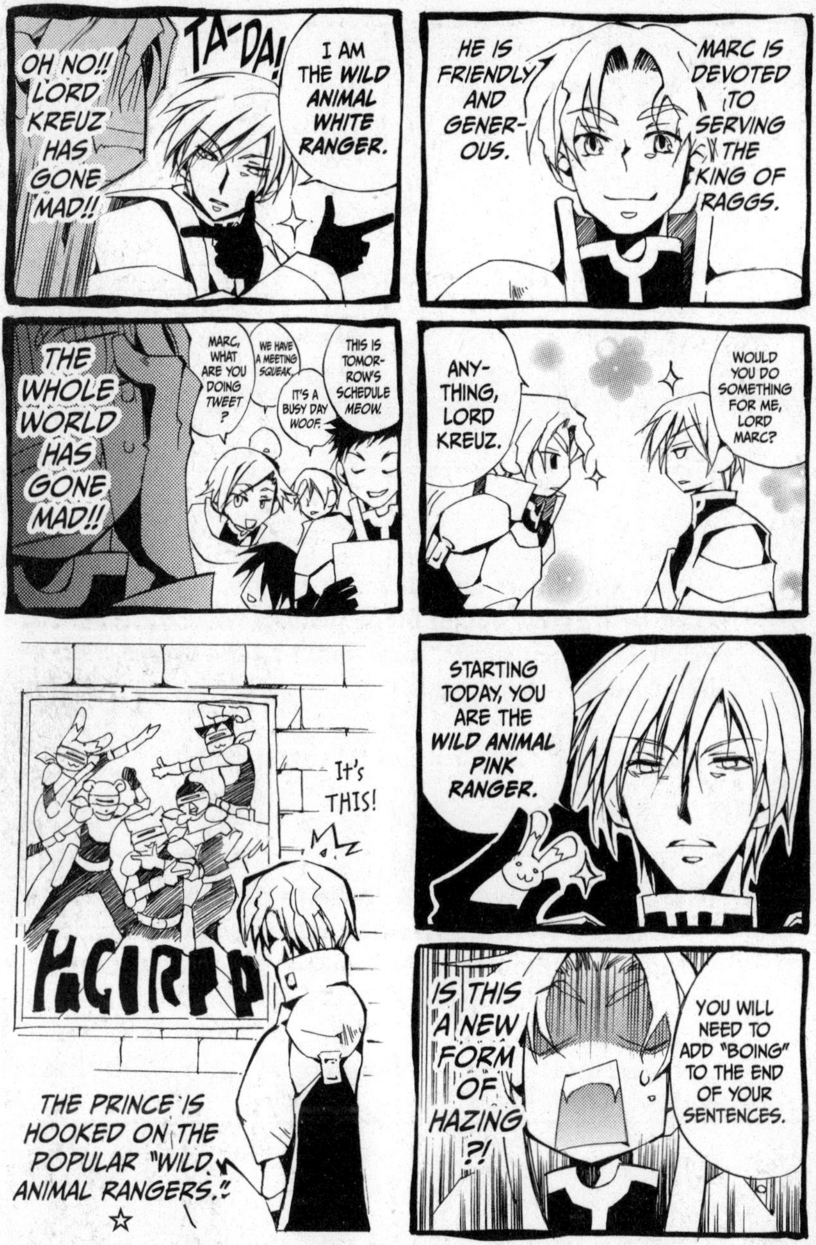
MARC IS DEVOTED TO SERVING THE KING OF RAGGS.
HE IS FRIENDLY AND GENEROUS.
I AM THE WILD ANIMAL WHITE RANGER.
TA-DA!
OH NO!! LORD KREUZ HAS GONE MAD!!
WOULD YOU DO SOMETHING FOR ME, LORD MARC?
ANYTHING, LORD KREUZ.
THIS IS TOMORROW'S SCHEDULE MEOW.
WE HAVE A MEETING SQUEAK.
IT'S A BUSY DAY WOOF.
MARC, WHAT ARE YOU DOING TWEET?
THE WHOLE WORLD HAS GONE MAD!!
STARTING TODAY, YOU ARE THE WILD ANIMAL PINK RANGER.
YOU WILL NEED TO ADD "BOING" TO THE END OF YOUR SENTENCES.
IS THIS A NEW FORM OF HAZING?!
It's THIS!
THE PRINCE IS HOOKED ON THE POPULAR "WILD ANIMAL RANGERS." ☆

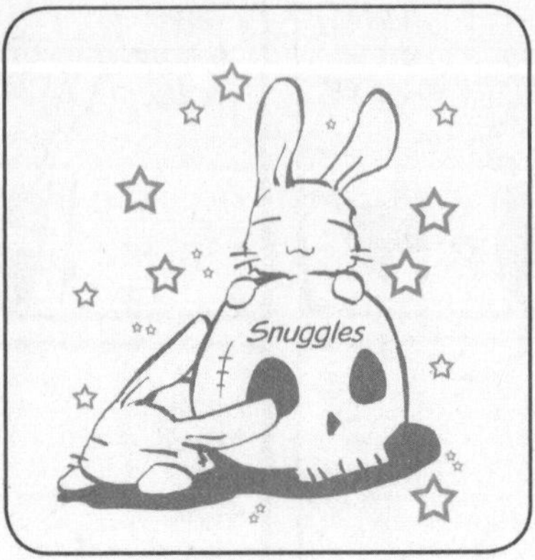
Snuggles

We saw kingfishers along the river in front of our house recently. We went out and took pictures while the old men were taking their strolls. It's so nice that the river is clean and natural… *(happy sigh)*

—Yuki Amemiya & Yukino Ichihara, 2008

Yuki Amemiya was born in Miyagi, Japan, on March 25. Yukino Ichihara was born in Fukushima, Japan, on November 24. Together they write and illustrate *07-Ghost*, the duo's first series. Since its debut in 2005, *07-Ghost* has been translated into a dozen languages, and in 2009 it was adapted into a TV anime series.

It's
trash day! ♪

?

07-GHOST

Volume 6

STORY AND ART BY
YUKI AMEMIYA and
YUKINO ICHIHARA

Translation/Satsuki Yamashita
Touch-up Art & Lettering/Vanessa Satone
Design/Shawn Carrico
Editor/Hope Donovan

07-GHOST © 2008
by Yuki Amemiya/Yukino Ichihara
All rights reserved.
Original Japanese edition published by
ICHIJINSHA, INC., Tokyo.
English translation rights arranged with
ICHIJINSHA, INC.

The rights of the author(s) of the work(s) in
this publication to be so identified have been
asserted in accordance with the Copyright,
Designs and Patents Act 1988. A CIP catalogue
record for this book is available from the
British Library.

The stories, characters and incidents
mentioned in this publication are entirely
fictional.

No portion of this book may be reproduced
or transmitted in any form or by any
means without written permission from the
copyright holders.

Printed in Canada

Published by VIZ Media, LLC
P.O. Box 77010
San Francisco, CA 94107

10 9 8 7 6 5 4 3 2 1
First printing, September 2013

PARENTAL ADVISORY
07-GHOST is rated T for Teen and is
recommended for ages 13 and up. This
volume contains realistic and fantasy violence.
ratings.viz.com

www.viz.com

Hey! You're Reading in the Wrong Direction!

This is the end of this graphic novel!

To properly enjoy this VIZ graphic novel, please turn it around and begin reading from right to left. Unlike English, Japanese is read right to left, so Japanese comics are read in reverse order from the way English comics are typically read.

This book has been printed in the original Japanese format in order to preserve the orientation of the original artwork. Have fun with it!

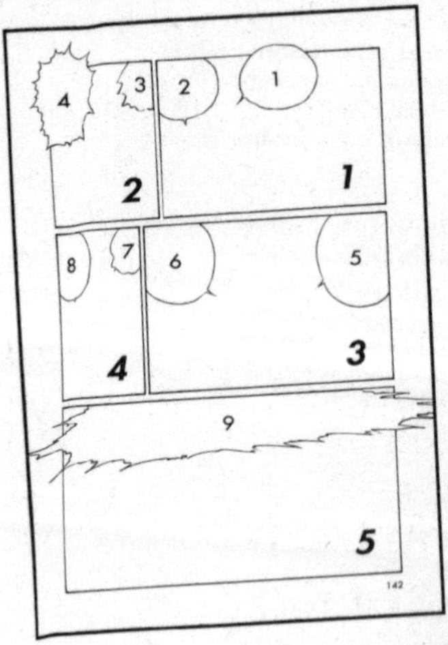
1
2
1
3
4
2
5
6
3
7
8
4
9
5
142

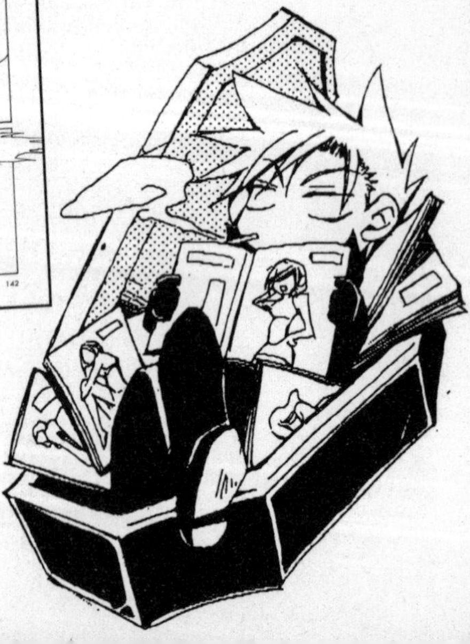